Real Reviews by Real People

What to Do When a Loved One Dies is essential reading that provides important information on the feelings and issues regarding death and loss. I congratulate Dr. Shaw for writing a wonderful book that will be of great assistance to so many people. — Robert M. Fells, External Chief Operating Officer and General Counsel, International Cemetery and Funeral Association, Reston, Virginia

ॐ

When my mother passed away, my copy of *What to Do When a Loved One Dies* became dog-eared with pages highlighted in various colors. As her caregiver for over a year, I thought I was ready for death. I wasn't. Eva's book kept my fragile world manageable. Over time, I've reached for the book again and again for guidance and support as life took away others in my family. Every home—no let me rephrase that—every heart needs a copy of this book. — Kathleen Shaputis, author of *Gramma Online: A Grandmother's Guide to the Internet* and *The Crowded Nest Syndrome*, Olympia, Washington

ॐ

As her veterinarian, I've consulted with Dr. Eva Shaw for years and in *What to Do When a Loved One Dies*, I have come to know her as a compassionate author. This book is not lighthearted, however Eva has somehow presented it so one wants to read it cover to cover. In the chapter "When Pets Die," Eva has absolutely covered the real-life drama all pet owners must go through; animals simply do not live as long as we do. This chapter alone should be available for veterinary hospitals and be beneficial to pet owners. — Lauren Bauer, DVM, Carlsbad Animal Hospital, Carlsbad, California

Eva Shaw's book, *What to Do When a Loved One Dies*, should be in the library of every pastor. Even though I have been in pastoral ministry over twenty-five years, situations still arise where I do not have answers. The first day I received this book, one of those situations arose and Dr. Shaw's book had the exact information I needed. Most books for pastors deal primarily with the funeral service itself. Dr. Shaw's book answers all the practical questions we must handle before and after the service. It is the most thorough, practical volume on dealing with death I have seen. — Joe Slaughter, Pastor of Assimilation and Pastoral Care, Hillcrest Church, Dallas, Texas

ଛଅ

As a clinical psychologist who specializes in grief and loss issues and who recently experienced the death of my father, I am recommending this book to clients and family alike. Death is a healing agent for life. *What to Do When a Loved One Dies* is a one-of-a-kind gift, a toolbox filled with comfort, guidance, and empathy. Dr. Eva Shaw has simplified the complex ordeal of "Now what?" She has illuminated the darkness of this sacred passage we call death. — CJ Johnson, Psy.D., Atlanta, Georgia

ଛଅ

My father died in 1980 after a mercifully short battle with virulent lung cancer. Your words, Dr. Shaw in *What to Do*, touched me numerous times as I read the book. I'll never forget sitting next to his bed shortly before the end, taking his hand in mine and feeling his surprisingly strong grip. Neither of us had ever been physically demonstrative because "real men" don't cry. As I sat there holding onto his hand, silently wishing I could take his pain away, a tear ran down his cheek.

"Why me?" he asked in a hoarse whisper. "I never did nothing to nobody."

There was no answer and with tears now streaming down my face, I brought his hand to my lips and kissed it. "I love you, Dad," I said for the first time I could ever remember.

"I love you, Son," came his almost inaudible reply, again for the first time I could ever recall. We then spent the new few minutes holding onto to each other's hand and silently weeping.

Shortly after that he lapsed into a coma and peacefully passed out of this world and into the next.

For the last twenty-four years, I have been living with the memory of this encounter, both cherishing and hating it. *What to Do When a Loved One Dies* has offered me insights into that all-too-brief communion of our spirits. I don't believe I'll ever again dread thinking about it. I am finally at peace. — Alan Fleming, Newark Valley, New York

❧

What to Do When a Loved One Dies is a must for anyone assisting those who have lost someone close to them. What a tool this would have been for me after the loss of my son, and subsequent seventeen years experience as a Bereavement Counselor for my church parish. The depth of coverage makes it an absolute essential in the library of any who deal with the bereaved. — Ruth Cate, Bereavement Counselor, St. Mary's Church, Windsor Locks, Connecticut

The death of a loved one is a time of great strain and more than a little confusion. Yet there are matters that must be attended to precisely at this time when survivors are not in the best condition to make important decisions. This gentle and sensitive book deals with matters mundane and monumental and offers cogent advice on both. Concerns such as grief resolution are treated caringly as well as questions of what to do if an autopsy is deemed necessary. There is even a chapter on dealing with the death of a pet and another about dealing with a death that has become a media event. Simply put, this book is a comprehensive treatment of the confusing situation of the recently bereaved and a most valuable resource for dealing with a situation that most of us will have to face at least once or twice in our lives. This, then, is a rare quantity: a practical how-to guide truly deserving of that designation. — Mike Tribby, reviewer, *Booklist*

જ઼

As a hospice nurse attending an elderly woman in her granddaughter's home, I was told, "I just want to love her, and walk her to the gate as she leaves this world." Dr. Eva Shaw's exceptional book, *What to Do When a Loved One Dies*, answers the question of "What now?" when a loved one dies, and we are left at that gate. The book gives readers assistance with feelings and necessary planning, whether death of parent, spouse, child, friend or pet. Thank you, Dr. Shaw, for an end-of-life resource like no other. — Margo Dillon, Registered Nurse, Elgin, Arizona

જ઼

As I type, we are on call. My grandfather is with hospice and their home health nurses now. The information in this book is of immediate concern to me. In *What to Do When a Loved One Dies: A Practical and Compassionate Guide to Dealing with Death on Life's Terms* Eva Shaw laces facts about death and dying as gently as she would lace her fingers in a mourning person's hand. Shaw swaddles the reader in hopefulness. — Dede Norungolo, Brain Injury Survivor, Seneca, South Carolina

What to Do When a Loved One Dies intensely, honestly, and directly approaches every facet of the death process we human beings will inevitably one day encounter. — Barbara Kinne, bereaved parent, Paris, Kentucky

ॐ

Our family has lost loved ones to death by disease, suicide, and accident. Though those deaths are in the past, the insights Shaw reveals in *What to Do* brought healing to our home today. I only wish we had had this book then. Everyone, beginning in their teen years, should have a copy and be required to read it. *What to Do* informs readers of what to expect, what to do, and where to get help, regardless of the type of loss. Thank you, Dr. Shaw, for writing a dignified, informative, empathetic guide to coping with the end of life. — E. Dian Moor, Christian writer, www.handsofhope.com, Moundsville, West Virginia

ॐ

Dr. Shaw's new book is an encyclopedia of information on handling the loss of a loved one. It is impossible to be prepared emotionally, but *What to Do* is the best guide to help in the process. — Dee Ondrish, Fortville, Indiana

ॐ

Eva Shaw's wealth of practical advice in *What to Do When a Loved One Dies* is best read, owned, and kept as a reference book. I found it especially useful and comforting as I grieve over the loss of my mother. — Mary Ruth Hammond, Administrative Specialist, Alameda, California

Why are we so afraid of death? Why are we so purposely ignorant about one of the few things we all do? If someone you know dies, this book will be a friend indeed. Nevertheless, I suggest you read it before "the time" comes. It is exquisitely practical. — Peter McWilliams, author, *How to Survive the Loss of a Love*

What to Do is an incredible, thorough, and much-needed resource. Death is part of life. This book can help you integrate all aspects of the experience into your life from the practical to the spiritual. — Bernie Siegel, M.D., author, *Love Medicine and Miracles*

ॐ

This is the most inclusive book ever written about loss; it is like having a good friend who has been through it before to guide the way. — Maniwa, Director, Buddy Program, AIDS Project, Los Angeles, California

ॐ

At last, a practical guide that recognizes death is not only about grief. I wish I would have read this book ten years ago and plan to keep it within close reach for ease of mind just in case I should be thrust once again into the stressful decision-making position when a loved one dies. After reading *What to Do*, I feel as prepared as anyone can be. — Jennifer Brown, Liberty, Missouri

What to Do When a Loved One Dies is a marvelous book. Everything anyone who has lost a loved one ought to ask is answered in a loving and direct manner; it should be in every clergy person's study. Dr. Shaw has done us all a great service by writing this book. — Very Reverend Lloyd G. Chattin, Dean Emeritus of Trinity Episcopal Cathedral, Trenton, New Jersey

Cleansing and therapeutic tears are easily evoked as a treasure of comfort unfolds in *What to Do.* It provides systematic action templates for those who face the reality of a loved ones death with balanced reference material concerning death entities requiring spiritual and practical helping hands. Sidebars by professionals and lay experts enhance the book offering a cornucopia of grief reality attestation and reassurance, sensitivity, personalization and counsel. This is an essential healing reference. — Robert L. Manniello. MD, MBA, Neonatal and Pediatric Medicine, Health Care Consultant, San Juan Capistrano, California

What To Do
WHEN A LOVED ONE DIES

*A Practical and Compassionate Guide
to Dealing with Death
on Life's Terms*

by Eva Shaw, Ph.D.

Writeriffic Publishing Group
Carlsbad, California

Writeriffic Publishing Group
info@writeriffic.com, www.writeriffic.com
760-434-6445, 866-244-9047 (orders)
P. O. Box 524, Carlsbad, CA 92018-0524

Originally published: Irvine, CA: Dickens Press, 1994.

All information in this book is given without guarantees on the part of the author or publisher, and the author and publisher disclaim all liability in connection with the implementation of this information. Every effort has been made to make this book as authentic and accurate as possible. However, the publisher has retained the right to acknowledge the titles of all contributors in appropriate places throughout the text and edit where necessary in order to maintain the literary style intended.

Excerpt from *Dealing Creatively with Death*, 12th edition, by Ernest Morgan, reprinted by permission from Barclay House, © 1990.

Excerpt from *If There's Anything I can Do: An Easy Guide to Showing You Care*, by Susan McClelland and Susan McClelland Prescott, reprinted by permission from Triad Publishing Company, © 1991.

Excerpt from *Coming Back: Rebuilding Lives After Crisis and Loss*, by Ann Kaiser Stearns, reprinted by permission from Ballantine Books, a division of Random House, Inc., © 1989.

Excerpt from *The Grief Recovery handbook*, by John W. James and Frank Cherry, reprinted by permission from HarperCollins Publishers, © 1988.

Cover and inside design/typesetting: Debra McQuiston and Matt Shaw. Author and cover photos: Cece Canton.

Library of Congress Cataloging-in-Publication Data

Shaw, Eva, 1947-
    What to do when a loved one dies : a practical and compassionate guide to dealing with death on life's terms / by Eva Shaw, Ph.D.
        p. cm.
    Includes index.
    LCCN: 2002117708
    ISBN 0-9705758-2-3 (trade) —ISBN 0-9705758-3-1 (lib.bdg.)
        1. Death—Psychological aspects. 2. Bereavement—Psychological
aspects. 3. Funeral rites and ceremonies—Planning. 4. Inheritance and succession.
I. Title.
        155.9'37-dc20

Distributed to the trade by Independent Publishers Group
Printed in the United States of America
Second Edition

Writeriffic books, including *What to Do When a Loved One Dies*, are available for special promotions and premiums.
For details contact Director, Special Markets,

*To Jennie E. Klein, my mother,
who taught me about life as well as death.*

CONTENTS

❧

ఌ

Chapter 3: The Expression of Loss 65

ఌ

Chapter 4: The Experience and Emotions of Parting 111

ॐ

Chapter 5: Support Techniques and Grief Resolution...157

ॐ

Chapter 6: When Death Becomes a Media Event 187

ACKNOWLEDGMENTS

No book is a singular effort. Through the gracious efforts of many, *What to Do When a Loved One Dies* has become a reality. To fully acknowledge, thank, and credit all those who have shared their experience, shared their expert advice, and contributed without hesitation would take another book of this size. Simply put: Here's a hug and a warm thank-you to each individual who has helped.

Special thanks to my publishers, editors, and all those who have lent a hand at Writeriffic Publishing Group for bringing out the best in the words I have written. Love and thanks to my husband, Joe, and our son, Matt, our beautiful new "daughter" El, and my good friends who stuck with me when writing and updating the book usurped almost every spare minute of my waking moments. And to our Welsh terrier, Miss Buttons Shaw, for helping me move through a thorny grief process by "just being there" for me.

Thank YOU, Frank B. Stewart Jr., Tommie Fagan, Linda Stewart Newton, and the incredible staff at Stewart Enterprises for help and support above and beyond any expectation. Our editorial graphic designer, Matt Shaw, the cover and internal graphic designer, Debra McQuiston, and our editor, Lois Swagerty have shared their gifts and talents to make this book supremely readable and beautiful, too.

It is with deepest appreciation to all those who provided information, support, and encouragement with this updated and revised edition. My gratitude, too, must be given to those who have told me how my words and advice have helped and brought comfort during a time of great sorrow, from casual acquaintances to good friends like Doris Engberg, Nora Lloyd, and Sally Mills. My love to all of you who are now facing the resolution of a loved one's death.

It is my simple prayer that the words found within these pages will provide comfort and assist you in a time of need.

May peace be with you all.

FOREWORD
By
Frank B. Stewart, Jr.

Chairman Emeritus, Stewart Enterprises
(A Leading Public Death Care Provider)

ح

Facing mortality is life's most complex lesson. I believe it is only second to accepting and understanding the physical loss of a loved one.

Human mortality is really physical mortality. The true and everlasting existence is our <u>spiritual</u> life, which is what we humans believe will never end but endure forever.

As a 69-year-old death care provider, I have spent decades serving men and women at a time of loss, at the separation of the physical and the spiritual life. It has also been the time of reflection, relief, rejoicing and most times, there has been sorrow. Based on my experience in attending thousands of funerals and burials over these years, along with the experiences life has offered, I am encouraged to share my earthly personal observations influenced by some of the greatest theologians, people who might be perceived as the most common human beings, as well as those who have carved out success, fame, and notoriety.

The advice of Eva Shaw, Ph.D., will help and hasten the healing process of our resultant human feelings of grief. This is a practical "how-to" book and with the thesis based soundly in "why to." One can immediately gain some helping tools, review the sidebars or find answers to issues overlooked or buried for some time. Hence, this book can help, whether one is moving toward accepting an imminent death of a loved one or even one's own death or recovering from the memories of a painful and unforgettable long-ago loss of someone who was loved. For those now suffering the open-wounded freshness at the recent passing of a beloved's life, this book is manna from heaven.

The book, *What to Do When a Loved One Dies*, as shown in the index, captures and communicates this vital topic in a format that provides a comprehensive resource of information and knowledge to be utilized by all. Dr. Shaw shares practical and thoughtful in-depth advice with compassion and experience that, I believe, can be applied to everyone willing to face life's realities and mandates. *What to Do* will increase confidence in our inevitable decision-making process. Reading the book will provide satisfaction and peace of mind for our emotions to bring physical and spiritual reassurance, along with calm at a time of loss, fear, and doubt.

Because I believe so completely in the thesis of Dr. Shaw's work, I will kindly ask your permission as I attempt to explain my philosophy of life and death. I believe that to understand and accept "death," one must first understand LIFE, EXISTENCE, and OUR OWN NATURE. Life, as we know it, is half physical and half spiritual. We humans primarily equate with "physical" existence, as "spiritual" existence is problematical to fathom.

Most of us truly believe or want to believe that in the beginning, life and all existence originated by an act of an Almighty Source and a Power, referred to as God, Deity, Creator, or whatever one's perception is of an origin or a beginning that has no limit, neither time nor space. In describing creation, <u>time</u> and <u>space</u> are the two words in our vernacular that have no beginning and no end.

As for the origin of <u>physical</u> existence, those who do not want to believe in an Almighty Source or Creator, or who call themselves atheists and secularists, reason that life is the result of a cosmic explosion or just a physical consequence of "chance." Yet, earthly laws dictate otherwise. For anything to be <u>physical</u>, to explode or to exist, it first requires pre-existence of <u>something</u>.

"<u>FATE</u>" is the origin of spiritual existence and is an act of our Creator, <u>our</u> "origin." Fate, from our perspective, is God's plan; it is the creation of a spirit. "Fate" is being in 1) the right place at the right time, 2) the right place at the wrong time, 3) the wrong place at the right time, or 4) the wrong place at the wrong time. Regardless of our belief to the contrary, we have nothing to do with our fate! No one chooses their mother and father, or one's timing in existence. Why was I born in 1935 in lieu of 1900 or 1999? No one chooses their birth environment, gender, race, opportunities, role models, personality, and on and on. <u>Fate</u> is God's choice for us to earn our eternal salvation. All we have to do in life is to be the best "you" you can be.

I believe the origin of existence can be described as "absolute perfection." In our language, the key word is <u>absolute</u>. Most words can have various meanings, thus we must define our understanding of the words we use for clear communication in each context. Let us now focus on the definition of the essential word <u>absolute</u> and what it means to you and me. To me the word <u>absolute</u> means:

> The be all and the end all
> The beginning and/or the end
> None other like it
> The one and only
> Unconditional
> Unlimited
> Complete unto its self
> Self-existing
> Free from imperfection
> Free from restriction
> Free from limitation

If one now accepts the meaning of the word <u>absolute</u> in this context, it is possible to move on and assume the word <u>perfection</u> speaks for itself. Perfection is perfect, meaning without failure or flaw. Now our understanding can then go on to explain the perception of GOD, or THE ORIGIN OF ALL EXISTENCE. It will also become easier to comprehend not only the "how" and "why" of physical death, but also physical death itself, with all of its associated, existing consequences.

How could a good and almighty Creator have allowed death, evil, or man's inhumanity to man to exist in a world or universe that He created? This question needs to be answered by each of us. For more than thirty years, I have been troubled by this concept. That thought often made me question my own faith. I believe our existence was truly intended to be as perfect as our Maker. However, it is not! The real question is how could an almighty, all loving, all knowing, all perfect Creator have allowed imperfection and evil to come into existence?

It is my belief all humans were given almost everything possessed by our Maker, including and especially FREE WILL, but without the almighty power and the ability to re-create a spirit. However, we do have the ability, in most but not in all relationships, to physically create through conception a new human life and existence by our own choice in an ACT OF PHYSICAL LOVE. Yet, even in that context, the gift and privilege of creating a new life is not as perfect as that of our Maker. How can identical twins conceived at the same moment by the same parents (cells and genes) come into this world looking exactly alike, yet possessing totally different personalities or spirits? This proves the two-fold existence of spirit and physical.

In my opinion, all of this is true because of the simple and logical reason that if God (the origin) is "absolute perfection," and "absolute perfection" is defined as "perfect love," and "perfect love" can only be defined as "the desire to share," then one must conclude that God, the origin, decided to share His/Its/Her existence with another. We are the "other" and He chose to give us the gift of life in His own image and likeness, with the key exception being that He could not make us the "Maker" or the "Origin" ourselves; yet, He gave us free will.

Consequently, it is logical that we were created in the image and likeness, and were intended to be as perfect as God, but we are not, nor can we ever be, as perfect as He. Even though He wanted us to be as perfect, we are one degree or one ion less than our Maker. Our problem is we awoke convinced we are in fact equal to God. We don't feel the necessity to say to our origin: "Thank you," "I'm sorry," or "Forgive me!"

However, God will never stop trying to bring our spirit back (redeem us) into absolute perfection! I believe He started existence first through angelic existence, then through the material universe, then through mankind in His incarnate son, and now in the continuation of His perfect love for us to be part of Him.

Although God desired us to be equally as perfect as He is, even God could not re-perfect Himself in absolute perfection with almighty power. Hence, he would not be "ABSOLUTE." By logic and by the very definition of the word "absolute," one must see that ONLY GOD IS ABSOLUTE.

ONLY GOD IS ONE. Yet, to those who believe Christ to be the Messiah, God is a triune God. God is father, His son, and Holy Spirit, all in one perfect trinity. Even faiths that do not accept Christ as God's son or as our redeemer still accept His existence as monotheistic, the source of all being.

Most of us accept the premise that once spiritual life is ordained to exist, it is eternal and forever in salvation or otherwise. Unlike animals that function on instinct rather than intellect, we humans are blessed with intelligence and the ability to differentiate right from wrong, along with a desire or appetite for the pleasures of existence. Nevertheless, we are not, nor can we ever be absolutely perfect. Our original sin is the fact that when we awoke, we thought we were perfect in ourselves and that we were equal to God, our origin and, therefore, our own Creator.

Humanity's original sin, in my opinion, can be defined as "EGO." EGO occurs when we *Ease God Out* of our lives and feel we are God, without the necessity of thanking Him, asking forgiveness, or being respectful. Men and women with "ego" problems, I believe, are the causes of all wickedness, sin, and humanity's unwillingness to accept an almighty source of goodness and power as our Creator.

Regardless of one's beliefs in the hereafter, many of us have first-hand experience with man's "will power." Try to move your finger and it moves. Where did that brainpower come from? The "will and desire to live" is a powerful force! Even the most high-tech medical procedures and the world's best doctors cannot come close to understanding or duplicating this "medicine." Further, I believe, God has instilled in every spirit that <u>will to live on</u> in one form or another. Those suffering physically or emotionally often opt to live on in a spiritual way. This is the only way to accept and understand why a human can and would commit suicide.

Man has a desire for eternal existence. If this were not so, history and experience would have no meaning. Therefore, one must also conclude that the future has a value and a meaning in the eternal process of existence and the generations to come. "Evolution" and unending growth in physical life is a reality and we must accept it as a "truth." The divine plan---that of our origin or Creator's actions, is the key to understanding life and its consequence,---namely, death; but death, as we know it, is only a physical experience! The divine plan takes on greater depth and meaning when contemplating our spiritual life's destiny.

The "death care experience" is a process in this modern physical world and is essentially not unlike the practices, of pre-civilized man's actions in the very beginning of mankind. Humans have always buried their loved ones' physical remains with respect and dignity, as "life" is a sacred existence and the body in which it dwelled is also sacred. In all my years, I have never met a man or woman who amounted to or accomplished anything or who fulfilled a purpose in being who honestly did not have a desire to be remembered as having been "significant." Please understand "significant" does not mean powerful, influential, or wealthy. Rather significance translates to mean: Fulfilling one's purpose in being. Something within us asks that we be remembered, hopefully, for having pursued our mission and our purpose in this physical life of existence. Discovering our vocation and achieving God's plan and intention for us will set our spirits soaring. Yes, the spirit does live on!

We are all creatures seeking long-term survival on this earth. However, we must face our life's motive, as a way to comprehend existence, both physically and then spiritually, which we believe and hope will never end, but be eternal. "Death" is a reality. We face it at our own time and in our own manner. In fact, each one of us wants to be remembered in our own way.

We only bury our body, not our spirit. Yet, our body is the sacred vessel, the tangible matter of substance. It holds the spirit. If we preserve physical objects in life, which have meaning, such as those artifacts filling our world's museums, we must conclude that the remains of our physical existence should be treated with reverence and respect. People of all nations travel the world over to visit the cathedrals, historical relics, pyramids, and shrines, which were constructed to honor and remind us of the individuals and the events that had a tangible meaning to our civilization, along with our own.

Please think and meditate on these thoughts before reading on!

Imperfect as we are, it is vital to know that death and life have practical sides. There are many options and alternatives available in facing the traumatic occasion of the physical loss (separation) from a life we love. It is in everyone's best interest to prepare and plan in advance of need for the inevitable event, especially so when we are planning for our own mortal ending.

With Dr. Shaw's practical style, one may browse through the table of contents or the index and find immediate help. One may read it to gather reassurance, comfort and information when preparation is the concern. As she writes, and as I often explain when consulting and meeting with families in pre-planning, or meeting with the bereaved at a time of loss,---there are three separate physical acts necessary in Death Care. These three components take place in every transition of life from physical living on this earth to spiritual existence in the hereafter.

They are:

The Funeral Service: Call it a ceremony, ritual or tribute. It is a celebration of a life that lived. The funeral service provides a time when the bereaved express feelings and grief to the living about the deceased. Family and friends are never relieved of their need to provide consolation until meeting those left behind in person so that visual, verbal, and physical contact can be made. Letters can be written, flowers given, contributions made, cards sent, but nothing will substitute for personal direct contact, a hug, a touch to the hand, a sympathetic pat on the back. If the funeral ceremony and visitation are held at a convenient time and location, the funeral service provides the opportunity for 70 to 80 percent of those who want to express their sympathies in person to do so. If a private funeral is desired, rather than one open to the public, or just for family, friends, colleagues and neighbors to attend, it will not be possible for the larger circle of friends to communicate their feelings of sympathy. Hence, omitting the funeral experience or making it private tends to act against the intention of returning to, as Dr. Shaw explains, the "new normal" of life and happiness. If the funeral is omitted, people will seek you out in the future to express their sympathy and condolences, socially or at business encounters, just when you are returning to some normalcy. This is true no matter what letters, flowers, contributions, and so on are sent.

The Cemetery Component: Our body is physical matter that cannot and will not disappear. It can be buried traditionally in a grave in the earth; or it can be placed in a vault above the ground in a mausoleum crypt. In every cemetery, there are countless arrangements available from which to choose. Alternatively, it can be cremated. Many families often misunderstand cremation and the actual process that takes place. The result of cremation is not ashes and gases, as most individuals believe. Our body is reduced to a cubic foot of calcium in the cremation process, after the maximum time allowed for incineration. Basically, our remains are reduced to a skeletal frame through this procedure, after which the skeletal remains are mechanically reduced to cremains. This physical matter is then placed in a permanent monumental urn, or placed in a less permanent container that can be buried or used to transport the cremains for traditional burial, burial at sea, or scattering at a designated and approved location.

The drawback to the scattering process is there is no place for the remaining or future family members or friends to equate with the physical location of the vessel that once held the spirit. Most people only feel the presence of the spirit when visiting the resting place of the physical temple that held the spirit. In any form, our physical remains are sacred material that once held the spirit. They should be treated with respect and dignity, no different than the millions of meaningful artifacts we preserve in museums, our homes, and public places.

The Monumental or Memorial Component: This is the memorialization, remembrance, or footprint of existence that validates we lived, or that our loved one lived and did inhabit this earth. People yearn to be remembered as having been significant. This is accomplished through a footprint in the form of a monument, inscription, or some private memorial according to the wishes of the individual and the family. As I have mentioned, this is evident by the fact that tourists travel the world visiting and viewing the resting place of those who meant something to them in life. The desire for memorialization is provided for family and friends with the chosen memorial, along with its location and aesthetics.

All three components of death care are a result of our human choosing and basically, I believe ceremony, cemetery, and memorialization are a way of fulfilling and honoring the one whose life is being commemorated.

This foreword is to commend Dr. Eva Shaw's magnificent summation of knowledge: to introduce, to instruct, to give comfort, and to give compassion when one needs to know what to do. I end with my own planned personal inscription for my own place of burial.

Those who reflect on the message, in which I believe, will know I am not in the grave, but,- - -rather, my spirit is in a far better existence. My inscription will read:

"I HAVE APPRECIATED EVERY MINUTE,
EVERY SECOND,
EVERY INSTANT OF THIS LIFE- -
ESPECIALLY NOW."

Frank B. Stewart, Jr.
Chairman Emeritus, Stewart Enterprises, Inc.
A Leading Public Death Care Provider

INTRODUCTION

In 1971, my mother died in my arms. It wasn't inspirational; it was terrifying. I felt completely helpless, sick physically and emotionally.

Being with a loved one at the time of death may not have been right for you—it may have been impossible. But looking back I wouldn't trade that time for any of the holidays, celebrations, or successes I've had. I'm very glad I was there. It was right for me. I no longer grieve for my mother, but I still miss her and miss other family members who have died, the close friends who are no longer here, and the loss of family dogs with whom I relaxed, shared secrets, and took long walks. The shock and grief for those who are no longer in my life have turned to memories. If someone you loved has just died that might sound preposterous, but it will happen *with time*.

After working months and months on a book about what to do when a loved one dies, what strikes so profoundly is not death but the miracle of life. Now I stare at babies and see precious, perfect human beings bawling to make their tiny selves heard. At children running and screaming and jumping and making noise. At young people strutting their stuff like tropical birds. At people "my age" with a deepening sense of value, acting as if they've suddenly found all the answers. And at old people—those well up in their eighties—wrinkled with lines of life. Once again, for the millionth time, I realize that this is the reality of life, the cycle of death, and the scheme in which we're all involved. As journalist Jack Anderson said, "I look at the universe and I know there's an architect." This is what writing a book about death has meant to me.

Intellectually, we know death is all around. However, when death comes close, over time, we forget it, ignore it, deny it. Perhaps like you, when I started to write this book, my own death and the death of those whom I love rarely entered my mind.

If someone you loved has recently died, you know it's not possible to prepare for the death. Yet with this book and the information within these pages, you should be able to handle the situation. In a difficult time, this book can help.

Within the pages we'll talk about how to manage during situations that are uncomfortable, new, and often heartbreaking. We'll discuss options for funerals and memorial services, what to do should the death become a media event, and the procedures when death occurs out of the state or country. We'll cover costs, discuss how to get your "house" in order, explain wills, hospice, and grief, and explore the issues of suicide, stillbirth, and AIDS. At various intervals throughout the book are sections called "Where to Get Help." These sections recommend self-help books and detail how to contact support groups or organizations that can be of assistance during this difficult time. Sometimes the help you need is as close as calling in a neighbor immediately after the death of a loved one, as recommended in chapter 1, Immediate Action. In another circumstance, you may need to call a representative of the United States Department of State, for example, if a loved one has died while traveling overseas.

Often after a loved one has died, survivors begin to understand the need to inform the public regarding the specifics of the death. While it might not seem remotely possible that you will want to bring a message on the circumstances of your loved one's death or be able to fathom how it might be presented to television newspeople, journalists, or a room crowded with men and women, this often happens. That's what Candy Lightner thought after the drunk driver killed her daughter. And yet from this horrendous event came the birth of Mothers Against Drunk Driving (MADD), which has become an international movement saving countless lives. Because survivors often become activists against the cause which has snatched the lives of loved ones, we've included a section on how to prepare for and give interviews.

Some of those who contributed to the book take a warm, caring attitude toward the transition that we call death. Others look it squarely in the eye and refuse to mince words, as illustrated by interviews with an American Baptist minister, Rev. Diana Cole Veazey, and Rabbi Maurice Lamm.

When reading the interviews and essays, you'll find a full range of expressions and euphemisms others prefer instead of the word death. Some of the terms sound more like a commercial for Kodak film or Hallmark: "She's with the angels" or "We lost him last year." However, within the text, we'll talk about death in plain terms. This is not done to be heartless, but so that you can understand clearly what has happened. If words such as death, dead, and dying offend you or you cringe at the term deceased, feel free to substitute words that you are more relaxed using. Personally, I like the euphemism of "passing on." It mirrors my personal philosophy of my loved ones moving from this dimension into another.

Throughout the book we will be talking about and referring to "family." Family in this context includes anyone who loved the person who died. One does not have to be related by blood or marriage to accept this term. While I have a small blood-related family, perhaps like you, I'm also "family" to dear friends, and often feel closer to many of these men, women, and children in my immediate circle than the distant relations I haven't kept up with in years. We have also attempted to avoid any sexist references. If there is anything you find offensive, it is unintentional.

With this revision, the contact information you'll find throughout the pages for self-help groups and other resources has been verified. It was decided that Web addresses (also called URLs) would not be included since they change, as do telephone numbers and addresses. Most self-help groups have Web sites, and you can contact the organization for newsletters and other materials that can help in a time of need.

Reading and applying the material can help you get through the experience of death and perhaps make the road a little smoother. With the information you can get a "handle" on the pain, but any death hurts, including that of a cherished family pet as we'll discuss in chapter 10. Additionally, my hope is that this book will help you understand what's going on "inside," as well as how to cope with and work with the external changes brought on by the death of someone you loved.

Let this book be your guide. It tells you *What to Do When a Loved One Dies*.

Immediate Action

There's been a death. It's someone you loved. You're frightened, confused, angry, distraught, numb, shocked, and dazed. You feel helpless, you feel powerless. You've never been through this before. Whether you like it or not, the responsibilities "to make the arrangements" are on your shoulders or, if you're lucky, to be shared with another family member or friend.

Life doesn't prepare us for death. However, we only find that out when someone we love dies. Since, as a culture, we often deny death, that's not much of a surprise. We just don't make plans for the inevitable. And as author Margaret Mitchell said, "Death and taxes and childbirth! There's never a convenient time for any of them."

Hindsight continues to be twenty-twenty, and most likely the "if onlys" bombard your head with what might have been if your loved one had been consulted on what he or she wanted done when death occurred. Because Mother was a veteran, would she want the tribute of having her casket draped with a flag? Since your spouse was under the care of a physician and an autopsy would not be required, would he want one to help further medical data about his disease and donate his body for medical research? Since Dad was a regular "golf-aholic," would anyone consider the family to be disrespectful if his favorite putter and golf cap were included in the casket? Would it be appropriate to have a small family service, then a memorial for your brother's friends later in the same week? These are just a few of the more obvious decisions to be made almost immediately.

When the death has occurred, take the needed time to call a supportive person, or to adjust to the situation. There is no rush. Taking care of yourself is what is most important now....

—Neighborhood Visiting
Nurses Association

Our marriage vow says "till death do us part," but who among us is ever prepared for that final parting?

—Dr. James Peterson, director,
Emeriti Center, Gerontology
Department, University of
Southern California

In order to survive the emotional crisis, you must mobilize all the elements in your personality that make for stability—your values, your outlook on life, and your faith. You have to face your grief honestly. You must not be afraid of a confrontation with reality.

—Therese A. Rando, editor,
Loss and Anticipatory Grief

Right now there are a million decisions which must be made within the first twenty-four to forty-eight hours—unanswered questions of what's appropriate, arrangements to be completed, and pressing details to work through. There's no time to extensively weigh the pros and cons, no way to research all the information. Suddenly you're thrust into an arena totally foreign to your experience and you're expected to make decisions that could affect your loved one's memory, youself, your family, and perhaps the future. We muddle through somehow managing the death of a loved one all the while adjusting to our own personal style of heartache.

If you and your loved one have preplanned what to do when he or she dies and have composed a specific list or letter of instruction, then consider yourself fortunate. Most of us don't think about the death of a loved one, for many reasons, until we are faced with the situation. Out of sight, out of mind in the instance of a death doesn't work. That's what this book is all about.

While this book cannot provide all the answers, it will help you in a difficult time. If you know that a death is forthcoming, then this book will prepare you with information when you need it and act as a reference volume when required. It will help you navigate the path so that you can handle the situation a little better. The death of a loved one is never easy.

This chapter concentrates on your immediate needs and responsibilities after a loved one dies in the hospital setting or at home. We'll also talk about the impact of death and immediate support for your own needs and others in the family. We'll provide information so that when you're asked specific questions, you can respond.

HELPING IMMEDIATELY AFTER THE DEATH

There are things you can do to help yourself through the impossible aftermath of the death of a loved one. Sandra L. Graves, Ph.D., A.T.R., director of the American Grief Academy—a teaching service on group recovery for health and funeral professionals—recommends:

- Within the first twenty-four to forty-eight hours following a trauma, engage in periods of strenuous physical exercise (physician permitting) alternated by relaxation to ease some of the symptoms.
- Keep busy.
- Don't label yourself crazy.
- Scream if you feel the need.
- Make as many daily decisions as possible that will give you a feeling of control. If someone asks what you want to eat, answer him or her. Make a decision even if you don't know what you want and don't think you can eat.
- Keep talking. Where were you when you heard about the death? If you were present, what is the worst part that keeps going through your mind? What did you think when it first happened? What did you feel when it first happened? How do you feel now? This is all part of "debriefing." It does help.

Following a traumatic death of a loved one, there is even greater need to reach out for emotional support. How do you know you need to join a support group or speak with a therapist? Anytime you have unanswered questions or sense you need a tool to help with the coping process, you will benefit from professional support.

Says Dr. Graves, "Don't be afraid or ashamed to get help. Your reactions are normal. When you break your arm, you go to the doctor. Part of your life now may be broken. Seek help. It is a sign of strength that you can reach out to take care of yourself."

WHEN DEATH OCCURS IN A CARE FACILITY

When death occurs in a hospital setting, a care facility, or hospice, there are trained personnel to help and a doctor on call or on staff. Most deaths, nowadays, happen in these settings. Should the death occur at a medical facility and you're not there, you or another designated next of kin or responsible adult will be called by a doctor, a nurse, or a patient representative.

FINAL WORDS

ॐ

"Beautiful," Elizabeth Barrett Browning.

"It's very beautiful over there," Thomas A. Edison.

"I'm so happy, so happy," Gerard Manley Hopkins.

"C'est bien," André Gide.

"I hope with all my heart that there will be painting in heaven," Corot.

"Had I a pen and were able to write, I would describe how easy and pleasant a thing it is to die," William Hunter.

"Oh, relief has come," Robert Owen.

"Calmer and calmer.... many things are growing plain and clear to me," Friedrich von Schiller.

"When you come to the hedge that we all must go over—it isn't so bad. You feel sleepy—and you don't care. Just a little dreamy—some anxiety about which world you're really in—that's all," Stephen Crane.

I DIDN'T SCHEDULE DEATH FOR TODAY

by Sandra L. Graves, Ph.D., A.T.R., director of the American Grief Academy

We live in an age of planning–financial planning, business planning, funeral preplanning, house planning, meal planning, diet planning. There is nothing wrong with planning. It gives us structure to the time we spend in life and a goal toward which to strive.

When a loved one dies, there may be a forlorn "no, not today!" escape through our lips. We may acknowledge death, and know that death occurs and will occur for us and our loved ones someday. The anticipation that the death may occur at any time gives us some control over the idea of death. If we can second-guess it, we can control our grief. We can plan emotions. Not likely!

What happens when a major event occurs at an unscheduled moment? First of all, our attention is shifted to a different reality. There is an automatic reevaluation of all else that is taking place. For example, it matters not that we may be late to an appointment now, because the appointment does not have the same meaning as it did before the death.

After the funeral is over, the casseroles eaten, the friends and family have returned to their own lives, we are once again faced with plans. Now what? How is life different now? What do I do today, tomorrow, and next week? For some of us, our routines are backwards. We schedule, but don't necessarily plan events. We schedule in eating,

Some care facilities have volunteers or a chaplain who is trained to inform as well as comfort the family members at a time of death.

Even if the occurrence is one you've expected, such as with a long-term or potentially fatal disease or disability, you will still experience emotional and physical grief. If the death is the result of an accident, homicide, or sudden illness, it is said that the shock is even greater. Yet in a time of bereavement, it's senseless to attempt to determine which types of death make survivors suffer more.

When the death happens, informing the next of kin is often done over the phone. Once the family is present, the hospital staff member may take the family into a special, comfortable room. Like the scenes we view straight from a Hollywood movie or television script, in metropolitan hospitals there are often limited private areas, and the family receives word of the death standing in a swarming, noisy waiting area.

Telling the family about the death of a loved one must be one of the most heroic responsibilities ever placed on a human being, and in a care facility it usually falls on the shoulders of a nurse, doctor, or chaplain. There's no easy way, there's no good way, and there's no "right" way to say a loved one has died.

The personnel in care facilities are expected to do and say the correct things. Nevertheless, their words are always wrong. The only sentences that could make a difference are: "She pulled through the crisis–she's stabilized," "He's been getting better every day," and "It was close, but the baby's going to be fine."

After the initial shock wears off, you may want to return to the care facility and talk with those who were present when your loved one died, were friends with your loved one, or with the staff who cared for your loved one. This is healthy and is part of the process of grief.

WHEN DEATH OCCURS IN THE HOME OR AT WORK

When death occurs at your home, in your loved one's home, or at work, and you are there, immediately dial 911 (or other emergency telephone number designated for your area).

In the face of a crisis, it is up to the individual who calls 911 to clearly state the location, including apartment number, and type of emergency, i.e., fire, accident, or circumstance, i.e., the loved one isn't breathing or has been dead some time. All 911 calls are traced to the telephone and the operator can at once dispatch assistance to the exact street address. Therefore, even if you are unable to give perfect instructions or you're too emotional to make much sense, stay on the line and help will be on the way.

Once the emergency staff—probably fire personnel and/or paramedics—is dispatched, most cities also send a police officer and a police detective to the location. Any death occurring without a physician or medical personnel in attendance must be reported to the police (or other law enforcement branch in your area) and an investigation held.

When the police arrive and the paramedics enter the home or workplace, you will be asked to wait and provide information. The police might snap some photographs of your loved one or the room or place where he or she has died to use later to complete their reports. It is not being inferred that you had anything to do with the death of your loved one; this is simply part of their difficult job.

It is all right to call family members, a friend, or neighbors for emotional assistance while the police are in the house. You do not have to be alone with the body of your loved one, the medical staff, and the police. If the police are busy, they may forget to recommend that you call someone to sit with you. And even if you feel like you're fine, trauma specialists suggest that having another person with you helps. Additionally, later, after all the chaos has subsided, you will have someone with whom to discuss the details and recall what happened. This is sometimes part of the healing process.

going to the hairdresser, writing thank-you notes.

We often think about our plans for the future, before they were altered by the death. We tend to reassess everything that we find important about life and give it a new rating. We may no longer want to plan at all. We may feel cheated by the plans we made that were unfulfilled and unfinished. Plans no longer motivate us, but are painful reminders of what we have lost.

What are your needs at this moment? If you have trouble answering this question, you are not alone. We who grieve are often at a loss for understanding and direction. After all, if information gives us control, then questions must cause chaos. You need to know that this is normal, even if unpleasant. When you or others around you push to make plans, be kind to yourself. Plan the necessary things to do. Keep it simple.

As time goes on you will "test" each new situation, asking yourself how you feel (mad, sad, glad, scared) and what you think (Is this really worth the effort?). Try not to punish yourself with whether you accomplish your old plans or not. If they still fit the new you, you will know it.

As you begin to add experiences to your daily routines, schedule in a time to stop and turn inward. Just breathe and be with yourself quietly. Your clues that you may need to push your stop button can be when you are experiencing fear, desolation, emptiness, and loneliness. Don't abandon yourself; grief recovery occurs in small ways over big amounts of time.

SHOCK AND DENIAL
by Elaine Vail, psychology
professor at Western Illinois
University, from *A Personal
Guide to Living with Loss*

ટ્⋙

*Denial, when it occurs, may
last for a few moments, a few
days or months, or it may
never go away. Some days, we
may be able to deal quite
openly with the impending
death, while the next week we
may be unable to face it
again. We all have good days,
when we feel strong and in
control, and bad days when
we are "down" and feel
impotent and ill-at-ease.
Surely you can recall one of
your own "down" days, when
you were already upset about
one or several things going on
in your life, or perhaps you
simply didn't feel good.*

*If someone walked in the
room and brought up the fact
that you are expected to
arrange a program for the club
meeting or fix the leak in the
basement or bake a cake for
the fundraiser at school, you
would probably kick him, at
least mentally, or ignore the
intrusion completely. At that
moment, you must deny those
particular responsibilities,
and you cannot or will not
deal with them. There are
other demands and difficulties
claiming your attention, and
anything else is overload and
must wait. Our egos accept
only so much assault. Denial
is a way of maintaining some
control in one's life.*

Recently in all police emergencies involving a death, there's
been a movement for a Trauma Intervention Program (TIP)
volunteer to stay with the family while the police are
investigating the circumstances of the death and await the
coroner, who is sometimes called the county medical examiner.
TIP volunteers are trained to understand the shock which
accompanies the death of a loved one and can be of assistance
helping direct you to the next steps.

If your loved one has been recently treated for an illness or
disease, you will want to call his or her doctor. The coroner will
want to know the doctor's name, too, since without a medical
history to help verify the cause of death, an autopsy or
examination must be performed. If you don't know the doctor's
name, you can often find this information on prescription
medicine bottles or on bills from the physician.

After the coroner (or one of the coroner's deputies) has
initially examined the loved one, the body will be transported to
the county or city morgue for an autopsy. Or in the case of a
loved one having a known and treated illness or disease, the
coroner will direct the body to be transported to a funeral home
of your choice.

For many adults who live alone and die at home, it is a
neighbor who finds the body. If this happens and the police and
coroner are unable to reach a family member immediately, the
house or apartment will be locked and a warning seal placed
over the doors. This seal serves to protect the contents of your
loved one's home. Once it has been determined that you are the
most appropriate person to enter the home of the person who
died, the seal will be broken.

The same procedures will most likely hold true if the death
occurs in the workplace. However, often the person who seems
to be dead can be resuscitated and thus paramedics will
transport him or her to the hospital.

DEATH AND THE HOSPICE PROGRAM

The hospice program provides an entire framework for
caring for both the dying and the family of the dying. It does not
seek to treat the illness, but to enable the dying to control pain

and manage the final stage of life. For those people who, while terminally ill, have been actively involved in a hospice program, the family members are given specific instructions and procedures to follow when death occurs. Instead of dialing 911, it is asked that a hospice staff member be called. Those people who die under the care of the hospice staff of doctors, nurses, and social workers have previously decided that they do not want heroic means performed to reestablish life. They sign a form that clearly defines their wishes, including not to be resuscitated. This is sometimes known as a DNR form, or do not resuscitate consent document.

One is "officially" dead when there is irreversible cessation of all functions of the entire brain, explains Fred Jordan, chief medical examiner of the state of Oklahoma, or when there is irreversible cessation of circulatory and respiratory functions. "Most people are pronounced dead when heart and lung function ceases. Brain death requires documentation by special equipment generally only available in a hospital setting."

Like most hospice programs, Hospice of North Coast, affiliated with Tri-City Medical Center, a suburban hospital in San Diego County, California, provides family members and those caring for the individual who is "actively dying," with a checklist of the signs of death. They include:

1. No breathing
2. No heartbeat
3. Loss of control of bowel or bladder
4. No response to verbal commands or shaking
5. Eyelids slightly open
6. Eyes fixed on a certain spot
7. Jaw relaxed and mouth slightly open

The staff members instruct the family to call the hospice worker to help confirm that death has occurred, and then the hospice will call the mortuary and the doctor. Explains Bonnie Gray, licensed social worker with Hospice of North Coast, "This information may sound frightening, but we explain to the clients not to call the police, paramedics, or the fire department. The

Our minds seem to try to protect us from the awful information of a loved one's death by fabricating a way out of it, or even if at a loss for a fabrication, we simply refuse to believe it. Sometimes we are buffered by a state of shock which temporarily separates us from reality. It gives us some time to absorb the emotional insult and begin to adjust to its impact.

SURVIVING THE GRIEVING PROCESS

by Nancy Zeidman, director of the Caring Program, featured in *Health Scene* magazine

ع

Although each individual has his or her own way of mourning the loss of a loved one, there are ways to help cope more effectively with the pain:

• Accept the loss. Some things in life have no basis in logic; they just happen. Accepting this can prevent much bitterness and self-blame.

• Acknowledge your pain. Try to live through it, not avoid it.

• Reach out to family and friends. Make your needs, both physical and emotional, known. Loved ones can be tremendous sources of support. Don't be too proud to accept their help.

• Share your thoughts and feelings. Don't keep your emotions bottled up inside. Talk, scream, cry—all grieving people need these outlets.

• Understand that each person has an individual timetable for grief. It is difficult to estimate a "normal" grieving period. Everyone moves through grief at his or her own pace.

• Accept that life is for the living. This is the final stage of grieving.

hospice team's goal is to prepare the patient and family for what is expected, for death. The physical and emotional well-being of the family is as important to us as the dying person's."

In Ernest Morgan's classic on a kinder, gentler form of death and dying, *Dealing Creatively with Death,* he explains that when the death is expected and a loved one has died in the home or in a hospice, it's often possible to transport your loved one's body to the funeral home yourself. (A funeral home is sometimes known as a mortuary; funeral directors are sometimes called morticians. These terms vary depending on your location.)

Depending on where you live, you may need a transportation certificate, available from the county health department before the body of your loved one can be moved. Morgan considers the responsibility of personally moving your loved one from the home or place of death to the funeral home as a final act of love, and he believes it enables family members to privately say good-bye. If this is something you'd like to do, talk with the funeral director or prearrange the details and transportation before the death of your loved one.

You are not making a "death wish" by preplanning the course of action following a loved one's death. On the contrary, at a tremendously hard time, preplanning will make the situation somewhat easier for all involved.

Where to Get Help

After the death of a loved one and during those chaotic first twenty-four to forty-eight hours, family and friends can help. Do not hesitate to call your own spiritual advisor or the clergy person of your loved one. Even if it's the middle of the night, he or she can probably help you cope through the immediacy of the death.

If your loved one was part of the hospice program, immediately call the nurse, social worker, or your representative. Although representatives at the National Hospice Organization will be glad to talk with you, your local representative can connect you with other social services and support groups.

Look under the type of support group in the index—you'll be able to access the name, address, and phone numbers for other organizations that will help you immediately. For example, if your loved one has died of homicide, lay counselors and chapter representatives from Parents of Murdered Children will assist you through the initial shock and become a resource throughout the ordeal.

DECISIONS AT A DIFFICULT TIME

In the first few hours after the death of a loved one, many people are unable to make decisions or discuss the reality of the situation. Denial is one of the stages of grief, as discussed by psychiatrist and internationally known expert on death and dying, Dr. Elisabeth Kübler-Ross.

If you are the responsible next of kin, you will be asked how you wish to dispose of the body of your loved one and what kind of funeral, memorial, or commemoration you would prefer. These questions are not easily answered, unless you've previously discussed what your loved one prefers to be done or you have specific guidelines outlined by your religious beliefs.

You may want to contact other relatives or close friends of your loved one to help share the load. Most people like to feel useful and delegating some of your responsibilities allows them to feel part of the process. This too helps process grief.

While hospitals, care facilities, and the county morgue are not equipped to keep or store the body of your loved one for any length of time, you can wait for a few hours to make a decision. You will have to let the staff know that you need some extra time. Further, it is possible to pay to have the body transferred to a mortuary, temporarily, so that you can shop for the best or most appropriate funeral services.

IDENTIFY AND EXPRESS THE EMOTIONS OF GRIEF
by David A. Crenshaw, psychologist specializing in grief, from *Bereavement– Counseling the Grieving throughout the Life Cycle*

෨

The bereaved must be helped to experience the pain of grief. This crucial aspect of the grief work consists of expressing in words the intense feelings that accompany the loss of someone important to us.

The healing process is very much aided when the feelings are shared with a trusted person. When the bereaved share feelings of grief, they are not just ventilating powerful painful emotions, more importantly in terms of the healing process, they are making an active declaration of trust.

Thus, the bereaved are taking a formidable risk. Grievers are confiding and unburdening their painful feelings and thereby are expressing the belief that their feelings can be accepted and understood by significant others. This declaration of trust removes barriers of isolation, cynicism, and mistrust that so easily get erected after a tragic loss heightens our sense of vulnerability.

IN THE FIRST FEW HOURS

At intervals throughout the book, we will provide information on what should be done next. Within the first few hours after the death of a loved one:

- Call or contact other family members and friends.
- Lock the home or apartment of your loved one or receive personal effects from the care facility where the death occurred. If your loved one has been living at a care facility, such as a nursing or Alzheimer's home, find out if a staff member will take charge of arranging for your loved one's possessions to be returned to you, or designated next of kin.
- Make sure your loved one's children or dependent adults have a responsible adult with whom to stay and everyone understands the situation honestly and *on his or her own level*. Although a death has occurred, for those children involved, try to keep everything as normal as possible. Do not use phrases concerning the death such as "a long sleep," or "he went away," which only confuse children and mentally disabled adults (see chapter 9, Preparing Children for the Death of a Loved One).
- Make sure your loved one's pets are taken care of, that they will be fed, given water, and be exercised. Pets grieve, too. What you see as misbehavior (such as chewing up a slipper or digging holes in the yard) is often an animal cry for help. Animals do not realize that their favorite person is no longer there.
- If you know that your loved one is a member of a memorial society or has prearranged a funeral and burial or cremation, contact the appropriate organization.
- If your loved one wanted to be an organ donor or body donor, you should inform the hospital staff or the organization for which the donations are meant.

Often a friend or neighbor, who shares the loss and feels helpless, will assist with these details. Most people want to help and simply do not know what to do.

THE DEATH CERTIFICATE

You will need a death certificate in order to go ahead with any funeral, memorial, or commemoration service. In some states, it is illegal to move a body unless a death certificate has been signed by a doctor, coroner, or medical officer. If your loved one has died in a hospice or hospital setting, a staff member at the facility will prepare the form. If your loved one has been under the care of a registered nurse or doctor, he or she will give you the form. If your loved one has died in an accident or of a sudden illness, the county medical examiner or coroner will prepare the form.

You will need the form for the mortuary, and the funeral director will fill in necessary information. Often he or she will be able to provide extra, official copies of the certificate, or this service may be part of the package you buy.

The death certificate will indicate the loved one's name and cause of death, including the underlying cause of death. It may also include other details such as the time and date of death, sex, occupation, date of birth, place of birth, residence, country of citizenship, social security number, marital status, name of surviving spouse, names and birthplaces of both parents, and ancestry. Some forms have places for the name and address of the individual who has furnished this information. The form will be signed by the attending physician or other medical professional. Some states require that the form be completed by two physicians. As with any official form, it is wise to double-check that all the information is correct and appropriate doctors or officials have signed and dated the form. For example, if there is a mistake, such as one digit of your loved one's social security number written incorrectly, a monkey wrench could be thrown in receiving benefits for dependent children, life insurance money, or pension funds. When the information doesn't jibe, the process will come to a grinding halt until the error is rectified. This may take weeks or months.

The search for a definition of death in the medical profession and in the courts is a testament to humankind's desire to know and control all the facets of life. Social history underlies the present-day legal systems that come into action subsequent to death, reiterating the same story of people's constant struggle to control their lives— and their own death.

—Richard G. Benton, from *Death and Dying*

ABOUT ACCEPTING DEATH
by Ernest Morgan, from
Dealing Creatively with Death

❧

If we were to walk across the fields in summertime to some undisturbed spot and mark off a piece of ground say four feet square then examine this little area minutely, we would find an astonishing variety of life. There would be many species of plants; possibly a mouse's nest, and other small creatures. Then resorting to a microscope, we would observe an incredible host of microorganisms functioning in association with the larger life forms.

In that little square of ground we would have seen an interdependent community of life in which birth and death were continuously taking place and in which diverse life forms were sheltering and nourishing one another. Written in the rocks beneath was a story of a similar process going back through eons of time.

Humankind is part of the ongoing community of nature, on a world scale, subject to the same cycle of birth and death which governs all other creatures and, like them, totally dependent on other life. Sometimes we tend to forget this. Birth and death are as natural for us as for the myriad of creatures in that little square of ground.

You or another designated next of kin will need an official copy of the death certificate to apply for benefits due the family, to sell or transfer ownership of property, to have access to safety deposit boxes and bank accounts, to receive VA benefits, for probate filings, and to prepare your loved one's final tax returns. We'll talk more about this and other financial details later in chapter 8, Practical Matters of the Death.

Official copies of the death certificate should be available at your state health department, at the county clerk's office, or through another designated city or county office. You can pay for copies or have a funeral director or your attorney obtain them for you. You will need approximately ten copies.

WHEN AN AUTOPSY IS NECESSARY

As stated, when a physician is not in attendance at the death of your loved one and/or he or she has not been under the care of a doctor, often a postmortem autopsy is required. There are other times when an autopsy is required, such as when the death occurs due to a result of an accident, criminal violence or other suspicious manner, or suicide, or if the death occurs in a correctional institution or at the discretion of the coroner.

In an autopsy, the body is dissected and organs are weighed and inspected. As medical technology continues to advance, other techniques that do not require the body to be dissected are being used, including magnetic resonance imaging, fiberoptic endoscopes, and ultrasound procedures.

WHEN AN AUTOPSY IS RECOMMENDED

An autopsy determines the cause of death. However, it can do more and many times a physician will ask the family for permission to have an autopsy performed. It is up to the family to provide consent for the procedure unless the autopsy is mandated by law. There are still many people who object to an autopsy for their loved one on antiquated grounds that stem more from the horror movies made in the 1950s than reality. Your doctor can discuss the complete procedure as well as the pros and cons, and you may need to ask for his or her advice.

Even after an autopsy, the body of your loved one can be prepared for an open-casket service should that be your wish. However, when there is a complete autopsy, including examination of the head, completed by coroners or medical examiners (called a medicolegal autopsy), an open casket may not be possible. Be sure to ask and/or let your wishes be known. If it is your desire, you can of course still see the remains of your loved one, however, most coroners suggest that you discuss what you will be seeing before the visit so you will be somewhat prepared.

While this sounds grisly to some people, postmortem autopsies reveal information and data that may help others. Through autopsies, science has learned about the correlation between obesity and arterial plaque and smoking and lung cancer, among other things.

Often, a family asks that an autopsy be performed. *The Autopsy Manual* suggests that you may want to consider this procedure for a number of reasons. Done with dignity and respect, the procedure is indicated when the loved one who died has been in good health; when there is the chance of a genetic disease or contagious diseases others should know about; when there is a chance of an environmental or work-related cause; when there is a question of misdiagnosis whether from a medical or dental procedure; if death occurred in a care facility; or if death happened before, during, or shortly after childbirth.

When the next of kin requests an autopsy, it must be paid for by the family. When it is required by law or asked for by a medical institution or a physician, there should be no cost for the family.

RELIGIOUS VIEW OF AUTOPSY

Protestants, Roman Catholics, Jews, Christian Scientists, and other religious groups have their own rules and preferences regarding autopsy. If your loved one has specific wishes regarding his or her religious philosophy regarding autopsy, it is best to make those desires known before death. That's not

When we have learned to accept ourselves as part of the community of nature, then we can accept death as part of the natural order of things.

We commonly act as if we, and those we love, are going to live forever. But we are wrong, for all must die—nor can we know when this will happen.

In our culture we tend to avoid the subject of death. This is unfortunate, for death is a normal and necessary part of life. Until we learn to face it honestly and accept it, we are not living at our best.

If we are to appreciate our fellows, if we are to live with patience, gentleness, and love, let us be about it today, for life is short.

always possible or even reasonable. Therefore, keep in mind that most religions view autopsy as a means of helping others.

In Judaism, for example, where there is a reverent treatment of the body after death and speedy burial, it is one of the biblical precepts that the body be left intact. Thus it might be theorized that an autopsy would be forbidden by Jewish law. There has been considerable discussion on this topic. Reformed Jews are not opposed, while Orthodox and Conservative Jews will approve it *when* the autopsy would save other lives, if there may be heredity causes, and/or if the individual has agreed to the autopsy before his or her death.

In the opinion of the Roman Catholic Church, there is no moral objection for an autopsy to be performed on the body of a loved one who has died to determine the cause of death or for the progress of medical science generally. The Catholic church also points out that an autopsy may be critical to detect a suspected crime. With such motives, autopsy is morally unobjectionable, as long as the consent of the next of kin or those having legal guardianship has been obtained.

Regardless of your religious or moral views, the decision to go ahead with an elective autopsy can be difficult. You may want to discuss the procedure with other family members, your clergy, and possibly your attorney.

Reading the information in this chapter and in the chapters that follow may not be pleasant or easy, yet by knowing what might be expected at the time of death of your loved one you will be better prepared to take charge of the situation or lend assistance.

❧

In the next chapter, Making the Arrangements, funeral and burial practices and procedures will be discussed. After a loved one dies, you will be asked questions on the disposition of the body, embalming, and services. If a loved one has recently died and you are in the planning stages, you may want to refer to the index and specifically read the information you will need right now.

Chapter 2

Making the Arrangements

"Instinctively and unconsciously, we reject the idea of death and assume (though we really know better) that we and those for whom we care will live forever," says author Ernest Morgan. This feeling is charmingly expressed in a popular ditty, made up by a five-year-old child, and currently sung in Russia:

May there always be sunshine,
May there always be blue skies,
May there always be Mama,
May there always be me!

This feeling of permanence leads us to take all our relationships for granted. The realization that all our relationships are temporary and should be cherished while we have them can profoundly enrich these relationships.

Not surprisingly, it will take days, weeks, and perhaps years for the pain of grief to subside or to resolve the death of a loved one. We never "get back to normal" or get over his or her death. We move on to a "new normal."

MOURNING AND RITUAL
by Michael A. Simpson,
from *The Facts of Death*

❧

Various acts of mourning have clear purposes. They openly acknowledge the reality of death and explain it once more in whatever way the current system of belief conceptualizes death. They allow for the open expression of grief, but in controlled and socially acceptable circumstances and forms; and they allow gestures of consolation and support from friends and relatives. For one final occasion, the dead person takes a central position in a social event, along with his or her bereaved relations. The rituals may honor the dead and define the shape they will take in our memories, or make preparations for the soul's journey or the life in another world.

Rituals serve to provide a temporary structure at a time when the removal of an important part of your personal and social structure has left you adrift. They give you something to do when there's nothing to be done and you feel you must do something—without your having to search to be creative in devising something to do. Rituals can give you a set of familiar practices to turn to when the shape of life has become unfamiliar.

There will always be an emptiness without our loved ones; with healthy grief and healing, it turns from pain to fond recollections. That's where memories help fill the void. However, after the immediate shock of the death, there are arrangements to be made for the final decisions that are best for you, your family, and the loved one who died.

The choices are numerous, overwhelming at times, and seem especially so in the numbed state so many experience at the death of a loved one. Although in most cases you don't have an extended period to consider the alternatives and the options that are available, you do have a little time to think through the options.

This is a very practical chapter. The information in the following pages will help you when a loved one has died. There's less fear of the known than the unknown. So for many people, knowing the hows, whys, whats, and whens of the decision-making process unshrouds the mystery of death. A few may criticize that discussing what to wear to a funeral is frivolous and flippant. Shopping around for the best buys on funeral/memorial services is inappropriate, profane, and blasphemous. Even the idea of sprinkling a loved one's ashes in the apple grove behind the house is contemptuous and the ultimate in intolerable taste. Like our differing lifestyles, death styles vary, too. Isn't it more important to please yourself, celebrate the life of your loved one, and do what you must do than worry about "what the Joneses would think"?

Death, like life, is filled with choices. The roads we select and the decisions we make should be based on as much information as possible. This is especially true when the decision for funerals, body burials, and cremations of a loved one is concerned.

When you're in the middle of coordinating all the details or involved with sharing the arrangements for the final disposition of your loved one's body, it's nearly impossible to think through each decision, weigh the alternatives, and look at the consequences. Thus, the topics included in this chapter will help you organize a funeral, memorial, commemoration, or other service. There can be a service, a pause, or a prayer that fits your loved one's life choices and his or her wishes, and/or accommodates the desires of family, friends, and religious affiliation. There are also other choices that require less decision making such as direct disposition of a loved one. While that might seem callous, it has an appropriate place in life and death, too.

SHARING THE RESPONSIBILITY

If everybody, including you, regards you as the wisest, the strongest, and/or the smartest one in the family, it may just *seem* logical for you to make all the arrangements for the service, to do everything, to answer all the questions. Or you may be standing on the sidelines while another family member has accepted or taken over this role. This happens in many families, especially when those who are grieving are in incredible pain. However, what might seem right, good, and thoughtful can be counterproductive to healing and the resolution of grief.

Sherry L. Williams, president and cofounder of ACCORD, Inc., a self-help network based in Louisville, Kentucky, specializing in aftercare and grief recovery, says, "By sharing the responsibilities of the services, decisions, and details, those who are mourning are able to begin moving through the stages of grief. The funeral helps provide a vehicle for this transition.

"Many funeral directors and those involved in counseling the bereaved are seeing the need to involve all interested family members, including children, in the planning stages and at the arrangement conference, where the funeral director meets with family to discuss the service. About half of all funeral directors and funeral consultants will actively involve as much of the family as possible and the percentage is increasing as more people in the funeral field became sensitized to the wishes of the family and survivors of a loved one.

"At a time of death, so much is out of control that by planning part of the service, helping with the details, and making decisions, family members can begin to put some control back into their lives. Even simple decisions, such as what food to serve after the funeral or who should care for the loved one's plants, can be healthful. By helping, those who are grieving are able to begin to cope with the situation and confront the death," explains Williams.

Delegating responsibilities for the service among family members and friends also serves other purposes, explains Williams, who is a registered nurse, holds a degree in psychology, and has devoted the last fifteen years to grief counseling and aftercare. Participating in the plans for the service, suggesting who will ride to the visitation with whom, or asking certain people to speak at the service helps loved ones face reality. Williams advises, "Through this participation, loved ones can move their thoughts about the individual from the present into the stage of memories."

CONTACTING THE FAMILY ABOUT THE DEATH

There's never a right way to tell family and friends about the death of a loved one. In this time, the announcement of the death is zapped over telephone wires. Some people blurt it out, "Mom's dead!" Others try a softer approach, "There's been an accident—it's Phil," or "I have some terrible news… about Jan." Quite often a friend or other relative can take on this difficult task. Working with you, as the individual responsible for all the details after the death, you can advise how best to tell the difficult news. A lot of times we feel we must do this ourselves (back to the strongest, smartest, most reliable family member trying to cope with all the responsibilities), but on the other hand, family members and friends truly want to help. This is one of those responsibilities that can be delegated while you attend to more pressing issues.

Basically, all family and friends who will want to attend the service should be called, including associates, clients, and colleagues. The executor of the will should be informed. Teachers and caregivers of the children involved should be notified as others who were close to the loved one who has recently died. If your loved one has many friends, such as someone who has been extremely active in community affairs, you may want to enlist the help of the president of his or her civic organization to make calls to other members. For example, the rotary membership chairperson could call all the members, or the bird-watching club's president could call the participants, instead of you making twenty-five more calls.

Except for close family and friends, you may want to wait to make most of the calls until after the details of the service are formalized. Call once with, "We'll be having the service on Saturday at ten at Our Lady of Hope on Elm Street. Then we'll return to Mother's after the graveside ceremony for lunch." This will save you considerable time instead of having to make the phone calls twice, first with the news of the death and then with the time, date, and place of the funeral.

DISPOSITION

When a loved one dies, a decision must be made on disposition, that is, how his or her body will be disposed. For some, it's a cruel, uncomfortable task, yet one that must be faced. For other people and those who have planned for this time of death, it is an extension of caring, a final act of responsibility, and a tribute to love.

The options include earth burial, entombment, cremation, direct disposition, donation of organs, or a body donation followed by cremation or burial.

Earth Burial

Commonly in America, the body of the loved one is embalmed and there is a time for viewing the body, sometimes called visitation. A funeral is planned, and depending on the services and religious affiliation, there is

ON AN OPEN CASKET

by Theodore E. Hughes
and David Klein, from
*A Family Guide to Wills,
Funerals, and Probate*

❧

*Some psychologists (and
virtually all funeral directors)
firmly believe that it is only
after viewing the body that
survivors accept the reality
and finality of the death and
that such viewing actually
facilitates the grieving
process....*

*Other psychologists (and
many clergymen), however,
argue the opposite point of
view with equal conviction.
They do not feel that viewing
a highly cosmeticized corpse
helps the survivors accept the
death, and they feel that in
some circumstances viewing
the corpse may be a traumatic
experience.*

often some type of commemoration service at the site of the burial. The body of a loved one is buried in a casket in a cemetery. This is called interment and is the most common form of disposition in the United States. Whether we personally agree or not, earth burials seem to traditionally fit what Americans believe should happen when a loved one dies.

Under United States law, burial is regulated by statute. While burial laws differ from county to county and state to state, there may not be a burial without a certificate attesting the cause of death by a physician, coroner, or medical examiner. Court decisions have confirmed and upheld the ruling that a corpse has no commercial value and is legally the property of the next of kin (in inheritance order). Some states demand that the family accept the financial responsibility of burial, which is regulated through charges or fines. Although cremation is growing in acceptance (in the western states cremation and scattering of ashes is now equal to earth burials), many Americans prefer the idea of a final resting place and of a grave site where they can go to remember the person who died. Quite often, those who choose earth burials have a "family site" so that members can be buried in the same cemetery. Many cemeteries offer "scattering gardens" for cremated remains.

Cost of a cemetery plot: The cost of a cemetery plot, like that of the funeral or service, can different widely from one area of the country to another. A number of cities have municipal cemeteries and there are cemeteries owned by religious organizations. If your loved one was a veteran, he or she and immediate family may be buried in a government cemetery. Not all family members choose to have their qualified loved one buried in a government cemetery, since plots are often unavailable and not convenient for the family members to visit as often as they'd like.

Selecting a cemetery is another difficult decision that must be made immediately or within the first few days after the death of your loved one. If this is your first experience with the death of a loved one, ask the funeral director or a representative from the memorial society for suggestions and recommendations, including pricing. This is part of the service the funeral home provides, and the funeral director will have knowledge about cemeteries.

Do not think you'll be considered a cheapskate or feel intimidated by selecting a plot that is adequate, but not at the top end of the scale. As with funerals, plots and cemeteries are available to fit all budgets. In addition to the cost of the plot, you will be charged for the opening and closing of the grave and there may be gratuity expected from those who conduct this service. You will also be charged for the marker and for its installation.

The Consumers Union's *Funerals: Consumers' Last Rights*, encourages everyone to consider the marker as a purchase. The book's editors say, "A buyer should insist on receiving the manufacturer's guarantee or warranty for a memorial so that a claim for repair or replacement can be filed if necessary."

Be sure to ask what other fees are involved. Like a funeral home or memorial service, the cemetery is in the business of sales.

When you talk with the funeral director (if he or she is making the arrangements to buy the plot for you) the cost of the plot will definitely be on your mind, as it should. You will not only want to talk about how much items and options cost (and whether they are necessary), but also discuss the type of marker to memorialize the loved one at the grave site. Markers vary from large granite or marble memorials to small, bronze plaques placed over a grave. Some families choose other personalized memorials such as placing a marble bench at the site or having the loved one's name inscribed on a bell or other marker at the cemetery.

Most cemeteries require that the family purchase a vault (or grave liner); the average cost is about $750. The vault liner is placed inside the grave, with the casket within the liner, so that the earth doesn't collapse around the casket. A vault liner is a boxlike structure, most often made of concrete, with a loose-fitting slab cover to support the earth that will be filled over it. A burial vault is a more substantial

In Europe an interest in cemeteries is not regarded as morbid or unnatural. On November 1 and 2 thousands of Parisians flock to Pere Lachaise to celebrate All Saints' Day and the Day of the Dead. Much French funerary sculpture is designed to be appreciated (and sometimes to give a warning or impart a private joke).

—Judi Culbertson and Tom Randall, from *Permanent Parisians, Permanent Londoners* structure, often steel reinforced and metal lined or coated, with a tight-fitting molded lid that provides a seal when it is put into place.

There are only a few local jurisdictions where legal requirements will force you to buy a liner, but since sunken graves add to a cemetery's upkeep costs, many (though not all) cemeteries require some kind of grave liner. Check directly with local cemeteries to find out what their requirements are. Do not necessarily rely on what a funeral director tells you.

If possible, personally visit a few cemeteries before you purchase a plot. Look around at the facilities; notice how the other sites are kept up and how the grounds are maintained. Within the cost of the plot you may see an item called "perpetual care," known in some states as "endowed care." Most cemeteries are required by state law to charge for this service.

Some people find it helpful during the stages of grief to go to the cemetery and visit the grave of their loved one who has died. Thus a cemetery that's conveniently located, even if it's not the first choice pertaining to facilities and the site, might be the best choice.

Keep in mind that some cemeteries do not allow headstones; others require them. Cemeteries sell urns or vases for flowers to be placed at the grave and some require that the family buy the cemetery's accessories instead of obtaining others at a lower cost. Some cemeteries have restrictions on the types of flowers, plants, or decorations at the grave site. You'll want to ask some questions on these points when you visit the cemetery or talk with the funeral director. Also, ask for a copy of the *Cemetery Rules and Regulations.*

Another reason to go to the cemetery before you buy is because you may be able to choose a plot that has special meaning. For example, you could select one near a grove of trees, close to a rose garden, or on a hillside that gets the first rays of morning sun. You may want to consider your comfort, too. If you are disabled, you may want a plot near the road, so you can park the car and not have to cross a hundred yards of grass when you visit.

For more information on funerals and other memorial services, including costs and options, refer to other sections of this chapter.

Where to Get Help

International Cemetery and Funeral Association
1895 Preston White Drive, Suite 220
Reston, VA 20191
800-645-7700   703-391-8400

ICFA is a nonprofit association of cemeteries, funeral homes, crematories, and monument retailers that offers informal mediation of consumer complaints through its Cemetery Consumer Service Council.

"Backyard" burials: Years ago, loved ones were often buried in the family plot near a small chapel located on the estate. We've all seen this type of family cemetery in movies and on television. Today, few of us own vast acres of land or have the property to consider establishing a cemetery of our own. However, it's not unusual for family members to think about "backyard burials" and deliberate the topic when discussing body burials in the earth or sprinkling of cremated remains.

If you or your loved one wants to be buried in the backyard, near the old apple orchard, or beneath the wild roses that grow on the thousand-acre ranch, check with the health department or medical examiner regarding the laws. The funeral director who takes care of your needs may also know whether it is legal to bury the remains of your loved one in the area you've chosen. Some experts say that sprinkling cremated ashes is a private affair and as long as you don't make "a big deal out of it," you can do it almost anywhere. However, there are regulations in this instance too.

There's no "generally speaking" other than to check with your own county health department or other regulatory board regarding burial regulations before a decision is made.

Entombment

When a body is entombed, the casket is placed in a mausoleum, or tomb, which is an aboveground structure usually made of marble or stone. Some are large enough structures for a number of caskets or for entire families. Most mausoleums are found on cemetery grounds and some cemeteries have areas where family mausoleums can be erected. The cost, as you can imagine, can be considerable.

Tombs are some of the oldest, most recognized forms of architecture. We all know or have at least seen photos of the Egyptian pyramids. They were built for the pharaohs before 2000 B.C., and are a classic example of a tomb. These tombs were included in the Seven Wonders of the Ancient World. In the seventeenth century, Saint Peter's Basilica in Rome was built over the grave of the first pope, which exemplifies the practice of building monuments to those of importance. More modern tombs include those of former U.S. President Ulysses S. Grant in New York City and Russian Communist leader Vladimir Lenin in Red Square in Moscow.

In recent times, mausoleums are often positioned somewhat away from the cemetery. As with the past, people choose entombment for various reasons, including the historical significance of entombment. When purchasing a crypt, it is important to understand that there is a distinct difference in cost depending on the level at which the casket is placed in the mausoleum crypt. Should you decide on entombment, the following terms refer to the levels: "eye," "heart," and (the highest) "heaven." Mausoleum space is often priced at about $1,500 and continues upward from there, depending on location, the city, and the extras the family wants to purchase.

Cremation

There was a time when it was the decided exception to the rule that one chose to be or have a loved one cremated after death. Cremation in the United States is gaining wider acceptance, and cremation is the choice for about 30 percent of all dispositions. According to a survey on "cremations and death" by *Cremationist* magazine, in some states, such as California (where 40 percent choose cremation), Hawaii (where almost 50 percent choose cremation), and Nebraska (almost 52 percent choose cremation), the acceptance of this practice is practically the norm. In Japan, cremation is mandatory and in England, earth burial is thought to be odd; cremation is the preferred method.

According to the National Funeral Directors Association (NFDA), some people choose cremation because they prefer quick reduction of the body rather than its natural return to the earth through decay. Others like the concept of ashes-to-ashes and dust-to-dust philosophy that cremation symbolizes. Still other people use cremation as a way to immediately dispose of the body without a memorial service or a tribute of any kind. (Funeral personnel decline to use the term *ashes* to discuss cremated remains, since the remains are technically fragments of bones. In "lay terms" the use of the word ashes is still accepted. After the cremation, the remains are often referred to as *cremains*. All terms are understandable to a funeral director and his or her staff.)

Some grief experts explain that sometimes people who choose cremation for their loved ones' bodies are doing so, they believe, to sidestep the grieving process. And yet the opposite can occur. One cannot jump over the physical and emotional stages of grief and those who try to, through a speedy cremation, often are left uneasy.

With cremation, you have several choices of what to do with the loved one's cremated remains. You can choose inurement, that is, the remains are placed in a container and

CREMATION
by Michael A. Simpson,
from *The Facts of Death*

❧

Different religious groups vary in their views of cremation. Though there is no prohibition against cremation in the Bible, ancient Judaism practiced earth burial in all but exceptional circumstances. Today, Orthodox Jewish tradition is opposed to cremation, and Conservative congregations share similar views. Reform Judaism does not oppose cremation. The early Christian Church followed the Jewish tradition of earth burial, and cremation came into rather unfair disrepute—having been in common use in Greek and Roman culture, it was regarded as a pagan practice. Later, some other objections to cremation arose from those who interpreted the idea of the resurrection of the body very literally, believing that it had to be buried completely intact to allow resurrection. Later still, the modern cremation movement at the end of the nineteenth century was often supported by rebels against Church authority. Accordingly, the Catholic Church enacted some canon laws forbidding cremation or even cooperation with the practice. It was made clear, however, that the objection was not theological, but a matter of Church

kept in a niche at a columbarium. The niche will typically have a glass door and an inscription on the urn will be turned to the glass. Some columbariums have urn rooms where many urns are placed on shelves and there are benches for family and friends to come and be with their loved ones. The cost of a niche can be almost the same as a grave and varies depending on location in the columbarium and section of the country. Some, but not all, cemeteries have columbariums.

You may decide to place the remains in a container and then bury them in a grave in a cemetery. The place where the urns are buried may be referred to as an urn garden. The cost of a spot in an urn garden is often the same as that of a grave. The urn garden is the choice of many as this allows some people to visit the grave and "talk" with the loved one who has died. There will be a fee for a memorial plaque, opening and closing the plot, and care of the grounds.

Quite a few families choose to have the remains scattered over an ocean. The funeral director you will be using can often care for the scattering or direct you to a memorial society, such as the Neptune Society, to assist you. Depending on county regulations, you may be able to sprinkle or bury your loved one's remains on a location that has held importance to him or her in life. Another option is to keep the remains of your loved one with you for disposition at a later time. One couple preplanned that their remains would be scattered together when they had both died, so when the husband died, his widow kept the remains. The family was instructed about their wishes so they could be carried out when the wife died.

Many funeral directors, where state regulations permit, will offer to prepare the body for viewing in a rented casket, then arrange a service, before cremation takes place. If cremation and a closed casket is chosen, embalming is unnecessary, but you must make this clear to the funeral director. FTC Funeral Rule requires authorization prior to embalming. Some funeral homes and some cemeteries have their own cremation facilities on the premises. In smaller towns, the funeral home will contract with a cremation facility. However, it's important to speak with the funeral director and be clear on what you are getting. Under law, funeral directors who offer cremations:

- May not tell you that state or local law requires a casket for direct cremations.
- Must disclose in writing your right to buy an unfinished wood box (a type of casket) or an alternative container for a direct cremation.
- Must make an unfinished wood box or alternative container available for direct cremation.

Authorization for cremation follows the state-mandated "next of kin" laws, i.e., spouse, adult child, parent, etc., unless otherwise designated. If there is a difference of opinion as to whether your loved one should be cremated or if one of the next of kin is not available, funeral directors will, sometimes, not proceed with cremation. For example, if you and your adult sister have decided that you will choose cremation for your widowed mother's body, but your brother is out of the country and unreachable, unless there has been a prearrangement, cremation may not be possible.

Historic and religious perspective on cremation: Evidence that our ancient ancestors used cremation as a form of disposition of their loved ones' bodies predates history with pottery vessels from the Neolithic period filled with the ashes of several individuals. Between 4500 B.C. and 200 A.D., cremation was the normal custom at the time of burial. Julius Caesar and his family were cremated. With the acceptance of Christianity, cremation lost favor since followers began to believe that only a buried body could be resurrected.

Even today, a number of religions prohibit cremations as a means of disposition. Islams, Orthodox and Conservative Jews, and some Protestant, fundamentalist, and evangelical sects forbid the practice. Conservative Protestant groups look on it with disfavor and Mormons may choose it, but it is not encouraged among the followers. Eastern Orthodox churches

discipline. The Second Vatican Council permitted cremation and authorized priests to take part in such services. Protestant denominations are more permissive of it, freely allowing cremation.

do not approve of it, the Greek Orthodox Church fervently disapproves of it, and the Russian Orthodox and Armenian Orthodox churches accept the decision of the individual and/or family on the issue of cremation. Roman Catholicism, Reformed Judaism, Buddhism, Hare Krishna, Hinduism, and other religions permit it (sometimes under certain conditions).

American Protestant denominations, The Society of Friends, Christian Scientists, Seventh-Day Adventists, and Jehovah's Witnesses, among others, permit cremation.

Each religious sect has its own specific requirements and recommendations. If your loved one hasn't prearranged cremation and discussed this with his or her religious advisor, it's recommended that you discuss specific instructions for cremations. For example, in Conservative Judaism, while the practice isn't advocated, the remains may be interred in Jewish cemeteries and the urn should have an opening so that the ashes come in contact with the earth.

The Cremation Process: At the arrangement conference with the funeral director, those who are making the decisions for disposition will be asked whether they want an earth burial, entombment, or cremation. Again, there can still be a service and if appropriate an open-casket visitation, too. After the service, the body is placed in a small rectangular furnace. The furnace is called a retort. The furnace is turned on extremely high, at a temperature of about 1,800 degrees Fahrenheit or more. The retort has special filters so that odors do not escape. Within an hour the body is reduced to a gritty combination of bone mass and ash.

The ashes, technically called cremains, are then calcinated (a pulverization of the remains). The funeral director will normally tell you what to expect when you receive the remains— somehow the word ash conjures thoughts of light, fluffy material, when in actuality once the ashes are calcinated, the body is reduced to about seven or eight pounds for an adult. Ordinarily, relatives do not watch the cremation; some counties forbid the practice. For some people the thought of watching the process is too morbid or emotional, but for others it is comforting to be there during the final minutes. If it is important for you to see or be there when the cremation is occurring, talk with the funeral director.

Some mortuaries had once insisted that the body be held within a casket during cremation. Most state health laws now regulate that the body, to be cremated, be held in some type of container, but it can be the same one that the body was transferred in from the place of death. If the crematorium is off-site of the funeral home, the body must be transported, and often this is in a cardboard or fiberboard casket. (In some states it is now illegal for the body to be transported in a regular ground-style casket.)

If there is to be a memorial service after cremation, and no service with the body present, it just makes sense to select a fiberboard casket. A fancy casket is an extra expense and unnecessary, unless stipulated by the family. However, you may be asked by the funeral director if you prefer to buy a casket. With an affirmative answer, you will be presented with a cost sheet of the prices and shown into a room that will have caskets on display.

When selecting cremation, an urn will be necessary as a means to hold the remains when they are returned to you. At the funeral home for the arrangement conference, you will probably be asked to purchase an urn. Some urns are elaborate, exquisite affairs worth many thousands of dollars. Others are simple. Urns come in a variety of materials from brass to marble. You can even custom order urns. With an extremely inexpensive cremation, the remains may often be returned in a plastic bag, closed with a twister, held within a cardboard box. As you select an urn, keep in mind that the amount you spend is no reflection on how much you respected or loved the individual who has died. Buy the one that suits your needs best.

If you have a special container in which the remains will fit, you may want to use that. Take it with you to the arrangement conference and ask if the remains will fit.

Should it be necessary to arrange for the disposition of a loved one's body "long distance," i.e., managing the

DEFINING THE COMPONENTS OF DEATH CARE
by Frank B. Stewart, Jr.
—Chairmain Emeritus,
Stewart Enterprises

ক৯

The funeral service can be equated as a celebration of a life that lived, that achieved, and that fulfilled its purpose in our God-givenvocation. "Life" and "Love" have always been celebrated and expressedin one form or another at death.

Burial is the physical disposition of our temple, the sacred vessel that held the spirit.

Memorialization is the third component of death care and is the fulfillment of man and woman's desire to be remembered as having been here and accomplished our God-given mission.

arrangements from another area and over the telephone with the funeral director, the remains can be shipped parcel post to you or to a cemetery or funeral home in your area.

Cost of cremation: If your loved one chose or you have chosen direct disposition (from the place of death directly to the funeral home for cremation) the cost of cremation is approximately $1,100, and varies depending on the area of the country in which you live. There are other costs involved for which you may want a price list, including transportation of the body to the crematorium, the casket, the urn, and space in the columbarium. These costs often make cremation about the same price as an earth burial, so if cost savings is one of your goals, try to establish which will be most cost effective.

For information on funerals and other memorial services, including costs and options, refer to other headings presented later in this chapter.

Direct Disposition

Direct disposition of the body is another method of putting a body to rest. Direct disposition is sometimes called immediate burial and does not require that the body be embalmed. In direct disposition, immediately after the death occurs the body is cremated or buried. Direct disposition is often selected by the loved one before his or her death.

The Neptune Society and other memorial societies found under memorial societies in the Yellow Pages of most telephone books can send information on this option. Those interested in prearranging cremation become members and pay an initial fee, which provides for administrative work as you choose the type of service you want. The cost of the service, when needed, is anywhere from $200 to $1,000 dollars.

Even with direct disposition, there can be a memorial or graveside service and the cemetery (if one is used) will charge for opening and closing the grave, transportation of the remains, and various administrative costs.

Grief experts, including ACCORD president Sherry Williams, have found that with direct disposition and without a service, family members often are unable to smoothly pass through the stages of grief and ultimately seek counseling. Take time to consider your choices and be aware that a memorial service can always be held at a later date if direct disposition is selected.

Donation of Body or Organs

In the last twenty years, medical science has made incredible strides in the ability to transplant and use organs, bones, and skin of donors. Who would have ever thought, even thirty years ago, that blind people would have the gift of sight from donated corneas? Patients who thought they'd spend their lives hooked to dialysis machines can now lead active lives with the donations of kidneys. And thousands now are thankful for the donations of livers, hearts, lungs, and pancreases.

Donation of organs and bodies for medical research has gained popularity and appeal because of humanitarian reasons and desires, and with the success of transplanted tissues and organs over the last few years. These donations are called Anatomical Gifts. There are two types of donations:

1. Body donation for medical research.
2. Organ, tissue, and bone donations for transplants. Usually, according to the NFDA, donations are made to one and not both. While healthy organs are in short supply, the organs can only be donated under certain conditions—such as the donation of a heart cannot be made after it has stopped beating and kidneys cannot be donated after they have failed.

When people become organ donors, they sometimes carry a designation with that desire affixed to their driver's license, have completed a uniform donor card to be carried in the wallet, and/or informed their families of their wishes before they died. About 25 percent of American adults have made this choice and carry the card.

Even with a donation card or sticker affixed to his or her driver's license or a uniform donor card in his or her possession, without the family's request, the loved one may not have this desire granted. If a person has not indicated that he or she would like to be an organ donor, a doctor can obtain permission from members of the family in this order of priority: spouse, adult son or daughter, parent, adult sibling, or guardian. And even if there is a great desire to have the entire body donated or various organs donated for transplantation, in some instances—such as those who die of cancer—only eyes may be donated.

Body donations, generally, are only accepted if prearranged; your loved one may have filled out an instrument of anatomical gift, or a form called a certificate for bequeathing body, which will have been signed and witnessed. The decision to be a body or organ donor can be reversed at any time. You will only need to destroy your card or form. You will want to let your family, physician, and medical school or institute know this, too.

After death occurs and if the body and/or organs of the loved one are needed and acceptable (with an accident or illness sometimes they are not), the organs are removed or the body is sent to the medical center or organ bank. Transportation of the body to the institution is not always covered by the institution and you may be financially responsible to hire a hearse, provide a transportation casket, and secure a permit to transport a body.

Some medical centers and schools will not accept bodies that have been autopsied or mutilated by a violent death. They may not want a body that is missing a limb or organ, such as a liver. Age, weight, and type of death are also considered when institutions accept bodies for research. Sometimes a medical school or other institute has too many bodies or the one being donated isn't acceptable. Therefore, you may have to have an alternate plan for disposition.

After the organ has been removed, the family can still

have an open casket funeral or other service, should that be their wish. If there has been a whole body donation, the body is often preserved with special embalming chemicals so that it will last longer, and obviously there can be no body for a funeral. Normally, cremated remains are returned to the family. Thus, a memorial service, graveside, urn garden service, or other ritual can be performed as the family desires.

EMBALMING

The purpose of embalming is to allow for the family to make plans and arrange a service or ritual without undue haste by limiting the breakdown of the body. When embalming is selected, it gives family and friends enough time to travel to the funeral or other service. It can often enhance the remains.

If whether or not to make the decision to approve an autopsy is a personal issue, embalming is another option you should know about and will have to consider. While it might seem that embalming is part of the funeral process, that is simply not the case, although normally most families request embalming.

Every state has its own specific guidelines regarding embalming and in most states a body does not have to be embalmed. You will need to consult with an official at the state or county department of health, or a funeral director or staff member at the memorial society for specific information on your state.

Generally, a body must be embalmed when it is to be transported, such as when the body must be flown to another area or country, when death has occurred from a highly contagious disease, or when there is a long period before the burial which may happen when family and friends must travel to the funeral. When direct disposition has been selected, there is an immediate cremation or a closed casket at the funeral, or if you do not choose to have the body of your loved one embalmed, let the funeral director know

EMBALMING INFORMATION
from the Federal Trade Commission

❧

The Funeral Rule requires funeral providers to give consumers information about embalming that may help them decide whether to purchase this service. Under the Rule, a funeral provider:

• May not falsely state that embalming is required by law.

• Must disclose in writing, that except in certain special cases, embalming is not required by law.

• May not charge a fee for unauthorized embalming unless it is required by state law.

• Will disclose in writing that you usually have the right to choose a disposition such as a direct cremation or immediate burial if you do not want embalming.

• Will disclose to you in writing that certain funeral arrangements, such as funeral with a viewing, may make embalming a practical necessity and, thus, a required purchase.

immediately. Typically, this service will be routinely performed within an hour after the body is received at the funeral home. As with other funeral services, including this costly one (priced in the $250 to $1,500 range), you should be notified of the price before the process is administered. If you do not choose embalming, you may want to confirm your decision in writing and send it to the funeral director.

Embalming only helps preserve the body for a short period of time and is used to keep the body presentable until after the funeral. Believed to have begun among the Egyptians about 4000 B.C., embalming as we know it is not a form of mummification, historically practiced by the Egyptians who honored pharaohs and royalty with this practice and the building of elaborate tombs. Embalming is performed by a licensed embalmer or licensed funeral director. Some states have dual licenses, one for embalming and one for funeral directing. In larger establishments, there are circumstances where a licensee is principally assigned the duties of embalming, dressing, beautifying, casketing and otherwise preparing for in-state viewing. In funeral homes in small towns, funeral directors usually do the embalming themselves.

Training to become a funeral director and an embalmer is extensive and requires a very multidisciplinary study. Specific educational requirements differ from state to state with a maximum of four years study plus an internship.

The Embalming Process

The embalming process is complex. First the embalmer washes and cleanses the body. The mouth, nose, and other openings are disinfected and closed to prevent excretions. Eyes and jaw are closed.

Chemicals, such as disinfectants like formaldehyde, are injected into the body through one or more veins. A machine injects and removes these fluids. Other body liquids are also drained. The chemicals are injected to convert the body's proteins from a liquid state to a gel state and prevent bacteria growth. Organs are removed and submerged in the chemicals then replaced in the body. The chemicals continue to seep into the body's tissues even after the body has been buried.

Once the body has been preserved, the next step is to prepare it for viewing. The object is to restore as natural an appearance of the remains as possible. If the remains are intact, meaning the body didn't suffer from a disfiguring accident or illness, this process is relatively simple. The embalmer will dress the body and apply cosmetics that are appropriate for the age and sex of the loved one.

If the body has been damaged by illness or an accident, then the embalmer must rely on "restorative arts." Experienced embalmers can rebuild sunken or fractured features, return a natural appearance to dehydrated skin, and replace missing hair. Depending on the damage, there may be additional fees which the funeral director should make clear during the initial conference.

The embalmed body retains a somewhat lifelike appearance for a short time. The real importance of embalming, according to a number of grief experts, is its ability to restore a natural look to a body for the viewing and funeral, so that mourners can accept the death of a loved one and get on with their lives.

RITUALS OF PASSAGE

Since ancient times, civilizations have acknowledged the passage of death. "Guidebooks" such as *The Egyptian Book of the Dead* and *The Tibetan Book of the Dead* have been written to help those who have died make it through the maze of dying and death and into the afterlife. Each culture has methods of finalization for the dead.

In America, a traditional funeral with family members and friends hugging, touching, crying, and finally burying the body of the loved one is still the customary method of marking this passage. The funeral is a ritual. However,

Rituals link us with the past and the future. We have rituals for graduation and marriages, and we need a ritual for this most important passage of life.

—Dr. Judith Stillion, professor of psychology at Western Carolina University memorial services, commitment services after cremation, or other direct disposition are all acceptable. There are many forms of rituals.

A funeral is the most commonly accepted ceremony, or ritual, for the dead. The body of the loved one is a part of the ceremony, either in an open or closed casket. A memorial service (without the body present) has gained considerable acceptance, since more people are wishing to be or have a loved one's remains cremated. A humanistic ceremony is often another name for a memorial service. Sometimes a funeral is held in one area of the country with memorial services in another, or a funeral is held for close family members and a more public memorial service is also offered. A commitment service (or committal service) is often held at the grave site or when the ashes are sprinkled.

Sherry Williams believes that these rituals of passage help heal those who grieve. The NFDA concurs. Like many others, they believe that a ceremony in celebration of the life of a loved one is a ritual that can help focus on our emotions and bring meaning to the experience of death. It can be a time to support the needs and emotions of loved ones, family, and friends who are in the midst of the grieving process.

FUNERALS

After a loved one dies, his or her body will be kept at the hospital, care facility, or morgue until a family member or designated individual makes a decision as to where the body will be sent. In the case of an unattended death, an unexplained death, or a death involved in violence or crime, the county medical examiner will release the body after examination or an autopsy.

If a decision has not been made beforehand regarding the plans for a funeral or other service and how the body will be disposed of, most care facilities will make recommendations for funeral homes. In some parts of the United States, funeral homes are referred to as mortuaries or funeral parlors. These are usually funeral homes that routinely deal with the facility and have been found to be reliable and efficient. You are not required to accept their recommendation.

As stated previously, while the care facility would like to have you make a decision regarding disposition immediately and the body sent to a funeral home, you do have a few hours. Whether or not the death was expected, the decision as to which funeral home to use can be extremely perplexing. For some, it is the most difficult one that will ever be made. Keep in mind that you have another option. You can have the body of your loved one transferred to and held at a funeral home until a decision has been made. You must specifically arrange for this service and there will be a cost involved. However, this will give you a little more time to consider options.

Even if your loved one wanted to be cremated, or you have selected this disposition method, you can still have a funeral with an open casket (if appropriate) and even a memorial service later or in another part of the country. Unless you plan to do everything yourself, you will require the services of a funeral home and a funeral director, sometimes called a funeral consultant or mortician.

The funeral is a ritual in which many people find great comfort and can help in the grieving process. It is not only a time to recognize a death, but it is time to remember a life and recognize that your loved one has lived and influenced many during his or her span of years.

A service, funeral, or memorial provides mourners with a place to express the feelings and emotions of grief. The work involved in arranging a service is sometimes recommended to help process the news and trauma of the death. It can be therapeutic in this sense. The service is a time to express those feelings, talk about the loved one, and begin the acceptance of death. The funeral brings together a community of mourners who can support each other through this difficult time. Many grief experts and those who counsel the grieving believe that a funeral or service is a necessary part of the healing process, and those who do not have this opportunity may not face the death.

Even though viewing the body in the casket may seem a barbaric custom, research indicates that there are times when this is extremely helpful to the bereaved. Dr. Judith Stillion, professor of psychology at Western Carolina University, says, "Nothing helps you accept the death as much as seeing the dead person. It helps with grieving because it shows that there is no return."

The Role of the Funeral Director

When there is a death, the family members and those close to the loved one who has died are likely to be overwhelmed with all the decisions. The funeral director does a job that most are not familiar with and, of course, is paid for his or her services. Among the duties of this professional, the funeral director plans and coordinates the details of the funeral and recommends disposition of the body. Contemporary funeral directors are available for advice on how to fill out necessary forms to claim insurance and Social Security benefits, file claims, and secure pension payments. While this is the first time you may have had to complete a claim form for Social Security benefits, the funeral director has completed many and with his or her experience in the area, your work will be made easier. This does not mean that you should give the funeral director "carte blanche" and not expect to be informed of the costs of services.

More and more funeral directors have extensive hours of grief counseling and can assist the family members as they begin to heal. At various times, they serve as advisors, administrators, supporters, and caregivers. Conversely, as a consumer, you must be aware that the funeral home is a business and the funeral director is a business person there to sell a service.

According to the NFDA's slogan, "Yes, funerals are for the living," and from the hour of death until the loved one's final disposition, a professional funeral director helps families through their times of crises.

When the funeral director is called, an initial duty is to bring the loved one's body to the funeral home. The director secures information for the death certificate which is then completed and filed with the proper offices.

The funeral director meets with the family to discuss arrangements for a visitation, if the family wants one, and for the funeral. This is called the arrangement conference. In accordance with law, religious customs, and the desires of the family and those of the loved one who has recently died, the funeral director helps to make choices to meet the family's needs. These choices may include a traditional funeral with visitation, a memorial service which is performed without the body present, or immediate disposition.

Should the family choose to have some other type of service, the funeral director helps select the place and time for a service and the clergy person or other individual who will preside at the service. The director also provides information to help the family choose a casket or other burial container, a memorial stone, or appropriate marker, and the means and the place for final disposition, burial, cremation, or entombment.

On the day of the funeral, the funeral director attends to a number of ceremonial and administrative details, including the matter of transportation. Both before and after the service, the funeral director helps the family complete necessary paperwork, including newspaper notices (obituaries), claim forms, veteran's and union benefits, and insurance forms. He or she will also be able to arrange for official copies of the death certificate to be sent to your home. With the emotional impact of the death and because we, as typical Americans, are not familiar with the routine, it is often comforting to have a professional assist us.

The grief counselors and therapists at ACCORD see the role of the contemporary funeral director as going beyond the funeral. He or she is there to help answer questions on grief, make suggestions for support groups, and discuss referrals to therapists.

Cost of the Funeral

Before the Federal Trade Commission passed a regulation (called the FTC's Funeral Rule, effective in 1984), funeral homes often sold *only* "package deals," i.e., their services were offered for a flat fee to take care of everything for a specific amount of money. There was no breakdown of the costs and many people bought more than they wanted or more than they could afford.

Since the passage of the FTC Funeral Rule, which strictly forbids the funeral industry from offering only this prepackaged one-price-only type of service, funeral homes must provide a printed price schedule so that those who are buying services know specific costs. This is most helpful when comparing costs and services.

The FTC Funeral Rule states, in part, that funeral homes must "allow consumers to select and purchase only those goods and services they desire....instead of predetermined packages." As a service many funeral homes still offer consumers the option of prearranged packages. These are sometimes 10 to 15 percent less than if each item is individually selected, and are worth consideration. Even with the package funerals, consumers can ask for an itemized cost breakdown to compare prices with competing funeral homes.

Just as with the price of any product or service, the cost of a regular adult funeral differs from one area of the country to another. (A "regular adult funeral" is one where the body of the loved one who died is delivered from the care facility, hospital, or home without the assistance of another funeral home.) It has been said that next to a wedding, a funeral is the most costly event provided by family for one member. At a time of stress when a loved one has just died, it's often difficult to comprehend the importance of "shopping around," however, that's exactly what more and more people are doing. This doesn't mean you loved that special person any less; it means that you are being a wise consumer.

While prices vary, generally speaking, cost comparisons can be made on the following information presented in the 1999 Survey of Funeral Home Operations. The data was collected and tabulated by Association Research, Inc., for the NFDA and is presented here. The price information is based on figures from members' current general price list, prepared to comply with FTC Funeral Rule regulations.

According to Carol Jennings, an advisor for the Bureau of Consumer Protection, a division of the Federal Trade Commission, "The FTC does not regulate the prices charged by funeral providers. The purpose of the Funeral Rule is to make price information readily available to consumers and to enable them to do comparative shopping for funeral goods and services. This disclosure, required to appear on the general price list, informs consumers that they may select only those goods and services desired. The rule seeks to promote informed decision making so that consumers are able to make funeral arrangements that are within their means."

The schedule of standard items, which together may be considered the approximate cost of a traditional, adult funeral, is summarized below:

Non-declinable professional service charges	$ 800
Transfer of remains to funeral home	100
Embalming	350
Other preparations (casketing, cosmetology, hairdressing)	100
Use of viewing facilities	350
Use of facilities for ceremony	200
Hearse (local)	125
Limousine	125
Casket, (18 g. steel, sealer, velvet interior)	2000
Total	$4150

These figures do not include the vault (about $720) or a grave liner (and either of these is within the grave to keep the earth from caving in around the casket), cemetery monument or marker, or miscellaneous items such as flowers, burial clothing, honorarium for the clergy, fee of the organist, or newspaper notices.

Even the NFDA says that it's hard to determine the average cost of a funeral. The funeral home owner's costs, including mortgage or rent, maintenance, staff salaries, supplies, and administrative costs, can vary greatly from one area to another. The NFDA also points out that the cost of the funeral is determined by the amount of "funeral merchandise" the family buys. The merchandise includes items such as casket, casket lining, vault, vault lining, announcements or memorial cards, and clothing items. The cost of the cemetery plot is not included in the cost of the funeral in most cases.

One point to remember: The Funeral Rule requires funeral providers to disclose to you in writing if they charge a fee for buying cash advance items. Cash advance items are goods or services that are paid for by the funeral provider on your behalf. Some examples of cash advance items are flowers and obituary notices. Some funeral providers charge you their cost for these items; others add a service fee to their cost.

The Funeral Rule requires the funeral provider to inform you when a service fee is added to the price of cash advance items, or if the provider gets a refund, discount, or rebate from the supplier of any cash advance item.

The materials from which the caskets are made vary. Handcrafted hardwood caskets in the south central portion of the United States go for about $2,100, while a similar casket on the Pacific coast will run about $300 less. Various hardwoods are more expensive than caskets of woods such as pine. The gauge or thickness and quality of metal also have an impact on price. The interior of the casket is a variable, too. Likewise, these considerations are involved in the selection and purchase of a cremation urn.

The funeral industry likes to explain that there is a service that's right for everyone. Would you or your loved one be happier seeing him or her for the final time in a velvet-lined casket? Would you prefer lily of the valley instead of carnations surrounding the body? Will you want to drive your own car to the cemetery or prefer to ride in a limousine arranged by the funeral director? Few work up a budget for a funeral, however, so as a consumer and family member of the loved one, it is up to you to make a number of monetary decisions at this difficult time.

The final physical parting is the hardest thing to face. There our most personal and warm feelings are tested and tried.

—Algernon D. Black, leader of ethical humanism

The Funeral Process

You and your family may have decided on a traditional funeral. The following is a "walk through" of what transpires at each step of the funeral process.

Charles Gass, director of the Warner Funeral Home in Spencer, Iowa, and chairman of various committees for the NFDA, explains that once your loved one has died, you'll be asked to make a number of decisions. Gass says, "The nurse or other medical staff members at the hospital or nursing home will ask what funeral home you would like to use. Often that answer isn't known, unless prearrangements have been made. The staff will be able to direct you and that's where the funeral home (or mortuary as it's called in some parts of the country) comes in."

In hometowns throughout the United States, it's not unusual for someone from the funeral home to meet with the family at the hospital or in the nursing home where the death has occurred. In larger cities and metropolitan areas, Gass explains, the funeral director or a staff member will call the home of the family. "The hospital or care facility will typically give us the name of the individual who will be in charge of making the arrangements and we will contact that person." This doesn't preclude other family members from sharing the tasks, it simply means that one person will be the contact for the funeral director.

"Shortly after the death, the funeral director will set up an arrangement conference with the family. This is usually away from the house and I believe that's best for two reasons. First, there are so many interruptions at the home....visitors, calls, extra family members, and, second, this may be the first visit to the funeral home, which is where the family will be spending some hours in the subsequent days."

At the arrangement conference, the funeral director will obtain information for the death certificate. "We do not go straight down the list as if we're filling in the form, but ask questions that provide the information in a less obtrusive way," says Gass. The information from the death certificate can be translated to the obituary or, in smaller towns, the radio news report of the death. The funeral director will also arrange to apply for survivor's benefits, pensions, and sometimes life insurance benefits.

"At the arrangement conference, the family members will be asked how they want to proceed with the disposition, such as cremation or earth burial. We will talk about the details of the funeral or memorial service. Decisions such as what music will be played, whether it should be open or closed casket, the type of cemetery plot, the type of flowers desired, visitation hours, and whether or not to have pallbearers will be made at that time, too." Gass explains that the costs are clearly available for these services, the casket, and the vault. "We then proceed into a room that has caskets and vaults. I discuss various options and then leave the family alone for a few minutes. I often excuse myself at this time and say something such as, 'I need to make a few calls.' I believe this gives the family the privacy to decide on the type of casket and other items they really want to purchase without the presence of the funeral director in the room." Once the arrangements have been made, the funeral home's staff will call and stay in contact with the family. "There's so much going on at home, that it's normal for a family member to call and double check on the logistics of the service. When does the family have to be at the church? Will the funeral home send an obituary to the newspaper? How do they get from the cemetery back to the church after the graveside service?"

While it's not absolute, family members typically make it known when they will be at the funeral home for visitation, i.e., when friends, family, and associates come to pay their respects to the bereaved family and to the memory of the loved one. There is always a staff member from the funeral home with the family and friends during any visitation time.

After the family returns home, it's time for the funeral director to begin taking care of the responsibilities to prepare the body for the funeral, arrange for a smooth-flowing service, file the death certificate and other forms, and contact the pallbearers, clergy, organist, florist, and newspaper.

The family will be asked to provide clothing for the body of their loved one. While your first thought might be a somber, dark suit or dress, if this type of clothing was out of character for your loved one, then give the funeral director the clothing that he or she would have worn in life. For example, a man who traveled on the rodeo circuit was recently buried in a bright plaid shirt, spanking new jeans, and his best bolo. A woman who loved and constantly wore flowing caftans was buried in one of her favorites—an African-print creation that she bought after going on a safari.

You may want to include an object or something special in the casket before burial; in the case of the cowboy, he was buried in his most favored ten-gallon Stetson hat. Some funeral homes provide a "memory table," where friends and family can place items that were important to the family member who has died and that may be included in the casket.

Sherry Williams says that she sometimes recommends family members include a remembrance in the casket of their loved one. "They might want to write a letter to the loved one or compose a poem. They might want to add a snapshot of a wonderful time they've had together. A child might draw a picture. Knowing that a loved one was an avid fisherman, a fishing buddy might want to add a favorite lure. These offerings encourage a feeling of connection with the loved one and celebrate that life in a personal way for everyone involved."

"After the service and here in middle America, the family

COMMITTAL SERVICE FOR THE AGED
by Rev. Robert Terry Weston

Beautiful are the youth whose rich emotions flash and burn, whose lithe bodies filled with energy and grace sway in their happy dance of life; and beautiful likewise are the mature who have learned compassion and patience, charity and wisdom, though they be rarer far than beautiful youth. But most beautiful and most rare is a gracious old age which has drawn from life the skill to take its varied strands: the harsh advance of age, the pang of grief, the passing of dear friends, the loss of strength, and with fresh insight weave them into a rich and gracious pattern all its own. This is the greatest skill of all, to take the bitter with the sweet and make it beautiful, to take the whole of life in all its moods, its strengths and weaknesses, and of the whole make one great and celestial harmony.

and friends normally return to the church or home for a lunch. This again, we believe, supports the mourners in a time of sorrow," Gass says. One of the services few consider "typical" of a funeral home is aftercare. "That's when a staff member, whose sole job is to visit with families after the funeral, goes to the home, helps to answer questions, and discusses support groups and grief therapy if necessary. This is a valuable service more and more community funeral homes offer, at no extra cost."

Religious and Humanistic Services. What to Expect.

Most funerals are based on religion. Even though they are largely similar, each has distinct differences. The NFDA has outlined the uniqueness of each in an information brochure called *The Traditional Funeral*. It explains:

The Protestant funeral ceremony is the most commonly requested in the United States. The services are as varied as the denominations themselves. Often a Protestant pastor will design a funeral service instead of following a particular book of worship. The pastor will usually ask the family members what type of service they prefer.

Protestant services are generally preceded by a visitation period. The casket will be opened or closed depending on the family's wishes, but it is usually closed during the actual funeral service. Those attending a Protestant service often send flowers or gifts as an expression of their concern and feelings for the family and the loved one.

Protestant ceremonies usually include scriptural passages that relate to death and the Christian concept of resurrection. The service may also include prayers, a sermon, and group reading or singing of hymns.

The Roman Catholic funeral follows relatively formal guidelines. On the evening before a Roman Catholic funeral, a wake is held at the funeral home. Friends of the family may send flowers or gifts, although it is not uncommon for the family to request a donation to charity in lieu of flowers. Friends from other parishes can also ask that a mass be said for the resting of the deceased person's soul, then send a mass card to the family.

The Roman Catholic funeral ceremony often begins at the funeral home, proceeds to the church for a mass, then moves on to the grave site, where additional liturgy is performed. The casket is closed at a Roman Catholic funeral service, but usually open at the wake.

Jewish funeral services vary somewhat among the Orthodox, Conservative, and Reformed branches, but in general the funeral itself is the beginning of ceremonies instead of the end.

The Jewish ceremony is relatively short compared to Christian ceremonies, lasting about twenty minutes. The ceremony usually consists of prayers that praise life and affirm that a life was lived. Jewish families sometimes prefer that friends make contributions to charity instead of sending flowers to a service.

Traditionally, Jewish families remain at home for seven days after the funeral; this is called the *shiva*. During this time, friends and relatives visit to offer their support. The emphasis is on people getting together to share feelings and memories, not on religious teachings. There is an observance period of thirty days after the funeral during which mourners resume normal activities, continue to recite certain prayers, and do not go out to places for entertainment. The *kaddish* is a daily prayer recited for the first eleven months after the funeral.

Some families may attend services every day for the next year to commemorate their loved ones. In doing so, they may become part of a community of bereaved persons with whom they can share feelings.

In contrast to Christian ceremonies, a deceased Jewish person's memorial stone or tablet is unveiled months or even a year after the funeral, which gives family and friends another opportunity to gather in remembrance. The deceased person's name is also read aloud during synagogue service every year on the anniversary of his or her death.

Humanistic services and ceremonies are especially suited for

In Judaism, we believe that your very presence in the mourner's home marks the beginning of consolation. If you feel uncomfortable, know that it is understandable and perfectly natural.

–The National Institute of Jewish Hospice, from *How to Console*

Certain things must be done after a death, whether it occurs in a very simple or in a highly complex society. The corpse must be disposed of, those who are bereaved—who are personally shocked and socially disoriented—must be helped to reorient themselves; the whole group must have a known way of readjustment after the loss of one of its members.

—D. G. Mandelbaum, from *The Social Uses of Funeral Rites*

those people who have not followed a religious bent, which include about half of the men and women living in America today. These people often request a religious funeral from a church they had a relationship with in the past. Sometimes they settle for a religious ceremony and deal with mixed feelings. Sometimes in this case they do without a funeral at all.

Because relating death to religious teachings is only one purpose of a funeral, many nonreligious people elect to hold humanist ceremonies. During this service, as in religious ceremonies, families and friends gather to acknowledge the death, offer support to each other, and express their grief. A friend or family member may preside over the ceremony or the family may ask a pastor to conduct a ceremony that avoids religious imagery. Humanist ceremonies commonly feature music, group singing, and readings of poetry or literature that held some meaning for the deceased. In fact, group participation is also becoming more common in all funerals and ceremonies, such as those of the Protestant and Catholic services, which don't offer as many informal gatherings as Jewish services. If you wish to personally offer to say something at a funeral, it's wise to discuss this with the family first in order to allow time to complete the ceremony.

While the form of the service is often tied to religious philosophy or personal wishes, the service seems to help those who are grieving come to terms with the death of their loved one.

Children and Funerals

Funerals and other rites of death, such as memorial services, provide a valuable function. Every society has some form of ceremony to help the living acknowledge, accept, and cope with the death of a loved one. Whether or not a particular child should be included depends on the child and the situation. If the child is old enough to understand and wants to participate, depending on the circumstances, being included in the plans for the funeral may help him or her accept the reality of the death while in the supportive company of family and friends.

Parents with children who will be attending the funeral with an open casket would do well to discuss this with their kids before the service. If you are a parent, you might want to follow these guidelines:

- It's best to gently describe what will go on and talk about what your child can expect to see.
- If you have not been to a funeral or one where there is an open casket service, tell your child that, too.
- Prepare the child for what he or she will see before, during, and after the services. Talk about the fact that this is a sad occasion and people will be expressing their sadness. Some people will be crying.

According to the situation, you may want to have someone your child especially feels comfortable with be close during the funeral to answer questions honestly. After the service, you will probably want to answer other questions about death. If the child prefers not to attend the service, don't coerce or make the youngster feel guilty.

Where to Get Help

Consumers do have an assistance strategy for complaints and concerns about the funeral industry. Complaints about funeral directors, prepaid funeral plans, or other services are heard by an administrator of:
Funeral Service Consumer Assistance Program
P.O. Box 486
Elm Grove, WI 53122-0486
800-662-7666

Every day, trained licensed funeral professionals help families through tough times. It's always possible for misunderstandings and lack of clear communication to cause problems. That's where the Funeral Service Consumer Assistance Program and the National Research and

Information Center enter the picture. NRIC is an independent, nonprofit, charitable organization that researches and provides consumer information on death, grief, and funeral services. It is not a funeral home or prearrangement contract "rating" service.

Volunteer consumer leaders and impartial funeral service professionals across the United States work with NRIC. They are not involved or paid by the funeral home that is under review. Complaints filed in 1991 included overcharges or price lists confusion, personal property loss, and discourteous treatment.

The NRIC never refuses to answer or provide suggestions for any type of funeral-related questions. Its goal is to help with questions and complaints. Complaints have included contracted-for-funeral services and charges, related merchandise, prefunded funeral plans, and shipment and receiving of remains. Complaints must be entered by the person contracting for services or otherwise through a power of attorney. NRIC will not investigate a complaint if legal counsel has been retained or the consumer has filed a lawsuit. However, it will provide supplementary assistance if the claim is on file with another dispute-resolving agency, such as a state consumer protection office. If the complaint is regarding a cemetery or cemetery-related merchandise, the NRIC will attempt to direct the complaint to the governing office.

What should be done regarding a complaint? According to FSCAP, there are three steps:

1. FSCAP's administrator will discuss your complaint with you and the funeral home separately and gather information. The basis of many

complaints reaching FSCAP oftentimes is a misunderstanding about obligations of two parties who have a valid contract, and can be resolved quickly.

2. If step one does not resolve the complaint or reaffirm obligations, FSCAP will review written evidence. They will consult with an impartial funeral service professional whose business is at least five hundred miles from the subject funeral home. Technical and/or pricing matters are reviewed. Either the programs administrator or funeral professional may contact the consumer to obtain more information.

3. If the complaint remains unresolved, the consumer and the subject funeral home submit the disagreement to binding arbitration. The process resolves differences between the two parties and generally is less costly and complicated than legal action.

Depending on the outcome of the arbitration, the FSCAP arbitrators can decide that the consumers are entitled to a full or partial refund or credit against the cost of the services or prefunded funeral plans. The arbitrators may decide that the consumer is responsible for all or part of the payment. They can also decide that there should be no action. Panel rulings are final.

The National Funeral Directors Association, a group representing the majority of funeral homes in the United States, maintains a consumer security fund, in conjunction with FSCAP. The fund ensures consumers of NFDA-member funeral services should the arbitrators decide in favor of the consumer and the member home fails to pay.

MEMORIAL SERVICES

Funerals are traditionally steeped in convention. The body will be prepared to look as peaceful, yet lifelike as possible. When the visitation, or viewing, is in progress, the family will sit in the front first pews in the church and there will be prayers or other religious rituals performed. A memorial service, on the other hand, can be less rigid, yet meaningful to the family and friends. Memorial services have been performed at a lake, on the high seas, in the mountains, in the neighborhood pub, or in church.

Memorial services are still held three or four days after the death, for the most part, yet are often held at a convenient time and day for those who want to attend. For example a service may be held on Saturday afternoon at 4:00 P.M., or at the beach at sunset.

At memorial services, family and friends are ordinarily allowed to speak. If this is something you'd like to include, you may want to designate a time for this. Since few like to be first, you may want to prearrange for one or two individuals who you know will want to speak to stand first and second. This breaks the ice. Speaking at a loved one's memorial service is a time to remember the deceased, and the tributes and remembrances shared at memorial services can be far more heartwarming for everyone gathered to celebrate this life than a formal funeral service if this has been out of context to the loved one's lifestyle. Sometimes the dearest stories are ones that make us chuckle; a tale about kindness the deceased offered to another, a favorite poem, a favorite song, or a story about his or her adoration with a hobby, sport, charity, or grandchildren.

Let's say that you and Joe were great camping pals and you had known him since you attended Outward Bound Training as teenagers. If you want to speak at his service, make a point of talking with the family member responsible for the service *well before the service*. The family may not have allotted time or may not think it's appropriate. Memorial services can also offer a chance for a spontaneous speech. You may want to make some notes or write out what you want to say since this can be an emotional time and your thoughts might become muddled when you stand in front of the group.

While there are few rules for a memorial service these days, typically, the body of the deceased is not present. Sometimes this is because there has been a direct disposition and the individual has already been buried or cremated, or the death occurred in another location and was buried or cremated there.

For instance, if the loved one was in the military and the family wanted him or her to be buried at a national military cemetery, there might be a memorial service for family and friends at home in Topeka, rather than a full military service at the graveside. Sometimes when a longtime resident of an area is buried (or cremated) out of the country or the area, there will be a memorial service in the town where he or she had lived and is still known.

Other times, the family may request a small "family only" funeral and then a large, public memorial service. This happens frequently when the individual was a well-known public figure or celebrity, and the family wants to say good-bye to the deceased without unnecessary publicity.

Should you decide on (or if your loved one has prearranged) a memorial service, you will still need the services of a funeral home or memorial society for the disposition of the deceased's body. Unless you want to care for the details of the death, you will need to make arrangements for such things as the earth burial, placement of ashes, and obtaining the death certificate.

A memorial service is customarily more simple than a funeral and can be less expensive. However, if you choose to turn many of the responsibilities over to the funeral home, you will incur costs, although they should be somewhat reduced. You will be expected to pay for the services performed by the funeral home, such as burial or cremation,

ॐ

Until last week there was nothing at all unusual about the corner intersection half a block from our house. But at 4:30 P.M. last Tuesday, an out-of-control Cadillac came speeding down the steep hill east of here. The ninety-one-year-old man at the wheel may have been dead already from a heart attack when his car hit a another, killing a woman inside and injuring four others, then collided with a Buick that exploded into flames. Suddenly four people including two children were dead and one was dying at the intersection.

When my daughter came home, moments later, she saw the old man on the sidewalk, the Cadillac upside down, diapers strewn across the intersection. Firefighters were working desperately to extract victims from the smoldering wreck. About an hour later, when I got home, the last body was just being removed.

That night I went out to walk the dog, choosing a route away from the accident site. The police flares and yellow ribbons were still up, redirecting traffic. As I returned, I saw that a city cleanup truck had arrived, and I knew that by morning there would be no sign of the tragedy that had occurred. People would pass this corner again, stepping

paperwork, and assorted administrative tasks (such as filing for Social Security benefits and obtaining the death certificate) completed by the funeral director. Keep in mind that a funeral home makes money when a full funeral service is performed; a memorial service bypasses some of the rituals and expense. Make your needs and desires clear to the funeral director so that you and your loved one will have what is wanted—and nothing extra.

If you and your loved one have prearranged the disposition through a memorial society (see Memorial Societies section in this chapter), your work will be streamlined and less costly.

OTHER VARIATIONS

When a friend's sister-in-law died from suicide, an apple tree was planted in her memory. At the death of an avid horticulturist, an herb plot was started at a botanical garden. A wonderfully illustrated (and incredibly expensive) book on dogs was donated in the name of the deceased to the public library in the memory of a young woman who loved animals (and especially collies). Other commemorations include scholarships, fundraisers for medical or educational equipment, awareness campaigns, and memorial funds.

When University of California professor Diana Dann Chadwell died of breast cancer in 1990, friends, colleagues, and family applied for a grant to inform the public about breast cancer. The book *Diana's Gift* is a result of their work, with five thousand copies of the book given free of charge to women in San Diego. This is part of the memorial to Diana's memory.

These, and other forms of commemoration, can be provided in addition to paying respects in a more traditional way or instead of any form of death ritual. Should you decide to donate money, time, or energy in a specific way to honor a loved one, it's up to you whether or not you want to inform others, or the survivors, of your effort. Sometimes the most private observances are the most meaningful.

Depending on the family and the religious philosophy, there can be commemorations of the death at yearly intervals or when the grave marker is put in place. You may decide to donate money or time on the anniversary of your loved one's birthday to a special, meaningful cause. Again, allow your love and creativity to have a hand in celebrating the memories you cherish.

COMMITTAL SERVICES

A committal service takes place at the grave site or when the remains are buried or scattered. There can be a full funeral in a chapel or church and another final service at the grave site, or only a committal service. The decision is that of the family or the family carrying out the wishes of the loved one who has died. With a religious ritual, there will be clergy present and prayers, and sometimes songs will be offered. There can be moments of meditation, or in a more contemporary way, family members may want to read a poem or say a few words to honor the deceased.

Most military services are held at the grave site and include a rifle volley, the playing of taps, and specific rituals of passing a folded flag to the survivors of the service member who has died.

MEMORIAL SOCIETIES

Memorial societies, such as the California-based Neptune Society, are nondenominational and provide a means of direct disposition at a considerable cost savings. There was a time when funeral directors hotly refused to work with memorial societies, because they presented a less expensive alternative (and some said less helpful to the bereaved); however that opinion has softened.

Memorial societies are open to everyone and you can find telephone numbers and addresses (to ask for an application)

on the concrete where the children, the women, the dead old man lay just hours before.

In another country, another culture, there would be an acknowledgment. Everything would stop for awhile. A ceremony would be held. A medicine man might burn cedar, a priest might burn incense to aid these souls on their travels to the other world. But what do you do in a polyglot city where people are killed daily by gunshots, knives, drugs, accidents? We have no common rituals here to help us.

In the morning I cut some flowers in our garden and headed to the corner. When I arrived at the corner, I found a bouquet of asters already there. I tied it, together with my flowers, to the stop sign. That afternoon, when my daughter returned from class, she saw dozens of bouquets piled around the stop sign. Someone had tied a small teddy bear to the pole with yellow police blockade tape. By evening a votive candle was burning. Then there was a whole row of candles. Looking out the front window, my daughter called out, "Look, it's a shrine!"

The moon was almost full and the street was bathed in blue light. A woman in a long black skirt, with a black shawl, was standing, her hands folded, beside the flickering candles and the mound of flowers. A new picture had superimposed itself on the afterimage of the accident.

OBSERVATIONS ON A DEATH

〵

Family, friends, associates, and colleagues often want to do more or something special in memory of the deceased. Susan McClelland and Susan McClelland Prescott, authors of If There's Anything I Can Do: An Easy Guide to Showing You Care, give some thoughtful ideas, including the use of "Remembering" Letters:

• Take quiet time for reflection about the friend who has died, and have the willingness to let your mind go back over the years as you remember having that friend as a very important part of your everyday world.

• Write remembering letters to the parents, children, or spouse of the loved one who has died or to all of the family members.

• Write it for yourself, as your personal tribute. You can start with something as easy as, "I think of Amy so often. I remember...." or "My brother and your Tom were the greatest friends...." You'll find that this letter almost writes itself as you recall the fine and funny moments, the loved qualities, special clothes, favorite expressions.

• You needn't censor your thoughts: "I never knew anyone else who could stay wide awake through an opera and snore through James Bond." Or "Mary taught me

in the Yellow Pages of your phone book, or you can contact the Funeral Consuer Alliance at (800) 458-5563. If you want to know about low-cost funeral or memorial services and societies in your area, write your request and send a self-addressed, stamped, business size envelope to Funeral Consumer Alliance, 33 Patchen Road, South Burlington, Vermont 05403. Run by volunteers, they suggest you make a small donation to cover costs. For two dollars you can receive a cost sheet of casket prices. The Funeral Consumer Alliance can provide information, too, on anatomical gifts, organ donations, and how memorial societies can be established in your area.

With a number of memorial societies, there's sometimes a one-time membership/registration fee. This is also called a "record fee," and will be about twenty dollars. Most memorial societies are nonprofit and their goal is to help consumers get a fair shake where the cost of traditional funerals is concerned.

Memorial societies provide one or a number of options for disposition—some are for profit, others are nonprofit. Some provide a "packaged deal" and others will advise members of the most efficient and economical disposition services available in the area.

One can arrange before one's own death exactly what services are wanted, even prepaying for these, and the family then contacts the memorial society to carry out the final wishes of the deceased. Or after death, whether or not an individual has been a member, the body of your loved one can be taken to the memorial societies' repository and, after legal documentation, cremation is performed. The remains are often scattered at sea, in the desert, or in the mountains. Some families choose to have a memorial service or mass at the time of death. The memorial society sometimes will help arrange it.

The entire cost for one of the societies to remove and transport the deceased body, hire the chapel for a service, prepare the body for viewing, scatter the remains, and provide cremation service is about $1,200, well under a "traditional funeral." This doesn't include the honorarium for the clergy, flowers, mass cards, or the membership to the society.

MAKING THE ANNOUNCEMENT OF THE DEATH

In "small town America," the announcement of a death in the city is called or sent to the local newspaper and sometimes read on the radio. Charles Gass explains that one of his jobs is to notify the radio station; however, you can make the call. Again, it's best to wait until a time for the service (and/or visitation) has been established. At this time, and in the obituary notice, you can say if instead of flowers donations should be made to a specific charity or funds, like hospice or the American Diabetes Society.

Obituaries are written by a staff reporter at the newspaper. However, just because someone else is writing the newspaper story doesn't mean you can't write an obituary that includes all the correct details of the person's life. Don't be surprised if what you've written appears in the paper as presented. Because a newspaper staff member may want information "out of order," when you call, it's always best to write out what you want to say before you call. Also that way you can give the same statement to two or three papers, such as a daily paper, a weekly paper, and a newsletter that goes to the members of the organization the deceased belonged to.

If a loved one has been a prominent citizen or a celebrity, a long, formal obituary is often included in the newspaper, with copies of the obituary sent to the radio and television channels.

Death notices are paid for by the family or friends and placed in the newspaper to announce the death; you'll want to call and find out about costs and deadlines. Obituaries are placed in the paper free of charge. Notices include the date of the death, names of survivors, important accomplishments, and time, date, and place of service.

A formal way to announce the death of a loved one is by sending printed cards, typically printed as one might with a wedding or birth announcement, but with a black border.

most of what I know about sticking to your guns—that awful car salesman—remember how she'd...?"

• There need be no topic sentences, no brakes on your heart because of the structural requirements you learned in English 101. You just sit and write as you think, picking out brief moments, small bits and pieces, without any order of time or importance.

You can write this letter weeks or even months after a death. Sharing your memories with the family is a beautiful, one-of-a-kind gift, and a gift to yourself as well.

We get so tangled in the "mechanics" that surround us after a death that we're not free to help as our best selves. The fact is, deciding almost has to be done before the need for action comes up. Time is a real consideration after a death.

—Susan McClelland and Susan McClelland Prescott, from *If There's Anything I Can Do*

The cards are sent to friends who live at a distance. A local printer should be able to provide these, or perhaps you can make them using your desktop publishing program. Sometimes the funeral director will take care of this matter, too. A personal note to each individual who receives a card is not necessary, unless you feel inclined to do so.

ETIQUETTE

Etiquette experts have varying opinions on the etiquette involved when there has been a death. Few of us are familiar with death and we're often tongue-tied with what to say, what to wear, and how to act at a commemoration service. Whether it's a funeral or a simple memorial service, etiquette experts all provide their learned opinions. Your best bet is simply to be thoughtful of others' feelings at this emotional and disconcerting time of life.

If you are reading this book because someone you loved has died, then accept the thoughtfulness as such. The words are never enough, but regardless of how shallow they sound, they are usually spoken with esteem and tenderness.

At a funeral or other service when you approach the bereaved, saying "I'm so sorry," is adequate and appropriate. It is not the time to come up with some personal philosophy of death, life after death, God's will, or anything of that nature. These responses, even offered from the heart, will often make matters worse. Instead, a hug, a handshake, a gentle squeeze of the arm provide more love than words. These touching condolences are appropriate for the loved one's family, friends, colleagues, spouse, or acquaintances.

Although there will be tears, don't feel it's wrong to talk about the person who died. Sharing a kind thought or a special memory can actually help the family. "Teddy was a great tennis player. We're going to miss her at the club." "I didn't know him long, but when Randolph and I volunteered at the same time on the AIDS hotline I was constantly in awe of his caring soul and love for other human beings. I'm terribly sorry."

After Christian funerals, the family will often stand outside the church doors and greet friends as they leave the church. Typically the spouse and children are closest to the doors, sometimes with the clergy person next to the immediate survivors.

Like a receiving line at a wedding, as a family member, you will be asked to speak to each person and acknowledge his or her comments. Many grief experts feel, as with the funeral, that this makes the death more of a reality and continues the healing process. You need not be philosophical or witty. A simple, "Thank you for coming," or "We appreciate your thoughts," is enough.

What to Wear

If it's mid-August, and the death has occurred in the desert area of Palm Springs, California, with a full, traditional funeral with services in a church scheduled for Tuesday at noon, wearing a dark wool dress or wool suit would be lunacy. And while it might seem more logical to wear shorts and a T-shirt, that's probably not appropriate either.

Wardrobe-wise, almost anything goes when it concerns what to wear to a service and depends on the service as well as the lifestyle of the deceased. Most people still choose somber-colored clothing; many widows and female family members choose to wear veils (or even sunglasses). The traditional colors of black, white, and mauve are still okay. You can ask the funeral director what he or she recommends, or most likely wear any business-style clothing. If the service will be at a church or synagogue of which you aren't a member, you can call to find out what will be appropriate.

The exceptions are obvious. If the service is at the beach at Nantucket, you'll wear flat shoes so you can walk on the sand. Some women will probably wear slacks. If the service is atop El Capitan in Yosemite Park, California, you'll probably wear more casual clothing than if it is in a Catholic church in downtown Manhattan.

Flowers

Flowers and funerals used to go together with lilies and daisies as the norm. In traditional communities, they still do. The funeral home will put the card on the arrangement and will probably make a note of the sender's name, address, and type of bouquet so you can respond with a card or word of thanks.

If you are sending flowers, "Please accept our/my sympathy at this time," is all that is necessary. Or, "Our/my prayers are with you and your family." "With loving thoughts," is good, too.

Condolence Cards and Thank-You Cards

Sometimes after a loved one dies, it is too difficult to respond immediately to condolence cards. Survivors often say that while they were unable to even open the cards right after the death of their loved ones, the cards were appreciated. You need not read the cards at once. Instead you can place the card, even unopened, in a basket, bowl, or box to be opened at a later date or to look at again when you have more time or are feeling up to it. Some survivors place the cards in a keepsake or scrapbook.

You will want to respond with thank-you cards for donations, flowers, food, letters, or other gifts of kindness given after your loved one's death. While it's not necessary to write a long letter, a short, personal note in a card will be appreciated more so than simply signing your name. You may want to say, "Your thoughtfulness is most appreciated," or "My family and I will always consider you a close friend. Thank you for your kindness."

Replying to and thanking people for their thoughtfulness when a loved one has died is more than good manners, it is a way to stay connected to family and friends. The actual tasks, however, can sometimes be delegated. Susan McClelland and Susan McClelland Prescott, the authors of *If There's Anything I Can Do: An Easy Guide to Showing You Care*, point out that when a friend or family member asks if he or she can help, you can say yes to that person becoming a personal secretary of sorts.

As a helper, the authors say, "You could certainly offer to take care of other miscellaneous correspondence as well [in addition to the thank you cards]. Write the checks to pay the bills, for example, so that only a signature is needed. Or tackle filing the insurance forms—always a tedious and time-consuming chore. Handle invitations, renewals, and requests for donations. A personal secretary may be exactly what [you or] your friend needs right now."

If you have not done so yet, your "secretary" can send out notices of the death of your loved one or find suitable blank cards at the nearest card shop. He or she can write, "We are sorry to share the news that Arthur died on Christmas day. As a friend and fellow member of the university club, we knew you would want to be told."

Whether you want to discuss the cause of death is entirely up to you and, again, this is a chore a friend or other relative can help you with. Or you may want to handle it as did one family when their adult brother died: "Will Lawrence and Carol Gregory have asked me to write to you to share the news that their brother, George, died on May 25, after his long challenge with kidney disease. A memorial service was held immediately after, as George wanted. I know the family will want to hear from you and would appreciate your staying in touch as you did with George. They asked me to invite you to visit the next time you're in the city as George wanted you to have his baseball card collection."

Not only will you be providing a valuable service to those who are sometimes overwhelmed with the tasks to be done after a loved one's death, but these chores could help you with the grieving process by acknowledging and validating the death.

Donations in Lieu Of

There was a time in the history of the United States when oversized bouquets of flowers would be sent to the church or funeral home when a loved one had died. Nowadays, people often are asked or offer to donate money to a worthy cause supported by the deceased or of the deceased family's choosing.

For example, because Mark and his wife Beth received

help from the hospice program while he was dying of lung cancer, it was appropriate for friends to make a donation of money to the organization in lieu of sending flowers to the funeral home when Mark died. Quite a few people sent cards and made a donation. Some still sent flowers, but made a contribution, too.

Some religions prefer that you not send flowers, some in the more traditional way gratefully accept them.

As a family member arranging the funeral or other service, you may want to tag or let the funeral director know which flowers you want to take to the grave site, which you want to send to the house, or which are to be donated to a nursing home or hospital.

Ushers

In a funeral that is held at a church, there will be ushers to help seat the family. Like with a wedding, close family sits in the front of the church, chapel, or meeting room during the service. Unlike at a wedding, the ushers do not offer their arms, except to someone needing assistance. If the funeral is held at a funeral home, the staff typically provides ushers. As with pallbearers, these honorary positions are traditionally taken by men. You are no longer bound by antiquated tradition, unless that is your desire. You may ask anyone close to the deceased to fill this honored position—women and children definitely included.

Pallbearers

There was a time when six to eight strong men carried the casket from the church to the hearse to the grave site. Muscles and strong backs are no longer the qualifications as the casket is carried by the funeral director's assistants. The pallbearers walk in front of the casket. As the family member making funeral/service arrangements, you can give the funeral director a list of those who you want to serve as pallbearers, including women and children. You'll want to provide the telephone numbers, too.

Recently a friend's grandfather died and there were nine grandchildren. He specifically wanted all his grandkids to be pallbearers. Each felt extremely honored to be part of the funeral—including the youngest—a seven-year-old granddaughter. While the funeral director will present guidelines, it is your "job" to make the ritual personal and a memory that you can think of as grief is resolved.

Prayers, Poems, Songs for the Dead

At funerals and services for children and young people, often special songs and/or poems are recited. At services for older people, especially those who have been active in their religious organizations, it is often known what hymns they liked or what psalms they preferred. This is a decision, as the family member making arrangements, you will have to make. The funeral director can tell you what is usually used.

Whether it comes from the Bible, Shakespeare, John Lennon, John Kennedy, Edna St. Vincent Millay, or Billy Crystal, if it's appropriate for the circumstances and/or the wishes of the deceased, then it's appropriate for the service. Ernest Morgan's *Dealing Creatively with Death* provides sample services and ceremonies that are touching as well as proper.

ें‌

In chapter 3, we'll talk about what to do within the first week after the death of a loved one, the complexities of emotional and physical grief, and the causes of death with regard to the effect on survivors.

Chapter 3

The Expression of Loss

Death becomes the expression on a million faces, with a size and shape just right for each of us and just right for our loved ones who are also survivors. We often hear of a good death, or a bad death, or an easy death, or a slow death, yet in reality, it is still death. It is a biological occurrence and one that can displace those who survive the death, perhaps irrevocably changing lives. We are affected as we move from shock to resolution.

Opinions vary as to the meaning of death and the meaning of life. At this juncture in time, you may be too numb to even venture a guess, even consider that you will recover....but you will.

Specialist on death, dying, and afterlife, psychiatrist Elisabeth Kübler-Ross, best known for her pioneering work with terminally ill patients and her book *On Death and Dying*, explains that there are five phases to grief: denial, anger, bargaining, depression, and finally acceptance. Although other grief experts do not use these exact terms, they discuss that grief has many facets. Some believe that the grief stages can be experienced simultaneously. While there is considerable discussion on how and why people

TEARS ARE A SIGN OF HEALING

by Alan D. Wolfelt, Ph.D., director of the Center for Loss and Life Transition

❧

Many people associate tears of grief with personal inadequacy and weakness. Crying on the part of the mourner often generates feelings of helplessness in friends, family, and caregivers.

Out of a wish to protect the mourner from pain, those people who surround the mourner may severely inhibit the experience of tears. Comments similar to "tears won't bring him back" and "he wouldn't want to see you cry" discourage the expression of tears. Yet crying is nature's way of releasing internal tension in the body and allows the mourner to communicate a need to be comforted.

Another function of crying is thought to be somehow related to the intent of bringing about a reunion with the lost person. While the function cannot occur, crying is thought to be biologically based and a normal way of attempting to reconnect with the person who has died. The frequency and intensity of crying eventually wanes as the hoped-for reunion does not occur.

Some investigators have suggested that suppressing tears may increase susceptibility to stress-related disorders. This would seem to

feel sorrow, all grief therapists caution us not to forget, not to hide the tears, not to be an ostrich, although the initial response after news that a loved one has died is denial. Like birth, death happens. Sometimes, it's painless; most of the time it's not, especially so for those who mourn.

Within this chapter, we'll talk about the effects of death on the loved ones, including physical and emotional grief so that there is a basis of understanding. Lots of people think they're "going crazy" after the death of a loved one, but it's simply not true—it's grief.

We'll talk in detail about grief in chapter 4 with specifics to help you through this time. In this chapter, we'll concern ourselves with the result of the death including various causes—suicide, homicide, sudden illness, and long-term sicknesses such as cancer. There's no right way for a loved one to die, no "easier way" for family or friends to proceed through the stages of grief.

You know if someone you loved has died there are no platitudes to make everything "okay again." You have permission to mourn, to grieve, to cry and wail. Postponing a confrontation with feelings by filling each day with hectic activity only prolongs cleaning up the issue of death.

WHAT TO DO IN THE FIRST WEEK

In the first few days after the death of a loved one you will have a herculean-sized list of things to do, decisions to make, details to finalize. You may also be trying to continue to carry your full load at work, at school, or with household responsibilities and feel control slipping away.

Once the immediate actions have been completed and the arrangements made, the hard work of sorting through feelings and the loved one's life begins.

The American Association of Retired Persons (AARP) provides a series of "what-to-dos." The following is an adaptation of their material.

1. ***Make funeral or memorial service arrangements.***
   The AARP stresses that the family doesn't need to have an elaborate funeral or service to show that the one who died was loved. They advise that Social Security and the Veterans Administration provide burial allowances and the next of kin should apply for any benefits immediately after receiving the death certificates.

2. ***Locate important papers.*** You will need keys for the car and house (and perhaps a resort house or storage garage), bank books, stock certificates. You'll also need the loved one's birth certificate, a marriage certificate, Social Security card, tax forms, and birth certificates of minor children.

   The AARP warns, "Don't throw anything out. If you don't feel up to the search, ask someone you trust to help. Don't let your fear or personal turmoil at this time jeopardize your or your family's financial future."

3. ***Start getting finances in order.*** If your spouse has died, ask the bank to release the funds (if they have been frozen at time of death). Immediately set up your own account.

4. ***Obtain at least eight copies of the death certificate.*** You will need "originals," not photocopies. Originals have the stamp and/or signature of an official. The cost is typically from five dollars to eight dollars each. You'll need the death certificate to apply for benefits and pensions.

5. ***Notify your insurance company.*** You will probably have to fill out a notice of claim and attach a death certificate to the paperwork. Depending on how and when you need the money, you may want to talk with a financial advisor about various payment methods and tax implications.

make sense in that crying is an exocrine process, one of the excretory processes. In reviewing other processes, such as sweating and exhaling, the fact is that they all involve the removal of waste products from the body. Crying may serve a similar function.

Not only do people feel better after crying, they also look better. Expressions of tension and agitation may seem to flow from their bodies. The capacity to express tears appears to allow for a genuine healing. The expression of tears is not a sign of weakness. The capacity of the mourner to share tears is an indication of the willingness to do the "work of mourning."

FAREWELL, DAD

Magazine publisher
Michael Tynan MacCarthy
talks about the death of his
father, H. Neil MacCarthy

❧

"Soon after I read Robert Bly's book, Iron John, Dad and I began trying to bond. We would write and call each other. He asked for a subscription of San Diego Writer's Monthly to show off to his friends. Dad's labored breathing into the phone told of his poor health. He admitted to a deteriorating lung condition, a legacy from his days as a production engineer in hazardous plants.

"Although now tethered to an oxygen tank, Dad would not curtail his routine. There was grocery shopping, biking, riding, and sailing on the Rappahannock, but most of all there was his writing. He was working on a new script for a children's play that he would once again direct and produce for the local library. Also, he was under contract to write a fifteen-hundred-word column each week for the local newspaper while doubling as their proofreader.

"I asked him for copies of old columns. Months passed. One day a big envelope containing a dozen of his vignettes arrived at the office. I showed them to the magazine's editor, and he thought one called 'Father, There Is No Good-bye' would work well for SDWM. When I

6. ***Apply to the Social Security office and Veterans Administration for benefits.*** These benefits are not automatically paid. You must ask and be ready to complete necessary paperwork. You can take a friend or loved one with you for support.

7. ***Write a letter to your spouse's or loved one's employer*** telling about the death. You may want to contact professional, union, fraternal, charitable, and academic organizations to which he or she belonged. Often friends say, "Is there anything I can do?" This is a responsibility others can assist with. Ask them to keep a list of those who have been contacted so the effort isn't duplicated at a later time.

8. ***Write letters to all creditors*** informing them that your loved one has died. You will want to call or write to credit card companies, too. If your loved one's house was mortgaged, there may be mortgage insurance which will pay off the outstanding loan. You must ask.

9. ***Talk with an attorney,*** perhaps a certified public accountant, and/or a financial planner. Most professionals will talk to you, free of charge, for the first half hour. Ask about this consulting fee waiver. This "free time" allows you to ascertain if you'll like working with the person. Family and friends, even if they've been through things like this "twenty times," are probably not familiar with estate law. Be a good consumer and if you do not like the answer to your questions or how much the services of the attorney will cost, find another one.

The AARP's *On Being Alone: Guide for Widowed Persons* instructs anyone who has had a loved one die to "postpone any decisions that can be put off until you feel better emotionally."

PHYSICAL GRIEF

The physical changes that occur when danger arises are something we've heard about. This is referred to as the "fight or flight" response to threat. We've all felt this when a child suddenly appears out of nowhere, dashes into the street to retrieve a ball, and barely misses being smashed by an oncoming car. Or when there is a stranger following us too closely on a deserted street, a weird noise outside our bedroom window at night, or any event that makes our breathing shallow or deep, our hearts beat faster, our palms sweat or become clammy, and our senses go into overdrive. The body continues to respond by pumping more blood to the heart and muscles, which increases the need for oxygen, nutrients, and energy to go deep into the muscles. As the muscles receive more blood they begin to tighten. Breathing becomes deeper, reserving oxygen for strength. The blood vessels on the surface of the skin constrict; this is the way the body protects itself in case the body is injured.

These same physical alterations occur in any situation concerning change …. hearing through the grapevine that you'll be forced into early retirement, being told that the plant will be closed, or receiving a letter from the school that your child's special education program will not be funded next year. That response also happens when there is a death and with the subsequent sadness and grief that is experienced with all the changes that occur afterward.

At a time of pain from the loss or change of a loving relationship, the body secrets chemicals into the bloodstream. You feel confused, unstable, on edge, and often depressed. These are the physical sensations of grief and they are just as real as the deep heartache of emotional grief. For a person who does not know about physical grief, he or she often thinks, "I'm going crazy." It's simply not true.

Death experts and those who counsel the bereaved, including Dr. Sandra Graves, explain that after a death,

called Dad to ask permission to use the piece, there was a long silence. 'You really want to use it?' he wheezed, his voice breaking. When the June issue finally arrived, he called and said how happy he was we had downplayed that he was my father. He could now believe his piece had been accepted on its own merit.

"A few days later, he and I began discussing the possibility of my sojourning with him after the summer. His hope was that the two of us could drive up the East Coast so he could visit and reconnect with all his eleven children while he still had the strength.

"Meanwhile, my editor and I were putting together the July issue, featuring poetry and essays about the male experience. Something told me I'd better publish in that issue the story about how I came to reconnect with my father. On Fourth of July weekend, SDWM arrived special delivery in Virginia. Dad had a virus. In his weakened condition, fever raced unchecked through his now frail body. Still, he found the strength to read his oldest child's essay. Nodding, he smiled and closed his eyes. It was the last thing he read. Two hours later he died.

"And so, dear Father, for you and me there is no good-bye either. Just a loving farewell and warm thanks to you for being my dad."

this period is called the Stage of Resistance. You are resisting the natural reaction to change. Your mind may be saying: How could she die now? Why couldn't his death wait until I had a chance to say I love you once more? And concurrently, your body is fighting the change just as hard by producing chemicals and creating hormonal imbalances that are released immediately and may continue as long as six to eight weeks after the death. Some experts believe that the hormones can continue to be released up to six months after the death. Thus every time your mind happens to recall the incident of the death, seeing your loved one dead, or the shock of the news, the hormones pump through the body as if it's the first time. The result is that you feel the pain afresh, as if it's happening all over again, and the tears, sorrow, and numbness are again foremost in your mind.

During the Stage of Resistance, the adrenocorticotrophic hormone (ACTH) is released by the pituitary gland, which controls growth and development. ACTH stimulates the production of the hormone aldosterone, causing salt to be absorbed by the kidney. This in turn leads to high blood pressure, water retention, and often shortness of breath. Thus, you feel flushed, perhaps have headaches, and sometimes experience dizziness. Cortisol production, which causes increase glucose (sugar) levels in the body, can cause your body to not fully process the sugar, leading to feelings of anxiousness and excitability. Cortisol also causes fat, protein, and vitamin B to break down, and subsequently energy levels drop. Muscles begin to feel weak.

While all this is going on, the immune system's ability to fight bacteria is weakened, making the body more susceptible to infections. People often say that after a loved one has died, they caught every cold anyone had in the office or at school. This is a manifestation of physical grief.

ACTH also produces thyroxin, released by the thyroid gland. Thyroxin causes changes in the metabolism (weight gain or loss are often the result), shortness of breath, and added stress on the heart. Thyroxin causes anxiety, confusion, insomnia, and feelings of discontent including suspicion and dejection. Increased levels of it can also cause a worried response, jumpiness, and exhaustion.

Physical changes can last a few days, a few months, or even years. As with emotional grief, there is no time clock ticking away so that "Bong! Sam can stop grieving now." The body and the mind do not work that way.

The important point here, as outlined by medical and grief experts, is to be aware of the physical changes occurring as a result of the death of your loved one. They recommend getting feelings out into the open with friends, family, and/or support groups; eating well-balanced meals (sometimes smaller portions more often than three meals are easier to digest); reducing or eliminating caffeine; and cutting out or down on alcohol. Try to get six to eight hours of sleep each day, preferably at night. Some people find the use of relaxation techniques can help restore their energy. A regular exercise program, such as taking long walks, can also help. Reorganize your day to reduce stress, break down large tasks into smaller units, and spend time relaxing.

EMOTIONAL GRIEF

On Death and Dying was published in 1969, and consequently changed (albeit slowly) the way people think of the death and dying process. Dr. Kübler-Ross also established the stages or phases we go through after the death of a loved one. Like other theories, these facets of the grieving process are controversial and some experts dismiss the notion that they happen separately. Some believe that one can experience anger and acceptance, or bargaining and denial simultaneously.

Experts do agree that there is no specific timetable or intensity that is acceptable. You do not suddenly finish grieving on the twenty-seventh of May when the clock strikes three o'clock in the afternoon. Six months before the

ॐ

If faith is part of your life, express it in ways that seem appropriate to you. Allow yourself to be around people who understand and support your religious beliefs. If you are angry at God because of the death of someone you loved, realize these feelings are a normal part of your grief work. Find someone to talk with who won't be critical of whatever thoughts and feelings you need to explore.

You may hear someone say, "With faith, you don't need to grieve." Don't believe it. Having your personal faith does not insulate you from needing to talk out and explore your thoughts and feelings. To deny your grief is to invite problems that build up inside you.

Express your faith, but express your grief as well.

acceptance stage is reached may be right for one father who has experienced the death of a child, while sixteen months later after he returned to work, another father's grief is almost as fresh as it was the day he buried his beautiful three-month-old daughter.

THE STAGES OF GRIEF

Emotional grief triggers incredible emotions and lacerates a survivor with such swift power that it paralyzes even the strongest, smartest, and most responsible individuals. Knowing the stages or phases of the emotion may help you to cope with the feelings and to understand that you are not going crazy, but are normal.

The grief stages include:

• Denial
• Anger
• Bargaining
• Depression
• Acceptance

After the death of a loved one, understand that you will be feeling many things. Basically, try to take very good care of yourself, talk to a facilitator at a bereavement group, and seek professional help anytime you feel that the problems of grief are too knotted to untangle alone.

Denial

"You're wrong—Linda wouldn't have taken her own life!" "I don't believe you. I felt the baby kick me just before labor started. He couldn't have died." Denial that death has occurred is the initial feeling of grief. There is shock, numbness, and disbelief and these emotions are experienced right after one hears the news of the death of a loved one. When the *Challenger* spacecraft exploded, tens of thousands of school children sat in utter disbelief, shocked at seeing real flesh and blood death on television screens. Without ever intimately knowing the brave men and women who lost their lives, they sat stunned in skepticism, denial, and began grieving.

During this first stage of grief, we sometimes experience a feeling of shock, as if our entire bodies and minds have been given a megadose injection of Novocain. The ramification of the death of our loved ones is so absolute, so horrible, so extensive that we are unable to grasp it. One grief counselor compares hearing the news of a loved one's death to a computer overloading, or "crashing"; there is no room for more information. Our minds are overwhelmed.

In the initial stage, the numbness, survivors say, deadens the immediate pain. Sometimes we feel our hearts race and sweat breaks out on our bodies. We cannot get enough air. We may faint or feel weak. Some people must be treated for the physical effects of grief immediately, as one would treat any victim of shock.

It has been said that this first wave of shock and denial helps us to slowly process the news that there has been a death. Often survivors report that the shock lasts through the time of the funeral. They remark that they couldn't have made it through the service, making all the arrangements and coordinating the details without that terrible numbness.

Do not be afraid of the disbelief and the denial. Having other family members or supportive friends with you during this time can help alleviate some of the responsibilities.

Anger

"If I ever see that doctor, I'll kill him!" "I hate God. He could have saved her!"

As children, before we learned what was acceptable and "polite," when we didn't get something we wanted, we struck out at those who denied our wishes. We screamed and fought; we became angry. This same basic instinct is evident in the second stage of grief. We are often incensed at other loved ones, at doctors, at God and, in the case of a violent

HELPING A FRIEND IN GRIEF
by Alan D. Wolfelt, Ph.D., director of the Center for Loss and Life Transition

è&

When a friend is grieving, listen with your heart. Helping begins with your ability to be an active listener. Your physical presence and desire to listen without judging are critical helping tools. Don't worry so much about what you will say. Just concentrate on listening to the words that are being shared with you. Avoid clichés and the temptation to say things such as "I know just how you feel," because you don't. Allow your friend to have his or her own feelings.

A vital role of those who desire to help the bereaved is to encourage and support the outward expression of grief. The grieving person moves toward reconciling him- or herself to the loss when he or she can attend to his or her emotional experiences, accepting them as a result of the privilege of having been capable of loving another person.

As a result of this death, our friend's life is under reconstruction. Considering the significance of the loss, be gentle and compassionate in all your helping efforts.

Accept the uniqueness of grief and accept the griever for who the person is, as he or she is, and where he or she is.

death, at the individual who killed our loved one, at the police, at anyone in authority, including the justice system. We are angry for other family members not grieving as we are, we are angry at ourselves for letting the death happen (even when it is clearly not our fault).

While knowing that this is a typical reaction, the anger is still a very real effect of death. Along with anger, survivors often experience another emotion. How can he or she possibly feel angry that his or her loved one has died? This anger often leads to guilt. Some people become "stuck" in the anger/guilt stage of grief. For their entire lifetime, some may stay angry and feel guilty that their child, sibling, or parent died.

Others idolize the loved one who has died. For example, the child who died may be used as the perfect example of behavior, and according to the stories and comparisons spouted by her parents, her siblings may pale in his or her shadow. Or a widow may idolize her late husband, forgetting that he was an alcoholic and a gambler.

Know that the stages of grief do not have a set timetable or sequence; you may not feel all the emotions or may feel them simultaneously. If the anger/guilt stage (or the other stages) seems to be excessively long, a therapist, a religious advisor, or a listening friend may help you move through your anger and release it as you reconcile with the death of a loved one.

Bargaining

In the bargaining phase, survivors often try to strike a deal with God or their Higher Power. "If I just concentrate hard enough (or pray hard enough), God will bring Sissy back to me." "If I keep his bedroom just like it was the day he died, I know he'll walk through that door. This is just a terrible mistake." "If I can just find out why Charlie was in that neighborhood, I'll know why he was shot."

During the bargaining stage of death, survivors often begin a search for information regarding the death. Grief experts explain that this is extremely normal and the search is part of the healing process. However, there is no bargaining with death. We can't be better, prettier, smarter, richer or any of the "ers." It is only through acceptance that we can turn the terrible reality of death into memories.

Depression

As stated before, the stages of grief can all flow together or be felt individually. Depression, however, is typically the hardest stage to move through and may last for a considerable time. This is the stage in which you realize that you will never see or touch or talk with your loved one again. This is also the time when you may experience the "if onlys," or the "should ofs." Grief experts agree that there are many signs of depression, including:

- Obvious unhappiness
- Inability to feel pleasure
- Crying and preoccupation with sad thoughts
- Feelings of helplessness, worthlessness, and hopelessness
- Periods of withdrawal and isolation
- Loss of energy
- Signs of self-neglect
- Loss of interest in things that were previously interesting, including sex
- Physical complaints and sleep difficulties
- Thoughts and talk of suicide

During the depression stage, you may experience the "firsts." That is, the first time you go to the cemetery, the first time you go alone to buy furniture or a bed, and the first time you travel alone. It's the time you celebrate your first holiday season without a loved one. This is the time you may sit in the audience, watch your child graduate from college, and know that her mother isn't there to share the bittersweet pride you feel.

For two years (after being widowed), I was just as crazy as you can be and still be at large. It was total confusion. How did I come out of it? I don't know because I didn't know when I was in it that I was in it....

—Helen Hayes, actress

During the stage of depression, the reality of the death settles in and can last from months to years. An airline pilot comments on her mother's death: "I still get jealous—and depressed—when I see other adult women with their mothers. They can shop, and visit, and become friends. I never had the chance to be anything but her little girl, never had the opportunity to know her as one woman to another. That hurts. It's been twelve years since she died of cancer, and I still feel that stab of depression once in a while."

Survivors often feel hopeless, as if they cannot cope with the reality of living. Many report that they feel suicidal tendencies or other thoughts of running away. It is at this time that support groups and other self-help techniques can be valuable. You need not be alone; others have walked the pathway before and can share advice on coping with this stage of grief.

Acceptance

During the reconciliation stage of grief, we come to understand that we are moving to a new facet of our lives. We will never experience things exactly as we did before a loved one died, but come to know a new normal of what we are and of what the future will hold.

It is often helpful during this time, when we begin to have feelings of hopefulness, that we carry out promises made to the one who died. "I always said that if anything happened to her, I would try to be a good grandfather as well as a grandmother. I actually baked cookies with the grandkids—using her recipe." "I told her I would finish college and get my bachelor's degree."

It may also be helpful to take on new hobbies, return to school, take classes, join clubs, get a pet, or take a more active interest in your church or other organizations. Additionally, many survivors find that through broadening their social circles away from those they knew before (especially in the case of one being widowed), they meet new men and women and thus begin to date.

Acceptance only means that you have acknowledged the death. You don't have to agree with it, but eventually as the grief is processed, there is an acceptance that a loved one has died. Keep in mind as you move through each stage, or see another person processing grief, that often you might feel a pang of guilt, or depression, or anger, even years later. This doesn't mean regression, it means that you still have deep, loving feelings for the one who died and that you are very normal, indeed. When a loved one dies of natural causes, there is a different feeling among survivors than if the family member has been a victim of homicide. Therefore, the second portion of this chapter examines how certain causes of death affect us.

NATURAL CAUSES

Back in the "old days," when our grandparents (and great-grandparents) lived, people died of natural causes. Today, we've moved to a civilization where there's no such thing. Every disease has a name and while we might not be able to stop the consequences, the result is known as terminal. Individual organs that wear out can be translated to a specific type of dysfunction. Each deviation internally and externally can be identified. Even a combination thereof can be cataloged and classified by a medical practitioner.

So our loved ones die as a result of cardiac arrest, kidney failure, breast cancer, internal bleeding. Loved ones die of a gunshot wound, an airplane crash, a boating accident, and other causes as far from natural as you can get.

"I've only seen a few people die of what I would call natural causes," remarks Mary K. Bernowski, a hospice nurse in the San Diego area. "These are the people who are at peace with the terminal illness, have made plans for their death, have said good-bye to family and friends. They peacefully die—of natural causes."

It's all right to cry, to question, to be weak. Beware of allowing yourself to be put on a pedestal by others who tell you what an inspiration you are because of your strength and your ability to cope so well. If they only knew!

—Father Kenneth Czillinger,
volunteer with Parents of
Murdered Children

PROLONGED DEATH FROM AN ILLNESS

"Death due to chronic illness, such as cancer, is rarely rapid," explains Robert E. Enck, M.D., past president of the Association of Community Cancer Centers in Columbus, Ohio, an organization affiliated with the National Hospice Program. "Dying usually lasts a few hours to a few days and is a continuous process as the body and brain are unable to cope....emotional, cognitive, behavioral, and autonomic function all slowly deteriorate and finally coma ensues before death."

Dr. Enck says that there are two roads to coma, as described in the dying patient—the high road and the low road. "The low road is the most common and is a path of increasing sedation to coma and death. This path does not appear to be traumatic for patients and survivors generally recall a peaceful death. If not controlled, the high road is much more traumatic." This resembles the organic brain syndrome of delirium and symptoms include restlessness, confusion, agitation, hallucinations, jerks, seizures, and finally coma. This preterminal delirium can start as early as nine days prior to the death with symptoms becoming increasingly frequent.

Within the hospice program, Dr. Enck points out, "More than one-third of dying patients experience some difficulties during the last forty-eight hours of life, with noisy and moist breathing, pain, agitation, and restlessness the most common. The great majority of these terminal symptoms can be managed by reassurance or drug intervention."

Does it make it easier when there is a prolonged illness that results in death? The answer is no. Some experts refer to this as "anticipated grief," but since grief is an emotion that happens after the death, other experts prefer the term, "anticipating the death."

UNEXPECTED AND SUDDEN DEATH

If a prolonged illness, which results in death, is fought and unaccepted, it may seem like a slow-moving, suffocating wave of lava. An unexpected, accidental, or sudden death can be compared to having one's spirit sliced into one-inch cubes with a switchblade.

In 2000, there were approximately 30 million victims of crime, including almost 6 million who fell prey to violence. The United States Department of Justice estimates that five out of six of today's twelve-year-olds will become victims of violent crime during their lifetimes. These painful statistics represent countless individuals whose lives are irrevocably altered by violence.

"Sudden death is easiest for the person who dies, hardest for the survivors," says David Carroll, author of *Living with Dying*. Survivors frequently experience a hysterical reaction or become stoically silent.

In the book by Mothers Against Drunk Driving (MADD) founder Candy Lightner, *Giving Sorrow Words*, Lighter details her shock when learning that her daughter had been killed by a drunk driver. On hearing the news, Lightner explains, "I didn't pass out completely, but I did collapse. They carried me into the house and I screamed all the way in." A few years before, she recalls her son Travis had been run over by a car and nearly died. As he was recovering, Lightner's mother had a heart attack after major surgery and died. "Somehow, I survived," she writes. "But I couldn't believe such a horrible ordeal would happen again, not ever, not even in a million years. I didn't want to believe it. I couldn't believe."

Lightner insisted that her husband and father were playing some inhuman prank. She remembers screaming, "You're lying to me, you're telling me cruel lies. Why do you hate me so much?" She was, according to her account, experiencing a classic case of denial and shock felt by most when they hear the news of a sudden or unexpected death.

As a nation of people who regularly deny death, it's rational that even when the death is a possibility, for example when a person is in the final stages of Alzheimer's disease, the family quite often reacts in the same way as if it is a totally unexpected death. Recently a friend in her late sixties, who had cancer and two mastectomies, suffered a

We will feel pain. We will feel loss. Our lives will be changed in ways that we could not have imagined.

—Paul Kent Froman, Ph.D.,
grief expert

heart attack. She convalesced enough to returned home from the hospital and two weeks later, she died during the night. To many of her friends and family, this still came as a shock. "How could this happen? I just saw Julienne and she was recovering!" they cried. In actuality, this lovely lady was slowly deteriorating, yet loved ones denied the fact.

It is not unusual when death has been unexpected for the family to lash out at the caregiver, doctors, the police, or other members of the family. This is a symptom of shock and has been compared to the survivors of a tragic disaster.

When a sudden death has occurred (or if the death seems to be "sudden"), those who have been close to the deceased are sometimes medicated and sedated because of the tremendous, heartrending drain on the body both physically and emotionally. There are strong arguments regarding this practice and each must be individually decided since the medication may prolong the shock, but without it the physical symptoms can be traumatic and debilitating. Your family physician can advise you on this, yet he or she may not be the best qualified professional. Don't hesitate to talk with a psychiatrist for specifics on antidepressants, sedatives, and the appropriate dosages.

DEATH BY TRAUMA

As anyone knows, death in all forms is traumatic. Death by suicide, homicide, accident, natural, or man-made disaster can take an even greater toll on the family.

According to Dr. Graves, who has done extensive work with survivors of large-scale accidents and disasters, "A trauma is defined as any incident in which your normal coping abilities do not work. This means that the intensity of all the experiences of grief is going to be greater. This also means that you will more than likely need to learn or relearn ways of dealing with acute stress."

Dr. Graves explains that it is important for survivors to understand that grief is physical and the body is attempting to adjust to a new set of reality standards, different ways, fresh concepts. It is also adjusting to the morality of death as your mind examines, perhaps for the first time, the consequences of your own mortality.

In addition to the normal physical stresses in grief, a traumatic death of a loved one can result in one or more of the following reactions:

- **Startling at any noise or disturbance** beyond the normal response we all experience. This usually means that it takes your body several minutes to calm down again and come back to "reality." Your mind also recalls the traumatic event which is causing the response.
- **Nightmares**: Night sweats, waking up with an acute sense of anxiety, and the inability to relax after the nightmare are included in this reaction.
- **Hyperactivity or agitation**: You may experience a need to pace or move around a lot and not be able to pinpoint why you are feeling restless.
- **Flashbacks** (seeing the incident over and over): These experiences are often total sensory reactions—you smell, hear, even taste the incident as well as have a vivid visual recall.
- **Difficulty making decisions**: Concentration may be poor and the little things we do each day become big decisions....what to wear, what to eat for lunch, which bus to take to work, which way to walk the dog.
- **Amnesia for the event** (especially prevalent for those who saw the traumatic scene): Our minds sometimes close out events that are too horrible for us to face. This is the way to protect us and a primary survival tool.

The questions produced by a traumatic death are never-ending. Will justice be done? What is justice under these circumstances? How can we deal with intense feelings of revenge? What role does forgiveness play? How could the event be prevented?

If your loved one has died as a result of trauma, for example in a hit-and-run accident produced because

Since nothing we intend is ever faultless, and nothing we attempt ever without error, and nothing we achieve without some measure of finitude and fallibility we call humanness, we are saved by forgiveness....

—David Augsburger, from *Caring Enough to Forgive*

someone was driving drunk, you may be experiencing fear or even terror because of these questions. The world is no longer safe. If murder or freak accidents or drunk driving can occur where you live, anything can happen. Terrible things can occur. Death takes place anywhere. Returning to that part of town, or anywhere similar, tends to strike terror into the survivor. You may be thinking that this is insane—but if you are feeling this way, you are not crazy. It makes sense that with your reality shattered, your deepest sense of fairness and safety have been taken away. It would be unusual should you not be afraid.

Dr. Graves explains, "When you were a child, you were taught that the world was fair. When something wasn't fair, you probably felt cheated. Do you remember how angry you became when you felt cheated? What did you want to do? More than likely you wanted to strike out at whomever caused the unfairness."

She says that by examining these feelings many survivors understand where their rage is coming from since the death of a loved one. "Our sense of fairness is buried deeply within the child in all of us. The child part of us remains throughout our lifetime. When that fairness is wronged, we are outraged with the anger of a cheated child. We grow up expecting fairness from life. We grieve at the loss of fairness in our lives."

A HOMICIDE SURVIVOR SPEAKS OUT

When a family member is murdered, survivors are not only caught up in the weight of incredible grief, the unwarranted death, and the breakdown of traditional ethical values, but are often faced with long legal battles. The trauma of the legal system tears open the wound and for many this halts the grief process from continuing, curtailing the possibility of closure and resolution.

Some people withdraw from life and living. They are angry and depressed. Some flounder. Some begin to intensely hate the system that has allowed the killer of their children, husbands, or friends to go free while that precious life has been snuffed out. Others become activists, start and join national support networks, or lobby on a state and national level for an overhaul of the system.

This is the storyline that Jack and Trudy Collins followed, with assistance from the Office for Victims of Crime, National Victims Resource Center, part of the U.S. Department of Justice, (800) 627-6872.

In a situation that statistically could have driven husband and wife apart, the Collinses now work together feverishly trying to right a system they believe has gone haywire and channeling their energy to right the wrong as part of the Judicial Reform Foundation. The Judicial Reform Foundation's primary goals are to analyze the ongoing operation of the national criminal justice system and to assess its impact on victims of violent crimes and their survivors.

Jack Collins explains, "For too long, there has been disproportionate attention paid to defendants and convicted felons and too little to victims. It is time to restore a proper balance to this system and place victims in a position of centrality.

"I have been convinced for some time now that for our own violent domestic war, nothing will afford the criminal justice system more force, more credibility, more integrity, than putting an end to the interminable succession of appeals that issues from the convicted and vicious murderers of our nation's death rows.

"Let me speak on a very personal note for a moment. On July 18, 1985, my wife Trudy and I buried our lovely and very special nineteen-year-old daughter, Suzanne. At age nineteen, she was brutally choked, beaten, raped, tortured, and murdered in Tennessee, on July 12, 1985. She now lies in Arlington National Cemetery, a young woman Marine who was so very proud of her professional military calling.

"Her killer was convicted and sentenced to death on March 17, 1987. The Tennessee Supreme Court and the United States Supreme Court, after full and fair review, denied his initial appeals. Now additional appeals are taking place in the state courts. Once these appeals are concluded, lengthy and repetitive habeas corpus appeals in the federal courts undoubtedly lie ahead. Is this justice? Or is this a second victimization of Suzanne and her family?

"Trudy and I quake with fear and anxiety as we reflect on the interminable path of habeas corpus appeals that we must still walk. While this process goes on, there can be no closure to our grief, no end to our emotional and mental suffering. Our nightmares will continue, the knots will remains in our stomachs. The leaden weights will remain in our hearts. We will continue to bleed."

The Collinses urge others who have had family members die from violence to join together and make their voices known to the government, and to their representatives, and to change the way the judicial system works. "I speak, not only for myself and my wife Trudy, but for all victims and survivors. I particularly speak in the name of our daughter, Suzanne, and in the name of the other daughters and sons, brothers and sisters, spouses and parents who have been so viciously and brutally murdered in our ongoing domestic warfare."

When death is the result of a violent crime, the Department of Justice's National Institute of Justice is an office that provides a toll-free access to highly trained criminal justice reference specialists who can help you find answers to specific questions. The referral service, (800) 627-6872, is staffed from 8:30 A.M. until 7:00 P.M., EST, Monday through Friday, with a message machine after hours. It provides referrals, statistical information, audiovisual, microfiche and written library materials, along with extensive free publications.

According to Brenda G. Meister, acting director of the Office for Justice Program, a division of the Office for Victims of Crime, "The Office for Victims of Crime is the central focal point within the United States government for all issues affecting crime victims. It also administers the Crime Victims Fund, a special account set up in the Treasury Department to meet the direct needs (compensation and assistance) of victims of crime."

Meister explains that the fund is truly unique. "It is made up solely of criminal fines, special penalty assessments, and the proceeds of forfeited appearance/bail bonds paid into the fund by criminals convicted of crimes in federal courts. Not one dollar of this fund comes from hardworking taxpayers."

The two major efforts of the office are a Victims Compensation Program and a Victims Assistance Program. These programs encompass the needs of surviving members of homicide victims. The Compensation Program reimburses the survivors for funeral expenses, as well as medical expenses incurred by victims before their crime-caused deaths. In addition, it covers the expenses related to needed mental health counseling for survivors.

The Assistance Program funds local agencies that provide a wide range of support activities for crime victims. This program funds homicide survivor support groups and grief counseling efforts. Meister reports that the Assistance Program "provides information/referral services and offers advocacy support for homicide survivors who must deal with the complexities of the criminal justice system during the trial of their loved ones' murderers."

The Office for Victims of Crime also awards discretionary grants for three programs of direct relevance to homicide survivors. The first, says Meister, is the "Spiritual Dimension in Victim Services, which provides professional training to clergy to help them respond properly and sensitively to criminal victimization, including homicide. The second grant is called the Assistance for Children Grieving Violent Death and recognizes that children grieve differently than adults and understands their special needs. The grant enables victim service providers, school staff, and other human service professionals to insightfully and correctly address these special needs.

"The third grant is directed to Parents of Murdered Children and Other Survivors of Homicide Victims (POMC), a national self-help organization for parents and their children who have experienced a violent homicide in their families. The goal, here, is to establish a national network of POMC chapters to assist survivors and increase services."

If you or a family member have been a victim of a violent crime, talk with a counselor or advisor at a victim's services office and seek out help on a local level such as with POMC.

WHEN DEATH IS ANOTHER'S FAULT

Sometimes death is another person's fault, such as a murder or homicide. Sometimes it is the result of the carelessness of another person, as with a work-related accident, or an individual has been driving drunk or using drugs. These are only a few of the ways a death can be attributed to another person, but the survivors feel a unique pain regarding the death.

When a death occurs in these situations, as with murder, in a situation that we formerly felt safe, we as survivors become especially frightened. Suddenly the streets are filled with terrifying possibilities, our places of work or where our loved ones worked are risky, and perhaps, as in the case of malpractice, the medical professionals whom we have so thoroughly trusted with the lives and health of our loved ones have been discredited so completely that it may take considerable time to work through the grief and fear.

If the Death Seems Like Malpractice

When a loved one is desperately hurt, for example after a serious car accident, we are overwhelmed by the technology involved in attempting to save his or her life. Tubes are connected to every opening of our loved one's body, monitors crowd us out of a place near the bed, and the medical staff rushes around grim faced as if we are unnecessary and definitely in the way. These are the life-and-death struggles they cope with on a daily basis, and we want to believe that everything humanly possible is done correctly. When there is cause for question, the very foundation of our intelligence is distressed.

If your loved one's death was caused by another, in a malpractice claim for instance, you will be faced with litigation and a lengthy judicial process. Since most of us put incredible trust in the medical community, scientific advancements, and the system that saves so many times, it's quite right that you will feel outrage as your basic values are shaken. When there has been an alleged malpractice allegation, it does feel like murder.

Grief experts and therapists who help families after a death explain that in a malpractice allegation, there is an intense sense of helplessness, a desire for revenge, paranoia, and lack of security and safety in this world that killed their loved one. Dr. Graves reports, "The most common phrase I hear under these circumstances is 'He might as well have held a gun to her head and shot her. He murdered her as sure as anything.' "

During the intensity of accusation, there is often a shortage of details regarding the death. In most cases, the information is "sealed" and not accessible by family before the lawsuit is filed. What this means is that it may be years before all the details and information regarding the death are brought to the attention of the State Malpractice board and because of the technicalities of medical malpractice, there are various obstacles that hinder the flow of justice. This triples the frustration felt by survivors.

Malpractice is a civil action, not criminal, and as Dr. Graves says, "The impact of the lawsuit and trial rarely meet the needs of the bereaved family members. There may appear to be little actual 'punishment' and many families feel like there is a conspiracy against them." This multiplies the breakdown of trust in society as a whole.

What can survivors do as a result of a malpractice death or other death that is caused by another person? Support groups, including Parents of Murdered Children, can help provide information as well as advocacy and counseling by telephone as well as letter.

You will not be alone; you will not be thought a social deviant by calling the death murder. Be persistent. Find an attorney who is willing to look beyond what is available. Become educated in the law and the reason for the illness or death. Talk with other doctors who specialize in the same area.

It is essential, too, that the matter and manner of the death are separated from the fact that your loved one is dead. It is normal that the stages of grief are postponed during the

TAP-TAP-TAP
by Diane Watson

❧

My mother had been ill with a lung disease for years. Her lungs could not throw off a constant infection. Many times she almost died. She'd used breathing machines and oxygen the last two years of her life. It was hard to see her body slowly weaken, to see my mother suffer.

The holidays passed and we knew these would be Mom's last; she knew it too. In the hospital for over a month, my oldest sister and her family had been in town since Christmas and were about to leave. It was then that Mom decided to quit taking her medicines and breathing treatments. With only 20 percent lung capacity left, only morphine and oxygen would now help her die in comfort. I remember telling Mom before she started taking morphine shots that I wanted her to tap me on the shoulder when she was out of her body so I would know she was okay. I told her twice. We were alone in the room when she assured me she would. Honestly, I thought it would be impossible, but it gave me a tiny measure of hope.

For the next twenty-four hours my sisters and I watched Mom struggle to breath, her lungs slowly filling with liquid. She would wake between morphine shots and the pain was etched on her

time of litigation, but the grief must be dealt with. Talking to counselors, your clergy, or a therapist about sudden death and the grief process will help, although you should never minimize the death—that only adds to your grief. Dr. Graves concludes, "It is vital that you understand what is happening to you, enabling you to reclaim some of the energy that is being expended in the entangled world of malpractice."

DYING OF SUICIDE

Official statistics show that approximately thirty thousand Americans kill themselves every year. The true figure, according to the American Association of Suicidology, is probably much higher. Suicide is the third leading cause of death among young people ages fifteen to twenty-four, and it is the eighth leading cause of death among all persons. Suicide shows no favorites—it cuts across all age, economic, social, and ethnic boundaries. And surviving family members not only suffer the trauma of having a loved one die, but are themselves at higher risk for emotional problems and difficulty with grief.

Adina Wrobleski, author of the book *Suicide Survivors: A Guide for Those Left Behind*, knows that bad parenting doesn't cause suicide, and good parenting does not prevent suicide. If it were the case, then all the children of "bad" parents would kill themselves, but they don't. It also does not account for why children of "good" parents kill themselves. Divorce and broken homes do not cause suicide. However, Wrobleski knows the personal pain. Her daughter died of suicide. And she understands the myth about being a suicide survivor. An internationally recognized authority on suicide and grief after suicide, she clearly discusses the grief and the guilt.

Wrobleski's points hit home for anyone who has survived a loved one's death by suicide. "There is nothing too awful to talk about; everything in the world has happened before." And she continues, "Research on suicide grief has found that suicide survivors have extra problems due to the taboo and stigma, but despite this recover as other people do. A case could be made that suicide survivors are sturdier than other grieving people because they recover despite all the extra problems they have."

No longer called "committing suicide," death by suicide produces all the anxious emotions and physical changes as other forms of death. Some say it is more intense. Along with this, as with the death of a child—especially of Sudden Infant Death Syndrome—there is a combination of anger and sadness which mix to form the emotion of guilt. Anger is often violently expressed, sadness is sometimes bottled up and shoved aside internally, as we try to understand the reason our loved one killed him- or herself.

Carol Cozart, coauthor of *The Widow's Handbook*, became a suicide survivor when her husband took his life. She relates, "There are as many reasons why a person would choose to end his or her life as there are suicide deaths. What all of these people did have in common, though, was a deep emotional anguish for which they felt suicide was the only relief. They did not so much wish to die as to get rid of the terrible pain." Cozart explains that suicide doesn't actually end the pain; it only places it on the shoulders of the survivors.

Special note: All unexplained deaths are handled by the police as if they are a homicide. Thus the death of your loved one by suicide will be examined in this manner until it has been made clear that the death is a result of suicide.

The Guilt Associated with Suicide

The guilt of a suicide is very real and is a normal reaction for some people, *but not everyone*. According to grief experts, during bereavement, the guilt helps to regain some control in an existence that has gone berserk. There are so many "what ifs," "if onlys," and unanswered questions to which you will never truly know the answer.

According to the grief therapy network ACCORD, most survivors search for the answers to three questions:

1. Did my loved one know what he or she was doing at the time he or she took life away?
2. Will I ever believe there was nothing I could have done to stop the suicide?
3. Is my loved one at peace?

face. I felt so helpless. All I could do was cry. Finally the moment came ... her last breath. The doctor pronounced her dead. She finally looked peaceful.

Everything seemed unreal. A priest came in to say a prayer with us. We made a semi-circle around Mom's bed and the priest had his arm on my shoulder. My mind was blank, thinking was too painful.

Then it happened. The priest tapped me several times on the shoulder. He stopped and he started to tap again. I looked up expecting to see something heavenly, perhaps an angel.

I saw nothing—no, that can't be from Mom. But I kept thinking about the taps on my shoulder. The priest had tapped no one else. With a start, I realized Mom couldn't have physically tapped me herself, but she had let me know she was okay.

My request had been answered.

These questions are *very normal* and *you are one among many survivors who feel exactly this way and search for answers to these questions.* ACCORD recommends attending your local Survivors of Suicide (SOS) group. If there isn't a group in your area, help organize one. You deserve to know you are not alone.

Feeling a Sense of Blame

Condemning yourself and blaming others is a human response, poignant in the case of a death by suicide. That blame is part of the grief involved in a suicide. Grief experts suggest keeping a journal of the guilty thoughts, writing a letter to the person who died of suicide, talking with friends who are not family members about the anger, guilt, and blame you are experiencing, and looking outside your circle to support groups specifically for survivors of a death by suicide.

Wrobleski explains the misassumption that survivors of a suicide death are guilty in some way that other survivors are not. "This assumption, from the Dark Ages," she writes, "that we should have some brand to show people our guilt and shame for having a suicide in the family lives on." Wrobleski, who is a suicide survivor, is quick to correct that erroneous thought. "How do [people] know how guilty you feel? Would they assume you must feel guilty if someone you loved had died from cancer?"

Other experts point out that before your loved one died of suicide you did not take credit for his or her achievements or successes in life, nor did you take credit for the failures that he or she experienced. Why then, should a survivor take credit (i.e., accept the responsibility) for the suicide?

Telling Others about the Suicide

"What will the neighbors (coworkers, family members, church friends) think about the death?" "How can I ever face anyone?" The truth is best. Lying, hushing it up, covering the death, only makes the situation worse. Wrobleski explains that if you've already lied about the situation, it's time to correct the situation, especially so with children. You will also need to tell children the method that was used; if you don't, they'll ask. Remember, violence is part of our daily lives—if not on television in cartoons, then daily in the newspaper and on the six o'clock news. Yes, they will probably be angry at you for lying, but once the truth has been established you can build a stronger relationship.

What do you say about the death by suicide? "Bill died. He took his life on Thanksgiving." "I didn't know how depressed Tiffany was. She killed herself last summer." While telling the method of the suicide can be nearly impossible initially, you may decide to tell people. "Mother had been unhappy for a very long time. She swallowed sleeping pills and died two weeks ago."

There will be shock on the faces of those you tell and you may have to console them. This is an extra burden the suicide survivor must carry. Wrobleski goes even further and encourages suicide survivors to "take care of them before they can turn around to console us!" She recommends saying, "Thanks for your concern. I know it's a shock."

While it is commonly thought that life insurance policies become void should someone die by suicide, that's not always the case. Many policies will pay the beneficiaries if the policy has been in effect for a period of time. Do not neglect to file for benefits because of your unfamiliarity with this issue. Check your policy; check with your agent or company. As with claiming Social Security and other benefits, you will need a copy of the death certificate to apply for the life insurance benefits.

Keep in mind that you may have to continue to make payments on the policy even after the death, until the necessary paperwork is completed by your insurer. You will be reimbursed for these extra payments, but unless you continue to pay, the policy may lapse.

A Religious Reflection on Suicide

While suicide is mentioned throughout the Bible's Old Testament, there is no opinion, condemnation, or condoning. Saint Augustine said it was a grievous sin and the Catholic Church and a few Protestant denominations

Suicide among elderly people is a major problem in our society.... the old do not make suicidal gestures; their ratio of suicide completions to attempts is the highest of any age group.

—Dr. Judith M. Stillion, et al., from *Suicide Across the Life Span* have, at times, taken a harsh view of suicide. All major religions have abolished the philosophy that suicide is a cardinal sin; however, you may have to forgive a few people who make comments about the religious aspects of suicide.

No one can provide an answer, from a religious view, of what happens to the soul when there is a suicide. You may find help by talking with a compassionate minister, priest, or rabbi regarding the religious view of suicide. Some of our deepest fears and hurts are the result of what some dictionaries still refer to as "self-murder."

As John Hewett, author of *After Suicide*, explains, "You need to rid yourself of the belief that all suicides go to hell. This often results from a rigid logic which teaches that forgiveness occurs only after repentance. I believe the wealth of the biblical evidence shows that God's grace and mercy are unmerited, given freely. We don't earn his love, we receive it! Already, in the midst of this tragedy, God is working to create goodness out of the ashes of your despair."

When the searing pain of immediate grief is finally channeled into a new awareness, as it will, survivors begin to see a deeper meaning to life and refuse to let the death mean nothing.

Suicide survivors say that while you'll never "get over this," you can work it through, with the help of talking to other suicide survivors, with the love of your family and friends. What will happen is that you will become more aware of the sensitive feelings of others. "There's a greater experience of cherishing love, now," says a woman whose father died of suicide.

Where to Get Help

There are a number of excellent books to understand suicide, including John Hewett's *After Suicide*. Personally, you can find out the truth (not rumors or gossip) about what happened, what he or she said, what he or she did before the death occurred. You can learn from support groups and therapists about the behavior and psychology of suicide.

In order to talk out the grief, refer to the other support groups and other programs and contact these groups:

American Association of Suicidology, 4201 Connecticut Ave., NW, Suite 408, Washington, DC 20008, (202) 237-2280, promotes research, public awareness programs, education, and training for professionals and volunteers. In addition to providing an excellent list of reading material and a directory of survivor groups which invite survivors to attend, it also serves as a national clearinghouse for information on suicide with a variety of programs for survivors.

The Samaritans: If you are despairing, in crisis, or contemplating taking your life, and need to talk to someone, contact The Samaritans. The Samaritans Suicide Prevention Center confidential hotline number: (518) 689-HOPE (4673) In Canada, call (800) 667-8089.

EUTHANASIA

Do we have a right to choose the time and method of our death? Do we have a right to refuse heroic medical procedures that could possibly prolong a painful life? Is this a form of self-murder?

If your loved one has elected to end his or her own life while suffering from a terminal illness, you may feel all the emotions associated with a suicide death. Perhaps during the long-term illness and subsequent death of your loved one, you learned and shared his or her views on the right to die. Regardless of where you personally or morally stand on this heated issue, there will still be a sense of loss, a recognition for the life and death, and the emotion of grief. To what extent and how it is handled is always a personal issue.

Euthanasia has been called mercy killing, self-deliverance, assisted suicide and other names, quite a few that are not so pretty. Much like the concept of abortion, the word provokes a series of emotionally charged arguments for and against this right to die issue. In most states the legal ramifications of a doctor-assisted and self-suicide are unclear. A "living will" is a document formally addressing what efforts should be made when the illness or diagnosis is terminal or irreversible in a hospital. The care provided in conjunction with hospice programs allows many to die at home with the care of a family member and ongoing support of hospice nurses and social workers.

Ernest Morgan, in *Dealing Creatively with Death*, points out that the right to die, or refused treatment "is based on the common-law right of self-determination and the constitutionally derived right of privacy. As long as the patient understands the nature and consequences of refusing treatment and can communicate those wishes, the patient's wishes control, even if doctors or family disagree." He explains that civil damages can be brought against health care providers if the patients' wishes are not honored.

When Derek Humphry wrote *Final Exit*, a manual of self-deliverance and assisted suicide for the dying, the upheaval of feelings was phenomenal and the book was banned, scorned, and objected to in many locations, countries, and religious communities. Yet the proponents of euthanasia say that there is little difference between informed refusal of life-saving medical procedures and choosing a time for one's death. Some authorities reflect that while suicide is a form of escaping from emotional or mental pain, euthanasia is a release from physical pain. Clearly there is no right or wrong, unless it is from a personal and philosophical standpoint. And clearly the arguments will continue.

The fifty-thousand-member National Hemlock Society, based in Eugene, Oregon, is the most public of voluntary euthanasia groups. Through public awareness and personal decisions the group strives to raise public consciousness on the topic with the public and media, by publishing books and pamphlets and providing members with free living wills and durable powers of attorney for health care. The society is quick to explain that it is not their goal to encourage suicide for any primary emotional, traumatic, or financial reason *in the absence of terminal illness*. It totally approves and supports suicide prevention. It believes that the decision to terminate life is ultimately one's own and that the timing of the decision is a personal one, and it works with family and loved ones when death is forthcoming.

"My God is a God of love and would not want people to go through the indignities of being kept alive by a mechanical system that gives no thought to quality of life," says Rev. John Prindonoff, current director of the Hemlock Society. "If someone feels that suicide is an abomination in front of God, I think that opinion should be respected. But it's not right for someone of that opinion to thrust his or her opinion on someone who is not of like mind." Provided there are sufficient safeguards, Reverend Prindonoff explains that euthanasia suicide should be an option for terminally ill patients who ask their doctors to help them die.

A DISAPPEARANCE DEATH

We've all seen the headlines:

"Woman Swept Out to Sea."

"Local Business Person Disappears—Plane Crashes in Asia."

"Honeymoon Couple Lost, Search Underway."

In a disappearance death, there are a myriad of conflicting emotions, and for those who have to experience it, there's no easy solution. Unless there is a body, there can be no death certificate. As most Americans know from television or hearsay, survivors, including widows, must wait seven years to have a family member declared dead. This means that in a disappearance death there can be no settlement of the estate, no benefits, no change in title on community property. There can also be no closure to the grief, no funeral, no final ritual.

Survivors of disappearance deaths sometimes find sanity in the madness that surrounds the death by working toward getting a clear legal status and finding professional legal and financial help. As with a homicide, often there are police or other authorities involved which can make the process considerably more painful. If the disappearance has happened out of the country, you will have to coordinate the search effort and verification of death through the authorities who may or may not understand your needs and seek counsel in that country. The State Department's Overseas Citizens Service can often help coordinate your effort (see chapter 7, When Death Occurs Away from Home, for more information).

Charlotte Foehner, coauthor of *The Widow's Handbook*, experienced a disappearance death when an Eastern Airlines flight to La Paz, Bolivia, crashed in the snow-covered Andes Mountains. The body of her husband was never recovered, no trace found. She was not able to publish a death notice, have a funeral, change title on property, or work through the grief properly. In a disappearance death, she writes, "You are not legally a widow until your husband's disappearance is proven to be a death. You won't have a death certificate, you won't be able to claim any life insurance proceeds or retirement or survivors annuity benefits. You are not eligible for any veterans or Social Security benefits. You have no access to any accounts or property titled in his name only. His will cannot be probated."

Foehner recommends finding the best legal counsel you can afford and one who has had experience in the red tape that accompanies a disappearance death. If you live in a rural area or small town, you may have to contact an attorney in a large city to get one who is experienced in these matters. Your attorney will probably recommend that you go to court to legally establish what has happened. Once the death has been proven, you will receive a finding-of-death certificate. This isn't a death certificate but can be used as one. As with death certificates, you will need official copies to apply for benefits and pensions and to transfer property.

As a result of the disappearance death, many survivors report that the search for their loved ones, the incredible amount of paperwork, the quest to make sense of the mystery and horror attached to this type of death, have delayed the grieving process. There's often a What-do-I-do-now? feeling when the ordeal is over. Participating in counseling, attending a support group of survivors, or talking with good friends and/or the clergy can help. Says Foehner, "Look for a new job, take a course in something you've always been interested in, volunteer to help other people. Above all, make every effort to get back that feeling of being needed by someone, someplace."

THE DEATH OF AN UNBORN CHILD

In our society, we go to great lengths to deny the occurrence of death, yet when it is faced, family members are allowed to work through the phases of grief. On the opposite end of the spectrum, grief for the death of a baby when the death is the result of an ectopic pregnancy, spontaneous or medical abortion, or miscarriage seems to be acceptable. It seems to be okay to talk about the death (often really referred to as a loss) in general terms. However, it is not "socially acceptable" to discuss the death after about a week or two of the event. These deaths are called "perinatal deaths," and are as real to those in the family as the death of a family member who has lived five, twenty-five, or eighty-five years.

Those who have not thought about the baby, not made even vague plans (or dreams or fantasies about "when the baby comes"), not felt the baby (or been touched by the fact that a fetus was quietly growing inside), find it almost impossible to sense the cavernous grief that is a part of the tragedy. This baby has been very real to the parents. He or she is precious and forever will be a genuine member of the family. Thus when the baby is forgotten by others, the result is that the parents and those very close to the parents can become angry, and feel tremendously alone and despondent. This isolation can create distress in the expression of feelings and, therefore, prolong and/or intensify the time of grief.

When death is a stillbirth, an abortion, or occurs through miscarriage or ectopic pregnancy, those who survive often have no one to talk with. Parents and siblings do not receive condolences; they are ignored. It is as if the baby did not exist at all. While it's hard to make excuses for other people in this or any death, the thoughtlessness can be perhaps attributed to the concept that if they do not discuss the death, you won't feel bad *or* they won't have to feel bad.

As with all grief, not discussing the death, keeping a stiff upper lip, and avoiding the reality of the pain are probably the worst things survivors can do. Talking helps. Support groups such as the New Jersey-based Miscarriage Infant Death Stillbirth (MIDS), founded by Janet Tischler, provide a way to speak with others who have experienced the unique feelings of the death of an unborn child.

After the stillbirth of her son Darren and two previous miscarriages, Janet Tischler realized that there was a particular need for grieving parents and others who have experienced miscarriage, infant death, or stillbirth. The group evolved from her despair and anger at the lack of support she received. At the first meeting in April 1982, five women were present. Today MIDS has over seven hundred members, including doctors, nurses, psychologists, social workers, clergy, and other professionals.

Says Tischler, "MIDS is a support group which is open to parents who have experienced miscarriages, infant deaths, or stillbirths. We are not a therapy group, however; we offer friendship through understanding and sharing with bereaved parents who have suffered similar losses."

She explains, "Death does not come in sizes." "Our children may not have been known to society, but they are real to us. When a baby dies, the parents go through an intense grieving process. The feelings of grief can be so severe that the couple is unaware of what has happened." MIDS understands that everyone handles grief in his or her own way and provides services to help toward that end with telephone friends, in-hospital visits, workshops and grief groups, library resources, and a score of other services.

Another group, SHARE, started in 1977, now has close to three hundred chapters nationwide. Based at St. John's Hospital in St. Charles, Missouri, SHARE is a pregnancy and infant loss support group which serves as a resource center for bereaved parents, group leaders, caregivers, and others. With materials in both Spanish and English, SHARE reaches out to fill the void that is left when a baby has died so that the child is not forgotten.

SHARE's executive director Cathi Lammert, a registered nurse and a survivor of an infant death, explains that the mission of the group is to serve those who are touched by the tragic death of a baby through miscarriage, stillbirth, or newborn death. "The primary purpose is to provide support toward positive resolution of grief experienced at the time of and/or following the death of a baby. The support encompasses emotional, physical, spiritual, and social healing, as well as sustaining the family unit.

"The secondary purpose is to provide information, education, and resources on the needs and rights of bereaved parents and siblings. The object is to aid those in the community, including family, friends, employers, members of the congregation, caregivers, and others in their supportive roles."

Sherokee and David Ilse know the pain. "On November 2, 1981, one day past our baby's due date, we were told the most heartbreaking news parents can hear: 'I'm sorry, your baby has died. There is no heartbeat.'

"Four long and grueling hours later we delivered a beautiful, peaceful boy. Our son, Brennan, never took a breath, nor greeted the world with a bellow. But he lived. And he will continue to live in our hearts and memories always." Sherokee Ilse, author of *Empty Arms: Coping with Miscarriage, Stillbirth, and Infant Death*, provides assistance with the difficult decision making that is entailed with an infant death. As Ilse says, "Babies are not supposed to die. Not your baby and not ours. But sometimes they do die." She urges parents to remember you are not alone; you are not crazy. You are grieving at a death that is very real. And you have permission to mourn.

Ectopic or tubal pregnancies, when a fertilized egg is implanted in the fallopian tube, in the ovaries, cervix, or abdomen, is a highly painful and critical condition for the woman. Once the condition is diagnosed, the pregnancy is terminated through surgery. Parents who have planned a

A BROTHER'S MEMORIES

by Shaun Lammert, at age 14, on the death of his infant brother

❧

One bitter November day, I welcomed the birth of my brother. Both he and my mother were very sick with various things I was not told and probably never will be told about. I never saw him, not one glimpse of what he looked like. All that was left for me to remember him by is a photograph.

I thought everything would be fine because, even though my sisters weren't in the greatest health when they were born, they still lived. Being seven, I was very confused; my sisters and I were jolted from relative to relative, friend to friend, as if we were unwanted orphans. Not once did anyone notice or ask how we felt about the situation.

Five days later there was an unexpected ringing of the phone, announcing the death of my brother. I, like my sisters, was abruptly awakened, only to find out the bad news. My aunt told us to go back to bed and worry about it in the morning. I didn't want to wait to worry about it; it was such a shock and I needed attention right then. Of course, there were tears, but also there was a feeling of guilt as if it were my fault. I couldn't get back to sleep so I sat in bed until dawn.

pregnancy quite often feel angry and even cheated, parents who have not planned the pregnancy may deny that there is a feeling of loss. There is also, for many couples, the fear that they will not have the chance to conceive again. In all cases, there are a myriad of feelings that are experienced. There's no good or bad in these emotions. It may take weeks or months to resolve the feelings.

Experts explain that parents and the siblings in the family must have the opportunity to talk about the pregnancy. If you have experienced an ectopic or tubal pregnancy in the family, you may want to name the baby or perform a special ritual for the unborn child. One couple donated, planted, and now personally tends a pear tree in a community garden in memory of a special being who was never born. Unknowing of the child's gender, they've called the precious memory Blossom.

In the termination of a pregnancy—an abortion—whether it is a decision made because of a serious genetic defect, a significant physical problem with the fetus, or through a conscious choice, there are still very real emotions involved in the death. The very word "abortion" provokes intense emotions in our society and can often end in heated, sometimes violent, arguments on both sides of the issue. For the mother and father and other family members involved, the aftereffect of an abortion is often a sense of loss, without examining the moral or ethical logic.

Regardless of the reasons for the pregnancy's termination, abortion is a death with all the accompanying feelings of loss. And grief, as we know, is part of death. If you have been involved in a pregnancy that was terminated, to some degree you will feel the emotional impact of grief. You may also feel saddened for the loss of a dream. You may feel guilty because of a sense of relief knowing that you will not have to spend a lifetime worrying about the future of a severely disabled person. You may feel a sadness for creating a child that was imperfect and fear that the next conception may also result in an abortion. And you may fear being criticized by others since abortion seems to infer some blemish on the character of the parents and family members involved. If you do not feel the emotions of grief, there is nothing unnatural about this either. Again, feelings are feelings....they are not good or bad; they just are.

If you do feel sadness at the death of this child, as others who have suffered the death of a child, you may want to name the baby, and plan a ritual or service. According to bereavement experts, this helps provide a means to heal the emotional scars. It may also help if you talk with a counselor or join a support group to openly examine your grief and work toward resolution.

Giving up a baby through adoption produces feelings of grief and cannot be discounted. The feeling of grief is real, but there is no closure, no funeral, no death. Sometimes that makes the most intelligent, the bravest, and purest reasons to release a child even more painful. There are support groups for parents and family affected by infant death as well as adoption. As with the death of a family member, the emotional help provided by the groups can give you an outlet for the emotional toll that is often a part of adoption. Talk with a counselor, a social worker at the hospital, or perhaps a close friend who will listen and not simply give advice.

Where to Get Help

The following are the national headquarters for organizations specifically concerned with the death of babies and children. If you do not find assistance or answers by talking with one group, contact another. Most of the groups have local chapters and their members have "been there," that is, right where your heart and mind are at this moment.

National SHARE Office (pregnancy and neonatal loss)
St. Joseph Health Center
300 First Capitol Drive
St. Charles, MO 63301-2893
(800)-821-6819 or (636) 947-6164
Fax: (636) 947-7486
Among the various resources available from SHARE: a one-hundred-page manual on starting your own SHARE group; a national listing of support groups and parents

In the morning we went to the hospital and, for the first time that week, we were able to see our mom and dad. We learned that our mother had just missed death herself. Feelings of thankfulness and grief were felt at the same time. We all were glad to be united after our minor separation.

A few days later the funeral was held. There was a closed casket so I couldn't see him even then. I felt as if I was a loner; no one could completely understand what I was going through. I was quite upset and mad at God for taking away what would have been my only brother. I kept to myself and avoided contact with everyone.

I learned two things from all of this: That it was fine to grieve and the only thing that could cure grief was time.

who are willing to help; a perinatal bereavement bibliography; *Bittersweet.... Hello–Good-bye*, a resource manual on planning a farewell ritual; and various stories, coloring books, and workbooks for children on bereavement.

Janet Tischler, perinatal bereavement consultant
Miscarriage Infant Death Stillbirth
16 Cresent Drive
Parsippany, NJ 07054-1605
(636) 947-6730

The Compassionate Friends National Headquarters
(child death for children of all ages)
P.O. Box 3696
Oak Brook, IL 60522-3696
(630) 990-0010
Toll Free: (877) 969-0010

Ways to Contend with the Death of an Unborn Child

Dr. Graves explains that there are four major ways we can cope with a crisis. The following are not listed in order of importance, but simply include:

1. ***Learn as much as possible*** about the event, what happened, why, when, if it happens to others. If the pregnancy resulted in a miscarriage or you elected to abort the child, talk with your obstetrician afterward for the details regarding the circumstances leading to the end of the pregnancy. If you suffered a stillbirth, talk about why it happened, the delivery, and the death.

   Dr. Graves says, "In many cases, there are no concrete answers available. Be aware that this does not stop you from asking." When we cannot find information or find the answers that put the puzzle pieces together at the time of a crisis, we turn inward and can blame ourselves. "If I'd only not gone out that day...." "If we'd lived in the country with clean air instead of living in a place with so much pollution, maybe the baby would have been...." Find a local chapter of SHARE, MIDS, or other support group, review the listings for self-help books in this book, and look for other books at your bookstore.

2. ***Follow a ritual or a remembrance rite***, such as the memorial services or a funeral for an older child or adult who has died. You may want to light a candle, take flowers to the cemetery, ask for the photo that was taken of your stillborn child so you can frame it and display it. This is your child, as real as your living children, as real as children you may have in the future, as real as all the children of the world.

3. ***Schedule "time outs."*** These are periods when you allow yourself to laugh, exercise, have fun. During your grief, you may not feel like emitting a belly laugh at a movie or watching ancient "I Love Lucy" reruns, but in time you will laugh again. British playwright George Bernard Shaw said, "Life does not cease to be funny when people die any more than it ceases to be serious when people laugh." You have permission to laugh even in grief.

    Everyone feels the death of a loved one differently. Just because your wife, husband, sibling, child, or parent doesn't grieve in the same way or intensity that you are grieving doesn't mean that there was any less love.

4. ***Reach out to others.*** Talk about the death. When asked how many children you have, you can say, "I originally had three. Billy died at birth." Or, "I was pregnant four times. Julie is our only living child." This may shock some people; what it will do for you is affirm that you did have a child and still keep that child in your memory.

Dr. Alan D. Wolfelt, author, educator, and practicing clinical thanatologist in Fort Collins, Colorado, explains, "Your baby deserves a name. If you had already decided on a name, keep it. The name truly belongs to this unique child. Having a name for your baby allows you to talk about your loss in a personal way. You are openly acknowledging that you have loved a child and will always remember him or her. You will find it easier to embrace your memories if you can refer to your baby by name."

The director of the Center for Loss and Life Transitions, an organization dedicated to teaching therapists, funeral directors, and members of clergy how to administer grief counseling, Dr. Wolfelt encourages parents and grandparents to gather important keepsakes from the child. "Memories are one of the best legacies that exist after a baby dies," he says. "You may want to collect some important keepsakes that help you treasure your memories. Some hospitals automatically offer to provide you with ways of remembering your baby, but not all. So be certain to request any items that you want to be able to keep."

Examples of keepsakes might be a photograph of your baby. ("Even if you don't want it now," encourages Dr. Wolfelt, "it can be taken and viewed later." Many parents find this extremely comforting and although some are initially repulsed by the concept, they later return to the hospital for the photo or pull it out to frame. It becomes a treasure of their special child.) You may want a birth certificate, a set of footprints, the plastic arm bracelet, the blanket your baby first came in contact with, and perhaps a lock of hair.

Dr. Wolfelt suggests that you might want to create a memory box. "Then, when you are missing your baby, you can open up your memory box and embrace these special memories. The reality that your baby has died does not diminish your need to have these objects. They are a tangible, lasting part of the special relationship you had with your child."

SUDDEN INFANT DEATH SYNDROME

Sudden Infant Death Syndrome (SIDS) is the sudden and unexplained death of an apparently healthy baby. It is the major cause of death in infants between the ages of one month and one year. In the United States, SIDS is sometimes referred to as crib or cot death. It is responsible for the death of approximately seven thousand infants each year. It has been estimated that up to two deaths per one thousand live births will be the direct result of SIDS every year.

While the death of the SIDS infant is sudden and without warning, there are probably some types of biochemical, anatomical, or developmental defects or deficiencies that cause the death. Currently, according to the National SIDS Clearinghouse information program, these problems are not detectable by a medical test or examination. One single cause for SIDS has not been discovered. Research indicates that SIDS is most likely caused by a combination of events.

Facts about SIDS:

- SIDS is a definite medical entity and is the major cause of death in infants after the first month of life.
- SIDS victims appear to be healthy prior to death.
- Currently SIDS cannot be predicted or prevented, even by a physician.
- There appears to be no suffering. Death occurs very rapidly, usually during sleep.

What SIDS is not:

- SIDS is not caused by external suffocation.
- SIDS is not caused by vomiting and choking.
- SIDS is not contagious.
- SIDS does not cause pain or suffering to the infant.
- SIDS cannot be predicted.

The National SIDS Resource Center is an affiliate of the National Center for Education in Maternal and Child Health, and funded by the United States Department of Health and Human Services. The center provides a network of information, resources, and technical assistance for professionals, health care providers, researchers, and the general public.

For information on SIDS, to get the SIDS fact sheet, to review bibliographic information from lay and professional sources, for informative videos, or to subscribe to the newsletter called *Information Exchange*, contact the National Sudden Infant Death Syndrome Resource Center, 2070 Chain Bridge Road, Suite 450, Vienna, VA 22182, (703) 821-8955, (703) 821-2098 (Fax).

Where to Get Help

As yet, medical advances have not uncovered the cause of SIDS, however many are working toward that end. Those who have had a baby die of SIDS can often help survivors understand. The following are national headquarters of the groups strictly dedicated to the SIDS survivors:

National Sudden Infant Death Syndrome Resource Center
2070 Chain Bridge Road, Suite 450
Vienna, VA 22182
(703) 821-8955
(703) 821-2098 (Fax)

Sudden Infant Death Syndrome Network
SIDS Network
P.O. Box 520
Ledyard, CT 06339

American SIDS Institute
2480 Windy Hill Rd., Ste. 380
Marietta, GA 30067
(770) 612-1939 or (800) 232-SIDS

Sudden Infant Death Syndrome Alliance
1314 Bedford Avenue, Suite 210
Baltimore, MD 21208
(410) 653-8226

SIDS's Traumatic Reactions for Family Members

When a baby dies of SIDS, there is a great sadness, and every family member experiences the death and walks the path toward grief recovery in a unique way. In the following pages, we'll talk specifically about this troubled time.

The parents' grief: After the initial shock begins to wear off, parents often fall into a prolonged depression. Melancholy can be triggered by a thoughtless remark from someone who does not understand SIDS or by remembering that it is the same day of the week that the baby died. At these low points, it may be helpful for the parents to talk with a member of a parent group. Another parent who has experienced a SIDS death can help a newly bereaved parent to see that things will not always be so grim. Time really does make a difference in recovering from a SIDS death or other death. A family physician, minister, rabbi, nurse, or therapist can be helpful as can the assistance of a support group for SIDS survivors.

After the death of their child, many parents find that it is difficult to concentrate for any length of time. Their minds wander, making it nearly impossible to read, write, or even make decisions. Sleep may be disrupted, leaving the parents extra tired and edgy. These are symptoms of physical grief. Even with sleep, the feeling of exhaustion can be persistent.

Grieving parents may experience muscular problems or physical symptoms centering around the heart or in the stomach. Loss of appetite is common; eating a chore. Mothers and fathers have reported that their arms "ache" to hold the baby.

As with other grief, there are times when there is an irresistible urge to escape, to run away. Some parents dread being alone. Others experience unreasonable fears that they are in danger. Parents may fear for the lives and safety of other children in the family and may not want to let them out of their sight. Because parents experience these conflicting feelings, they may show extreme irritation and impatience with surviving children's behavior. When friends and other family members offer to watch their other children or the house, this can make the SIDS parent survivors feel more guilty, and doubly so when they cannot accept the help. The situation is made worse, according to the National SIDS Clearinghouse because most Americans do not understand SIDS. Friends and acquaintances say or infer things that are thoughtless and inconsiderate.

The grief of the husband and wife may be different. At a wedding of a close friend or a family member, the wife may cry. The husband will brim with joy, but no tears sparkle in his eyes. It's quite normal that husbands and wives express their emotions in different ways and we accept that. The same holds true when there is a SIDS death. Women are more inclined to "talk out" their grief. Men tend to grieve more silently. Parents working outside the home may be diverted by their work, while parents who stay at home are surrounded by constant reminders of their baby and the death. Very often the death of the infant is the first grief that the adults have experienced and it can be a profound experience.

Children's reactions to SIDS: Children will be affected in some way by any death, SIDS included. Children who are too young for complete explanations need love from their parents to feel secure about the change. Some young children may be very frightened about SIDS, cling to parents, and misbehave to get attention. Children often feel guilty about the death as if they were responsible, "If I'd only looked in on the baby...." "Maybe I scared the baby by playing ball next to the baby's window...." Older children should be told as much as they can understand. Surviving siblings need this information and need to be made a part of the funeral or other service. SIDS is not a secret, it is not a sin; it is a terrible tragedy but one that needs open communication between all family members.

Some children feel great insecurity when a baby in their family has died of SIDS. Bed-wetting, problems in school, and nightmares are warning flags that the child needs help. A family doctor or a counselor can often assist at these times.

Surviving siblings may not outwardly show their distress, or show their grief. They may even deny that they are troubled by the death of their baby brother or sister.

This is normal. It is important to talk to children about the death and explain that the baby died because SIDS is a serious medical problem that occurs suddenly, unexpectedly, and only to a few babies of that age. Siblings should be reassured that older members of the family— themselves included—will not die from SIDS. Where there is a surviving twin, the family may need professional counseling.

Seeing children as a source of strength, comfort, and joy at a time of a SIDS death can help.

Close relatives, caregivers: Sometimes the baby is in the care of relatives, a baby-sitter, or other caregiver at the time when SIDS occurs. This is a special problem and therapists recommend that the caregiver seek counseling. It is often helpful for him or her to read information and talk with the physician. At first parents may blame the relative or caregiver or themselves for leaving the child with someone else or leaving the child at all. It is through understanding that the myth about SIDS can be eliminated.

❧

In chapter 4, we'll talk about coping with the loss of a loved one. There is information on specific aspects of grief and how grief affects us. Within chapter 4, we'll also discuss how to work through the stages of grief and when and why to join a support group.

Chapter 4

The Experience and Emotions of Parting

Death is an unknown quantity for most of us *until* we meet it when our loved one dies. We view the devastation of death, but we do not encounter the truth of death, unless the experience of grief follows.

While we look at and acknowledge the result of actual violence and death recorded in the newspaper, on the six o'clock news, and at various times throughout the day on CNN, we do not really examine it. Most will agree that televised death has become a fact of life. Once in a while there will be a shot of a woman, head bent—possibly dressed in black—obviously crying at the death of a loved one.

Unless we've personally experienced a death or have an extremely sensitive nature, we do not identify with the "big picture." Sure, we see the woman. Perhaps our hearts feel an uncomfortable stir, but most likely that's as far as we think about grief. We do not consider the daughters and sons, fathers and wives, aunts, uncles, sisters and brothers, coworkers and colleagues who also hurt. The children who

Feelings of loss are caused by feelings of love.

—Margaret Edison, from
Living with AIDS

hurt. The friends who hurt. We do not think about everyone who is personally affected by the death when we view that two-second televised glimpse of a tormented woman struck and shocked by grief.

In this chapter, we'll talk about death and present theories including those of the renowned Dr. Elisabeth Kübler-Ross. We'll talk about how death affects us when the we experience the death of a spouse, sibling, grandchild, companion, and other family members. Also, we'll provide a unique project to help look at the death with love and memories as you organize and write in a keepsake book.

GRIEF

Why would anyone want to read about the incredible barb of grief? That's a real sentiment for many who have recently experienced the death of a loved one. Others want to know what good it does to read about it *beforehand*? Yet, reading about what is happening (or will happen) emotionally and physically can help each of us adjust to the newness that is felt when there has been a death.

Pain is normal, loneliness is normal, sadness is normal. Reading about these feelings will not take them away. Reading about grief and knowing what to expect can provide a measure of control in a situation that may seem to have gone insane.

Everyone Grieves in His or Her Own Way

In one family, a mother and son cry constantly, are too upset to eat, and aren't sleeping well. They're unable to help with the funeral arrangements. On the "flip side," another family member experiences these emotions to a lesser extent. This *does not* mean she is not grieving nor did she love the person who died less. Just as we all experience joy and exhilaration at various levels and intensities, everybody knows grief and expresses it in distinctly different degrees and ways.

Not everyone grieves. And there's no right or wrong way to grieve. For instance, let's say a longtime companion has been extremely ill and is in considerable pain. He has been diagnosed with a terminal illness. When he dies within a few months, there may be a sense of relief for this loved one when his pain is finally gone. Sure there are feelings of sadness, loss, and regret. There are feelings of missing how you shared joy and friendship, the future good times, and love of being with that person. Yet the grief and shock may be considerably less then when his illness was originally diagnosed.

In another instance, we experience grief when a grandparent dies. As children, we usually see our grandparents as "old," especially at a time when anyone over forty is archaic. If we're lucky enough to still have the love and friendship of grandparents when we become adults, these special family members continue to appear old—perhaps not as old as they were when we were children, but definitely old. Emotionally and intellectually, we know old people die. It hurts, but it is admissible for grandparents to die. This doesn't make the time less distressing, simply more allowable than, say, when a child dies of AIDS, a teen chooses death by suicide, or a family member is killed in a car accident.

Those who study death and grief explain that the age of the person who dies relates to the intensity of grief for family members. When a baby dies of SIDS, for example, parents who have had great dreams for a beautiful, perfect child grieve deeply, often for a long time. They feel cheated of what might have been, for the reality of their hopes and aspirations. They mourn the uncelebrated birthday parties and never being able to teach the little one to ride a two-wheeler. This same deep grief and unfairness of life are often felt after the accidental death or terminal illness of a young spouse. "It's just not right. They were only married two months!"

When death comes suddenly, from suicide, an accident, violence, or a crime, such as those involving murder, the emotional and physical grief are often far more intense then when, as with the example of a long-term illness, loved ones have time to know and come to terms with the emotion of grief. As to whether we are ever ready, emotionally or physically, to accept grief, the answer is

CARE AND LOSS
by Margaret Edison,
from *Living with AIDS*

❧

When somebody dies, and family members and friends experience shock or despair or a sort of tightness in the chest, it is because they loved him. Human beings naturally gravitate towards safety, happiness, and good times.

But people who have watched someone they love die are going to feel sad, and there is no reason to pretend otherwise.

The deep, sad feeling that comes to people upon the death of a loved one is called grief. The process of trying to sort out all the emotions and events that connect their lives to the person's life is called grieving. It can be hard work, and it can take a long time.

TWENTY-FIVE SUGGESTIONS TO HELP CONQUER DEPRESSION

by Teen Age Grief, Inc.

૨&

1. *Think of something you want that is available, then make a plan to get it.*
2. *Go for a long walk.*
3. *Think of people who bring you up; call one of them.*
4. *Listen to your favorite music.*
5. *Sing, chant, dance.*
6. *Take a shower or a long, warm bath.*
7. *Make a list of your strengths. Spend at least an hour concentrating fully on appreciating yourself.*
8. *Love a pet expressively.*
9. *Think of something you would enjoy doing for someone. Then do it.*
10. *Read a book on higher consciousness, love, or another enjoyable subject.*
11. *Forgive someone.*
12. *Consult a nutrition book and consider what you might add to your diet for pep and vitality.*
13. *Plan a trip that you think you would enjoy. Spend an hour anticipating in fantasy and savor the exciting aspects of the experience.*
14. *Think about ways of relaxing. Choose one and do it.*
15. *Get a massage, or give yourself a body massage or a skin brush.*
16. *Begin something you've been putting off for a long time.*

probably no. By knowing that what you feel is normal, that you're not insane, you will feel better. However, it won't make the misery you're feeling right now go away—that will take time, weeks, months, and even years—but you will heal.

When a loved one dies, it is natural to experience a wide range of emotions that we lump together as grief.... guilt, anger, denial, fear, shock, disbelief, depression, and, finally, acceptance. You may be unable to work, unable to think clearly, unable to carry on a conversation. When a stillbirth has happened, many mothers report that their arms are painful—they ache to hold and caress the child that they've carried for nine months. If your loved one died of a heart attack, you may experience heart pain. Your family doctor can help to determine if your pain is related to grief or if there is a physical problem that must be addressed.

Pain and physical discomfort are genuine symptoms of grief. Any major life-affecting change produces hormones to provide extra energy, quick thinking, faster reflexes. These are the fight-or-flight responses, the responses that make it possible for a young woman to lift a car off her child, or for that matter when our predecessors stalked wild game with flimsy bows and arrows.

When the necessary hormone, adrenaline, is pumped into the system, it causes a chain reaction to fight the enemy that is stressing in us. According to grief experts, the body sometimes "misreads" the crisis and produces the hormone each time we think about the death or confront the situation surrounding the death. The sensations may be replayed for weeks or months, and even, to a lesser degree, may occur years later.

Coping with Physical Grief

Understanding that there is physical grief and that you are quite normal will help in managing these sensations you are feeling after the death of a loved one. Don't ignore the physical signs of grief and stress. You may want to talk with your doctor. His or her reassurance that what you're feeling are the symptoms of grief may make you feel better. He or she may prescribe something to temporarily help you sleep if your symptoms are profound. You may want to use some relaxation techniques such as deep breathing and imagining yourself in a peaceful place before you elect to take a prescription drug. Listening to a ticking clock, tensing and relaxing muscles, and listening to relaxation tapes often are as useful as taking medicine. As always, you must listen to your body and consult with your doctor as you think best.

After the death of a loved one, even if you don't feel up to making even small decisions, such as what to eat or when to eat, do so. You need food to nourish your body. Eat well-balanced meals, drink lots of water, and keep coffee, tea, and colas to a minimum. Alcohol is a depressant and, while it might dull the pain temporarily, it will make you feel worse after the effects wear off. Walking, especially brisk walking, or another form of active aerobic exercise will make you feel better. Vigorous exercise interrupts the stress cycle, uses the bottled up and misplaced adrenaline, and helps provide a natural tranquilizer.

Begin keeping a journal, as soon as possible, after the death of a loved one. In it, write your feelings of that day, do not attempt to edit your comments. You can be angry, resentful, furious, scornful, and write to the person who died, too. The journal or series of letters will help you understand yourself. The journal will provide you with a way of looking back and seeing that you are making progress working through the grief.

Death and grief experts, including grief counselor Sherry Williams, divide the stages of the grieving process into many pieces. Williams explains that almost everyone who has experienced a death feels some or most of the following physical and emotional occurrences, but some people do not. She cautions that it's counterproductive to compare grief intensities with others:

- *Sadness*: "I'm lonely—so alone, now." Sadness is one of the four basic emotions—anger, sadness, gladness, and fear. The function of sadness is to deal with death or the loss of a relationship.
- *Appetite changes*: "It's impossible for me to eat."

17. Consider ways to make yourself more enjoyable to live with.

18. Stop doing anything and just be for awhile.

19. Give something away.

20. Tell someone you love him or her.

21. Surprise someone!

22. Do breathing exercises for energy and calmness.

23. Clean up something. Organize part of your life.

24. Think of the most difficult person in your life. Concentrate at length, perhaps a day, on looking for ways in which he or she is actually good and admirable. Share these thoughts with that person.

25. Stare at the stars on a lovely evening and feel your oneness with the universe. Know the limitlessness of being.

"I'm always hungry." Weight change often occurs with appetite change.

• *Nervousness*: "I pace—I can't sit still." People are often frightened by the physical experience of grief. Fear heightens the flow of adrenaline and you may become more fearful.

• *Sleep problems*: "I'm afraid to fall asleep." Exercise or relaxation methods often help. If your loved one was dying at home and you were "on call" twenty-four hours a day, it may take your body several months to return to a regular sleep cycle.

• *Anger*: "Why would his mother let this happen?" Anger and rage are also often directed to people we love—a spouse, grandparents, siblings, caregivers, and God.

• *Confusion*: "I forgot to lock the apartment when I went to work. I never do that." Often making a list of what needs to be done or leaving reminders around the house or office helps overcome the confusion accompanying grief.

• *Constant thoughts of the death*: "Every night before crawling into bed, I had always fluffed my husband's pillow. Now seeing that flat pillow reminds me that he was murdered." Whether it's the anniversary of the day your loved one died, first birthday, or other day or circumstance, it's normal to think about the death of your loved one. These are memories. Some are bad and some are good.

• *Thoughts of why*: Self-doubt and reexamining religious beliefs are a normal part of the grief process. "Why didn't my husband just leave me like he threatened he would instead of the suicide?"

• *Fear*: The function of being scared is to help us in attempting to find a solution, understand the situation. In grief, the fear is the result of no longer understanding our relationship with the deceased, our position in the family, or what will happen in the future. Thus, "I'm so afraid of being alone," is part of the grief process.

- *Jealousy*: Jealousy is a very common segment of grief and part of the "why" portion. "Why didn't it happen to somebody else?—look they have three healthy children."
- *Dreams*: We dream to help process information, especially so with grief and the resolution of the emotions we experience. Whether we think we're "handling it" or not, dreaming sorts data. Where the death is traumatic, dreams may reflect that horror with raging storms, sheer cliffs, and "bogey people." "In my dreams I see her twisted body under the car," is not an uncommon statement.
- *Exhaustion*: Processing grief is work. It is tiring. You have a right to be exhausted. "I feel like my legs weigh a thousand pounds—I'm so weary."
- *Depression*: "If we had another baby, he'd die, too." Sometimes our depression is so scary that we're afraid to talk with other people. But this is exactly the time to do so. While some suicidal thoughts are often part of intense grief, it's important to share those feelings with friends or a therapist.
- *Self-confidence*: "I don't look like I did *before*." The death of a loved one shakes our confidence, but it's okay. You can regain confidence one step at a time. Sometimes it helps to wear an article of clothing that makes you feel assured, or to buy one that will do this. Get your hair cut or nails done. Practice smiling. If you can smile back at yourself, you can begin to heal.
- *Communication*: "I can't explain how I feel." Try anyhow; people, friends, family, and those in support groups also can't communicate well at times. You're not alone.
- *Humor*: Humor is healing and laughing is a signal that you'll survive. "I feel guilty when I laugh— George just died last month. But when I remember some of the silly things we did, I have to chuckle."
- *Someone else is handling the grief better*: "Mom is fine—but I cry for Daddy every night." Don't compare yourself with others. We all handle and

process grief at different speeds and in different fashions; some "shelve" grief until the funeral is over.

- ***The need to take care of others***: "I'm so worried about my husband." It's natural to nurture others, but make sure you're taking care of your needs first.
- ***Hopefulness***: "I woke up this morning and the sunrise was lovely—absolutely hot pink!" Hopefulness is a sign that grief is lessening in its intensity. The hopefulness of the future will happen in time.

Knowing what you may expect as you walk the pathway toward grief recovery and the acceptance of your loved one's death can only help the process. You may not experience all of these fragmented emotions; you may encounter all of them. In the next days, weeks, and months, remember not to compare your recovery to others. You are unique, as is your grief.

Where to Get Help

Knowing that death can have a profound effect on a survivor both physically and emotionally, it makes sense to reach out to others, to support groups and friends in this difficult time. The following are a few agencies or groups that may be of assistance:

Kübler-Ross Center
South Route 616
Head Waters, VA 24442
(703) 396-3441

The Kübler-Ross Center contacts workshops and seminars and sends a newsletter to those who are interested. Kübler-Ross's books, *On Death and Dying, Questions and Answers on Death*, and *Death: The Final Stage of Growth*, among her other books, may help provide some further insight on the dying process and for survivors. They are available at libraries and through bookstores and the Kübler-Ross Center in Virginia.

Wendt Center for Loss and Healing
(Formerly the St. Francis Center)
730 Eleventh St. NW
Washington, DC 20001
(202) 624-0010

Providing help on death and dying, the center conducts workshops and offers support. A group of forty men and women—building managers, homemakers, typesetters—are the professionally guided volunteers of the Center Friends Program. They are aware of the feelings of people who are living with life-threatening illness; they understand the loneliness of loss for friends and families; they provide personal and practical support. A unique program has been developed at the center for children whose parent(s) have AIDS.

Make Today Count
c/o St. John's Regional Health Center
Mid-America Cancer Center
1235 E. Cherokee
Springfield, MO 65804-2263
(800) 432-2273

A national network of groups dedicated to those who have life-threatening diseases and the survivors. Chapters meet throughout the country and can be accessed through the national headquarters.

In addition to those books by Dr. Kübler-Ross, the following books may also provide some answers on death and dying:

There are many reasons why we don't talk about the future. Some people are afraid to bring up unpleasant subjects with family members. Others have unspoken agreements about issues they do or do not talk about. Some children are afraid to approach parents with the need to plan. And sometimes parents want to plan and find their children are afraid.

*—from AARP's
Tomorrow's Choices*

Living with Dying by David Carroll (New York: Paragon House Publishers, 1991) is a complete sourcebook for all the questions you have on the dying process and contains excellent information on how death affects those who are dying as well as families.

Men and Grief by Carol Staudacher (Oakland, CA: New Harbinger Publications, Inc., 1991) is written for men who are experiencing the death of a loved one. It is insightful for any woman who wants to help a man through the emotional process of grief.

CHILDREN AND GRIEF

"When a loved one dies, even a child not yet born, everyone in the family is affected, though in a different way," remarks Dennis Klass, Ph.D., professor of philosophy and religion at Webster University, St. Louis, Missouri, and coauthor of *The Need to Know: How to Teach Children about Death*. He explains that knowing how children respond to death and how to talk to children about death can help everyone in the family.

According to Dr. Klass, the best research available shows that if death is explained clearly, children can understand what death is almost as soon as they can talk. Very young children, of course, will understand death with the same thought patterns they have about anything— concrete operations. Therefore, if a child is told that "a star in the sky is your brother," or "Aunt Sue's body is in the ground," the words are taken literally as a fact, not symbolically. The child may draw logical conclusions that don't quite match our ideas.

By the time a child is in the first grade, research indicates his or her understanding is the same as an adult's, provided the child has been told the truth. If the death is explained in a confusing manner, it's not surprising that children do not understand. For example, both children and adults may go to sleep for a long time, but that's not what they do when they die.

Children's emotional responses are more complex and change as children develop. The ages used to describe these changes are to be taken loosely. Not all children develop on a strict time schedule. Dr. Klass explains, "Up to about seven years, death seems like a separation and thus a threat of abandonment. We have all seen the separation anxiety children show at points in their lives when parents leave them with a sitter. Human children need the protection of parents for several years to survive, so nature has given them an instinct of the fear of being abandoned.

"Children may be 'clingy' or need an extra lot of time and contact after a sibling's or another family member's death. As a way of assurance that the parents are still there, children may regress to earlier patterns of behavior and need and actually demand the kind of interaction with parents the children had when life seemed more secure."

From about seven to twelve, death is often seen as a personified external threat that may come and get you. This developmental level is played up in movies with the personification of death as the Terminator and Freddie Kruger. Dr. Klass says, "To overcome death or get on death's side, the child believes that he or she must be good, noble, brave, and in touch with a Higher Power. But at night in the dark with shadows on the wall or noises under the bed, personifications of death can be very frightening."

Teenagers respond to death very much like adults, Dr. Klass states, because they are in a stage of finding their own selfhood. They have already begun to understand a sense of themselves being alone (hence the need to herd together and be like everyone else), that the death of a loved one presents a particular existential threat. "One choice may be to adopt a religious faith which promises to overcome external death. Another choice may be to engage in death-defying behavior—either legal or illegal."

Should a child be "sent away" when a loved one dies? The impending death or actual death of a family member puts considerable emotional and physical stress on everyone involved. It can be nearly impossible to cope with everyday responsibilities, such as packing a school lunch or doing the laundry. It is even more difficult, at times, to care for young children and there's a temptation to send the children to visit relatives or friends until you can "pull yourself together." Keeping children at a distance may also be a way to avoid talking to them about the death of a loved one.

Before placing children in the care of others, carefully consider the immediate and long-term results. This is a time when they most need the comfort of familiar surroundings and close contact with family members, even family members who are not themselves. Children need time to adjust to the death and if feasible they should be prepared in advance of the death. The topic may pose hard questions and if you don't know the answers, be truthful. Tell them you'll find out the correct answer.

Even young children who do not understand the full implications of death are aware that something is seriously wrong: "The paramedics came in an ambulance and took the baby to the hospital. And the baby didn't come back. Now Mommy cries and Daddy's so quiet. I'm scared. Will the paramedics take me away, too?" Having familiar and caring people nearby before and after the death can reduce the fear of abandonment.

While adults may be deeply mourning the death of a family member, children continue to live and work through their grief as they naturally will. Children still need to run, jump, yell, and play even after the death of a parent or other close family member. This doesn't mean that they are not upset or that they didn't love the person who died; it means that they are children.

"Though it makes no rational sense to adults, some bereaved children may unconsciously believe that they are at fault for the death and so deserve punishment. Or, if the person who died was the family's primary disciplinarian, the acting out may be seen as a way to get that person to 'come back' and mete out punishment," explains grief expert Dr. Wolfelt.

Many children work through their grief in an on-and-off manner through an extended period of mourning. We must give them permission to be children. This is the greatest gift we can provide.

Common Expressions of Children's Grief

All children are affected in some way by the death of a family member, including the death of a family pet. It's not uncommon for a child to reenact a funeral or pretend to be sick or dying in a play situation. Regardless of this ability or inability to express themselves, children do grieve, often very deeply.

"Everyone who is touched by death," explains Susan Woolsey, associate director of the Maryland SIDS Information and Counseling Project, "experiences these emotions to some degree, grandparents, friends, physicians, nurses, and children. Each child's reaction to death is individual in nature."

Some common reactions are:

- *Shock*: The child may not believe the death really happened and will act as though it did not. This is usually because the thought of death is too overwhelming.
- *Physical symptoms*: The child may have various complaints such as headache or stomachache and fear that he or she too will die.
- *Anger*: Being mostly concerned with his or her own needs, the child may be angry at the person who died because the child feels he or she has been left "all alone." The child may also be angry because God "didn't make Daddy better."
- *Guilt*: The child may think that he or she caused the death by having been angry with the person who died. Or the child may feel responsible for not having been "better" in some way.
- *Anxiety and fear*: The child may wonder who will take care of him or her now, or fear that some other person in the family will soon die. The child may cling to parents or ask others who play an important role in life if they really love him or her.
- *Regression*: The child may revert to behaviors he or she had previously outgrown, such as bed-wetting or thumb sucking.
- *Sadness*: The child may show a decrease in activity. The child may be "too quiet."

Woolsey says, "It is important to remember that all of the reactions outlined are normal expressions of grief in children. Six months after a significant death in a child's life, normal routine should be resuming. If the child's reaction seems to be prolonged, seeking the professional advice of those who are familiar with the child (for example, teachers, pediatrician, clergy) may be helpful."

Helping Children Cope with Death

As adults who have been around for a while, the death of a loved one is still very hard. Dr. Klass explains, "If children feel death is a foreign outside force which comes to get people, we also feel death as the invader in our lives and our families. If adolescents wonder what life is about if it includes an untimely death, so do we. As we face the death, we are more like children than we are different from them."

Dr. Klass tells us, "That means that we serve our children best if we include them in the family as we grieve. There is an idea in the modern world that childhood ought to be a time of innocence and we should protect our children from knowing about death and all the other bad parts of life. We wonder if we should read them the old stories about how the wicked woman in the woods wanted to throw Hansel and Gretel into the oven and cook them for dinner. But the world does include death.

"If death comes to our house, children deserve to live in the real world. If we keep secrets from children they will know we are upset and that something has happened to a loved one. What they can invent in their imaginations can be far worse than what really has happened. Neither children nor adults can come to terms and resolve what we imagine but do not share. Both adults and children can come to terms with and resolve what really happened when we have a community of open communication and feelings."

Explanations That May *Not* Help

Well-meaning adults may give a child an explanation hoping to justify why a person he or she loved has died. Unfortunately, simple but dishonest answers increase the fear and uncertainty that the child may be feeling. Children tend to be very matter-of-fact. If an adult says, "Grandpa died because he was old and tired." The child may wonder when he too will be too old. He certainly gets tired when he rides his bike up the hill. What is tired enough to die?

"Grandma will sleep in peace forever." This explanation may result in the child's fear of going to sleep.

"It is God's will." The child will not understand a God who takes a loved one. "God took Daddy because he was so good." The child may decide to be bad so God won't take her, too.

"John was sick. He went to the hospital and he died." The child will need an explanation about the "little" and "big" sicknesses. Otherwise, she may be extremely fearful if in the future she or someone she loves has to go to the hospital.

Explanations and Ways to Help Children

As in all situations, the best way to deal with children is with honesty. Talk to the child in a language that he or she can understand. You might say, "You know that Uncle Mark hasn't been feeling well for a long time. The doctor just called to say that the cancer, a very bad disease that is in his liver, is much worse. It looks like he may not live much longer. We're going to the hospital to say good-bye to him. Do you want to go, too?"

Grief experts explain that it is important to use the correct medical terms. Knowing the name of the disease or reason for the death helps a child differentiate between everyday sicknesses and the sicknesses and causes of other deaths. A hug accompanied by the information is always appropriate.

Remember to listen to the child and try to understand what the child is saying. If asked, "How do you feel about Jim's death?" and the child responds, "I don't know," help the child to know. You can ask, "Let's see if we can know together. Do you feel mad, glad, sad, or scared?" You can also ask how much the child already understands, "How did Mary die—do you know?" According to grief experts, this encourages the child to gather information and clarify misinformation.

If you are reading this after the fact, i.e., you've haven't told the child the reason for the death, it is not too late. Depending on the age of the child, the result may be anger that you lied. Accept the anger and apologize. This is another lesson for the child that adults do make mistakes. A mistake can be forgiven and an adult can ask for forgiveness.

Here are a few ways adults can help children face the death of someone close to them.

- The child's first concern may be "Who will take care of me now?" Maintain usual routines as much as possible. Show affection, and assure the child that those who love him or her still do and that they will take care of him or her.
- The child will probably have many questions and may need to ask them again and again. Encourage the child to ask questions and give honest, simple answers that can be understood. Repeated questions require patience.
- The child will not know appropriate behavior for the situation. Encourage the child to talk about feelings and share how you feel. You are a model for how one expresses emotions. It is helpful to cry. It is not helpful to be told how one should or should not feel.
- Allow the child to express his or her caring for you. Sometimes children are open with the death and even tell strangers. They may be doing this to seek support or to check the reactions of other people— especially grown-ups—so that they can make a judgement about how they themselves should feel.
- The child may not know what to say to other people about the death. Prepare the child for the questions school friends may ask, which are often inconsiderate and curious. When asked why the child hasn't been in school, he or she can say, "My uncle (or whatever relation) died." Since other questions may follow, you can rehearse how to answer them and the words that seem right.
- The child may fear that he or she also may die or

that he or she somehow caused the death. Reassure the child about the cause of the death and explain that any thoughts he or she may have had about the person who died did not cause the death. Reassure the child that this does not mean someone else he or she loves is likely to die soon.

- The child may wish to be part of the family rituals. Explain these to him or her, the best you can, and include him or her in deciding how he or she will participate. Remember that the child should be prepared beforehand, told what to expect, and have a supporting adult along. Do not force the child to do anything he or she doesn't feel comfortable doing.
- Your child may need to see or touch the body to help him or her understand the reality of death.
- The child may show regressive behavior. Support the child. These regressions are temporary.
- Some children may want to sleep in their parents' bed for reassurance after the death of a loved one. If it's not possible for the child to sleep with you for a short time, suggest that he or she "camp" on the floor next to your bed. Gradually, the campsite will move back to the child's room.
- Comfort the child, hold the child, and give plenty of hugs. Say "I love you" as much as possible.

It is extremely hard as you, too, are grieving, but try to understand what is not being said by the child. Children need to feel that the death is an open subject and that they can express their thoughts or questions as they come up.

The American Cancer Society's booklet, *When a Loved One Dies....A Family Guide to Helping Children Cope*, provides some of the following ideas that have been found helpful. In reality you are giving the child a chance to say good-bye with respect to his or her own understanding and truth about death. You are also providing the model of the effect of grief on an adult; this is a gift which the child will need to perhaps duplicate later in life.

- Talk to the loved one.

- Write a letter or draw a picture.
- Place a picture or a favorite toy in the casket or in the grave. Or later, take it to the cemetery and bury it at the grave site.
- Bring flowers to the grave at a later date.
- Plant a tree or a bush in memory of the loved one.
- Complete a project that the child was working on with the loved one before the death occurred.
- Bake a cake and/or sing "Happy Birthday" on the loved one's birthday.

"In helping children understand and cope with death, remember four key concepts: be loving, be accepting, be truthful, and be consistent," concludes Susan Woolsey.

THE DOUGY CENTER

Once upon a time there was a boy named Doug Turno. He was nine years old and had an inoperable brain tumor. He knew he was going to die.

He wrote to Dr. Elisabeth Kübler-Ross. He wanted to know more about death. He asked her, "Why aren't there any books for children about dying? If you're old enough to die, you're old enough to read about it!" Dr. Kübler-Ross responded to Doug by writing his very own book entitled *A Letter to a Child with Cancer*, affectionately known as the "Dougy Letter."

Doug had a profound message to share about life, living, and love. All who met him fell in love with him. It was impossible not to be touched by his message. As ill as he was, Doug reached out with affection. He said, "I can go to the hospitals and tell other kids not to be afraid to die!" On December 5, 1981, at thirteen years old, Doug died. He received his wish: A new life for Christmas.

The Dougy Center, based in Portland, Oregon, is a tribute to a boy who knew about suffering and fear and realized with the rare insight of a child that both could be met with love, understanding, and the joy of life.

The programs at the Dougy Center are for children as

well as adults. Donna L. Schuurman, Ed.D., executive director of the Dougy Center explains, "Since 1982, we have been providing support groups for children grieving the death of a parent or sibling, and their adult caretakers or parents. The groups are age-specific and loss-specific. We currently have more than two hundred children per month involved in weekly, biweekly, or monthly groups."

Since its inception, the Dougy Center has served more than five thousand individuals in direct or indirect grief support services. The center receives from five to ten phone calls each day from parents, teachers, school counselors, and family members in the Portland area seeking help in dealing with a child or children in grief. Dr. Schuurman explains, "Increasingly, we are called on to provide training and education to schools, mental health programs, youth service programs, hospitals, and churches." As a result of those requests, the Dougy Center now has a network of twenty-eight "sister" spin-off centers and has formed a Children's Grief Support Network to share information and training among the centers. The centers are located in cities across the United States.

In the hearts and thoughts of all who come to the center and know about the good work there for grief, Doug continues to live and bring cheer and love. It's just like he'd want it. It is because of Doug that there is the Dougy Center in Portland and other programs throughout the country to provide loving support during difficult times. It is because of Dougy that there is a place where children grieving death can share their experiences as they move through the healing process.

Doug Turno's memory lives happily ever after.

Where to Get Help

Through the efforts of people like Doug Turno and his family and friends, the Dougy Center for Grieving Children and those who love children was established.

RESPECTFUL LISTENING
by Joan Borysenko, Ph.D., from *Guilt Is the Teacher, Love Is the Lesson*

&

Stop and zero in on what you are actually feeling. If the emotion is not obvious, ask questions to help direct your attention to its source. For example, if you are feeling restless or bored, ask yourself what the restlessness is all about. What led up to it? What were you thinking? What do you really need right now that you haven't got? Maybe the restlessness will turn out to be anxiety, anger, or some creative urge that needs expression. Keep open to the inquiry. If you can't actually feel an emotion or identify a need, ask yourself, What could I do right now that would make me feel better?

There are many recognized and recommended ways to deal with grief, but there is no one way which will help all people. Any method which is appropriate and emotionally healthy for an individual may be used.

—the directors of
Loving Outreac
to Survivors of Suicide

The Dougy Center for Grieving Children
3909 S.E. 52nd Avenue
P.O. Box 86852
Portland, OR 97286
(503) 775-5683

In addition to contacting the national headquarters of the Dougy Center for Grieving Children, the following books, suggested by the American Cancer Society, may help you explain death and grief to children.   You'll find many of these and other informational books on death at the bookstore. Also, your public library may have a "parent's library" or bibliographic listing of books recommended for children about death and dying.

For ages 3 to 7:
Freddie the Leaf by Leo Buscaglia (New York: Holt, Rinehart, and Winston, 1982).
The Tenth Good Thing about Barney by Judith Viorst (New York: Atheneum, 1972).
About Dying by Sarah B. Stein (New York: Walker and Company, 1974).

For ages 8 to 14:
My Grandpa Died Today by Joan Fassler (New York: Behavioral Publications, Inc., 1971).
Straight Talk about Death for Teenagers: How to Cope with Losing Someone You Love by Earl A. Grollman (Boston: Beacon, 1993).
Tell Me about Death/Tell Me about Funerals by Elizabeth Corley (Santa Clara, CA: Grammatical Sciences, 1973).
A Ring of Endless Light by Madeleine L'Engle (New York: Farrar/Straus/Giroux, 1980).

For adults who care about children:
Talking about Death: A Dialogue between Parent and Child, by Earl Grollman (Boston: Beacon, 1970).

Explaining Death to Children by Earl Grollman (Boston: Beacon, 1967).

How It Feels When a Parent Dies by Jill Krementz (New York: Alfred Knopf, 1981).

They Need to Know: How to Teach Children about Death by Audrey K. Gordon and Dennis Klass (Englewood Cliffs, NJ: Prentice-Hall, Inc., 1979).

TEENAGERS AND GRIEF

By the time a person reaches the age to be called a teenager, he or she probably understands death. A family pet may have died, a friend's grandparents were killed. Death and dying are seen in videos, magazines, movies, television, and in school. Teenagers know that loss cannot be avoided.

Teenagers are not mini grown-ups and are not children, but separate humans, and they go through the feelings and stages of grief just like everyone. When the death of a loved one occurs, it can be extremely frightening to anyone, especially if the death is someone approximately the same age.

Teenagers often "bottle up" their feelings, believing that no one has ever experienced anything similar before, which causes the emotions to become more intense. Some teenagers do not think that their parents or teachers understand the trauma of death. A counselor, a family member closer to the teenager's own age, a family friend, or a clergy person can sometimes be a sounding board. Who is the right person with whom to talk? The one who actively listens, asks questions, and doesn't criticize.

A widowed father of a teenager recalls taking long drives at night, during the time he and his wife would have normally been watching television. That time in the living room was too painful so he avoided it.

One evening, his fifteen-year-old daughter needed a ride to the library and he came along. Neither spoke for some time. Then within the blackness of the night, in the safety of the car, the daughter mumbled, "I hate our house."

"Why?" he remembers asking. He had become an expert in one syllable replies.

"Because Mom isn't there," she sniffed, and he could see her face in the reflection of the car widow. He could see the tears on her cheeks.

"Me, too." It was the first conversation they'd had in days. Both sensed it was a start.

When they arrived at the library, he explains, she didn't jump out and run toward the doors. "Want to go for a ride?" he asked. Again she didn't move or say anything. After a time he started the engine. For the next two months, father and daughter drove around the city at night.

The father says, "Sometimes we talked, sometimes we shouted at each other—we did a lot of yelling. A lot of times I had to pull over to cry. After a few weeks, I began stopping at a convenience store to get a couple of soft drinks or a candy bar to split. Another time, we got fast food. Now we're driving less but going more places together *in the daytime*. Sure the emptiness of losing a wife and mother continues to be with us. Sure I still live with a teenager—and she lives with a father who doesn't always understand—but from what we've been through, we're closer than most and we're friends. I think we're moving into the acceptance stage of grief."

There are scores of blunders bereaved adults make as they deal with their teens. However, it's important to remember children do not need perfect parenting, rather they need "good enough" parenting. If you are reading this after you have experienced the death of a loved one, and you feel you've handled the situation badly with your teenager, realize that like raising children, you do the best you can at that time. You just do "good enough," and do it with love.

Signs of Abnormal Grief in Teens

Absence of grief that continues well beyond the numbness and shock initially encountered after the death of a loved one can be an indication—a caution flag—that something is amiss. It doesn't mean that the grieving teen is mentally ill; it means that he or she is reaching out to an adult or caregiver for help.

Some of the signs of abnormal grief in teens are:

- Severe guilt or other persistent anxieties
- Destructive and/or aggressive outbursts
- Unwillingness to talk about the deceased
- Dysfunction, or turbulent or profound behavior in school
- Taking on the role of the adult/caregiver.
- Accident proneness
- Illegal acts, stealing, drugs, promiscuous behavior
- Depression, lethargy

These are the signals that a loving adult should be concerned about. Not all teenagers who are abnormally grieving exhibit them, nor should you discount them if a teenager has only two of the eight. It is the intensity and duration of the behaviors with which to be concerned.

THE MENTALLY DISABLED AND GRIEF

Many mentally disabled adults and children have a difficult time dealing with death; this is also true for elderly adults who may be affected with diseases that undermine the thinking process or must take medication which alters perception of life and death.

If these people have a limited ability to reason about what has happened, their thoughts and feelings about the death can be profound. The mentally disabled often continue to see death through the eyes of children.

Mentally retarded children and adults go through all the emotions and stages of grief. According to Patricia L. Papenbrock, R.N., and Robert F. Voss, M.A., Q.M.R.P., coauthors of *Loss: How Children and Teenagers Can Cope with Death and Other Kinds of Loss*, "The mentally retarded have something to give. Although they need to grieve....they may be able to teach you and others something because their perceptions are simpler and their reactions uninhibited. They often help others to express their grief."

If one of the survivors in your family is disabled, you may find it especially helpful to review the section on

Grief makes many memories bittersweet. As you heal you will develop a great capacity to decide which dimension dominates.

—Joe Healy, executive director, THEOS

children and death. If the death is eminent and you are having trouble finding ways to explain that a loved one will die shortly, you may find reading sections of chapter 9, Death After a Terminal Illness, helpful.

WOMEN AND GRIEF

In the 1940s, 1950s, and part of the 1960s it was thought that women and men grieved differently. It was sometimes believed that generally men were less in touch with their feelings, and there was less straightforward talk and openness between the sexes. Yet, after all this time, grief experts explain that while the concept of men grieving less than women is false, it is correct to say that the sexes grieve in distinct ways.

Carol Staudacher, author of *Beyond Grief: A Guide for Recovering from the Death of a Loved One* and *Men and Grief*, explains that an average woman survivor "has a more overt period of working through" the stages of grief. "Her grief may *appear* to take longer. But once again, appearance is often deceptive. Because a woman's grief is usually more evident, it may seem prolonged." According to Staudacher the reverse is actually true. "Grief which is repressed or suppressed may take a much longer time; it may in fact take a lifetime."

Why do women process grief, typically, more easily—if easily can be used as a term when dealing with the death of a loved one? Staudacher explains, "In general, women are more communicative about their losses. They usually exhibit a wider range of emotions than men. They more often seek and accept support in one-to-one relationships or as members of a grief support group. When their grief subsides and they have integrated the loss into their changed lives, they will frequently assume supportive roles for other survivors. They may do this individually, as a part of an organization or group, or within the parameters of their occupation."

As with many men, after the death of a loved one, some women throw themselves into their careers or other work. While there has been a considerable amount written about how grief affects work, this has mostly centered on men.

Nonetheless, at work, women are just as distracted as men.

On the job or in school, women might find that they are staring into space, making mistakes, and feeling short fused. If they are lucky, they may have a coworker who can relate to or empathize with the grief. If not, it's not that they don't care. Most people don't have firsthand knowledge of the pain grief produces.

Throwing themselves wildly into certain tasks after the death is part of the grieving process and it may help many women work through the anger and denial stages. Yet, some people get "stuck" in the mode and are unable to examine their feelings openly. This is a time to seek the support of a social worker, counselor, and especially a group to talk about the death of a loved one.

MEN AND GRIEF

The death of a loved one can profoundly affect men, often called the silent grievers. Because the grief is, at times, suppressed, it is never "processed" and resolved. Some men grieve their entire lives.

According to Staudacher, "It is generally true that the man who expresses, releases, or completely works through grief is the exception rather than the rule. He is less likely to talk about, cry about, and *appear to others* to think about his loss. He'll probably be reluctant to seek the support of others, either individually or in a group. Instead, he's more apt to assume full responsibility for his bereaved state and depend only upon himself."

A man's grief is as immeasurable as a woman's, however, it may not be apparent. Therefore, a man's grief may appear to take a shorter time to be resolved. Yet, says Staudacher, "The pressures it creates are still there and the grief is real." She says that men have five coping styles:

1. To remain silent
2. To engage in solitary mourning, or "secret" grief
3. To take physical or legal action
4. To become immersed in activity, such as a job
5. To exhibit addictive behavior

After years of saying, "big boys don't cry," we've finally learned that real men do. One of the great pictures of the 1970s was of Rosie Greer, the huge hulk of a football player and bodyguard to Senator Robert Kennedy. Rosie is sitting on a bench, crying. Men like Rosie told us it was OK to show our feelings and OK to cry....

—Rev. Terry Moore, et al., from *Fathers Grieve, Too*

Men, traditionally, have thrown themselves into their jobs after the death of their loved ones. They return to work a few days after the funeral and it seems that they are handling their grief in the "grown-up way." Grief isn't an emotion better handled by grown-ups. It just is and it must be processed.

If a man has experienced the death of a loved one and has returned to work, he might find that he's being more aggressive while driving, bumping, or hitting himself with tools, or having little patience with coworkers or customers. Coworkers don't understand because for many, they have never personally felt the intensity of grief.

Throwing yourself into work after the death of a loved one is part of the grieving process and can be good therapy. However, we must take time to candidly examine feelings, too. As you may have noticed, family and friends withdraw when a man is "too busy," or is "always so darned crabby." However, this may be a time when the male is crying out for someone to help, to throw him a life preserver or offer a gentle word or a tissue.

Men often find they are better able to process grief by talking with other men who have had a similar experience. Compassionate Friends, a support group with chapters throughout the country, provides a caring, conducive environment for men to address grief, sometimes to cry, and eventually to move forward.

COUPLES AND GRIEF

Lots of people think that when a family experiences a death of a member, especially a child, it will bring the husband and wife closer together. In reality, the opposite is true. Both husband and wife, or committed couple, are so exhausted from the physical and emotional effects of grief that they have little energy to lean on each other. It can even be scary to see the turmoil in a partner and feel so helpless.

In the booklet *Fathers Grieve, Too*, the Rev. Terry Morgan, Chaplain James Cunningham, Dr. Ray Goldstein, and Earl Katz explain that there are things you can do to help your partner, even in this period of intense sorrow. Some of the points they recommend include that couples remember that it's important to:

- Keep on courting....even now.
- Talk about how you met. Remember how you fell in love.
- Share what you like about each other.
- Go out on a date, even if it's a short walk.
- Touch and hold each other.
- Realize you each grieve differently—respect each other's way of grieving.
- Accept your first sexual sharing after the death as a warm, gentle caring that brings you close, affirms your tears, and quiets your sadness.

Couples who are grieving separately may find help by talking with their clergy, attending support groups such as Compassionate Friends, or talking with a family counselor. While it is impossible to help another through the grieving process, it is possible for husbands and wives to openly communicate and thus lean on each other for support in this great time of need.

GRANDPARENTS AND GRIEF

When a child was young and he or she fell, grandparents picked up the youngster, blotted the tears, cleansed the boo-boo, and hugged those shaking shoulders until the pain subsided. When there has been a death of a grandchild or other loved one close to the adult child, as a grandparent, there's a triple dose of grief. A grandparent grieves for the grandchild, hurts for the torment the grandparent sees mirrored on the face of his or her child, and anguishes over the emotions felt by his or her spouse.

There's a helpless feeling, too, many grandparents feel. As a grandparent, he or she wants to provide support, perhaps even coordinate the funeral arrangements. Grandparents want to take on the agony, but that pain isn't theirs. Sometimes they have to "share" this time with the other set of grandparents and don't know where they can help....or even if they can help. It is distressful and there are no right answers.

As older citizens, they may have experienced death before and intimately understand the time it takes to move through grief. Nevertheless, when a grandchild dies, part of grandparents' dreams for the future die, too. They've made mental plans to take the child to football games and buy presents when they travel on vacation. Hopes and dreams and desires perish when a grandchild dies. Grandparents need to remember that they have a right to be angry; they have a right to grieve.

Sometimes the emotions they see in their own children, after the death of a loved one in their family, are difficult to accept. The adult child is probably going through all the facets of grief and he or she may lash out or vice versa. During grief, it is not unusual for a grandparent to blame the parents for something they didn't do for the child who died.

Grandparents of "blended families," that is with children from previous marriages mixed into a new unit, find their roles more complicated. It's important for them to try to help the child and the children of the family through the ordeal of the death and grief. Grandparents need to talk about their grief, talk to all the grandkids with openness and honesty, offer advice when asked, and offer hugs and love whenever close.

Grief experts say that grandparents are often angry at themselves. Because they are older, they may be thinking that they should have died, not the child. Intellectually they recognize that life doesn't always turn out as we plan, but grief turns thoughts around. This is a time that requires extra caring and love as a grandparent. Grandparents should try to be nonjudgmental, and see themselves as support, especially as a mom or dad to an adult child who is crying inside and out.

If there are other grandchildren, they need you, too, as will those grandchildren yet to be born. The heart is truly amazing. It stretches as wide as we ask and makes room for memories of the child who died with plenty of space left over for those who can physically light up our days.

SIBLINGS AND GRIEF

The Compassionate Friends believe, "As steel and glass are made stronger by going through fire, there seems to be a strengthening effect of those children who have suffered the death of a brother or sister. They have faced grown-up issues. They know the importance of family, a gift to be cherished. They know life is precious. They are generally more sensitive and compassionate than most kids. They have a different perspective on life."

Grief expert Dr. Klass explains that it is not the job of the surviving or subsequent child to live the life we had hoped for the dead child. "Each child deserves to live a life of his or her own, and not have to live out the unfulfilled promise of a dead child. There is a good deal of research showing that 'replacement children' suffer more than their share of emotional disturbances as adults."

When one child dies, bereaved parents often fall short in dealing with their surviving children. Surviving siblings are sometimes referred to, by grief experts, as the neglected mourners. They are left alone. Their parents are too involved in their own pain to recognize others are grieving.

Dr. Klass says that children deserve their own grief, not their parents'. Parents have lost a child, a part of them, the hope of their immortality and future, a child they chose to have and whom they had promised full care and protection. "The other children in the family grieve as siblings, not as parents. Their loss is different from an adult's. Children have a right to be judged on their own terms, not against the standard of an idealized dead child."

"Perhaps, besides including them and letting them have their own life and grief," says Dr. Klass, "parents help their surviving and subsequent children best by trusting them. Sad to say, but often the death of one child makes adults less good parents to their other children. In their grief they are short on patience, long on anger, and too often distracted. Many times, the children catch the brunt of it.

Parents need to trust that what they gave them before the death, what they will give them after they have resolved their grief, and what they are giving them now as they

RIGHTS OF CHILDREN WHEN A SIBLING DIES
provided by Cathi Lammert, executive director of SHARE

1. To be acknowledged as a person who has feelings that need to be expressed.

2. To be given the choice to see and hold a sibling before and after the death within reason.

3. To be considered in the choices parents are given. They may have an opinion.

4. To be informed about the feelings of grief in their terms, giving them the choice of a support group or counseling.

5. To be recognized by our society that we will always love and miss their siblings.

confront this most difficult reality is good enough." It is the best parents can do at this place and at this time.

ADULT SIBLINGS AND GRIEF

Adults take on many roles—father, mother, spouse, and worker. Many times the role in the original family—oldest, youngest, or middle child, the smartest, the most athletic, the prettiest—continues into adulthood. The feelings a sibling experiences when another sibling dies can be profound, and those birth roles or original roles become changed forever. When an adult sibling dies, it's confusing. Most adults feel cheated, feel angry, and feel a pronounced sadness that the past is gone forever.

If the relationship with a sibling wasn't a good one, and that is quite possible, the adult may suffer from regret that he or she never had the time or opportunity to resolve the problems. Because of the age difference or a geographic distance, the adult may not feel the death for some time or less intensely as someone who was closer to the sibling. This can produce feelings of guilt.

The death sometimes brings back feelings of sibling rivalry or uncomfortable memories. Even as adults, these feelings can still be deep inside and in a time of stress, they often surface. The feelings are not logical, but they are there nonetheless.

If the sibling was younger, there seems to be a real injustice happening. The baby in the family is gone, even if the "baby" was a gray-haired, slightly overweight, wrinkled man or woman. A sibling may be emotionally affected by the incongruity that older people usually die first, yet this is simply hasn't happened.

Additionally, if a parent has died, the sibling may have to help the surviving parent at the time of the sibling's death. While filling in the role as the "parent," he or she may not have time to process and resolve his or her own grief. If the sibling had his or her own children or if the sibling was a single parent, he or she may be needed to help provide emotional support for nieces and nephews as well as the surviving spouse. This may increase feelings of anger.

Siblings need to take time for themselves, nourishing their bodies, resting, and providing love and support to others, as they work through their grief. They need to ask for support from others who want to help, and get outside assistance from professionals to help meet the needs they cannot provide.

Dr. Sandra Graves tells that when an adult sibling dies, the surviving sibling should "try to remember feelings of a child have a lot of power, but as an adult you are far more powerful than you were as a child. Acknowledge the child within you, but forgive those feelings as the adult you are. When we put to final rest a part of our family of long ago, we also bury part of ourselves, a part of our past. Memories, however, are forever, and memories may lighten your load."

Shrinking away from death is something unhealthy and abnormal which robs the second half of life of its purpose....

—Carl Jung, Swiss psychologist

THE DEATH OF A CHILD

Grief is an intense, lonely, and personal experience.

Everyone learns about grief and grieving in the course of natural separations that occur during infancy and childhood and through encounters with the deaths of loved ones. The death of an elderly loved one is mourned; it is usually expected. The death of a child including the death of an adult child, however, especially the death of an apparently healthy one by accident, violence, suicide, or illness is a shock. When a child dies, not only does the death destroy the dreams and the hopes of the parents, but it also forces all family members to face an event for which they are unprepared.

Most parents who experience the death of a child describe the pain that follows as the most intense they have ever experienced. Many mothers and fathers or those close to the child wonder if they will be able to tolerate the pain, to survive the misery, and to ever feel as though life will have meaning again. They cannot imagine a future void of that person.

The intense pain that parents experience when their child dies may be eased somewhat with insight into what has helped others overcome a comparable death. That's why joining a support group often makes the grief more manageable. When the child is an adult, the death can be just as painful, especially when you reflect back on the nurturing you gave this person while growing up.

Often the first reactions after the death of a child are shock, disbelief, denial, and/or numbness. These responses are instinctive and soften the impact of the death until the survivor is better prepared to face the reality and the finality of the child's death. These reactions, as normal as they are, can be deceptive to others who are unacquainted with the grieving process. They may incorrectly assume that the parent is either strong and holding up well or insensitive and incapable of expressing feelings about the death. What these critics fail to realize is that the deep emotions allow the grieving parent to face the tragic occurrence without losing control. Many parents have said that they seem to be "functioning in a fog" during the first few weeks after their child's death.

"Some parents describe their experience at the wake or funeral as 'being an observer' or 'not really being emotionally involved,' " explains Margaret S. Miles, author of *The Grief of Parents When a Child Dies*.

All of these reactions are nature's way of helping the parents confront the death of their children. These reactions may last minutes, hours, days, or weeks. Parents determine subconsciously when they are ready to face the death, ready to face life without their children. Grief experts report that crying, sobbing, and wailing, or some other emotional release usually marks the end of this initial period of grief.

When the child's death becomes a reality to the family, acute suffering and pain usually start. During the weeks and months that follow, many say that they are frightened by the intensity and the variety of the feelings that they experience. Crying, weeping, and incessant talking are all normal reactions. A feeling of aloneness, even when other people are close by, is experienced, too.

Each parent may talk about his or her grief differently, or he or she may have trouble talking to others and expressing feelings. Relatives and friends are sometimes too uncomfortable with the actuality of the death to talk. They may be busy with their own lives. They may be unable to meet the needs of the parents. For some people, help can be obtained by talking to the clergy, physicians, counselors, or caring friends. Talking to other bereaved parents and finding out how they cope, and the practical matters of life that must also be dealt with may be extremely beneficial for many parents.

There are no quick fixes. Yet we all grieve in different ways and with various intensities. The death of a child or other loved one has been compared to having surgery. Parents need to be assured that they will heal, but there will always be a scar, a weakness, tenderness.

The emotions of grief when a child dies are the same as those when an adult dies; however, with a child, parents often feel the grief with more intensity. The emotions are:

Guilt: As parents try to understand the reason for the death of their child, feelings of guilt can arise. Mothers and fathers blame themselves for something they did in the present or the past, or for something they neglected to do. Each parent might blame the other. Parents may also feel guilty about not giving the child something he or she wanted. In most cases, there is no rational basis for these feelings.

Anger: Feeling rage to expressing mild anger may occur. Parents are angry at themselves, their spouses, the physician, the caregiver, or the child for having died. Religious beliefs are often questioned. Anger that is left unrealized, however, may manifest itself in abusive behaviors. Anger can be expressed by screaming in private, hitting something, or strenuous exercise.

Fear: After the death of their child, many experience an overall sense of fear that something else just as terrible or even worse can happen. Parents with other children become extremely overprotective. At the same time, they may find themselves fearful of their responsibilities because they believe they've failed as a parent.

After the death, often concentration is difficult. Sleep may be impossible and parents feel exhausted which makes them edgy with their other children, their spouses, family, and coworkers.

**COPING WITH THE
DEATH OF A CHILD**
common advice from death
experts and support groups
nationwide

ॐ

*As a survivor, there are ways
you learn to cope with the
death of a child.*

*1. Learn as much as
possible about the death. For
example, if your child died as
a result of suicide, you can
talk with therapists and those
at Survivors of Suicide. Learn
details of the death and people
he or she talked with.*

*2. Establish schedules in
your life and include rituals,
such as going to the cemetery
every Saturday to place a
bouquet of flowers on the
grave.*

*3. Take time to laugh. At
first you may have to work
hard at something to laugh
about, but laughter is a
natural tranquilizer and will
make you feel better.*

*4. Reach out to others,
especially those who have
experienced the death of a
child such as people who are
Compassionate Friends. Later
on, maybe you can lend a
hand to someone who has just
experienced a death.*

Depression: As parents continue to work through grief, depression often occurs, taking various forms. Some parents may feel constantly "down," unhappy, lethargic, or sad. Others may feel worthless. Suicidal thoughts are not unusual. Parents report that their arms ache to hold the child, or they hear the child playing outdoors or their skateboard's wheels rattling down the driveway.

Resolution and recovery: As the finality of the child's death becomes a reality, recovery follows. Parents begin to take an active part in life and their lives begin to have meaning once again. The pain of the child's death is less intense—but not forgotten. Birthdays, holidays, and the anniversary of the child's death can trigger periods of intense pain and suffering. The emotions that can surface every time a parent realizes that he or she has not thought about the child who died can bring on feelings of grief.

Painful days become less frequent. There's no set time, no schedule for resolution and recovery when a child dies. The only comforting thought that one can give is that the resolution does occur.

Parents will recover best by being patient and loving with themselves and others, with their spouses, and their families. If at any time they believe that they are not handling grief well, as few as one or two sessions with a counselor or therapist might help.

Why is this terrible pain necessary? "Grief allows us to let go of that which was, so we'll be ready for that which is to be," explains Therese Rando, Ph.D., clinical psychologist and author of *Grief, Dying, and Death*. "Mourning allows us to disentangle ourselves from the bonds we had with the person we've lost."

THE DEATH OF A PARENT

"The death of a parent heralds a new phase in our lives," explains Elizabeth Turner Haase, Ph.D., who is on the counseling staff at the St. Francis Center, Washington, D.C., and cofacilitates the Thanatology for Professionals training, workshops specializing in death counseling. "As adults, we can no longer rely on our parents' wisdom and we face the stark reality that they no longer stand between death and us. Now we assume the mantle of protector and defender of our own lives—and the lives of our children's if we are parents ourselves. Sometimes this happens before we are ready."

When adults experience the death of a parent, the bonds of their childhood are broken, and the memories and stories they've come to love (or cringe at) are no longer repeated. Life becomes single-generational rather than multigenerational.

In teaching and counseling Dr. Haase talks about the fact that many adult children feel as if there is no one left who truly thinks of them first and loves them unconditionally when the parent they feel closest to dies. "They cannot imagine how they will continue in this world without that parental support. If that parent was also the last surviving parent, they have to learn who they are in this world without a parent.

"Adult children may begin the process of separation even while the parent is ill or dying. This isn't easy. Suddenly, they may have to provide physical, emotional, and even financial support to the parents who provided those things to them in their childhood. Contrary to popular mythology, we are not reversing roles and becoming the parent, but our roles and relationships do change dramatically."

Dr. Haase relates that the intensity of grief when a parent dies varies—not all parent-child relationships are good ones. This intensity depends on the investment the child had in the family and with the parent. "In the case of a stormy or complicated relationship, the adult child must deal with this complicating factor during grief."

If the parent dies without warning, or the child does not understand that the parent was ill (or wasn't even told about the gravity of the illness), often the surviving child feels intense guilt. There were things left unsaid, things that shouldn't have been said, and love not expressed. There was no opportunity to say thank-you for a lifetime of gifts, joys, and pleasures. "When that happens, they often want to learn everything they can about their parent's death as part of the grieving process."

Parents by their nature stand on the borderline between the mortal and immortal sides of existence; the mortal because of their kinship with men and other animals through the perishableness of the body; the immortal because the act of generation assimilates them to God, the generator of the All.

—Philo, fourth century Roman politician

As an adult child who is surviving the death of a parent, the world may not understand the grief. The grief seen on the faces of the widowed or of a parent whose child has died is comprehended, but not an adult's. When a parent dies and one is an adult, there is a general feeling that this is the natural order of life.

This is not true. Adults whose parents have died will be helped by reviewing the steps of grief and the emotional and physical reactions they experienced. Grief doesn't make allowances now that "you're all grown up."

Coping with the Death of a Parent

Survivors will find comfort in knowing that this is a time to be kind to themselves, to take every day one day at a time. The feelings of loss and grief will be replaced by memories.

Grief experts say that if adults expect their adult siblings to suddenly join together to cement the family, they may be in for a disappointment. They suggest that adults look realistically at the dynamics of the family before the death and don't kid themselves that they can instantly change. As an illustration: If before Mom's death, brother Dave couldn't be in the same room with sister Amy without criticizing her newest boyfriend, her hairstyle, or her current career choice and she responded in kind, little will have changed after the funeral.

Some siblings may even revert back to how they acted as kids and in the family order. If Carl, the oldest, always told his siblings what to do and when to do it as everyone was growing up, then seemed to mellow with age, he may go back to this emotional state after a parent's death. Sisters and brothers are related by circumstances, not by choice; however, as adults it is possible to laugh at the problems. It's possible to make behavior changes.

"When a parent dies, his or her relationship with the children does not cease," explains Rabbi Marc D. Angel, author of *The Jewish Orphaned Adult* for the National Institute for Jewish Hospice. "Each of us continues to live with 'the parent within.' Many years ago, I attended a dinner honoring a prominent philanthropist who was then about seventy years old. When he received a plaque, his first words of response were: 'I wish my father were here to see this. He would have been so proud.' His father had died long ago; yet this distinguished and influential man was still profoundly influenced by and attached to his father.

"Parents continue to live within us in our memories, our attitudes, even in our gestures and mannerisms. As time passes, the initial pain and confusion of mourning lessens; a deeper, wiser understanding emerges."

THE WIDOWED SURVIVOR

"It's not supposed to be like this—she was only thirty-one."

"We'd worked so hard to scrimp and save in order to make our golden years together just that—golden. Now he's dead. The future looks so bleak."

Concepts such as growing old together, planning vacations, traveling at retirement, buying a first home, and dreams that will not be realized are extremely painful when a person is widowed. Widowed survivors can still do many things alone, but it's not the same. Not only has a husband or wife died, but survivors see themselves in a completely different light.

When a husband or wife dies, a life change occurs. There is no longer a team. There is a single person. Whether married a month or five hundred months, widows often feel like half a person. They feel incomplete. And they have no choice in the matter. Being widowed requires time for readjustment. They must work through the feelings which accompany grief—sometimes it is hard just to believe this has happened.

Because the pain of grief is numbing (and some say it is a blessing), those who have been widowed typically make it through the arrangements and funeral or other service okay. Then as days go by and they think they should be getting better—getting over it—they feel worse. This is normal.

Little things become enormous reminders of the loved one who has died. The first trip to the dentist as a widowed person. The first new pair of slippers. The widow, alone, has

LIVING WITH YOUR CHILDREN
from AARP's *Tomorrow's Choices*

❧

For many people, moving in with their adult children is the best choice when living alone is no longer possible. Think through these questions.... and discuss the issues together before agreeing to join their household.

• Does your son or daughter want you to move in? If not, and you move in anyway, will the emotional strain be too much on you?

• How will living expenses be shared?

• What will you use for transportation? Will you have easy access to shopping, a place of worship, friends, and other interests of your own?

• Do you have friends in the area? Are there people close by with whom you can create friendships?

• Will you be able to accommodate your child's lifestyle?

• Will you be able to live with your children's children?

• Can your children afford to have you live with them?

• How will your presence affect family relationships?

• How much time will you expect your child to spend with you?

🐌

*What's a person to do in order
to avoid the fifty-plus and fat
syndrome? How can a person
who's a little down pick him-
or herself up again? Here are
some tips for battling
depression and the slump that
can come from early
widowhood:*

*1. Select low-fat food
choices, like fish and chicken
instead of fatty red meats.
Reduce consumption of
processed foods, snacks, and
desserts. A healthy diet will
give you a healthy mental
outlook.*

*2. Exercise aerobically four
times a week for forty minutes
each session, always starting
slowly in any new or different
exercise plan. Walking is the
best over-fifty workout.*

*3. Include "sneaky" fitness
into your day. Wash your car.
Mow the lawn. Rake leaves.
Walk to the store. Join a
senior exercise program. Take
dance lessons and join a
dance club. Learn a sport.*

*With these easy steps you'll
meet trim, energetic people
and add a youthful bounce to
your step, too.*

to coil the garden hose, feed the pets, send out the family birthday cards, and a zillion other things the spouse previously took care of. Now each responsibility makes a survivor remember him or her and reflect how deeply he or she is feeling the loss of companionship.

Not only do those who have suffered the loss of a spouse experience the shattered dreams of a cozy future, but suddenly they're "single"—financially, physically, and emotionally alone. Family dynamics change. Friendships change. They may feel like outsiders when everyone is a couple. Jealousy is a part of grief.

The widowed often suffer from what grief experts call "secondary losses," in addition to those felt as a result of the spouse's death. For example, a woman who is widowed didn't just lose a husband—she's experiencing the death of a best friendship, a co-provider, a confidant, a companion, and someone to help with the responsibility of the children. These secondary losses often leave the widowed panicky and confused. For this reason, they should use caution making major decisions. Financial experts and other family members are probably suggesting that they postpone the decisions until they have a handle on the direction of this new, and changed, life without a mate. They are right. There is time later to make changes.

"Widowhood is a process," says Dr. Graves. "It's like relearning to walk after an accident. Widowers must take it one step at a time." The first step is often the hardest, but there are other hard steps along the way. As marriage is a commitment, a commitment to themselves is another phase of life. Often that commitment is assisted by reading about grief, knowing the signs, and working through the process.

Ways to Cope with Widowhood

Widowhood is a challenge—one of the greatest any adult may face. If the survivor has never handled the couple's finances, he or she should talk with an accountant or someone at the survivor's bank. He or she will advise how to manage a checking account and give references to other financial specialists. If the widowed person doesn't know about car care and worries about being stranded, the community college probably has basic auto classes.

Widowers need to reach out to others. Right now they may be feeling intensely dependent and they should allow others to help. Depending on where he or she lives, the local hospice program, as with other organizations, probably offers support groups and counseling. Often the counseling is free of charge. Loneliness is a familiar concern of those who are widowed and support groups can help work through this stage.

Another way to work through the loneliness is to volunteer. Volunteers are desperately needed and especially valued. Often groups are listed in the Sunday paper. Widowers can make inquiries and create a place for themselves. For instance, they respond to calls coming to a suicide or runaway hotline, plant trees in a reforestation area, deliver books or meals to shut-ins, hold crack-addicted babies in the neonatal wards. They can use their energy to help others and in turn heal themselves.

Said one widow who volunteers in clinics for the homeless and battered women, "Every time I felt sorry for myself and began to worry—which I did a lot after Frank died—I was slapped in the face with the realization that the people who come to the clinic have no worries. They have no T-bills to manage, no checking accounts to balance, no pension money to invest, and no need to plan a trip to Hawaii or with whom to spend the holidays. The clinic isn't the right place for everyone who is widowed, but for me it is. I leave each day, not only with the feeling that I've helped others, but they've helped me."

Some people find that traveling is helpful after they are widowed. While they may not have unlimited funds to take that cruise, there's no reason why they can't begin to plan it and read about all the places they'd visit. The widowed might want to go alone or ask other family members to go with them.

Senior programs such as Elderhostel, a travel and study program, plans trips that are affordable and informative in the United States and abroad. All registered Elderhostel participants must be sixty years or older, although younger people may accompany registered participants.

According to Mildred L. Hyman, author of *Elderhostel,*

God does not die on the day when we cease to believe in a personal deity, but we die on the day when our lives cease to be illuminated by the steady radiance, renewed daily, of a wonder, the source of which is beyond all reason....

—Dag Hammarskjold, from *Markings*

each year hundreds of thousands of older Americans take part in Elderhostel's program at one of the more than one thousand host institutions worldwide. Accommodations and curricula can, and do, vary greatly from program to program.

Lodging can vary from a bunk bed in a dormitory to a luxury hotel room with a private bath. Quality of food and ease of access are equally diverse.

The Elderhostel organization founded in 1975 has been called the greatest social movement of the century by *Time* magazine. Headquartered in Boston, it is based on the premise that people of all ages should have access to education. Founder Marty Knowlton, a social activist and educator, patterned his program on the European youth hostel movement. Like the European model, there is no charge for membership and the organization is nonprofit. Many golden-agers would dispute the adage that life begins at forty—for them, through Elderhosteling, it begins at sixty.

The widowed go through a tremendous shock. They will need time to heal. Grief isn't like a cold. One can't take a cough drop or an antibiotic and feel better. Like anyone else suffering from the loss of a loved one, the widowed should take each hour one by one, each day at a time, and attempt to become independent. Survivors will weather this phase of life. If they don't reach out to life, they'll never see who is out there ready to take their hands.

Where to Get Help

The American Association of Retired Persons provides a free list of books on widowhood, titled *Bibliography on Loss and Grief* (D435), available from AARP fulfillment on request. Contact them at:

American Association of Retired Persons
AARP
601 E St., NW
Washington, DC 20049
(800) 424-3410

While your local public library and bookstore will have many titles on grief and bereavement for the widowed man or woman, the following are book services that provide catalogues free of charge on topics of interest to caregivers and those who are in the grieving process.

Centering Corporation
7230 Maple St.
Omaha, NE 68134
(402)553-1200

The Centering Corporation also sends an inspirational newsletter called *Caring Concepts*, available for the asking.

Compassionate Book Service
216 Via Monte
Walnut Creek, CA 94598
(510) 933-0830 or (510) 284-2273

Know that there is no right way to grieve.

—Enid Samuel Traisman,
grief counselor

SURVIVING THE DEATH OF SOMEONE SPECIAL

Those who have just experienced the death of a special person in their lives may not fit into the role of family in the old-fashioned context of the word. For a fiancee, live-in lover, companion, best friend, ex-spouse, stepchild, or business partner, the death of a loved one is as real as it is to the children, sisters, brothers, fathers, and mothers who are related by blood.

Often there is no "place" for these caring friends at the funeral. They are lumped with "other grievers" who must cope with the emotions of death alone. They may be feeling like they're being ignored, and, truthfully, this does happen. When a death occurs, family members find support with relatives. They erroneously believe that others do not share the pain with the same magnitude or they didn't know the loved one that long. In reality, a friend's pain can be as overwhelming as a family member's, and yet a friend is often left out because he or she is just "someone she shared the house with," "someone he worked with," or "someone she was going to marry eventually."

If the relationship was one in which the special person planned a future together, he or she is feeling like his or her dreams have been shattered. Depending on the person's status in the family, he or she may not be able to make decisions regarding the funeral or last wishes, or be included when personal possessions are distributed to other loved ones. Many people without a spouse or children often become especially close to other children in the family, or the children of friends and they, too, are falsely thought not to be grieving as fully.

Coping with the Death of That Special Person

People who are not family members should understand that they are grieving and the death of their special person will make a change in their lives. How often did you see this person, talk on the phone, share a holiday? Of course things will be different and they'll miss the closeness, love, and companionship.

Depending on the situation, friends need to ask to be included with the loved one's family at the funeral or service. If that's not possible, they should perform their own rituals and/or memorials for their loved one, alone or with friends. There are other ways to remember the person who has died through a donation of funds for medical research, establishing a scholarship, creating a remembrance album, or planting a tree or special garden. If possible, friends should continue the relationship with the loved one's family. They should ask to be included, and invite family members to spend time with them. This takes work and it is painful, but no one said grief was easy.

As "anniversaries" come around, friends will probably experience the sense of grief once more. Anniversaries are not just days of celebration such as Thanksgiving or the Fourth of July, but can be the first time a kiss was given, the day the divorce was final, or the afternoon two people always went Christmas shopping together.

Those who have recently lost loved ones can find support talking with counselors or friends who know how to listen, or by attending support groups with people who are also survivors. They should go to a group and discuss their connection with the person who died. If they do not feel at ease, they should visit another group. Sometimes, self-help groups are made up of people who all have had children die, or all of suicide survivors. It is advised that grievers talk to a facilitator about their needs and find a group where those needs are met.

GRIEF WHEN A GRANDPARENT DIES

"Over the river and through the woods, to Grandmother's house we go...." We all know that catchy song and the nostalgic vision it reflects: a safe, loving retreat, filled with warmth and comfort.

For those children and adults who have been fortunate to have this type of relationship with a grandparent or other elderly adult, the death of that special person is extremely touching. It feels like we must be grown-ups now. Our safe harbor is gone forever. That makes the death of a grandparent extremely poignant.

Those "over the river" images aren't possible in the dynamics of every family, however, and if your relationship with a grandparent wasn't ideal, then grandchildren may feel cheated from some "Hollywood version" that didn't happen in their family. This can make them feel angry when a grandparent dies because they've lost the opportunity for unconditional acceptance and love. They may be grieving that fact as much or more than the actual death. This might make them feel guilty.

Now that the population is growing old, survivors may find that they are in charge or must take an active role in caring for their own parents, and watch as grandparents begin to deteriorate. They may be responsible for decisions on nursing homes or other care. And they may be confronting their own mortality. This may be the first death in the family and they are not familiar with grief. All the while, there's is a child inside screaming, "Not fair!"

SAYING THE NAME, SHARING THE MEMORIES
by Suzanne Howell, M.A.

❦

Have you "created silence" by saying the name of your recently deceased loved one?

Friends and family who are silent or who change the subject are demonstrating discomfort with talking about the loved one who has died.... a reaction that comes from a desire to help you. They think that by not talking with you about your deceased husband (wife, sister, brother, father, mother, child, or friend) they are keeping you from thinking about the person. As with others who counsel in grief and bereavement, we have a very technical term to apply to that reasoning, "Hogwash!" Unfortunately it may be up to you, the griever, to inform your friends that you need to think, talk, and share memories about the loved one who has died.

One of the reasons it is important that you are able to say the name of your loved one is so you can tell stories about your life and how he or she was a part of it. Have you ever thought how you would tell your favorite family stories without mentioning a now deceased family member? Not telling those stories takes away a part of your own life.

Telling stories helps in accepting the reality of the

As bereavement specialists explain, the feelings of anger and guilt are normal. The "if onlys" are normal. The stages of physical and emotional grief are normal. Dr. Graves suggests, "If you can confront the anger that feels out of control, but know you have controlled it; if you can confront sadness that makes your insides hurt, and know you can eventually soothe yourself; if you can confront fear and know you have learned from it, you have learned to cope. This is a skill that will last a lifetime."

Grandparents gave unconditional love. And with the death of grandparents, grandchildren have acquired the ability to live through life's crises and survive.

WHEN YOU DON'T KNOW WHAT TO SAY

Whether you are grieving or someone you love is experiencing the emotions that are provoked after the death of a loved one, there are times when everything you can think to say sounds wrong in your head....and will probably be worse when the words leave your mouth. At these times when there is nothing to say, grief experts tell us to say nothing. Instead:

- Stay in touch, physically and emotionally.
- Listen. You are not expected to have the answer or any answers.
- Ask questions.
- Continue to call, to bring food, to share a story.
- Talk about the good times. Share your memories.
- Mention the name of the loved one who has died.
- Say things like, "We were thinking about you."
- Be patient with yourself and others.
- Say, "We love you." Don't say, "We know how you feel."
- Tears are healing. Don't be embarrassed if during the conversation, tears flow.
- Offer a box of tissues, keep a few in your pocket or purse.
- Hold a hand. Give a hug.
- Sit close.

- Take a ride in the car.
- Drive home a different way.
- Go out to eat.
- Meet for a cup of tea.
- Let them pay sometimes.

A KEEPSAKE BOOK

Up until now, we've covered the emotions and experiences of parting, of the death, of one with whom we've shared love, laughter, trouble, and jubilations. We've talked about the effects of grief and the stages with which we must cope. But there are "hands-on" ways to cope with grief, too. One such method is the keepsake book. It is a project you can begin right as you are working through the stages of grief, or you can use later when you find that you want a special place for the treasury of memories you hold dear.

Like a scrapbook, a keepsake book, sometimes called a remembrance album, provides a real, tangible memory log of your life with the loved one. Grief counselor Enid Samuel Traisman's *I Remember....I Remember* is such a book. It's an activity project for those who are grieving to help with the grieving process. Traisman, who holds a master's degree in social work, writes that a keepsake journal is a special place for you to share your feelings that have arisen since the death of your loved one. It provides a place for you to go over your private feelings about the death.

"There is no wrong way to use your journal," Traisman says. "The journal is a memorial to your loved one. The pages will reflect the memories shared. You can keep it privately and show it to no one, or you can pass it down from generation to generation to offer those yet unborn the opportunity to know an important person in their family. Traisman's beautiful little book is filled with space to provide intimate information about the person who died, with photo spots and areas to write your own special feelings.

death. Making mention of how "Charlie loved seafood," confronts you with the fact that he no longer is here to enjoy it. It also helps you change your relationship with a dead loved one from a relationship of daily inter-action and contact to one of memory.

The next time you mention the name of a loved person who is dead and are greeted with silence or a change of subject, tell your good friends that they can help you by sharing your memories. And, because each of us wants to know that others remember someone who was so important to us, maybe you can get your friends to share some of their memories, too.

You can make your own keepsake book, organize a scrapbook, or set up a memory box. Simply find or buy a special scrapbook or a beautiful box and fill it with information and items that reflect your love and the personality of your loved one. Sometimes antique or craft stores have hand-crafted scrapbooks and boxes that will add to your pleasure.

Some grief experts recommend a journal of thoughts and feelings, letters written to the deceased after his or her death, and poems or drawings that reflect the journal keeper's feelings at the time. The physical activity of organizing a keepsake book, scrapbook, or memory box helps in the grief process and can become a special place for you to enjoy the memories you still have. Since this is your keepsake book, you may want to keep its contents confidential, or you may want to share the memories with others. This is for you and should reflect how you feel and your feelings for the one who has died.

ॐ

In this chapter we've concerned ourselves with the effect of death on individuals and within specific relationships. In chapter 5, the theme will take on a how-to aspect. As with your own stages of grief, it may be time to find help.

Chapter 5 concerns how to work through grief with a hands-on, practical approach. The topics include how to borrow some methods from proven self-help programs, find emotional support groups or find personal counseling that can fit your specific needs, plus what goes on behind closed doors. Because their needs are unique, we'll discuss a specific program for teenagers who are in the middle of the grieving process.

And if you need a hug *right now*, in the final portion of the following chapter "Dr. Hugs," a specialist in the healing power of hugs, provides information on how to give and receive therapeutic embraces. Actually there are three thousand ways to hug, but we'll concern ourselves with seven of the best.

Chapter

5

Support Techniques and Grief Resolution

There is no time limit on grief. There is no clock ticking down the minutes until all will be better and everything will be "normal again." You'll never be the same after the death of a loved one. With time, your memories will replace some of the pain. You'll laugh again. Yet, there will also be a new special place in your heart, a memory depository in your brain for the loved one who has died.

Within this chapter we'll talk in a practical manner about how to work toward the resolution of grief, including how to locate a grief support group or therapist to fit your needs, borrowing some recovery techniques from Alcoholic's Anonymous, the world's leading self-help group. Additionally, we'll discuss the distinct needs of teenagers during a time of bereavement. Greg Risberg, a.k.a., "Dr. Hugs," will provide some special methods to reach out and embrace others.

WORKING TOWARD A NEW NORMAL

Bereavement makes a major change in every life. If you have experienced the death of a loved one, you know it has made a change in yours. In his. In hers.

Nothing is ever the same after a loved ones dies. There will be a new normal with good days and bad days, days to remember and plenty you'll probably choose to forget. Grief therapists tell us that most people do not believe that life will ever be okay again, and typically the grieving do not want to hear it. But it will.

Some bereavement causes major changes: you're single, childless, orphaned, penniless, in the middle of a red-tape strewed judicial system, and confused. Depending on your circumstances and the loved one who died, the changes may be major or minor. Grief therapist Dr. Sandra Graves suggests that we look at this time as one of challenges. "This is not to minimize your feelings in any way, but to help you put a new perspective on the experience you are having," she says. "Stress is the perception of threat. If you can change your perception you can change some of the stress reactions you are having."

In the essay "How Can I Cope?" by Dr. Graves, she explains that there are five ways to cope with a crisis, in this case the crises of grief. They are:

- Information
- Attitude
- New rituals
- Reaching out
- Spiritual searching

Let's look at each coping mechanism individually. With this data, coping may come a bit easier. To paraphrase Snoopy, that famous philosophical pooch, "This is good grief work, Charlie Brown."

Information: You probably have an intense need to find out everything you possibly can about how your loved one died—what was the exact nature of the illness or the circumstances of the accident or the details of the homicide or crime? What really killed your loved one? How have others in this state survived? What is grief? How will it affect me and other members of my family? How long will it last? What is happening?

Information does give you some sense of control over yourself and the state of grief. With the data and an intellectual view, you distance yourself from your feelings.

Attitude: This facet helps us examine what truly happened, or what we perceive has happened. The attitude you take is your choice. Attitude is dictated in part by the physical experiences of grieving, but only in part since it also involves determination, hope, denial, or helplessness and a feeling of being victimized.

New rituals: When you can rely on simple behaviors you begin to feel more in control. Human beings like habits or rituals; we like to know pretty much when and what will happen so that we can put our limited energy to the unknown. When a death of a loved one changes our lives, we seek out new rituals and ways of performing habitual acts.

Reaching out: Express and share your grief with friends. Also look to supportive people who are in your life. These special people may help guide you through your early days of grief. As time passes and you assume an attitude of understanding and accept new rituals, you will want to reach out to other people, with a wider circle of friends. You may even find that old friendships, even those who first came to your aid after the death of your loved one, "just don't fit." Death changes people and you are changed. People who have been widowed find this especially true.

Spiritual searching: The search for the spiritual meaning of life and afterlife takes many forms and those who are in the process of coping with the death of a loved one often move to this phase. Some people deeply question God, their church, their synagogue. Some totally lose faith—at least for a time; others find it and zealously follow a completely different dogma or sect. Some men and women consult with psychics. Some search for a heaven, looking for answers as to what it could be like for their loved ones. There is a deep concern over whether they'll ever meet their loved ones again, and searching out answers to an afterlife helps restore their confidence and faith. Spiritual seeking is a positive part of the grief process.

ON RELIGION AND SPIRITUALITY
by Rachel Naomi Remen, M.D., Ph.D.

❧

The spiritual is not the religious. A religion is a dogma, a set of beliefs, about the spiritual, and a set of practices which rise out of those beliefs. There are many religions and they tend to be mutually exclusive. That is, every religion tends to think that it has dibs on the spiritual—that it's "The Way."

Yet, the spiritual is inclusive. It is the deepest sense of belonging and participation.... One might say that the spiritual is that realm of human experience which religion attempts to connect us to through dogma and practice. Sometimes it succeeds and sometimes it fails. Religion is a bridge to the spiritual, but the spiritual lies beyond religion.

- *Helping is not a commodity to be bought and sold.*
- *People who have the problem know a lot about it from the "inside." Competence is based on experience.*
- *People are helped by helping others.*
- *There is an optimism regarding the ability to change.*
- *The group is key: de-isolation is critical.*
- *The focus is anti-elite, antibureaucratic, anti-impersonal.*
- *Small may not necessarily be beautiful, but it is the place to begin: the small group, the personal, the informal, the simple, the direct.*
- *Do what you can. One day at a time. You can't solve everything at once.*
- *The consumer is a producer of help and services.*
- *Helping is at the center— knowing how to receive help, give help, and help others.*
- *The orientation is non-competitive and cooperative.*
- *People who have the problem are part of the solution.*

LOOKING AT SELF-HELP

The self-help movement, as viewed by the Self-Help Clearinghouse, a national network for referral services, has rapidly increased in the last twenty years. Currently there are over an estimated five hundred thousand members nationwide. The underlying self-help philosophy is that "You are not alone."

Self-help groups are consumer-oriented, peer-oriented, problem-centered, and rely on the member to be both a helper and one who will be helped. The groups provide a way for individuals in a collective setting who are facing similar life situations to assume responsibility for their own bodies, psyches, and behavior and help others do the same.

The Clearinghouse publishes a comprehensive book which lists by category the self-help groups throughout the United States. This book also provides information on forming support groups. To obtain information, contact the Self-Help Clearinghouse, Saint Clares-Riverside Medical Center, Denville, NJ 07834, (201) 625-7101. Ask for *The Self-Help Source Book* for finding and forming mutual aid self-help groups.

BORROWED RECOVERY AND THE TWELVE-STEP PROGRAM

Alcoholics Anonymous (AA) was established in 1935 for those who had become addicted to chemicals, and now most have heard of the Twelve Steps which AA describes as the foundation of recovery. It is probably the most well-known self-help group. Other groups have adopted the AA philosophy, primarily because the steps offer what people are seeking—straightforward answers and simplicity in life when it is most turbulent. Dr. Graves suggests those who are grieving can glean advice from the program and "borrow" their recovery.

"I have noticed that some individuals quite naturally follow something like the Twelve Steps of AA very naturally in grief recovery. I think we can borrow some wisdom from the millions who have followed and continue to follow this program," says Dr. Graves.

For those who are in recovery from a chemical dependency, the Twelve Steps embrace the concept that human beings are powerless under certain circumstances. As we now know, an alcoholic has a physical allergy to alcohol, making his or her body react to alcohol differently than those without the disease. Therefore, the man or woman is defenseless to control the effect of alcohol on the body.

Dr. Graves believes that just like people with cancer who are powerless to stop the increase in malignant cells without some intervention, people who grieve are powerless to stop their grief. "This doesn't mean that grief is a disease, but another human experience which we cannot control." She suggests the following as a Twelve-Step program for grief recovery:

1. Recognize that you are powerless to stop the thoughts and feelings of grief and don't deny them. They are "unmanageable" when you try to alter them. On the other hand, personal unmanageability relates to the attitudes and beliefs that you have about yourself, your environment, and the people you live with. There is a world of difference between the people who say, "I will never get over this!" and those who say, "I will never be the same as I used to be. But I want to do what I can so I won't defeat me, so I can be the best I am able to be at the moment."

2. There is a power within and outside you that can make this experience of grieving have purpose and meaning. Regardless of your religious convictions or lack of them, find peacefulness and truthfulness.

3. Make a personal commitment to your greater power to "recovery," to the healing process of grief.

4. Get to know yourself. What is important to you? And what is unimportant? If you realistically assess yourself, all strengths and areas that need strengthening, you know more about what you are capable of doing. You understand your own human needs more and your human deficiencies.

THE TWELVE STEPS OF ALCOHOLICS ANONYMOUS

We admitted:

1. We were powerless over alcohol, that our lives had become unmanageable.

2. Came to believe that a Power greater than ourselves could restore us to sanity.

3. Made a decision to turn our will and our lives over to the care of God as we understood Him.

4. Made a searching and fearless moral inventory of ourselves.

5. Admitted to God, to ourselves, and to another human being the exact nature of our wrongs.

6. Were entirely ready to have God remove all these defects of character.

7. Humbly asked Him to remove our shortcomings.

8. Made a list of all persons we had harmed and became willing to make amends to them all.

9. Made direct amends to such people wherever possible, except when to do so would injure them or others.

10. Continued to take personal inventory and when we were wrong, promptly admitted it.

11. Sought through prayer and meditation to improve our conscious contact with God, as we understood Him, praying only for knowledge of His will for us and the power to carry that out.

12. Having had a spiritual awakening as the result of these steps, we tried to carry this message to alcoholics and to practice these principles in all our affairs.

Through self-knowledge, we learn to strengthen the links between the conscious self and the Higher Self, bringing the personality more in line with the soul.

—Donald Watson, from
The Dictionary of Mind and Spirit

ᔥ

God made the world round so we would never be able to see too far down the road....

—Isak Dinesen,
Danish author

5. Be totally honest with yourself, your God, and another human being. Let go of any compulsive needs to control your life or the lives of others. Realize your choices through prayer or meditation and make them honestly.

6 and 7. Accept life with grace and faith. For some this means turning to God and telling Him about who you realistically are—impatient, intolerant of yourself, lacking faith. Make use of your own will—the power to love and to choose.

8. Restore your relationships and develop new ones. You are a different person than you were before your loved one died and before your recovery. Be willing to make the choices. If the death of your loved one was sudden, finish your unfinished business. Say the things to a trusted friend that you need to say to lay that relationship to rest.

9. Make amends to the living and the dead. Most people want to feel loving and lovable. Carrying a grudge or feelings of guilt make loving very difficult.

10. Live in the moment, one day at a time, paying attention to yourself.

11. Seek through prayer and meditation to strengthen your relationship with God as you understand Him. Pray for the knowledge of His will for you and the power to carry that out.

12. Help others who are just beginning their journey of grief and recovery. Reach beyond yourself, from within. These steps take time, probably more time than you can imagine. This is why it is doubly important to live in the moment.

SUPPORT GROUPS

It's been said that grief shared is grief diminished. Although we are all alone in our grief and how it personally affects us, talking, sharing, and allowing other people inside our hearts as we grieve can lessen the pain. For some, the pain is considerably reduced. For others, just knowing that there are people who have felt hopelessly alone is a significant step in their recovery.

The family structure has changed significantly and where once there was internal support during grief, merely by the fact that families were large and death was not an unknown quality, now there is very little. Today, few of us live with a large, extended family and the death of a loved one may be our first occasion to experience grief. It may be harder to grieve today than a hundred years ago for those reasons.

If you have reached a point in your grief that you are ready to reach out for support, you may want to understand that there are different types of groups with various dynamics. Here's an overview of mutual support groups presented by grief counselors and therapists at the grief therapy network ACCORD:

A mutual support group. Throughout our lives our need for stability, control, and support remain constant. These needs seem more important during bereavement.

A mutual support group is a gathering of people who need to share a similar experience, interest, or concern. Through their shared experiences comes an atmosphere of acceptance and knowing that their pain does not have to be a solo burden. A special bond develops among the members who help each other find more effective coping strategies.

What happens at a meeting? Groups typically hold regular meetings. They determine their own goals and structures and there is an unwritten code of confidentiality. At a support group organized by a San Diego hospice program, the confidentiality of what goes on in the meetings is discussed each time and participants only use their first names. While not everyone chooses to "bare the soul," it's comforting to know that what is said goes no further than the meeting room. The meetings last between one and three hours and are usually free of charge. (You may want to ask if there is a cost for the session or if a donation is expected, including how much is expected.)

A variation of the following was originally offered by the American Association of Suicidology and may help you understand some general, similar characteristics of various groups. They also suggest various pointers to make your experience more rewarding.

Bitterness imprisons life; love releases it. Bitterness paralyzes life; love empowers it. Bitterness sours life; love sweetens it. Bitterness sickens life; love heals it. Bitterness blinds life; love anoints its eyes....

—Harry Emerson Fosdick, American clergyman, from *Riverside Sermons*

1. The information shared is confidential.
2. You must give yourself a chance. If the first meeting doesn't meet your needs or expectations, give it three more times before you decide whether or not it's right for you.
3. Intensity of emotion is not the only measure of grief. Be careful that you don't compare your feelings with others in the group. Everyone's grief is important and unique to him or her.
4. Everyone in the group warrants time. If you are feeling left out or that you don't have enough time to express what's going on in your life, in your heart and in your mind, ask for it. You can do this over the telephone to the facilitator, or talk to him or her before or after the meeting or during the session.
5. The group needs time to share, too.
6. Be open to help from others in the group, not just the facilitator or leader. Everyone experiences death and grief uniquely, however, you can learn how others have handled or coped with their situations.
7. In addition to accepting suggestions for recovery from others and the group leader, take responsibility for helping yourself find solutions.
8. Adults learn best by hearing the experiences of others, not simply getting advice. The group leader will probably tell what he or she had done in a similar situation, not just what you should do.
9. Share even if you are unhappy about the outcome of some action you've taken. It might help prevent another person in the group from repeating your error or taking your detour.
10. Respect the opinions and experiences of others. What doesn't work for you may be the best advice possible for another group member.
11. Ask questions. If you don't understand, let that be known. Don't point out the faults in another's thinking or actions.

Programs can include group discussion on topics such as loneliness, anger, guilt, changing identity, the stigma of the death, relationships, saying good-bye, and coping strategies. Sharing, study groups, visiting speakers, and other planned activities are sometimes included. There is an atmosphere of friendship, compassion, and acceptance.

Participation is voluntary but everyone is given the opportunity to draw on the strength of the group as needed or to extend strength when possible. The facilitator, often a clergy person or trained counselor, channels the conversations, actively listening to members, asking questions, encouraging them to see that they are making sense of the often disturbing process of grief.

During one of the sessions group leaders may ask participants to bring photos of their loved ones who have died to share in the support group. Why photos? Group members feel alone in their loss partly because no one else knew the deceased. Bringing a picture encourages each to tell the group about the person. It helps the group members feel a deeper sense of other members' loss, it makes the loss more real to the others. It can also provide an affirmation of the relationship with the survivor and the deceased. Additionally, often humorous anecdotes are recounted and valued personality traits are described. Group members can be encouraged to ask any questions they may have about each deceased person as the picture or memento is passed around.

The traumatic death support groups (such as those for survivors of homicide and suicide, for example) are and should be lead by a professional counselor. These groups need the help of a facilitator with specific knowledge of the trauma to help survivors of a violent death.

Some groups have hotline or "help line" services. Others may have a "buddy" or referral system. Many groups publish newsletters and other written materials to help survivors be more aware of the issues and interests of their group.

When is it appropriate to join a support group? There is no set time to begin attending meetings. Some people attend right away after the death of a loved one. Others don't feel comfortable about going until months after the death. This decision is as individual as your grief.

Where can a support group be found? It is important to find a group where the members' interests and concerns are similar to yours. Many groups are listed by subject in the phone directory. The names and phone numbers of many more are available through churches, newspapers, hospitals, local health and social service agencies. The local funeral director is a good source for referrals, too. Check this chapter for the national headquarters for a number of support groups.

When should one stop attending a support group? There is no specific timetable, and no one will say, "Hey, you've been here six months. Isn't it about time you give somebody else that chair?" If you believe you've learned all you can from the group format, talk with the counselor or facilitator. You may want to attend future meetings once a month or every six weeks *or* the counselor may suggest that you seek one-on-one grief therapy.

Where to Get Help

The following names, addresses, and telephone numbers of national support groups can perhaps help you locate the right group for your needs and other survivors in your family:

National Sudden Infant Death Syndrome Resource Center
2070 Chain Bridge Road, Suite 450
Vienna, VA 22182
(703) 821-8955

Sudden Infant Death Syndrome Alliance
1314 Bedford Ave., #210
Baltimore, MD 21208
(410) 653-8226

American Sudden Infant Death Syndrome Institute
2480 Windy Hill Rd., #380
Marietta, GA 30067
(770) 612-8277

Federal SIDS Program, Office of Maternal and Child Health
Bureau of Maternal and Child Health and Resources Development

Parklawn Building, Room #7A13
5600 Fishers Lane
Rockville, MD 20857
(301) 443-2170

National SHARE Office, Infant and Pregnancy Loss
St. Joseph Health Center
300 First Capitol Drive
St. Charles, MO 63301-2893
(800) 821-6819
(636) 947-6164

The Compassionate Friends
National Headquarters
P.O. Box 3696
Oak Brook, IL 60522-3696
(630) 990-0010
(877) 969-0010

Parents of Murdered Children
100 East 8th Street, B-41
Cincinnati, OH 45202
(513) 721-5683
(888) 7818-POMC

THEOS International Headquarters
P. O. Box C
Pasadena, CA 91109-7107
(626) 797-7817

American Cancer Society
1599 Clifton Road, NE
Atlanta, GA 30329
(800) 227-2345

Make Today Count
c/o St. John's Regional Health Center
Mid-America Cancer Center
1235 E. Cherokee
Springfield, MO 65804-2263
(800) 432-2273

The National Hospice and Palliative Care Organization
1700 Diagonal Rd., #625
Alexandria, VA 22314
(703) 837-1500

Hospice Foundation of America
2001 S St. NW #300
Washington, DC 20009
(800) 854-3402

Association for Death Education and Counseling
342 North Main St.
West Hartford, CT 06117-2507
(860) 586-7503

American Heart Association
National Center
7272 Greenville Avenue
Dallas, TX 75231
(800)-AHA-USA-1
(800) 242-8721

American Lung Association®
61 Broadway, 6th Fl.
New York, NY 10006
(212) 315-8700

Grief Recovery Institute
P.O. Box 6061-382
Sherman Oaks, CA 91413
(818) 907-9600

SAVE - Suicide Awareness Voices of Education
7317 Cahill Rd., #207
Minneapolis, MN 55424-0507
(952) 946-7998
(800) 784-2433

Grief and Loss Programs
AARP
601 E St. NW
Washington, DC 20049
(202) 434-2260

NOVA – National Organization for Victim Assistance
1730 Park Rd. NW
Washington, DC 20010
(202) 232-6682
(800) TRY-NOVA

TEENAGE SUPPORT GROUPS

Grief is unique for each of us and in 1984, Teen Age Grief, Inc. (TAG) was founded to offer support to the bereaved teenager in an atmosphere that is safe and familiar. According to Arlene Anthony, executive director of TAG, the reason why teens need specific help is that their lives are lives in transition. Says Anthony: "They are saying good-bye to their childhoods, their emotions are experiencing a 'roller coaster' effect, and their self-images are striving to be established. The teenager is extremely vulnerable to stress. Add to this the loss of a loved one or classmate and frequently you are left with an individual who is frightened, insecure, and isolated....isolated because there are few places a teenager can go for help.

"It is often assumed that because the teenager is young he or she will 'roll with the punches' and come out of the experience relatively unscathed. This is dangerous thinking! Grief must be dealt with head on. If there is no support and closure, unresolved grief will resurface over and over again as new losses are experienced. Unhealthy behavior patterns may develop and grades may drop. Additionally, if the heart is not given permission to grieve, the body may then grieve, manifesting itself in any number of physical symptoms of stress."

Why a group for teens? TAG was formed because most teenagers are uncomfortable with the idea of going to a therapist, period. The fees involved can be prohibitive and there may be times when the teenager does not want to

Faith is a belief in something that cannot be proved. It is a belief in something not yet known as an accomplished fact. Faith includes a sense of possibility, of potentiality, of what might be. Faith is the readiness to live and the conviction and the commitment that by one's life and effort one can help make the possibility into actuality. One should be willing to stake one's life on one's faith.

—Algernon D. Black, leader of ethical humanism

share the idea of therapy with his or her guardian. Therefore TAG meets in schools or other neutral settings such as community centers. It is free of charge to any teen. "In this way," explains Anthony, "The teenager is already familiar with the campus/community facility and feels more comfortable attending the group. When TAG groups meet on campus, the student will not have to find a way to return to school or attend the meetings. It is important that the TAG groups meet on familiar turf where friends and faculty are available for support."

In the TAG groups—which are support groups and not therapy—there are normally one or two adults and the meeting is often cofacilitated by a teenager who is a survivor. TAG's material points out that when teenagers come to the group and show signs of pathological grief, they are referred to professional counselors. "Teen Age Grief not only focuses on loss, but more importantly on new life....the *new life* that comes out of honest confrontation and the willingness to face the future with courage and enthusiasm," assures Anthony.

Where to Get Help

Teenage survivors can talk with counselors at school, a clergy person, or sometimes peer counselors. For more information on TAG, specific books and manuals to help teenage survivors cope, and to contact the group, write:

Teen Age Grief, Inc., TAG
P.O. Box 220034
Newhall, CA 91322-0034
(661) 253-1932

BRIDGING THE GAP IN SELF-HELP

Whether you're eighty or just a quarter of that age, self-help programs can help provide you with confirmation that you are on the right course toward resolution. Yet there are other ways that you, personally, can help yourself move ahead as you live in the weeks and months following the death of a loved one.

Those who are in mourning often ask, "Is one-on-one therapy better, quicker, more confidential?" Self-help groups, in which many members are encouraged to talk through grief, work extremely well. However, they are not a one-size-fits-all recovery plan. Another option which may be best for your needs is individual counseling with a therapist.

Getting personal referrals to a therapist is a good way to begin finding someone with whom you think you can work. Perhaps your family doctor can advise you, too. During your counseling appointment, you will be charged at the therapist's hourly rate. Depending on where you live, that can be from fifty dollars an hour and up. Be sure to check with your health insurance carrier. Some policies may pay for all or a portion of private counseling sessions for yourself and dependent survivors.

Remember that no matter what options for recovery you look into, you will recover at your own speed, in your own time. Isn't it strange how some people still think that there is a certain timetable for grief? A few actually verbalize the myths and wonder why you are still grieving.

It's actually not that unusual for someone (even a survivor) to believe that: If a parent dies, a survivor may grieve for 9.5 months. If a spouse dies, a survivor may grieve 13.2 months. If a baby dies, a survivor may grieve for 19.6 months, and so on.

Grief has been provoked from a traumatic event. Grief is a very biological, physical, and emotional process. Grief is a new state of now, a mind change and a physical change. In actuality, unresolved grief knows no limit and some people carry the intensity of their grief work throughout their lives.

The following "time lines" are suggested by grief therapists to provide encouragement, hope, and a little light at the end of the tunnel in which you might now find yourself.

There are no rights or wrongs for grief work.... grief is a process.

—Sandra L. Graves, Ph.D., A.T.R.

WEEKS ONE THROUGH FOUR
FOLLOWING THE DEATH

You are normal, and what you are feeling is normal. You may still be experiencing shock, disbelief, numbness, anger, devastation, and an "unreal" sense that you're in a nightmare. But while the nightmare continues, you are awake.

During this time, you may have lots of questions about the death, why it happened, and if what you're feeling is similar to those feelings felt by other survivors. Books in your library or local university research center may help you solve some of the questions. National support groups often provide free or low-cost material on the disease or cause of death.

A time to write out your grief: It's often suggested that you keep a journal to record your feelings. Some people buy beautiful, cloth-bound blank books and others use three-ring binders. Some people put their feelings straight into the disks of their personal computers. Often people find a release to feelings by drawing or sketching them. This isn't an art contest and no one will be judging your work—you need not show it to anyone. The method doesn't really matter, it's the process that does.

Therapists recommend writing out your feelings at a certain time every day, at your "worst" time. This is a new ritual.

A time to establish a daily schedule: Although you still may be feeling numb, it's likely a therapist will tell you that going back to work could help. This is likely to occur in the second and third week after the death of a loved one; however, if the death has been traumatic, you will probably need more time. You will not feel like your "old" self at the workplace, but the routine will help provide a feeling of control in a portion of your life.

If you wait too long to return to work, there may be feelings of fear. Only a fool would think it's easy to return to the office or to school. It's going to be hard to face the people. Some will have questions. Some may offer condolences or repeat trite phrases supposed to pacify your aching heart. Some may even ignore the fact that your loved one has died. If this were your first experience with death, would you have known what to say to a coworker when he or she became a survivor? As awful as it is, try to put yourself in your peers' place.

What survivors say is that when they've returned to work or school, to a scheduled atmosphere and begin to concentrate on the work that must be done, they have moments (perhaps even if only a few scant seconds) when things "feel" regular. These times are essential and affirm that there will be new normal times ahead.

For those who are not employed outside the home or are retired, counselors suggest making a schedule. This is the time to get a job, or volunteer so that your volunteer work becomes a job. Even in this distraught state, perhaps you can think back on the things that you had thought, someday I'll do that.

For those who are not employed out of the home, counselors suggest making a chart—from 8:00 A.M. until 8:45 A.M., brisk walk and breakfast; 8:45 A.M. to 9:00 A.M., drive to college; 9:00 A.M. to 12:00 noon, class. What does all this "busy work" do? It provides meaningful activity that gives you the self-confidence to carry on.

Whether your work is in your home or out of it, with a class of ten-year-olds staring at your every move or in a cubicle office tucked away in a vast sea of other cubicles, there may be times when you are tearful, are unable to concentrate, are late for work, or miss appointments. It's okay—remember, in addition to being a survivor, you are a human being and under a hardship right now. Grief is exacting work, so excuse yourself, forgive whatever you think you have done wrong. You may want to physically give yourself a hug or get one from a friend, then continue. Carry on.

A time to maintain a stable environment: Try not to change a thing, primarily your residence during the first weeks after a death. This isn't the time to sell the house, move out of the apartment, junk all the furniture to go live in the woods. Many people who are newly widowed think that they must sell their homes to move into efficient condos or retirement centers. They often regret it, and

Suffering isn't ennobling, recovery is.

—Dr. Christian N. Bernard, heart surgeon and specialist

grieve losing the memories that brought them tears but produced pleasure, too. Your home can be a source of security for you right now when the world is too chaotic. This is especially so if the death involved a crime or was traumatic, unexpected, or sudden. You may desperately need a safe haven to revitalize your life.

A time to renew the bonds with family and friends: Many survivors report how lonely they feel without the companionship of their loved ones, although friends and family of the survivors say they've called and visited and stopped by only to be thwarted in their attempts at closeness. These people sometimes become frustrated when you don't want to come to the party, celebrate a birthday, or even visit for a few minutes over the back fence or on the phone. They may be experiencing grief for the loved one who died, but not in the same way or with as much intensity as you. Or they may not be processing the grief at all. They cannot understand your feelings, and in reality, there is no way we can fathom someone else's emotions.

Call your family and friends back when you need to talk. They're probably waiting patiently to hear from you, yet they may be afraid to call *once more*. Toward the second or third week after the death, say grief experts, you will probably find that your friends, and even a few family members, stop calling as much as they did during the time right after the death. This is normal, especially if you have not reciprocated or taken time to talk. It doesn't mean that they don't care for you or your loved one—they are simply giving you the time and space you need. Keep in mind that when one has had a tragedy, people come together to help and support the immediate needs; when the crisis has subsided, energy is put in other areas.

Those who are also survivors of a previous death may know that after the initial weeks of grief and shock ebb, you need friends and family. Others may not realize that you will continue to need the opportunity to talk about your experience—to debrief the death in order to process the grief. It may be up to you to educate your family and friends, to say, "I need to talk about Dennis and how he was killed. It will help me if you will listen." You can help them by being open about the death, and the feelings around it. You can help them by letting them know you appreciate their using the name of the individual who died, especially a baby who had been named. Thank your friends and family for listening, for asking questions, and for supporting you during this time.

A time for investigating support groups in your area: Some people think you can "fix" grief by getting busy. It's not true. Therefore, many would have you immediately seek out a support group after the death of your loved one, in the first month or so. However, you may not physically have the energy to do so, or be able to stretch your energy any further. You may still be feeling the effects of physical grief. This is quite natural, and do not become alarmed if you're sleeping more or sleeping less. As discussed previously, your body is going through a major change.

Therapists maintain that for some of those who join support groups immediately after the death of their loved ones, the help may not seem worthwhile. The death is still too fresh and with the immediate emotions of shock and denial, survivors may not realize as much from the group as hoped. Sometimes it's more beneficial to wait for awhile after the death to join a support group.

ONE TO SIX MONTHS AFTER THE DEATH

Keeping in mind that there is no specific time or way each of us works through grief, from one to six months after the death of your loved one, you may be ready to:

Search for more information. Continue your search for more complex information on the cause of death. Your need for information is natural and it is a way to gain control of the feelings and experiences of the death. It is an excellent way to cope.

People who are in shock only hear about 10 percent or less of what is said. A few are the opposite, and remember distinctly everything that was said, the people who were there, the color of the clothing someone wore. If either of the reactions are troubling you, take heart because these are normal reactions during the bereavement period.

It is true that grief is a teacher. For awhile it may be our master and a hard one as we learn each lesson. Grief teaches us to find options and to reach within to depths we probably did not want to explore. Grief teaches us compassion so that we may become the guide for others who will follow, for others who need our help to make choices in life, to accept challenge and change as part of living.

—Sandra L. Graves, Ph.D.,
A.T.R.

Everyone who loves is vulnerable to the pain of grief, for love means attachment, and all human attachments are subject to loss. But grief need not, should not, be a destructive emotion....

—Dr. Joyce Brothers,
psychologist

ART THERAPY
by Betty Kronsky, Ph.D.

᚛

For art therapy exercises to provide an accurate mirror of the workings of the mind, it is important to let go of any concern with the quality of the finished product. Any shape or form or line is acceptable. If it proceeds spontaneously from the self, it will reflect the complementarity of conscious and unconscious processes and thus will provide an opportunity for grounding and integration.

Anxiety may be a natural accompaniment of art therapy exercises, especially at the beginning of a session when inhibitions and blocks may be operating.... You may find that this anxiety transforms into energy and excitement when you stay centered.

If you feel that you would be more comfortable pursuing self-help exercises with professional guidance, you may be able to arrange some practice sessions with a registered art therapist in your community. For more information, write The American Art Therapy Association, 1980 Isaac Newton Square, Reston, VA 22090.

Continue to use your journal or sketch pad. Proceed with writing or drawing out your grief during the time you have put aside for sketching.

Dr. Graves, who teaches counselors and clients how to use art to resolve grief, coaches the grieving to add pictures to their journals of what seems important as they relate to the deaths or the people who died. "Tearing or cutting pictures out of magazines and gluing or taping them into your journal can also be helpful, especially if you don't feel comfortable drawing. Many times the visual image is easier for us to work with than the written word."

Make plans. Format intentions and set goals for the next six months. During the next six months, you will be going through some of the most difficult times since the death. It will be a time of many firsts—the first Christmas, the first birthday, the first Valentine's Day since your loved one died. If you have a plan of action, you can ease some of the depression natural to this time of grief.

Dr. Graves says to make up a wish list—don't worry about financial resources or responsibilities. If you've put aside family and friends, children and spouse, or put them off, this is the time to rekindle that closeness. She explains that after you've finished your wish list, "Begin to erase or scratch out the impossible dreams. Be careful, though, that you are not overlooking alternatives available to you. Be creative in your thinking."

Your next step is to narrow down your plan to two or three realistic things you can do within the next six months to one year. "Take out a calendar and mark down the dates when you will accomplish part of your goal. Then set your goal date. You may not be able to make your exact deadline, but it gives you something to aim for. Having a deadline will provide some sense of security and control when you need it."

Get your "house in order." Update your will, make your own prearrangements for your funeral, write or rewrite your letter of instructions so that your wishes are carried out specifically as you desire after your death. During these months you have confronted one of America's most dreaded fear: death. It is now time to make a portion of the pain positive by setting your own "house in order." Confront these issues, write a will, including a living will. Planning for your eventual death will provide a feeling of control.

SIX MONTHS TO ONE YEAR AFTER THE DEATH

You may now be ready to talk about and read more about grief. By understanding what you and others in your family have been through, you will be better able to grow from the experience.

It's okay if you still need to be gentle with yourself. You need to know that it's natural to still feel depressed and often tired. By reading about grief and the grieving process this will reaffirm that you're okay.

Even though you may feel more terrible than you thought possible, most likely it will not get worse. You won't have to go through the intensity of grief for this loved one again. Grief is a process without an actual end. Why is that? It is extraordinarily hard to let go of someone we love, to say good-bye, to know life will never be the same again. Thus, the grief process is at the phase of resistance. And while you may say a final farewell, you will always have the memories of this person. From the pain comes a new beginning—not better, but new.

Keep your "wish list" handy. During these months, refer back to the goals and your wish list. You may feel like you're on automatic pilot, without a quest and, if so, revise your goals. Set long goals and break them down into small, workable fragments.

Continue to rely on the secret or not-so-secret plans you made. During these second six months after the death of your loved one, rely on the plans you made. It is your road map—but it's okay to take a detour, too, if something interests and excites you.

AFTER THE FIRST YEAR

You've made incredible progress. The first-year anniversary of the death of your loved one is a landmark. You've made it through holidays, Sundays, birthdays, lots of days. Experts agree that you must celebrate your success,

AN AUTOBIOGRAPHY IN FIVE CHAPTERS
Author anonymous

&

Chapter 1
I walk down the street.
There is a deep hole in the sidewalk.
I fall in.
I am lost.... I am helpless
It isn't my fault.
It takes forever to find a way out.

Chapter 2
I walk down the same street.
There is a deep hole in the sidewalk.
I pretend I don't see it.
I fall in, again.
I can't believe I am in this same place.
But it isn't my fault.
It still takes a long time to get out.

Chapter 3
I walk down the same street.
There is a deep hole in the sidewalk.
I see it is there.
I fall in.... it's a habit.... but my eyes are open.
I know where I am.
It is my fault.
I get out immediately.

Chapter 4
I walk down the same street.
There is a deep hole in the sidewalk.
I walk around it.

Chapter 5
I walk down a different street.

FORGIVENESS

by Robin Casarjian, Ph.D.,
psychotherapist

ଏ୬

The psychological case for forgiveness is overwhelmingly persuasive. Not to forgive is to be imprisoned by the past, by old grievances that do not permit life to proceed with new business. Not to forgive is to yield oneself to another's control. If one does not forgive, then one is controlled by the other's initiatives, and is locked into a sequence of action, a response of outrage and revenge. The present is overwhelmed and devoured by the past. Those who do not forgive are those who are least capable of changing the circumstances of their lives. In this sense, forgiveness is a shrewd and practical strategy for a person or a nation to pursue, for forgiveness frees the forgiver.

and incorporate that feeling into celebrating with the memory of your loved one.

On the anniversary of the day your loved one died, you may want to set aside time to grieve, light a candle in his or her honor, or add a special entry into your journal. You may want to visit the cemetery or talk with friends.

One woman spent time on the first anniversary of the day her twin sister was killed by running on the beach (something they loved doing together) and then entertaining a few close friends for dinner. For dessert, she made a Bavarian chocolate cake with a gooey cherry filling (her sister's favorite). Later when she was alone, she framed a lovely photograph of the two of them together just before the homicide occurred. Yes, she cried as she knew she would, and she also knew these would not be the last of the tears, but finally she tucked the photo under her pillow and slept. The next morning, with a bittersweet pleasure that the memories of her twin and those reflected in that photograph would always be part of her life, she kissed the likeness of her sister, placed the photograph on the mantel, and left for work.

During the second year, you will probably experience some of the same feelings you had during the first year after the death of your loved one. You may have thought that when you lived through the first anniversary of the date that he or she died, you could leave all the grief behind. But it's not true because the grief becomes part of our essence as people.

With each experience, each reflection, each memory of your loved one, the days will become easier to examine. After the first year, while you'll still feel the intense sting of grief from time to time—it may feel just as terrible—it will no longer be felt with surprise. You have had the feelings before. There will be a period, too, when you will not be grieving and you may have twinges of guilt because you've forgotten to grieve. This is part of the resolution.

Dr. Graves says, "As the months and years go on, you will find that you are a special part of the population. You are among others whose grief has given them a better appreciation of life."

BAD GRIEF

Even though grief is a tremendously painful, bleeding gash in every sense we have, as humans we move through it in phases as discussed by Dr. Elisabeth Kübler-Ross. If there is such a thing as "good grief," that is, the type that eventually meets with resolution, what about "bad grief"? Therapists say that while almost anything is normal during the initial stages of grief, from violence to drastic changes in behavior, over a period of weeks and months the behavior of individuals should return to most of the characteristics shown before the death.

While different people may experience various intensities or combinations of the following, some of the most common consequences of avoidance and "bad grief" patterns are:

- Deterioration in relationships with friends and family
- Symptoms of chronic physical illness, either real or imagined
- Symptoms of chronic depression, sleeping difficulties, and low self-esteem
- Symptoms of chronic anxiety, agitation, restlessness, and difficulty concentrating

Anytime we, as grievers, feel that we are confused, regardless of the intensity of the confusion over grief, then an expert's advice or listening ear can probably help. One counselor compares grief therapy to a long road trip, something like driving to an unknown part of the country. Let's say you want to drive to Bangor, Maine, but you don't know which roads to take, so you continue down that open stretch of freeway and get lost. You could miss Maine completely; you could end up in Miami. Or you could stop every now and then to ask directions or look at a map. You could write down a few instructions and you'd eventually find your destination; A survivor may need only a single session to find that destination; another may need more than one "glance at a map." Not everyone needs session after session of grief therapy; sometimes all that's needed is

Gently care for yourself. Be as tender toward yourself as you would hope to be toward others. You need not feel apologetic because your pain makes you the center of your own attention. Now as at no other time, you are your most cherished possession and your own richest resource.

–Joe Healy,
Executive Director
THEOS

to know that you're on the right road, heading in the right direction. Remember, there is no timetable for grief to be processed or reconciled; we each move at our own speed.

Where to Get Help

The following are a few books and publications that can help during this time of grief. Often at the back of the books are lists of recommended reading or bibliographies which can assist in your search for more information.

Bereavement Magazine
Bereavement Publishing, Inc.
4765 North Carefree Circle
Colorado Springs, CO 80917-2118
(888) 60-4HOPE (4673)

Caring Concepts Newsletter
Centering Corporation
7230 Maple St.
Omaha, NE 68134
(402) 553-1200

The Healing Power of Humor by Allen Klein (Los Angeles: Jeremy P. Tarcher Publishers, 1989) is a warm, entertaining look at the way humor has the potency to heal mentally and physically, especially during the period of bereavement. Klein has personal experience with the death of his beloved wife, Ellen, which clearly colors this highly recommended book.

GETTING "UNSTUCK"

Dr. Ann Kaiser Stearns, author of *Coming Back: Rebuilding Lives After Crisis and Loss*, who holds a doctorate in clinical psychology with clinical training in pastoral counseling services, talks about strategies for becoming "unstuck" in a stressful mode after a death or a crisis.

She explains, "The following guidelines can help you take some positive action in order to regain a degree of control in your situation," and recommends that attempting even just a few of the concepts will give you a more extensive feeling of personal strength, confidence, and faith for the future.

To those who are rebuilding after the loss of any kind, including the death of a loved one, some of the suggestions Dr. Stearns recommends are:

- Make a conscious effort to identify what is *not* making sense to you about your loss or crisis. You might ask yourself: What is it about the situation and/or about his or her death that is most puzzling or troubling me? What part of grief is troubling me? What other things are troubling me? Write down your questions. Leave space to jot responses.
- Put a name to the emotions you are feeling as precisely as possible. Hurt? Anger? Shame? Guilt? Regret? Yearning? Are you wondering, why me? Labeling your emotions will cause them to lose much of their power.
- Specific actions promote healing. Ask yourself what actions in the past were helpful to get you moving.
- Confide in someone. Be sure to choose someone who is a good listener and a nonjudgmental, caring, positive individual.
- Search out the opinion of an expert or professional who is knowledgeable about problems like yours—a doctor, clergy person, social worker, financial advisor, or lawyer. You want someone who is qualified to address your particular concerns and human characteristics. If you must get advice from an expert lacking in such human qualities, take a caring friend along with you to humanize the encounter.
- Look for books that pertain to your situation, or ask your physician, counselor, or clergy person to

WHEN WE DREAM ABOUT THE LOVED ONE WHO DIED
by Sherry Williams, R.N., founder of ACCORD

Dreams can be understood in a number of ways. Human beings must dream to keep healthy. We don't always remember our dreams, however. When we do, they sometimes are easily read and sometimes very confusing. The things we dream about are often combinations of events from the past, current experiences, and symbols for our thoughts, fears, and anxieties.

After the death of a loved one the body chemistry has been altered substantially. It affects sleep patterns and dream cycles. Many people find themselves waking up several times during the night.

Some people dream about the person who has died, others do not. Sometimes our dreams are frightening and we experience nightmares, or those things that we fear the most. Some dreams are violent and reflect our own inner sense of being violated by the death.

Dreams can recall the physical relationship that has been lost. In dreams we can do what is not possible during our waking hours, such as see and hear the loved one. Our deepest wishes are thus granted in our dreams.

Sometimes dreams help us discover things that need to be talked about, and by focusing on the things that bother us the most, the healing can begin.

DISPELLING FIVE COMMON MYTHS ABOUT GRIEF

by Alan D. Wolfelt, Ph.D., director of the Center for Loss and Life Transition

≈

Being surrounded by people who believe in these myths invariably results in a heightened sense of isolation and aloneness in the grieving person.

Myth #1: Grief and mourning are the same experience. There is an important distinction between them. We have learned that people move toward healing not just by grieving, but through mourning, the actuality of the grief.

Myth #2: There is a predictable and orderly stage-like progression to the experience of mourning. That stage-like thinking about both dying and mourning has been appealing to many people. We understand that different people die in different ways, and likewise, each person mourns in his or her own way, too.

Myth #3: It is best to move away from grief instead of toward it. Many grievers, unfortunately, do not give themselves permission or receive permission from others to mourn, to express their feelings. We continue to live in a society that often encourages people to prematurely move away from

recommend reading material. Throughout this book are self-help and inspirational books that have made a difference to many people who are grieving; your local library or bookstore has more.

• Bring more order into your life. There's a great scene in the old movie classic, *I Remember Mama*, that illustrates this. For a child who is near death, Mama plots how she will enter the hospital ward that is off-limits to all visitors. She begins to bring order to her life by feverishly scrubbing the wooden floor of their tenement. And with the physical task and order being restored she comes up with a solution....she poses as a scrub lady and sneaks in.

Scrubbing the floor may be inappropriate for you, although it may help you feel better to simply straighten up the house, clean out the garage, balance your checkbook, pay the bills, return books to the library, sort a desk drawer, or accomplish other practical tasks. While there are certain stressful events over which you have little control, it is especially important to take charge in other ways.

• Take a positive action that will lead to a better understanding of your situation or help to resolve some lingering troublesome feelings. For example, write a letter, speak to a particular person, make a necessary decision. If you only make one necessary decision a day, you will feel an immediate sense of control returning to your life.

• Take a good look at the positive qualities that have gotten you this far in life and will carry you the rest of the way. What long-standing strengths and new perspectives will enable you to go forward? How did you handle or cope with other traumatic times? Can you apply these same coping techniques to the death of your loved one?

• Make plans for the future. Start to reinvolve yourself in life. If the big things, like going back to college, seem impossible, start small. Pick up a catalogue, study it, and circle the classes you'd like to take or the majors you'd like to investigate. Another small step would be to take a workshop or sit in on a class you might be interested taking next term.

Aid your own survival by doing something of benefit or helpfulness to others. Also you can do something for yourself, something you've always wanted to do.

DOCTOR HUGS TELLS HOW TO EMBRACE LIFE

A great day, says Greg Risberg, a.k.a., "Doctor Hugs," is when you get a dozen hugs. Traveling around the country talking about the power of touch, especially the hugging kind, Risberg has a lot of great days.

"Many of us don't touch even when we feel like it and when the time would be appropriate. When was the last time you hugged your best friend just for the sheer pleasure of it? What about your children? Colleagues? Spouse?" asks Risberg, a social worker, educator, and author in Elmhurst, Illinois, a suburb of Chicago.

Touch is withheld for many reasons. "Some people hold back because they've been taught that touching others isn't 'proper.' Others enjoy it so much they become slightly afraid of it—the old 'too much pleasure must be sinful' idea." Still others are caught in feeling that to admit a need for touch is to admit a need for other people. That admission makes them feel weak or silly, and nobody wants to appear vulnerable—especially men.

Obviously, there can be "bad" touches, the type that is controlling and abusing. "In good touch, it feels like someone has given a gift. In bad touch, it's as if something has been taken from you."

Risberg continues. "Touching can be silly." In fact, we hope it is playful some of the time because that's half the fun!" Risberg believes that the overriding reason people hold back is the fear of being rejected. "The fear of rejection is complicated and it is affected by how we were raised, the experiences we've had, and how we feel about ourselves. If

their grief instead of toward it. The result is that many people either grieve in isolation or attempt to run away from their grief.

Myth #4: Following the death of a loved one, the goal is to "get over" your grief. We've all heard it, "Are you over it yet?" Or the even cruder comment, "Well, now, shouldn't he be over it by now?" To think we "get over" our grief is preposterous. For the mourner to assume that life will be exactly as it was prior to the death is unrealistic and potentially damaging.

Myth #5: Tears expressing grief are only a sign of weakness. Unfortunately, many people associate tears of grief with personal inadequacy and weakness. Yet crying is nature's way of releasing internal tension in the body and allows the mourner to communicate a need to be comforted.

Only when we as a society are able to dispel these myths of grief will grieving people experience the healing they deserve!

we can deal with our fear of rejection, we can expand and enrich our lives."

Risberg says, "One of the times in our lives when we need touch is when we're grieving. Touch that is given in comfort is one of the most allowed kinds. The value of touch to the grieving person can't be measured and we all know how it can relieve despair, depression, and the feelings of loneliness and isolation that accompany grief.

"At times all of us may have difficulty meeting our touching needs, but for those who are widowed, alone, or feel alone especially after the death of a loved one, it can be a touchy problem." He believes that a touch can be a matter of self-affirmation and a confidence builder, too, explaining these theories in his book, *Touch: A Personal Workbook.*

"We must remember that touch affirms us. It lets us know that we are somebody. Touch can ease the pain of loneliness and can hasten the healing of grief. Receiving touch from caring friends can help those who have gone through a separation (from death or divorce) to feel worthy of love and affection from others. They also need to know that others believe in them and care enough to want a touching relationship with them."

What can people who are alone or feel that way do to increase the amount of nonsexual touching in their lives? What steps can they take on their own behalf to enrich their lives through touch? Risberg has several ideas to try:

- Approach a friend with whom you would like to share more touch and say, "I'd like to hug you more often. I don't want to wait until I need comforting."
- Arrange to spend more time with family members who are "high-touchers," that is, people who routinely touch others.
- Pick new friends partly on the basis of how much warmth is projected. Seek out sincere, high-touch people.
- Go dancing. If you don't know how, learn and touch at the same time.
- Get a massage on a regular basis. The benefits of massage are many and it is a way of saying, "Taking

care of myself is important and the expense is worth it."
- Become a volunteer. The disabled, the elderly, and children need a helping, caring touch.

Risberg quickly explains, "These aren't empty suggestions that sound good on paper. They are workable and beneficial. For example, dancing is great exercise which promotes a sense of controlling one's self and is very healthy. Massage reduces stress. Both are very important as we move on to resolve grief." He says you don't have to stick with just one suggestion, but try them all or as many as you need. He also offers that some of those he's talked with find that touch is a habit.

Research indicates, Risberg explains, that there are over three thousand types of hugs and for his purposes, he's narrowed that field down to a well-defined Seven Basic Hugs, from the least intimate to "downright friendly." He says, "There is much more to the importance of touching than a 'hug-fad' would indicate. Let's always remember that we can touch with our eyes, hands, feet, hearts, and voices, too. Have you ever heard a song that 'touched your heart' or saw a movie that was 'touching'?"

Risberg teaches all Seven Basic Hugs, illustrating how many different kinds of hugs we can give and receive.

- *Hug #1–The A-Frame Hug*: Two people are touching at the shoulders. Sometimes they are patting each other's back. Their rear ends are out. The A-Frame Hug is considered a "safe" hug that is nonsexual.
- *Hug #2–The One-Sided Hug*: Done along with the A-Frame, but the two people are touching one side of each of their chests.
- *Hug #3–The Two-Sided Hug*: Here people are touching both sides of their chests, but usually the lower part of their bodies are still sticking out.
- *Hug #4*: People are drawing closer and holding tighter. Usually their bellies are touching, too.
- *Hug #5*: The lower half of the body is drawing closer now.
- *Hug #6*: Now they're touching down to their knees.

- *Hug #7*: Everything is touching now, and the two people are smiling and happy. This is generally a joyous embrace.

Risberg says it's never too late to learn to hug. "Several years ago my father was taken to the emergency room and I was told over the telephone that he wasn't expected to live more than a few minutes. I raced to the hospital and miraculously he was still breathing. I held his face in my hands and told him I loved him. It had been so long since I'd said that. He opened his eyes and in a weak, hoarse voice, he said, 'Yeah, I love you, too.'

"We had a second miracle that day. My dad rallied, and not only didn't he die then, he went on to live seven more years. That moment in the hospital made me realize how much I cared about him. I began telling him that I'd like to give him a hug when I came to see him and give him another one when I left. He thought it was strange, but he indulged me.

"One day, I was rushed and started to leave his house without exchanging our hug. But he followed me out of the door and called, 'Hey! Hey! You forgot that thing—you know, that thing you like to do.' He'd never been able to remember what to call it, but he missed our good-bye hug and came after me to get it. So when people ask me if it's ever too late to learn to touch I say, 'If a seventy-six-year-old Swede can become a hugger, anyone can!' "

ॐ

While a hug can't cure everything, it can go a long way to make you feel better when it's given with love and compassion after the death of a loved one. But what happens when something so very personal as a loved one's death becomes front-page news? In chapter 6, we'll talk about the specifics of death becoming a media event and how to cope when the public invades at a time when all you may want is to be alone in your grief and sorrow.

Additionally, like many who have become survivors of the deaths of their loved ones, you may find yourself willingly in the role of spokesperson, activist, or lobbyist. Thus, we'll also provide information on how to give print and television interviews.

Chapter

When Death Becomes a Media Event

We've all seen it. There's a terrible accident and the survivors, witnesses, and spectators are thrown in the middle of what might feel like a publicly viewed circus. Their eyewitness reports seem to be broadcasted around the globe faster than you and I can even switch channels. Sometimes that's good— we need to keep abreast of what's happening in the world. Sometimes, grief-numbed families and survivors are too overcome to make sense of the horror they've just witnessed.

Or it happens closer to home....in your own living room. First there was the traumatic death of your loved one, so needless, so unexpected. Then you had to cope with the arrangements of a funeral or service. Finally, and without any warning, the media jumps in and, suddenly, what should have been a family affair with tears shed in privacy is now splashed across the front of the morning newspaper.

Today almost any death can become a media event. That fact is made clear by the nightly news and through the "insider"-style television shows that reenact the tragedy, murder, or crime. Whether we agree or not, death is news.

This chapter's focus is on what happens when the death of your loved one changes from personal moments of grief to a public event. The chapter provides information on catastrophic accidents, deaths of our heroes, and celebrity deaths. Why is it that the death of someone we only know from television or magazines may have such a profound effect? Why do people still grieve for Patsy Cline, Elvis Presley, Malcolm X, and John Kennedy? Additionally, because so many survivors become activists and/or need to speak publicly about their ordeal, public relations experts will advise us on how to talk with the press, inform the media, and meet with television reporters and other journalists.

Since the death of any loved one is a difficult event, it is logical that our faith in a Higher Power can reach a low or nonexistent point in our lives. Rev. Diane Cole Veazey talks about a crisis in spirituality which may make some sense out of the disaster in which you're currently involved.

THE PUBLIC ORDEAL OF A VIOLENT CRIME

When a loved one dies, the family and friends—the survivors—go through a period of intense grief. When a child or other loved one is murdered or involved in another form of violent crime, the anger, guilt, and confusion are complicated by the realization that another person intentionally took the life of someone who was loved. Parents of Murdered Children and Other Survivors of Homicide Victims (POMC) is one of the national network groups that intervenes in support of the family.

Nancy Ruhe, executive director of POMC, says, "We have found that losing a loved one to murder is one of the most difficult experiences anyone ever has to face. Part of what makes it so difficult is that few people know what it's like and many don't want to talk about it, so we go through the pain relatively alone, wondering if our feelings and reactions are normal and whether we will ever find meaning to life again."

Adding to the family's trauma, point out POMC's members, are intrusions into their grief. Police, lawyers, and other members of the criminal justice system need information, evidence, and testimony. Television and newspaper reporters focus upon the victim and the grieving family. When a suspect is apprehended, preliminary hearings, postponements, trials, and sentencing all force grieving families to face what seems to be a lack of justice. In situations where the murder is unsolved or lack of evidence prevents an arrest, family members are emotionally forced to make their own closure. In either case, there is additional pain.

POMC not only helps the family and other survivors cope with the pain and move forward toward resolution of the grief, but also helps with the justice system, too. Ruhe and others at POMC explain that the staff of the national office of POMC writes or phones any survivor and if possible, they link the survivor with others in the same vicinity who have survived their loved one's homicide.

St. Paul resident and president of the POMC Minnesota Hope chapter Dick Barrett explains that while some parents contact the chapters, "Generally, we receive the survivors' names from funeral homes or perhaps through the police. We simply send a sympathy card and place their names on our newsletter mailing list." When his and wife Beverly's son Dennis was murdered eight years ago, Dick says it took him four months to even say the word "murder." The anger consumed all his energy, with none to spare for support groups. "I was awfully angry and frustrated." But when he could reach out, POMC was there.

"When there is a murder, survivors often believe that they are guilty," says Barrett. "They should have been watching their children, should have done this or done that....and the should ofs or if onlys make them feel worse." Also, since murder is grist for the media mill, sometimes the dynamics of the family are questioned in the press and even in court when the case is tried. "When the parents already feel guilty and shameful for somehow being neglectful people—although in reality it's not true—

THE TRAVELING MEMORIAL WALL

❧

So that our loved ones are not forgotten, say members of Parents of Murdered Children and Other Survivors of Homicide Victims, the Memorial Wall travels throughout the United States. The Memorial Wall consists of plaques made of solid walnut, 20"x30", each holding 120 brass plates which are inscribed with a loved one's name, date of birth, and date of death. It is publicly displayed as a reminder of how the world has been impoverished by their passing.

the parents easily become victims, too. We've seen this when old friends turn away after a child has been murdered. And the fact that the personal support system crumbles leaves the parents with substantiation that they are partially responsible for the homicide. It's as if the parents have some horrendous contagious disease and others might catch it by associating.

"Therefore, when the media is involved, the parents are already feeling frustrated and angry at themselves, the judicial system, and the alleged murderer. Suddenly they have no one to turn to. No one really understands. That's the compassionate role of members of POMC. We do understand. And we've all been there."

In addition to talking and supporting grieving, frustrated, and disillusioned survivors, POMC staff is available to provide individual assistance, support, and advocacy. Once hooked into the POMC network, survivors can communicate with professionals to assist in the grief process as well as the judicial process.

Like other advocacy groups, POMC was founded by survivors. There are currently well over forty thousand family members, and all except three are strictly volunteer. In 1978, Charlotte and Bob Hullinger of Cincinnati, Ohio, started the group three months after their daughter Lisa died from injuries inflicted by her former boyfriend. Father Ken Czillinger, a Roman Catholic priest active in leading support groups for the bereaved, directed the Hullingers to others whose children had been murdered. Through the shared support both personally and through supporting denial of early release for the convicted murderers, the group is united together.

An editorial in the June 1992 issue of the POMC newsletter *Survivors* gives more than any explanation of what this support group does:

"Leslie Allen Williams is an alleged serial killer molded out of the inadequacies of the Michigan criminal justice system. The story told here plays out again and again in every courtroom and with every parole board in every state in America.

"In 1971 Leslie Allen Williams was convicted of attempted burglary, but he was released from prison early. In 1973 he was convicted of burglary and given another prison sentence. Again, he was released early. In 1976 he was convicted of rape, sentenced to fourteen to twenty-five years in prison, and released early. In 1983 Williams was convicted of assault, kidnapping, assault to commit rape, and being a habitual offender. These crimes were committed *just fourteen days* after he was released early from the 1976 sentence. This time he was sentenced to five to ten years for assault and kidnapping and seven to thirty years for being a *habitual offender*. On August 15, 1990, Williams was paroled after a favorable recommendation from a therapist.

"On May 24, 1992, Williams was arrested after he allegedly assaulted and abducted a woman from a local cemetery. It was during this arrest that he confessed to the murders of four teenage girls and the rape of a nine-year-old girl, crimes he committed between September 1991 and January 1992. Once again he is being held for trial.

"Each time Williams was released his subsequent crimes became more serious in nature. If the parole board had been doing its job—if Williams had been required to service his prescribed sentences and if he had not been released early time and again—these four young women would be alive today.

"For two years now POMC has been struggling against this tide of criminal justice apathy. Our Truth in Sentencing Program has kept sixty-five violent offenders off the streets of America, with many more parole hearings still pending. Our success confirms that every signature and every letter counts and that we can make a difference.

"It's time our nation's parole boards start taking seriously their number-one priority of protecting society and stop handing down these deadly decisions of early release. It's time to keep these violent offenders in prison where they belong."

"Because our nation's parole boards do not adhere to

the original length or terms of the murderer's original sentencing, there is no truth in the sentencing. It is not unusual for a convicted murderer who is given three life sentences to come up for early parole in *eight years.* Thus, the criminal element has a stronghold in this country. If criminals are not held accountable, no one in our society is safe."

Where to Get Help

For more information on becoming a part of a national support group, refer to the index and/or Parents of Murdered Children and a local chapter near you and for national as well as local victim assistance:

Parents of Murdered Children
100 E. 8th Street, Suite B-41
Cincinnati, OH 45202
(513) 721-5683

For resource and research data, including computer-based information, contact:

Office for Victims of Crime Resource Center
National Criminal Justice Reference Service
P.O. Box 6000
Rockville, MD 20849–6000
(800) 627–6872

WHEN THE PUBLIC INVADES A PRIVATE DEATH

Not too long ago, on her afternoon talk show, Oprah interviewed the children of Betty Broderick. Until disaster struck, Broderick was just another ex-wife, a neighbor you might meet at a club or supermarket or wave to pulling out of the driveway in the morning. This person who seemed to be just like you and I is serving a prison term for murdering her former husband, the children's father, and his new wife. Death can invade any life, and in this case has touched the children, relatives, and friends of the Brodericks.

When a Murderer Becomes a "Celebrity"

As Dick and Beverly Barrett and others involved in POMC will attest to, there are times when alleged murderers become some sort of deviant celebrities or folk heroes. "There is immense anger and personal frustration," reports one parent of POMC, "seeing the story of our child's killer as a somewhat sympathetic character on a made-for-television movie."

Others report that there is an incredible feeling of injustice when a killer financially profits from the sale of movie rights and books. Yet through the legal systems, these things are acceptable; in the current trend of "shock television shows," this is becoming more common.

Depending on the circumstances, the news and the media can intrude even in the most orderly lives when death becomes an event. Not all interviews are of the sensational type. Often survivors speak out against the issue or reason that their loved ones have died. The survivor becomes an activist and lobbies against the cause of death. In order to be as prepared as possible, you need to know what happens during an interview and when the media becomes involved.

TALKING WITH THE PRESS

When dealing with the media, if possible, plan out what you are going to say. Melba Beals, public relations expert in San Francisco, California, and author of *Expose Yourself* says, "Simply treat the reporter as the person he or she is: someone to whom you have recently been introduced. Don't for one moment believe that because this person is charming, wonderful, and delightful, he or she is your long-lost friend. Absolutely not. You know nothing about the reporter, but perhaps the reporter knows everything about you."

Beals explains that when giving interviews and talking to the media, "Firmly usher your interviewer away from the issue you find offensive. Hold the line with a gentle smile—and silence, if necessary. Nothing fuels a reporter's urge to dig into your background more than saying 'no comment' or 'I don't want to talk about that.'" She says, "It's like shooting off a gun and declaring the beginning of a war you are not likely to win. If you remain calm, you can arrest the reporter's urgent hunch that there is something to be uncovered by digging into your business. Behave as though you are undaunted, even when the question asked scrapes your very soul."

Diane Gage, president and managing partner of the San Diego-based Gage Group, and author of *Self-Marketing Secrets: Winning by Making Your Name Known*, says, "Don't use the 'no comment' strategy. Instead provide the information you do have and be as up front as possible. At the very least, tell the media you will get back to them as soon as more information becomes available. This is your best chance of coming through the emergency in a forthright way while controlling damage and not making a bad situation worse."

Herbert Schmertz, author of *Good-bye to the Low Profile*, says that the press wants substance, and they want facts, but "when they can't get substance, they'll settle for color." He goes on with an example of just how that worked with Hubie Brown, football coach and a master of turning the press around. When the New York Knicks were on a bad losing streak, a reporter cornered Brown and demanded, "What changes do you see in the lineup?"

Brown's expression became wise and knowing. "Well," he responded, "We'll have to see how the bagels taste tomorrow."

Schmertz provides alternatives to "no comment" with:

- I won't even accept the question.
- That question is unanswerable.
- The premise behind your question is so erroneous that I can't possibly give you an answer.
- To answer that question I'd have to do all your research for you.

When the death of a loved one concerns a crime, legal experts recommend consulting with your attorney before you make any statements to the press. If and when the criminal is captured or on trial for the crime concerning your loved one (or if your loved one was killed during a crime) what you say may be used as evidence.

In the language of public relations experts, this is called crisis communication or crisis control. Public relations specialists Stan Sauerhaft and Chris Atkins, both with the giant PR firm of Burson-Marsteller USA, authors of *Image Wars*, advise, "If the reporter's line of questions comes as a shock to you, don't shoot from the hip in return. Tell them you'll get back to them as soon as you have had time to review the situation—then start digging."

In Black and White—a Print Interview

If the death of your loved one becomes local, state, or national news, you and others in your family may suddenly be thrown into a media frenzy, a public circus of an event that most see best handled alone. While you may shake your head and swear this will never happen to you, "not in our family!" it can.

There are several ways, according to journalists and those who mould the images of personalities, that you can talk with the press.

On the record: Whatever you say can be quoted directly, in any context and in any way. And if it's spicy, provocative, or catchy, it probably will be. "He was such a dirty, low-down so-and-so!" "We'll miss her terribly, except for that gosh-awful habit she had of cracking her knuckles." The cue here is to watch what you say. And if you don't feel really comfortable revealing a tidbit about your loved one, don't. The default assumption with "on the record" is that unless you instruct the reporter otherwise, it is assumed that what you say can be quoted or included in the interview.

Off the record: This is for information that you are telling the reporter that he or she may not use. Off the record doesn't work retroactively. Let's say that you've just said that your loved one, Jane Smith, the financial wizard of Wall Street, deserved to die because she owed you $2 million. Suddenly you realize the words that have come from your mouth and quickly try to remedy the situation by saying, "Oh, you're not going to say that, are you?" Most likely your complete statement will include scandalous prattle of that unpaid debt.

Do not credit or quote: The reporter may use the

information but not quote you or attribute it to you. "It was said that Jane Smith died having owed a considerable sum of money to family members, reports a close connection to the deceased," the article may say.

This is the type of quote often seen in the tabloids when the quote is attributed to "a friend of the family," "a former roommate," or "someone who was at the event."

It will be up to you to make it very clear to the news person that you do not want to be quoted, nor credited with the information. And that you do not want your name used. The journalist may or may not accept the statement you provide as truth since you refuse to take credit for it. Journalists want facts, not hearsay or rumors.

Background information: In a print interview you can provide a printed description of your view of the death, with any details you'd like to bring out. This will not guarantee that the reporter or the newspaper/magazine will use the material, but it will give you a better chance to have your view stated as you wish. This type of information is referred to when you see, "According to family friends, Jane Smith had at one time amassed a fortune only to lose it just last month by investing in highly speculative stock."

If you know you will be interviewed, it makes sense to consult with your attorney, if applicable, write out some background information (keeping a copy for yourself), and rehearse the interview (see this chapter for tips on interviews when you have a message you want to get out). You can even write down all the questions the reporter may ask—even outlandish ones so that you will be prepared and avoid saying something inopportune.

"60 Minutes" Called.... The Television Interview

Somehow your loved one's death has become news and as a survivor your comments are newsworthy. Perhaps she pulled three children out of a burning building and perished while trying to get the fourth. Perhaps he had a heart attack, died, and the plane he was flying crashed into a school. Perhaps your loved one died of a suicide and now headlines in your local paper shout that there is implication of embezzlement of business funds. Any scenario is possible, few of us are immune to embarrassment or disgrace, and there is really nothing new under the sun.

Now one of the television investigative news shows has called and their reporters want to talk with you, maybe even do a segment on the death. Suddenly it would seem that you'll be on television—a famous star, or shown as a contributor, somehow, to the cause of the death. What should you do? If you have yet to talk with an attorney about what you should and shouldn't say, you may want to seek legal counsel now.

D. Wayne Brechtel, an attorney with extensive background in the criminal justice system, in private practice in Solana Beach, California, says that as a general rule, he wouldn't recommend that clients talk to the media about the death. "There's no law against it, but I wouldn't advise it. You don't want the case to be tried by the press." And after there has been a verdict in the case, you may want to withhold comments until you and your attorney are absolutely certain that everything is settled. "Hold off appearances on the investigative reporting shows," says Brechtel. "There may be an appeal that would throw the case back in court and in the public eye of the media."

After receiving the telephone call from a television producer, the producer's staff member, or someone on a news program, it's acceptable to say, "You've caught me at a very busy time. May I call you back in ten minutes?" Then, depending on your circumstances, quickly talk with your attorney or other counselor.

Public relations guru Herbert Schmertz provides a checklist of advice for anyone being interviewed by a television news show. Although he consults with businesses, the advice is sound for any individual who must face the camera.

He cautions that you should take copious notes on everything that is being discussed with the television show representative. And he suggests that you keep a written record of the questions you're asking as well as the responses—even if you do not get a response to every question.

Media interview? Follow the scout's motto and be prepared. It doesn't matter if you have a doctorate on the subject, the power of the media can bring on a severe case of amnesia....

—Diane Gage,
public relations expert

According to Schmertz, some of the questions you may want to ask before saying yes to an interview are:

- Exactly what is the segment about?
- What is the thesis? What will you be centering on? What's to be covered during the segment?
- Who else will you be interviewing? Why?
- Who is the producer and reporter for the segment?
- How long will the interview last?
- Will you be introducing any documents or evidence that are not commonly known?
- Would you be willing to write a letter confirming what your interview will include and the thesis of the segment?
- Will you allow me to talk with the producer or reporter, well beforehand, to explain any background concerning the death that you will want to clarify?
- When will the show air?

You can also ask questions as to why the show's representative has called you and what he or she hopes to illustrate in the segment. Another question you have to consider, says Schmertz, is if you decline to be interviewed or do not want to be part of the show, will they do the segment without you? If they do that, what will be the consequences?

Schmertz shares advice from *Mastering the Public Spotlight* by Arnold Zenker. "One of Zenker's best points is that you shouldn't listen to those well-meaning friends and colleagues who urge you to simply 'be yourself' on television. That advice makes sense only if the real you is particularly effective in front of the camera. But what if the real you is so incredibly nervous that it undermines your interview? What if the real you talks too much?"

More so, what if the real you talks without thought to what you've said or answered? Public relations experts point out that while it does not happen often, things can go wrong. If you feel that you are being used or abused during the interview, you have the option of terminating the interview at any time. Should you make this decision, do so politely and explain why you are doing it. You can then take off the microphone and walk away—the camera may still be running, but you will no longer be interviewed. In truth, the camera will not be running long because nonproductive television time is extremely expensive.

After the interview if you believe you have said or stated something incorrectly or perhaps inferred something that may not be true, do not hesitate to contact and write to the producer to clarify the issue. If you have legal counsel, this will probably be his or her job, but you may have to inform the attorney of your concerns and actions you wish to be taken. It may not work, it may be too late, you may still be misquoted, but it is worth a try.

GETTING YOUR MESSAGE OUT

Depending on the circumstances of your loved one's death, you may have a message to share with the world. For example after a woman's child died as the result of an individual drinking and driving, MADD was born. Candy Lightner took her message around the world. Other people who have experienced the death of a loved one become activists, too, producing public service announcements, campaigning for reform of the justice system, speaking to groups of survivors.

Just now, you may not think that you'll ever want to discuss the details of your loved one's death with anyone outside of family and friends. And most assuredly not the Senate, Phil Donahue, Larry King, or the viewers of CNN, but that may change.

According to public relations specialists, such as Diane Gage, even though you know your subject best, it'll pay to do your homework. Gage talks about preparation when you want to make the right impression.

It's your message, it's your passion, it's your determined effort to make the world aware of the cause of your loved one's death, so why, Gage asks, when a reporter starts scribbling or the TV camera starts rolling does your mind suddenly go as blank as a dark computer screen?

10 SURE-FIRE WAYS TO GIVE A LOUSY SPEECH
by Ed Wohlmuth, from
The Overnight Guide to
Public Speaking

❧

1. Come ill-prepared: After all, you're a busy person. They can't expect you to ignore all your important duties at the office just to prepare a little five-minute speech. Or, can they?

2. Waste everyone's time: Within thirty seconds, most audiences can tell whether a speaker means business. When the initial moments of the talk fail to give this evidence, even an important message can be buried in an avalanche of audience indifference.

3. Talk to yourself: You don't care who the audience is or what they would like to hear: What you have to say is important—at least to you. In the end, that'll be the sum total of your audience: You!

4. Talk to your boss: Who cares what all those nobodies think? The boss is out there, and that's who you're going to impress.

5. Use opinions instead of facts: Cite some fancy names, and say they all endorse your position. After that, who cares what the facts are? Your opposition, that's who—and that's the next speaker on the schedule!

6. Ramble away from your subject: That story good old Charlie told you yesterday just

"It happened to me once. There I was doing a phone interview on a Florida radio station ready to espouse the tenets of my new book. I knew the material. I had co-written the book with my public relations colleague Henry DeVries. I had given talks on the topic. It was information that I had imparted to my clients daily. But when the energetic radio personality began firing away random questions, it was as if she had read someone else's book, not mine. Before nerves completely silenced me, our connection went bad. She blamed it on AT&T; I bowed in thanks to a Higher Power.

"That humbling experience taught me that, when it comes to media interviews, I should never take my knowledge of a subject or the knowledge of my clients for granted. You've got to be overprepared for such occasions, because giving a good interview is tougher than it looks."

Gage recommends that you practice what you'll be saying out loud. "Although I had written a book on my interview topic, I realized that I needed to work on a good media interview of concise, meaningful answers. I had to practice the way I learn best. For me, that means writing down notes on the topic. The 'brain-to-keyboard' experience is what emblazons things on my memory. For others, preparing for an interview might mean talking with a tape recorder, then popping the tape into the car's tape deck while driving around town. Still others ready themselves for the media by highlighting notes or talking out loud.

"If you don't have a few days or weeks to practice for a media interview, you still can prepare. Call in your inner circle of friends or colleagues and brainstorm your approach. Talk out loud about how you will address certain issues. Let them fire away questions at you under pressure.

"No matter how you prepare you've got to practice out loud, not just to the bathroom mirror or an imaginary passenger in your car, but to someone who will ask you those questions that seem to appear from out of the blue and who will candidly critique your response.

"It's only when you are put on the spot that you realize that maybe you haven't approached the topic from all angles. Only when you and someone else hear your answers will you know if you really are positioning things just as they should be or if your comments could use a little more thought."

Gage explains that while you may understand the angle you want to take, the reporter may have another approach in mind. "You will only frustrate a reporter or producer if he or she plans to take the story in one direction and you are prepared for another." She says to find out the slant beforehand and to keep in mind that editors want a specific slant that makes your story different.

Speak slowly, says Gage, and state your main points first. "Your mind is buzzing with facts, statistics, and anecdotes. You're ready to spew forth everything you know on the topic, but in a two-minute television interview or even a longer electronic or print interview, there's just not time or space to really strut your stuff. So, how do you use the clock to your advantage?

"Begin by stating your main thesis or your conclusion, followed by a brief supporting statement. Even though you are accustomed in conversation to build up to the conclusion, in a media interview—especially on radio or television—it's best to do the opposite to insure that the points get made.

"Especially in electronic interviews, it's helpful to have three main points you want to make. That way, you, the interviewer, and the listener or viewer can mentally track what you've said and where you are going. Briefly reference each of your main points first, then explain them individually, as simply and succinctly as possible.

"A good interviewee often 'shows' the story with intriguing anecdotes rather than just telling the facts." As you know anecdotes are personal stories and examples, not jokes or silly narratives.

For example, a father whose child died of SIDS recounted the minutes before the discovery. He remembered that Saturday morning as if engraved in his mind. He was relaxing on the patio, his wife had a cold and was still asleep. He thought, "The little guy really tuckered himself out

has to be in your speech today. Trouble is Charlie told it to half the people at the convention, the other half have no idea what you're talking about.

7. Forget your objective: You love the sound of your voice so much, you've lost your main point amid a bouquet of sweet-sounding metaphors. You're not the only one who's lost!

8. Ignore the setting: The head table is crammed with speakers—seven of whom will follow your talk. Do you recognize this immediately, and win over the audience with a short-but-sweet address? No way! They gave you fifteen minutes and you're going to use every last second of it!

9. Ignore the clock: You've made your point, but still you go on and on—unaware that the audience wants to move on to another topic (or adjourn the meeting). Result: the only thing they'll remember is that you didn't know when to quit.

10. Conclude inconclusively: "Well, I guess that's all I have to say...." You guess? If you don't know, you're really finished!

yesterday." He never dreamed why nine-month-old Billy wasn't demanding attention, clamoring for breakfast. Not wanting to disturb the sleeping child, the father read the newspaper. Only a half hour later, after the comics and sports section were tossed aside, and a second cup of coffee finished, did the father realize that his baby had died of SIDS sometime during the night.

This type of account, when shared during an interview, helps people see what you're talking about. The father could have said, "My baby died of SIDS," but the description of the quiet morning's dreadful discovery makes the experience more terrifying to anyone with children. Gage explains, "People love word pictures. If you have examples prepared ahead of time, you can tell a quick story to further illustrate a point."

Make sure that your answers aren't too short. Yes and no answers don't make for good interviews or conversations. "But don't get on a tangent and forget to stop and let the reporter ask questions. Answers should be long enough to get the point across, but not so long that you belabor the point. If the reporter wants to pursue a line of questions, he or she will do so.

"Above all," Gage admonishes, "listen carefully to the questions. Try to focus on what the interviewer is asking, rather than your answer. After the question is asked, let yourself pause for a moment and take time to formulate what you want to say.

"Always use easy-to-understand language. No jargon. If a twenty-five-cent word pops up, explain it in nickel terms. Speak slowly and articulate your words well so they don't become muffled over the air and so the interviewer can easily understand what you're trying to say. Allowing yourself time to pause between thoughts will help avoid the 'ums' and 'ahs' that you'll dread when you hear the interview.

"If there is a point you want to make and the right question isn't being asked, you can segue into it by making a transition such as 'That brings up another important point,' or 'I'd also like to add....' "

Interviewing, getting your message across, and doing it right, even though you're not specifically trained, is possible.

It takes practice and preparation and if you're message is important to you, it's worth pursuing.

What to Wear

You've practiced your message, you know all rebuttals to all possible questions, you're confident and ready to face the press. Now what should you wear? Gage responds, "Dress in business attire. For cameras, avoid busy designs (plaids, checks, houndstooth). Don't wear all white, but a white shirt or blouse with a darker jacket is fine.

"Keep your pockets free of pens, pencils, and other paraphernalia. If you have contact lenses, wear them. That way you won't have to worry about bright lights bouncing off your glasses. Be careful how you sit. Make sure everything you want covered is."

Richard and Deanne Mincer, authors of *The Talk Show Book*, recommend these wardrobe tips. Both men and women should take advantage of viewing themselves on any previously taped shows. "You will then critique not only your performance but also your appearance," say the Mincers. Men should make the necessary changes if they find themselves looking like a ghost of Christmas past and women should be weary if they look like punk rockers. TV candidates should ask:

- Is my clothing consistent with my message?
- Are my clothes comfortable and do they fit properly?
- Have I chosen colors conducive to television?
- Have I considered travel needs in planning my wardrobe?
- Am I avoiding jewelry that will be distracting?
- Can a lavaliere or lapel mike be attached to my clothing?

Almost every first-time speaker has the same urgent question: just what *do* I do with my hands? Author of *The Overnight Guide to Public Speaking*, Ed Wohlmuth has a simple answer: whatever comes naturally. Would you like a great seminar on hands and gestures? You can attend one

Guilt and blame not only waste time, and don't result in cleaning up the problem, but they also tend to perpetuate the problem, all but guaranteeing that the mistake will happen over and over again.

—Paul Kent Froman, Ph.D., grief expert

that lasts only thirty seconds and will tell you everything you need to know. If you own a video recorder, just tape any Johnny Carson (type) monologue and play it back in the "fast-scan" mode. You'll see his hands flying all over the place: behind his back, grasped in front, waving, pointing, at his belt, at his face, you name it.

"That's the name of the game when it comes to gestures: You name it! If it's appropriate, allow yourself to do it. And don't worry about how it looks. The audience will simply absorb your gestures as part of the entire package of words and movements—you being you. That's exactly what you should want," says Wohlmuth.

Where to Go

"If your interview is not in a studio and the reporter is coming to you, make sure you know ahead of time where there is a good location for the interview. For television, pick a room free of clutter (or quickly pack overflowing papers into your drawers or closets). Make sure the room is big enough for a camera, lights, and about four people—you, the producer, the reporter, and the camera person," Gage advises. Have someone hold calls, or take the phone off the hook. Even if the answering machine is picking up the calls you may be distracted when you hear the phone ring or the message being taken. This could be counterproductive at a time when you're answering a complex or crucial question or right when you're making a point.

"For TV, it's also nice to think ahead of time where the reporter can do a stand-up ending to the story. Is there an outside spot that he or she could stand next to?" Gage recommends finding a place with a view or a busy setting that reinforces your story. Again tell with pictures. For example, if you're taping the message of terminally ill patients receiving hospice care, you may want to ask if the reporter can do the ending of the story in front of hospice patients doing exercises or being entertained by children.

What do you get for all this preparation and arranging, the hours spent planning a two-minute interview? Your message comes across loud, articulate, and important to the people who need to hear your cause.

DEATHS THAT TOUCH EVERYONE

Whether we've followed a notable person throughout his or her entire career or if there is a terrible natural disaster and an entire town is swept clean from the map, we are affected. This is not the personal form of grief and some less caring people might discount the effects, but it is death nonetheless. Often, those who are affected by grief become activists and work to stop the suffering of others who are far closer to the grief. Others seek inward solace, sometimes very much alone and in pain, because their grief doesn't have any pattern of acceptance.

Two of these occurrences are when a notable person dies and when there is a major tragedy, or a catastrophic death.

Catastrophic Deaths

Catastrophic deaths produce a moment frozen in time. The event shakes us deeply and we are faced with the question of Why? Suddenly the world is scary, unsafe, inhospitable. We face our own mortality and feel helpless against the future. Although we may not know the individuals involved or the families who suffer and are now survivors, we grieve. We must work with the stages of grief.

Grief experts tell us that as with more personal deaths, we may want to perform a ritual of closure to acknowledge the death. This can be done by finding a quiet place and meditating on what the tragedy means to you and the families involved. It might mean attending mass or reciting a special prayer. You may want to personally help survivors by raising money to establish medical or other aid or donate money to a cause supported after the dreadful calamity. And if you have any unanswered questions or feel you could profit by professional help, don't hesitate to talk with a counselor, clergyperson, or friend who will listen.

Just because you didn't personally know anyone who died in the tragedy, just because it happened halfway around the world, it does not mean that you were untouched by death. If the deaths disturb you, or

BEREAVEMENT AND CATASTROPHIC LOSS
by Ernest Morgan, from
Dealing Creatively with Death

ε❧

Individual responses to loss can be multiplied in social upheavals to become powerful social and political forces. As an administrator of refugee relief in the Middle East in 1950, I was responsible for twenty-five thousand homeless people. I became acutely aware of the grief they felt. The loss of home, country, livelihood, and sometimes of family members as well represented great bereavement. Many clung to denial, fantasizing a return to the homeland. There was a vast reservoir of bitterness and anger against those who were blamed. I believe that terrorism, nationalism, and warfare grow, in part, from these collective grief responses.

Along this line, many forces in our modern world create tragedy on a massive scale, shrinking forests; displaced cultures; expanding deserts; rising populations, war and genocide; vast poverty and exploitation. Thus we find grief far beyond the normal. Grief which must be dealt with at its roots. It is the responsibility of all of us to seek healing for this in whatever ways we can.

perhaps bring forth unresolved grief from a previous death of someone you loved and you are not processing these emotions, then your questions are serious and deserve attention.

Linda Probus, M.A., A.T.R., a grief counselor who works with families and friends after catastrophic loss, shares her insight. She talks from a counselor's view when she describes how she flew to the aid of families and friends coping with the accidental death of members in a small city south of Chicago.

"The commuter plane lifted smoothly and settled into its familiar rhythm and wobbled gently side to side. I closed my eyes and leaned back into my seat overlooking the plane's right wing. My eyes saw the beautiful clouds of East Tennessee as we flew below them. Within minutes we magically crossed over into the rarely seen view of our planet from above the clouds. An endless sky of robin's egg blue capped all that was visible. My eye caught a most remarkable image glimmering in the feathery cloud bank below the plane's wing. Following me was a fuzzy but brilliant circular rainbow with the plane's darker shadow right in the center. I watched it, deciding it was a good omen for this journey. I had been asked to assist a community just devastated by the sudden death of six women who were killed in a drunk driving accident. I knew we would all need that rainbow.

"On a Thursday in mid-September, two women school teachers, their high school daughters, and two other girls were returning home from playing volleyball when their van was rear-ended by a man whose blood alcohol level was nearly twice the legal limit. This small town was plunged into an experience for which it, or any other community, was unprepared.

"The school administrators had requested assistance in lending emotional support to students as soon as possible. Four of us professional counselors were joined by eight volunteers from local and regional chapters of a national support organization, who donated their time, training, and personal experiences with drunk driving deaths in their own families. Most of all they gave a priceless gift during this time of need. They donated their hearts.

"While scanning the silent world outside the small window from my pane, some of my own memories emerged of working in Radcliff, Kentucky, as the grief counselor following the nation's worst drunk driving incident which killed twenty-seven children and seven adults.

"How easily these memories bring themselves forward, unbidden and unwanted, I thought. Again, as in the past three and a half years, I employed my faith in a Higher Power to keep these events emotionally manageable in my own heart. I cannot resist asking the tempting, unanswerable question, Why? Why did these thirty-four people, none of whom were even known to me, but whose names and faces will always remain in my heart, have to die? All grieving people struggle to respond to this cry of disbelief. I am comforted by knowing it is a normal human response to not believe such a truth for as long as possible.

"The concept of time and healing was the therapeutic essence of what the critical response team hoped to bring to the rural town. Family members, high school and elementary students, and community leaders were frozen in the immediacy of what had happened. Research has proven that trauma victims and bereaved people can experience altered perceptions about time and events happening around them. Time will help restore balance if permitted.

"On a more intimate level, we were permitted into a private world. Shock and profound sadness were visible in hundreds of family members and friends who attended the seven-hour visitation service held in the high school gymnasium for five of the seven women who died. Friends waited over an hour to offer caring tears, hugs, and love to these families. Perhaps the gift of time will only reinforce the protective veil lovingly placed around these grieving families by their community. These moments were often captured by smiles and gestures because words of consolation sometimes fail to convey what the heart so earnestly yearns to say.

"As Monday drew to a close, we searched out the small

memorial of handmade crosses, flowers, and cards which had appeared along the side of the two-lane highway where the accident happened. A quiet group of teenage girls was already there, speaking in hushed tones. We waited patiently at a distance as they shared these moments together with their friends who had died four days earlier. Along the road's shoulder, grass was blackened or missing over a frighteningly large area. All that could be seen that might have belonged to the van were the remains of a steel-belted tire and a few snippets of wire. A man's light blue, very soiled work jacket had been tossed carelessly close to the fragile memorial, unknowingly contaminating the spirit of the place. Who were these young girls and women of my own age I would never be permitted to know?

"I returned Tuesday morning, privileged to step away from this nightmare of sudden, violent death that had blanketed an innocent community. Gratefully I leaned back into the softness of my bus seat and gazed absentmindedly into the blue sky above. There, waiting for me to see, was an enormous feathery cloud formation that did not look like anything in particular. It grabbed me with its abstract beauty. Maybe it was an erupting fountain filled with the whiteness of joy and hope that I alone could see.

"It was so comforting against the clear blue sky that I was compelled to sketch it so as not to forget its secret message. To me, its arching beauty was certainly a message of hope, perhaps an unspoken reminder that I, as well as the people who had spent three days here, had given all that I knew how to give during this period of intense pain and sorrow.

"Within this brief moment of reassurance, or escape, my eyelids closed easily as the bus snaked its way through the traffic, taking me once more to the airport and back to my own small town in East Tennessee."

The Death of a Hero

When a person dies who was noted for an accomplishment—a famous entertainer, a politician, a sports figure—often we are deeply touched. Lots of folks shake their heads and smile kindly, but they really want to know, Why are you crying? You didn't know her. But in fact you did know the public image of this person.

Who hasn't seen on television or known someone who has visited Elvis's, John Kennedy's, or Martin Luther King's grave site? Few of us knew these heroes and all the others, yet we've all been affected by their words, their heroism, their music. Grief experts and those who study the effect of a celebrity death on the population say we are influenced and grieve because part of what was seemingly safe and secure is gone. Few our age may remember the sobbing throngs who took to the streets when silent movie heartthrob Rudolph Valentino died. Some of us remember the tears shed when John and Robert Kennedy and Martin Luther King were assassinated. Most of us including millions of school-age children will never forget the horror and tears when the *Challenger* exploded. Public and private grieving for a celebrity, and other heroes, isn't new.

Some people grieve as deeply for the notable person as if he or she were a close friend or relative. While not in all cases, sometimes the death of the celebrity is the first encounter with death and graphically illustrates that we are all mortal—even those who are beautiful, rich, and powerful. This is a shock to some.

Grief experts suggest that for those who are greatly affected by the death of a celebrity, they may want to talk with a close friend, a counselor, or a therapist if the death is producing as many grief indications as the death of a loved one. It's also suggested that if it is impossible to go to the funeral, memorial service, or grave site, they may want to plan a small ritual to help provide a closing for this person's life. Celebrities have families, too, and a compassionate letter from an admirer might mean a lot to the survivors. Yes, it's appropriate to send a note with a sympathy card. Even the rich, beautiful, and powerful feel the effects of death and grief.

After the death of a great conductor, one woman lit a few candles and spent an evening listening to the music he has conducted. We've all seen people singing and swaying to Beatle John Lennon's music as they stand outside the Dakota, the apartment house in New York City, where Lennon lived before he was assassinated.

Dr. Sandra Graves says that we need heroes. "Some very interesting research has been conducted in recent years which shows our desire for heroes and their value to us. Heroes provide a means of identifying with the power around us and through identification, empower us."

She identifies women and men as heroes—using the term "hero" to apply to both genders. "Heroes give us a sense of reference in a world of confusion, a renewed security and a trust in our environment."

Why is it important to feel powerful, secure, and trusting and why is there a section on heroes in a book on death? A survivor of a death, herself, Dr. Graves explains, "The answers are simple. These are the characteristics of mental health, and these are the goals as we process our grief, to renew self-confidence and identity, to know we are safe in a world in which reality has been so altered, and to trust ourselves and those around us again. Trust is the foundation of relationships and hopefulness. We must find trust to find attitudes which lead toward healing."

Who are our heroes? "It may come as a surprise to you, but most people find their heroes quite close to home. A survey shows that the number-one heroes in the American public are our parents. We also find heroes in politics and in religion. Our heroes are close to us....either physically or psychologically filling a need or displaying an attribute we admire.

"Heroes have special characteristics. They are courageous and strong. They must show a loving, generous nature. Intelligence, skill, and expertise are essential, and they demonstrate an honest approach to the world. Finally, a hero must be affectionate as well as adventurous and daring, a risk-taker in life."

So why do we need heroes? Dr. Graves responds, "Coping with grief is a consuming and exhausting experience. One of the most challenging things we have to deal with is making the decision to find meaning in the deaths of our loved ones and rebuilding our lives for ourselves." Those who live on after the death of a loved one by traumatic means, such as homicide or being involved in a crime, find an even greater challenge in turning from that bitterness and resentment—and with moving forward transform the grieving energy into self-empowerment and fuel for proceeding with life. "We cope, therefore, by finding support around us, identifying with and nurturing others, and reaching out to make meaningful changes in our world. We look for role models—for heroes—to give us guidance." Unaware of our quest, we look for heroes and we find them all around, including those who have very public personas.

"Look inside yourself and find your courage—not to handle the death itself, but to handle all the life events which remind you of your loss on an hourly and daily basis. Look to those around you who have been so caring, those who have still been there for you as the weeks and months go by." Dr. Graves challenges each of us to become a hero, our own heroes. "Acknowledge your survival skills, your ability to solve problems you may never have dreamed you would deal with. Measure your tears and sadness by the amount of love you felt for the person who has died, for grief is the consequence of loving."

"Be specific about your heroes. Who are they? More importantly, why are they your heroes? What do you admire about them? How do they have power in their world?" Dr. Graves asks. "As you do this simple exercise, you will begin to discover something—the power within yourself. Look around you and find all the powerful things in your environment, from telephone poles to aircrafts, from lightening to computers. If you spend five minutes listing the power around you, you will gain hours in a renewed sense of security and a renewed energy. Too often we are caught in a tunnel of grief which has only one ray of light. We tend to focus on the obituaries, robberies, murders, financial losses, destruction, etc. This is a normal reaction to the death of a loved one as we identify with feelings and circumstances we are experiencing. However, we can alter our focus and regain some balance in our lives.

"We can discover the hero within as we identify with the people we admire. We think we admire qualities in others we do not possess. Just the opposite is true. Look outside yourself and you will see a reflection of your own inner

❧

It has been three months since a terrible triple tragedy had befallen us. Our two oldest sons, along with the lovely young girl our eldest had planned to marry, had all died in a house fire at Eastern Illinois University.

We were still suffering from shock, incredible grief, and disbelief. Somehow, we managed to go through the motions of the holidays. Now the New Year was here. Reality was sinking in. We could hardly stand to think of the rest of our lives without our boys. They were honor students, star athletes, and good and loving sons. We were at our lowest ebb.

The night of January 18 was cold and crisp. The stars were bright when I went out for a walk. As I made my way through the darkness, I thought constantly of the three we loved and missed so much. I walked and talked aloud, cried and tried to pray, but it seemed all my former faith and trust were gone. I felt as if I could not go on any longer unless I could be assured that they were all right. Soon I could not tell if I was shaking from sobs or the cold. I felt as if I just had to know they were safe and happy somewhere.

strength, courage, determination, generosity, intelligence, and love."

SPIRITUAL DISASTER IN A TIME OF CRISIS

Many people experience the questioning of their spiritual convictions at the time of their loved one's death and this is especially so when the death becomes front-page news.... or viewed by curious onlookers.

At this time a fundamental faith in God, a faith in a Higher Power, and the scheme of life are shaken. Sometimes it crumbles to pieces, it is irreparable. This is poignantly clear when the death involves violence, an accident, a homicide, kidnapping, or other "newsworthy" material on which the media may wish to capitalize.

"For each of us there comes a moment in life when a line is drawn that cuts us off from someone we love. The name of that line is death," says Rev. Diana Cole Veazey, minister with the American Baptist Church and chaplain at Children's Hospital of the Kings Daughters, a trauma hospital for children located in Norfolk, Virginia. "It can come in one sleek move, or in jagged strokes. In one swift moment, we are cut off from someone precious. The moment in which this separation takes place is so infinitesimal that it seems we should be able to reach across that line and pull that one back to life. But we cannot."

When the death involves an iniquity, says Reverend Cole Veazey, "The death draws its line in irregular dashes and punctures which robs us piece by piece of someone very dear. At other times, the moment of death comes almost as relief, yet leaves us no better prepared to face the reality of that loss. Whatever the case, the end result is the same. A new reality has begun for us for which there is no way to prepare.

"We have lost not only those we loved, and by whom we were loved, but we have lost our identities. We have lost the way we understand ourselves in relation to the world, as well as the way we understand ourselves in relation to God, a Higher Power, or the 'Other' which is beyond ourselves. The illusions of 'once upon an time' and 'happily ever after' no longer exist.

"There is a loss of innocence as our fingers are pried loose from persons, relationships, and dreams which gave our lives structure, form, purpose, and meaning. Adrift amid a turbulent sea of emotion, we hold on to remnants of what is left of our shattered existence and search for some glimpse of shore.

"Overwhelmed by reality, we seek to gain some control. Hence, often our first thoughts are who can we blame? Whose fault is this anyway? Someone should have stopped this from happening. Sometimes we become involved in lawsuits in an effort to prevent this from happening to someone else, but also as a way of focusing our anger. However, when all is said and done, we still must confront the question of the injustice of life. There is no lawsuit which can address this concern. Ultimately, we are led to the question of where a Higher Power is in this. Who is this Higher Power? Or, is there a Higher Power? All of the unresolved losses of our lives come together in their collective grief, and we become overwhelmed by what feels like a world out of control.

"We find ourselves at a doorway of one of the most difficult losses one must face….the lost of faith. For some, this experience comes gradually as a part of life's journey. For others, it is brought on by a specific event. Regardless, it is a journey each of us must take. It is an experience that takes a kind of courage we have rarely been called upon before to use. It threatens our existence, our understanding of life at its deepest level. It challenges us to question the very essence and meaning of life."

Reverend Cole Veazy compares the challenges faced in a private death turned public to the story of St. Ignatius.

"St. Ignatius speaks in his autobiography of an experience he had on a journey. Having lost his way, he found himself traveling beside a path with a riverbank down below and the road up above. The farther along he went the more narrow the path became. Finally, he could go neither forward nor backward. His only resort was to get down on his hands and knees and crawl. Fear tore through his body for with each move he thought he would fall into

I realized I was freezing cold and utterly exhausted. As I turned to walk back toward the house, something off to the side of the road caught my eye. A bright light seemed to be moving toward me on the left. It was like a very large star. It was low, at the level of the tree-tops, traveling parallel to the road. It was moving very slowly on a straight path, and not at all like any falling star I had ever seen.

I watched in awe as it kept steadily moving toward me. Then, just as it was directly across and above the spot where I stood, it stopped and broke into three separate stars. They disappeared as quickly as they had come.

I was suddenly convinced, beyond a shadow of a doubt, that Bob, Mike, and Carla were with God. I began sensing a peace I had not known for months. A million stars seemed to close in around me. I was over-whelmed with a tremendous feeling of warmth and love and began to weep tears of joy.

My faith was restored. I'm forever grateful for that symbol of light in my darkness. There is no more fear or doubt in my life. Only an unshakable trust that, someday, we will be reunited with our loved ones for all eternity.

MOVEMENT AWAY FROM TRADITIONAL RELIGION

by Algernon D. Black,
from *Without Burnt Offerings*

❧

Many human beings who are no longer part of any traditional religious community may strive for meaningful lives through work and devotion to their families and the community. Some turn to careers of service. Others make their contributions to a better life in their avocational activities. There can be no one definition of "the good life" for all people.

For some it means acceptance of and obedience to a particular moral code, one of conventional conformity. For others it means a life guided by a conscious choice of values and priorities which include respect for every human being, a recognition of the interdependence of all life, and a treasuring of the relationships and interplay of differences which can enrich and enhance life, the life of all.

the river and drown. Agonizingly, he felt his way along in what seemed like an endless journey. At long last he found his way out. St. Ignatius compares this physical journey to his spiritual journey through which he struggled with the loss of meaning and the purpose of life. This second journey in St. Ignatius's life lasted seventeen years. He often wondered if he was following some crazy dream, or God's leading. He even thought of suicide. Yet, St. Ignatius is one of the spiritual giants of history."

Reverend Cole Veazey refers to this story when consoling those who are on the journey to clarify the details of their loved ones' deaths while their deepest faith has crumbled. "Coming to terms with the reality of this loss of faith is like a second death. The pain and grief are equally as powerful, but less clearly defined. They are thus more complicated to deal with. Most of us are aware that relationships to parents, friends, and children change, but rarely do we give consideration to our relationship to God or a Higher Power changing. We repeat rituals we have used for years, but they seem hollow and empty. Clear answers do not exist. Unfortunately, organized religion has not been as helpful as it could in assisting people as they name, confront, and struggle with these disillusionments in the way they see exemplified in the Old and New Testaments of the Bible.

"We are so uncomfortable with pain that we eagerly move on to the resolution which follows. It is in losing faith that we find faith and in losing God that we find God. We are freed to encounter that Higher Power in a new way, with new knowledge, new truth, and new wisdom.

"This journey is marked by four stages. The first is recognition of the reality of the loss. The second is experiencing the grief and pain. The third is struggling with the disillusionment, and the fourth is beginning to rediscover meaning and purpose in life in relation to oneself, others, and a Higher Power.

"Through this process, we find that our perspective on spirituality changes. Our understanding of what is sacred may broaden. Our traditional words and symbols may no longer express adequately the meaning of life. New symbols, which are less clearly defined, may enter our lives.

"For me, spirituality is the way we understand our lives in relation to the mystery of both the good and the evil of the universe and how that gives our lives meaning. It is living life by values which come from within rather than values that are imposed from without. It is letting go of control, trusting in the mystery, and believing that there is a Higher Power who is 'for me,' not 'against me.' It is being in a relationship with that Higher Power in a way which leaves me feeling neither victimized nor totally self-sufficient. It is a relationship which invites me to participate and be engaged in the mystery of being and becoming."

Throughout this chapter, we've focused on the circumstances of a death that changes from a personal, family event into one that is put under a magnifying glass by the media. With the steps and how-to information, your own emotions can be handled in a smoother way, and you can avoid having the media dictate your feelings.

In the next chapter, we'll talk about what happens and what to do when death occurs away from home, whether you are with your loved one or not. There is information on what to do when death involves a member of the military and other unique circumstances. The chapter provides material on how to handle funeral arrangements, burial details, and the effects of grief "long distance."

I have known good people who believed in God. I have known good people who didn't believe in God. But I have never known good people who didn't believe in people.

—John Lovejoy Elliott
leader of ethical humanism

My religion is very simple, my religion is kindness....

—Dalai Lama,
Buddhist religious leader

When the Death Occurs Away from Home

It had been *the* vacation they'd planned for months. Like the honeymoon they'd never had. They talked, ate, and breathed the holiday, right down to the last detail as they spent hours pouring over colorful brochures. Ah, the tropics. Ah, Shangri-la. Trade winds, swaying palms, and an accident, a fatal collision that robbed adult children of their parents and children of their beloved grandparents. Like a pebble thrown into still water, the circles of grief followed by this death could be felt in many families.

Death can occur any time, anywhere. In our mobile society, it's not unusual for a family to be scattered in five states or five different countries. Telephone calls are exchanged along with birthday cards and holiday wishes and we stick together thanks to modern telecommunications. When death happens away from home or away from other family members, it's often a telephone call that announces the shocking news.

The death of a loved one is always difficult to face. An unexpected accident, a sudden death, or a death that consciously we know is to be forthcoming, but we have not resolved, can be a frightening, shocking experience. When the death occurs away from "home," that is, away from where you are physically, there are tremendous emotions that must be resolved along with the logistics of the death. A death away from home is a special circumstance.

In this chapter you'll find information on how to cope with a death that occurs away from you, when you are not personally with the loved one when he or she dies, or when you're traveling and a companion dies. We'll also touch on military deaths along with some of the resources you have in foreign deaths.

We've provided a separate chapter on advice to consider when death occurs away from home because when one dies far away from loved ones, survivors often not only feel intense shock, but panic as well. Most who have been through the experience say, "I didn't know what to do." This chapter provides some of the answers so that you can be informed and prepared.

WHEN A TRAVELING COMPANION DIES

If you are traveling and a companion dies, you first need to get emergency help. How you should do this depends on where you are. Howard Raether, former executive director of the National Funeral Directors Association, says, "If you are in a hotel, you should call the front desk. The desk clerk will know where to call for an ambulance. In most other public places, such as restaurants, museums, or theaters, you should ask the nearest waiter, clerk, or usher to notify the manager, who will then call for help."

The manager will ask for your assistance accompanying your companion to the hospital and providing the staff with pertinent information such as where your companion lives, any known illnesses, and so forth. As with any unexplained death or a death that occurs out of a care facility, the death will be reported to the police. Just because you will be asked questions by a police officer does not indicate that you have had anything untimely to do with your loved one or friend's death. It is part of the procedure. See chapter 1, Immediate Action, on the procedures that may be followed when death occurs.

At a campground or other outdoor facility, you should notify the nearest staff member or law enforcement officer, such as a park ranger. He or she will call for emergency help. If you are where there is no staff to assist you, find the nearest telephone and call for help, either 911 or "O" for the operator.

What should be done if a death occurs in an isolated area, with no telephone or emergency help for miles? There are differing opinions. According to law enforcement agencies, it is recommended that you cover your companion with a blanket if possible and immediately seek emergency help. This makes the best sense. However, as one man replied, "There was no way I would leave my brother in that forest, alone and dead after the lightning killed him. I carried him from the campsite to the car, then drove the fifty miles to the nearest fire station. I could not—no, would not—leave him."

Authorities say that even if you believe that your companion is already dead, it's always best to call for or get emergency help. There may be a chance, however slim, that he or she can be revived by emergency personnel or a doctor at a hospital. In any case, in some states a doctor must be present to declare your loved one dead and state the cause or causes of death. If the doctor isn't sure of the cause of death, or if he or she thinks the death may have been caused by suicide, homicide, or an accident, a coroner or medical examiner will be contacted to examine the body.

A key function of talking while in the grief state is to work through negative emotions such as hate and guilt. The aid of another person, whether friend, relative, or the clergy, may be required, both as listener and as interpreter of such emotions; but the end effect to be sought is that catharsis in which, according to the acclaimed Albert Switzer, "speech becomes a substitute form of the emotionally charged acts that need to be performed, understood, and accepted."

—Richard G. Benton, from *Death and Dying*

According to Raether, "After getting emergency help locally, you need to notify close relatives who don't already know about the death." He suggests that you personally call the "inner circle" of family—close relatives such as parents, grandparents, children, siblings, and companions or partners of the deceased. While you may feel you shouldn't wake others if the death occurs at a late hour, Raether says that grief experts and researchers explain that those close to the deceased may feel cheated if they aren't told until the next morning. "Though you may not realize it, telling others of a death is therapeutic for you. By saying aloud that your loved one has died, you confirm the death in your own mind—an important first step in the grief process."

After calling the immediate family, you can let the calls "branch out," that is, asking others to call those who need to know or who will want to know about the death. It's not practical for you to call all your loved one's friends and relatives, and by sharing this responsibility you allow others to take an active role in the rituals that will help in the grief process.

Raether points out that news of a death travels quickly. People far down on your loved one's list of family, friends, acquaintances, and colleagues will probably have already been notified by the time you reach them. For example, if your loved one was a member of the local rotary club, having a family member call the chapter's president and letting him or her make any calls would be a service. Often it's best to have relatives or friends call others after the time and place for the service has been decided so that only one telephone call needs to be made.

"If the person who died was a family member and your family is active in a church or synagogue or other religious affiliation, you should call the clergyperson as soon as possible. He or she will help you with the details of the death. Although many people hesitate to call the clergyperson in the wee hours of the morning, most clergy say they prefer to be notified so they can be a consoling presence to any family members who are back home and just heard the news," says Raether. He explains, "This is, after all, not a time for them to be alone."

One of the first calls back home should be to your funeral director. Your clergyperson can help provide you with a referral or perhaps make the first call. The funeral director, in your own city or the city in which your loved one lives, can make arrangements to have the deceased removed from the place of death by a funeral home in that area.

Someone from the staff of the hospital where the death occurred may ask for you to name a funeral director in that city. You can tell the person that your local funeral director will contact a firm immediately. When you do call your hometown funeral director or the director in your loved one's hometown, you will need to know certain things such as the full name of the deceased, the place of death, the location of the body, and your location so you can be reached by phone again.

Raether suggests that you let your hometown funeral director be your agent and make the arrangements for you. He or she knows about the procedures required, such as how to obtain a permit to transport a body, contact airlines regarding requirements, and meet the flight when the body arrives. Your local funeral director can help coordinate with the funeral director in the out-of-state location in order to obtain copies of the death certificate, select a casket, and prepare the body. He or she can help you file for any pensions or benefits that may be due.

Before a body can be transported by air, rail, or sea by a common carrier, it must be embalmed; your funeral director can tell you other requirements while working out any details. Check with your funeral director before you decide to pick up the body of your loved one; some states require that only licensed funeral directors can claim bodies that have been transported from one area to another.

The cost of sending a body from one area of the country to another is approximately three hundred dollars, and according to the law, no one need accompany a body being transported. While some airlines offer discounts to family members traveling with a body, you must tell the ticket agent when making reservations.

Your local funeral director will then give the instructions for transportation of the deceased to your hometown or other location you choose for services and burial. If your loved one wanted to be cremated or this is your decision, it should be considered very seriously as it is much easier and will save money. Be sure to check your billing to verify that you have not been charged twice for the same service performed by the funeral director in the location of the death as well as the funeral director you have selected in your hometown.

In a time of great stress, letting the funeral director help with the service can make things easier for you and other family members. If you would like to participate in any of the decisions normally handled by a funeral director, including those of transporting your loved one's body, you can talk with the funeral director. Sometimes there will be a cost savings, sometimes not. Make your wishes known.

WHEN A LOVED ONE DIES WHILE TRAVELING ALONE

If a loved one is traveling alone and dies *and* has identification, conveying the news of the death is made much easier. Should this occur, the police will notify the county or city medical examiner, an investigation will be made, and the family will be sought out and notified as promptly as possible.

If the loved one lives in the same county as where the death occurred, a coroner or law enforcement officer will actually go to the address on the identification, a driver's license for example, and substantiate that the person who died actually lives there. From neighbors, the officer will try to find the next of kin.

If the next of kin live out of state or if there is an "in case of emergency" card in the wallet of the individual who has died, the coroner will call the local coroner in the loved one's hometown and the family will be personally notified this way. If there is no identification on the body, fingerprints will be taken and run through a computer check, and verification will be made in that way. To verify the correctness of the identification other forensic methods may used, such as dental records. This is the case except if your loved one was a member of the military, where a chaplain and a fellow service member will personally call on the family and coordinate the arrangements for transporting the body back home. For more information on military deaths, see the section later in this chapter.

For those foreign travelers visiting the United States, their passports indicate country of origin and whom to call in an emergency. From this information, a local coroner calls the embassy representing the country of the individual who has died and the embassy contacts call a local agency within the country of origin to contact the family.

While coroners and law enforcement personnel try to explain the news of the death personally, sometimes that's not possible. In cases where the department is short on personnel or in a large, rural area, you might hear the news over the telephone. If possible, during this traumatic time, try to write down the name, telephone number, and department of the individual who is calling. As horrendous as it sounds, there are some people who gain perverse pleasure by telling a family that a member has died or has been in a terrible accident. With the telephone number of the coroner or law enforcement officer, you are able to double-check the validity of the awful news.

Should you receive news that your loved one has died away from home, you will need to call a local funeral home director and let him or her make arrangements with a funeral director in an area where the death occurred. Often this is the first time you'll have to call a funeral director when you do not have one chosen. A family member, clergy, or friend can often recommend a funeral director he or she has used.

It will be up to you or another designated next of kin to have your loved one's personal property sent home. As mentioned previously, if the death seems unexplained, there will be a police investigation. If the death has been the result of a crime, you may find it helpful to contact an attorney in your area to help with the arrangements and provide information regarding the death. The Office for Victims of Crime may be able to help, too (see chapter 5).

WHEN A LOVED ONE CALLS MORE THAN ONE PLACE HOME

Charlene Harris lived in Phoenix, Arizona, and had a successful career as a hairdresser, but always referred to Buffalo, New York, as "home." That's where her father still lives along with her cousins and other relatives. When she died, Harris's body was flown back home and cremated in Buffalo as per her wishes.

When the husband of a couple who always spent five months "wintering" in Florida died of an aneurysm, Harold's body was flown back to Toronto, Canada, for burial. A funeral according to the couple's religious faith was held there; there was no other service in Miami.

Raether points out that some people call more than one location "home." It's very common for the body of a loved one to be transported to where his or her relatives reside. "After all, funerals are for the living," says Raether and, as grief experts explain, the rituals are necessary for closure and grief work to begin as the death is affirmed.

In the case where a loved one lived in one area but wanted to be buried in another, hopefully, those wishes were known before the death. Often the local funeral director will coordinate the activities with his or her counterpart in another location. If the loved one is to be buried or cremated in the location where he or she resided, then it's up to the close family to instruct the funeral director on the details of the arrangements. Additionally, if the family wants the loved one buried in the place where the death occurred, the local funeral director can be instructed to published death notices in both the hometown newspaper and the newspaper in the city in which the death occurred. Often there will be a funeral in one city and a memorial service in another.

As you consider making arrangements for the funeral or other service, talk to the clergyperson who will preside. Sometimes family and friends make all the arrangements *then* call the clergy and hope that he or she will be able to oversee the service.

OTHER CONSIDERATIONS WHEN DEATH OCCURS AWAY FROM HOME

If your loved one belonged to a memorial society, check the telephone book for a branch of the society. They will provide you with information on lower cost services.

If your loved one wanted to donate organs, anatomical gifts, or give his or her body to a medical or research center, you must make the notification immediately. However, if your loved one is out of the area and away from the medical center to be given his or her body, the center may decide against accepting it because of the transportation time and costs involved. Also, keep in mind that although the gift of organs or a body was your loved one's wish, that may not be possible because of the circumstances of the death. For example, if your loved one was in an accident, his or her organs may not be in satisfactory condition to be transplanted to another.

WHEN DEATH HAPPENS ABROAD

Americans traveling abroad on business, pleasure, or a study program rarely think about death. Nevertheless, approximately six thousand Americans do die outside of the United States each year. The Citizens Emergency Center assists with the return of the remains of about two thousand.

When an American dies abroad, the Bureau of Consular Affairs, with the United States Department of State, in Washington, D.C., must locate and inform the next of kin. Sometimes discovering the next of kin is difficult. According to Robert K. Heaps, an officer with the Overseas Citizens Services, part of the Department of State, says, "If an American's name is known, the Bureau's Office of Passport Services will search for his or her passport application. However, the information there may not be current." Some travelers have enough wherewithal to understand the importance of keeping emergency information up-to-date and keep a copy in their passport as well as their wallet and suitcase.

Heaps explains that the Bureau of Consular Affairs provides guidance to grieving family members on how to make arrangements for a local burial or return of the remains to the United States. "The disposition of remains is affected by local laws, customs, and facilities that are often vastly different from those here in the States," says Heaps. "The Bureau of Consular Affairs relays the family's instructions swiftly and as efficiently as humanly possible and necessary private funds are forwarded to the embassy or consulate to cover the costs involved." The Department of State has no funds to assist in the return of remains or ashes of American citizens who die overseas; however, it acts as the liaison between the family and the local officials in the country in which the death occurs.

"When the formalities have been completed, the consular officer abroad prepares an official Foreign Service Report of Death of an American Citizen, based on the local death certificate. The report is then sent to the next of kin or legal representative for use in United States courts as verification of death and to settle the estate," says Heaps. The Report of Death will be necessary for the family to claim various survivor benefits, life insurance, and Social Security, if applicable.

A United States consular officer overseas has statutory responsibility for the personal estate of an American who dies abroad if the deceased has no legal representative in the country where the death occurred. The consular officer takes possession of personal effects, such as money, apparel, jewelry, personal documents, and papers. The officer prepares an inventory and then carries out instructions from members of the deceased's family concerning the effects. A final statement of the account is then sent to the next of kin.

The Bureau of Consular Affairs, and the officer who has been appointed to work with the family regarding the death, instruct the next of kin on how to provide legal evidence so that personal effects can be claimed.

After notification, the Bureau's officer will discuss the costs of shipping the remains or ashes back to the family working with a funeral home out of the country and coordinating the delivery of the body to a funeral home of the family's choice in the United States. In order to export the remains of a body from Guatemala, for example, there must be a Guatemalan burial transit permit, embalming of the body, hermetically sealed box, zinc casket, outer wooden casket, and shipping container. The cost from Guatemala to Los Angeles can easily exceed four thousand dollars. The estimated burial in Guatemala is about fifteen hundred dollars.

Since it's quite costly to ship a loved one's body home, most Americans who die abroad are buried abroad according to the local custom of that country and with the presence of an embassy officer who carries out the family's wishes. The officer from the Bureau of Consular Affairs

Denial following a violent and unanticipated loss should be considered normal and functional. You should be allowed to travel through this part of grief at your own pace because denial will serve you well until you are stronger and better able to cope. It is impossible to push through any part of grieving in order to "get it over with." If you cannot think clearly, seem forgetful, and seem detached, be patient with yourself. If you need help, ask for it.

—Janice Harris Lord, from
No Time for Good-byes

will explain the options for burial or cremation available. However, in some countries, specifically the Islamic countries, cremation facilities as we know them are not available. Other countries do not embalm bodies. Some do not have perpetual care for cemeteries.

The Bureau of Consular Affairs can be very helpful. *Tips for Travelers* pamphlets provide advice prepared by the Bureau on travel to specific areas of the world.

Depending on the region discussed, a *Tips* pamphlet will cover such topics as currency and customs regulations, entry requirements, dual nationality, import and export controls, vaccination requirements, restrictions on use of photography, and warnings on the use of drugs. Single copies of *Tips* are for sale for one dollar from the U.S. Government Printing Office, Superintendent of Documents, Washington, DC 20402, (202) 512-1800.

WHEN THERE HAS BEEN A DISASTER

You hear about it on the news.... "earthquake hits Mexico City" and suddenly your heart is in your throat. Your loved one was spending her vacation in Mexico's capital. But it's after 6:00 P.M. and there will be no one around to provide information or help you make contact.... or will there? Yes—that's where the Citizens Emergency Center can help.

After a *major disaster*, a tidal wave, hurricane, airplane crash, political upheaval, or act of terrorism abroad, the Center, which is part of the Bureau of Consular Affairs, immediately sets up a task force to begin working on lines of communication between loved ones perhaps caught in the disaster and the family at home. In a task force, the immediate job of the State Department's Bureau of Consular Affairs is to respond to the thousands of concerned relatives and friends who begin to telephone after the disaster abroad is broadcast.

Relatives want information on the welfare of family members and the disaster. Through the Citizens

Emergency Center family and friends can obtain hard information from embassies and consulates abroad. These installations are often affected by the disaster and without electricity, phone lines, and gasoline; however, it is the Center's goal to get information back to Washington as quickly as possible. Often this process seems far too slow for the family who wait nervously for that phone call about the welfare of their loved one; however, the foreign service office cannot speculate—its information must be accurate.

During a foreign disaster and as relatives call in, officers of the Bureau of Consular Affairs collect the names of the Americans possibly involved in the disaster and pass them to the embassy and consulates. Officers at the foreign post attempt to locate these Americans in order to report on their welfare. The officers work with local authorities and, depending on the circumstances, may personally search hotels, airports, hospitals, or even prisons. As they try to get the information, their first priority is to determine if the American is dead or injured.

The Citizens Emergency Center and consular officers are sympathetic and helpful. As can be imagined, during a disaster, their energy is spread extremely thin. Should you have to call, to be most helpful it's beneficial to have the full name of your loved one, where he or she is traveling (and possibly staying), and the arrival and departure time from the area.

Where to Get Help

The Citizens Emergency Center is staffed by twenty-five officers and clerical personnel. In addition to being a liaison when there is a death, the Center also is involved in Americans who die, become destitute, get sick, disappear, have accidents, or get arrested while traveling abroad. To contact the Citizens Emergency Center, call:

(202) 647-5225, Monday-Friday 8:15 A.M.-10 P.M., Saturday 9:00 A.M.-3:00 P.M.

(202) 647-5226, 5:00 P.M. to 10:00 P.M.

(202) 647-1512, 10:00 P.M. to 8:15 A.M. during the week and at all times during weekends and holidays.

THE PRIVACY ACT

The provisions of the Privacy Act are designed to protect the privacy and rights of Americans, but occasionally they complicate the Center's efforts to assist citizens abroad. As a rule, consular officers may not reveal information regarding an individual American's location, welfare, intentions, or problems to anyone, including family members and congressional representatives, without the expressed consent of that individual. Says Heaps, "Although the Center is extremely compassionate and sensitive to the distress that this can cause anxious families, consular officers are forced to comply with the provisions of the Privacy Act."

LOCATING A MISSING PERSON ABROAD

The Citizens Emergency Center receives approximately twelve thousand inquiries a year concerning the welfare or whereabouts of Americans abroad. Many are from worried relatives who have not heard from the traveler and think the worst has happened. Others are from relatives attempting to notify the traveler about a crisis at home.

According to Heaps, "Most welfare/whereabouts inquiries are successfully resolved. However, occasionally, a person truly is missing. It is the responsibility of local authorities to investigate. The State Department and

United States consuls abroad do not conduct investigations. As in the United States, sometimes missing persons are never found." (See chapter 3, A Disappearance Death, for more information.)

THE FAR-REACHING EFFECTS OF DEATH

Few are alone on this planet. The death of a loved one affects the close family personally, and it affects a wider range of those who have known the one who died, whether for five minutes or fifty years.

Dr. Sandra Graves says, "For all who grieve the death of a loved one, it is important to know that we all stand together in an ever-widening ring of circles." She compares the impact of the death to the ripple effect of a pebble on a quiet pond. "The incident has many layers and reaches far beyond what may be expected. Each circle stands alone, yet is connected to the center. The circles touch each other before they radiate outward."

Each circle in our lives has a different significance because we are unique and also because each circumstance is different. For example, when a young friend dies away from home—at college, away on business, away on holiday, or during relocation, that death has many tangents. Within the inner circle is the immediate family. Perhaps there are three generations who were all bound by disbelief; perhaps the friend has two very young children, a wife, and two parents under the age of fifty. Dr. Graves says, "The next circle represented includes those close relationships of business partner, employees, best friends, associates in civic organizations, the teachers who remembered my friend when he was a boy in their classrooms, and the minister who baptized him, wed him, and only a few years later conducted his funeral. Further outward, but still near the center are those whose lives were affected by the life that has just left us—colleagues, dignitaries, and friends of friends. The circle then reaches the community as a whole,

THE NEED FOR TIME
by Bertha G. Simos,
from *A Time to Grieve*

ès

Grief is an active, not a passive, process; Freud rightfully labeled it "work." It is mental and emotional labor. It is exhaustive and exhausting, not only for the bereaved but also for those about them and those who would be of comfort to them. Ideally, it should allow for an emotional return to the helplessness of a safe infancy, a kind of symbolic rebirth which a new chapter of life can be woven out of the fabric of the old, the pain and struggle of the grief process itself, and the hopes for the future.

Grief is so painful that people will attempt to flee from it by any means. Flight from the pain of grief, however, can offer only temporary relief; eventually the price is costly.

The ability to grieve is also the ability to enjoy life!

those who knew him and those who did not, who mourned the loss of an expectation that life was the way it was supposed to be."

Dr. Graves asks, "How do each of us in each circle cope with his or her loss? How are you, who stand in your own circle in another city, coping with yours, and are you feeling unconnected to the main circles? My guess is that we are all similar in some ways, which means that the ripples are ever-larger as we grow to understand how death is and can become the symbol of our definition of life and living. Who among us has not been a part of his own circle and put events, things, and people in perspective according to the shifting values following a death? Who among us had not shook her head when she learned of the death, when she stood together with the family at the visitation and the funeral, and when she gets together with other loved ones to share memories?"

Whether the death occurs close to home or happens half way around the world, Dr. Graves explains that shaking our heads in disbelief is actually a form of coping. It is a ritual that is performed which is nonverbal and universally understood. The gesture speaks clearly, "I don't understand. Why did this happen? This isn't right! Make the nightmare stop." The gesture allows us to touch each other. It is a universal movement that transcends the necessity for words. It indicates, in an acceptable fashion, that a major change has occurred. She reflects that we all resist change. With the shaking of our heads we are saying no to change, and particularly to a change that is painful. "In the face of no we can question how and why. These are universal words that help us search for meaning—not just in death, but in life."

The field of psychology asks questions about concrete living and it is an outgrowth of philosophy, which questions life in the abstract. Dr. Graves says, "We need our questions, our outcries, our sometimes feeble attempts toward explanation." She explains that when those around us in the circle use platitudes and talk of God's will, "They are seeking purpose, as much for themselves as for those who they believe they are comforting, while others around us in the circle talk of details in the coroner's report or the medical examination. By seeking out this information, we are searching for reasons, whether concrete or abstract, which lead to the event of the death. The search is another of our basic coping characteristics." This is especially poignant when death happens away from the immediate area.

Each of us must experience his or her own pain alone while keeping the delicate balance necessary in reaching out to others for support. "When those in the inner circle find themselves smothering each other, telling each other what should be done, becoming too dependent or too isolated, it is time to remember those first critical moments when we reached instinctively from the heart and from the strong survival instincts with us." When those in the outer circles feel helpless and lost, feeling the emotions of grief because of this death, they need to reach to their own circle for support because survival in any society depends on each member of that society.

Dr. Graves asks us to reach into the next circle and those circles at a distance, too. "These are the 'historical people' who share memories with you, who can tell you stories you have heard a million times and loved, or can tell you new stories about the one you loved. In reaching out to others who grieve with you, you are also giving the care and respect toward other human beings in pain. If you listen you will hear their need for others in other circles."

When we are grieving, especially in the initial shock of the death, we tend to ignore the relationship our loved one had with friends and other close acquaintances. These people in the outer circles—perhaps thousands of miles away—grieve for expectations, hours spent in debate, or shared laughter with our loved one. They grieve for the plans that must be changed and the financial arrangements which must be altered, the same anger you experience when that "pebble" was dropped in the water too soon. Their grief and sorrow is as real as yours.

While it might seem impossible at this time, if your loved one has recently died away from home, you may want to contact his or her friends, colleagues, and neighbors. A note or phone call about the funeral or service, a shared memory, will help those who also grieve process the death and build new memories.

A MILITARY DEATH

When a member of the military dies, the designated branch of the services has, as you can imagine, a full operation procedure to take care of all the details. But after reviewing the manuals, there are real, warmhearted human comrades who grieve and experience the pain of separation and change. The manuals do not mention them.

When a death occurs involving a member of the U.S. Marine Corps, for example, a Casualty Assistance Calls Officer (CACO) is immediately assigned the responsibility to tell the next of kin about the death and help coordinate the funeral arrangements. But a CACO is more than the messenger of bad tidings, he or she is typically a close friend of the deceased or someone with whom the deceased has served.

According to a command chaplain with the navy, typically the CACO and another officer or a chaplain will personally visit the immediate family of the deceased. Arriving in uniform, the CACO will have as many details of the death as possible. While it might seem to "outsiders" that there should be a specific person who always calls on families after a death, every man and woman in the military has the opportunity to be a CACO and assuming the role immediately takes precedence over other jobs which are assigned. Telling a spouse or parent that a military member has died isn't a position anyone chooses, yet part of the code of honor in the military service is that each member cares for his or her service members and the dependents of those members, too.

The military makes allowances for travel to the funeral or burial, provides an escort for the body if it is to be returned, and makes arrangements for the family to be given timely information on the status of the death or impending death. When there has been any type of death, including those involving hostilities and casualties, the family is kept abreast. The military keeps the names of the service member and next of kin out of the press until the family has first been informed.

The officer who informs the family of the death makes a commitment to stay with the family until other help arrives. He or she returns to visit with the family and becomes their liaison to untangle the maze of paperwork and helps secure the benefits and services provided by the military. If the loved one died of unusual circumstances, the CACO discusses their rights and helps the family file an investigation report.

A visit from a chaplain and a CACO isn't one any military wife or husband welcomes, however, the CACO stays with that family and devotes as much time as necessary to help solve the problems incurred by the death. On the second visit—within forty-eight hours after the first— the officer or other person who has been appointed to help the family provides support for the disposition of the remains, whether it will be done in a military fashion or through a private funeral home. The officer helps determine if it is appropriate to have a visitation and viewing of the loved one's body. Obviously, with a military death, that's not always possible.

The officer or other appointed individual helps with funeral dates and times, the location of the service, and the choices available if the family wants a full military funeral or a memorial service. The family is also informed about survivor and Social Security benefits, including a lump-sum death gratuity issued immediately to help the primary next of kin of active duty staff to meet immediate living expenses. Other money paid to next of kin varies in amount depending on the disposition. For active duty military, approximately three thousand dollars is paid to the family for interment in a private cemetery, two thousand dollars is paid for a memorial service (for example if there are no remains), and there are allotments for headstones and markers. As previously discussed, military personnel and their dependents may be buried at no cost in a government cemetery, provided there is space. All benefits and payments are made to the designated next of kin without the assistance of a civilian attorney. In some cases, attorneys have collected half of the money due survivors when the attorneys' services were unnecessary.

Depending on the military survivor's closeness with the deceased, he or she may be eligible for other benefits including employment preferences and educational opportunities from scholarships to grants. This information may be available through the help of the CACO or by contacting the nearest Veterans Administration office.

The military does not issue death certificates, but a Report of Casualty is issued within three weeks after the death. This Report of Casualty is used in the same way as a death certificate, such as to change title on property and obtain life insurance benefits.

A marine chaplain explains that when a military member has died away from his or her home, the body is returned home or to another location designed by the family. The personal effects (of the nonmilitary variety) are sent on to the family. The military dependents of the deceased are reimbursed for travel expenses back to the home of record of the service person, as are the household goods.

For example when a marine lieutenant died in a car wreck in Germany, his remains were escorted back to a suburb of Portland, Oregon, by a service member. Personal effects, such as clothing, books, and electronic equipment, followed shortly. Right after the death, the headquarters in Germany contacted a military base in Oregon and the deceased's parents were contacted personally by a CACO from the Portland area. She assisted in the funeral arrangements, sat with the family during visitations, and found the answers to matters regarding death benefits. She attended the funeral. But her personal responsibility didn't stop there. She checked in on the young man's mother and father off and on for two months, making sure she telephoned them on Christmas Eve right after speaking to her own mother. While she didn't know the lieutenant, she became good friends with the family. She went above and beyond what the manual says must be done, and not every CACO goes to this extent. She knew that should something happen to her, the time she spent helping the family through a tough period would be repaid by another marine.

THE MILITARY FUNERAL

It is the responsibility of the closest military unit, whether that is a reserve unit or a unit on a military base, to officiate at a military funeral, if the family desires one. Some families, according to a spokesperson from the chaplain's office at Camp Pendleton, California, are so angry they want nothing from the military. The CACO and chaplain understand the anger and frustration survivors feel. Other families believe that a military funeral is a closing ritual and a tribute to their loved ones who loved their country.

At a military funeral, as with a civilian one, the family must make certain decisions, such as visitation (if appropriate), who will preside at the service (a military or civilian chaplain or clergyperson), and whether there will be flowers or donations in lieu of flowers. The military provides a flower arrangement.

While there may be a ceremony or service in a chapel, the military ceremony is typically at the grave, with a seven-person firing party for the salute or volley, a bugler to play

WHAT YOU THINK—YOU ARE!

by Therese A. Rando, from *Loss and Anticipatory Grief*

ठ&

We have cried, mourned, protested, and retreated deep within ourselves; we have been angry, anxious, and depressed. Now we have to ask ourselves what viable options are left open to us. We can think of committing suicide, mourning forever, or escaping to another part of the country or the world. Or we can get back into life with hope in the future, determined with self-management, knowing there is no alternative. We can say, "There's no use in trying. I'm through, finished with living." Or we can say, "No matter what, despite everything, I will go on and declare with the Psalmist, 'I will not die, but live.'"

At times it may still seem that all hope is lost, that life is a covenant with sorrow and that there can never be joy, love, or a better tomorrow. Jeremiah felt that way when the land was devastated and the Temple in ruins: "My heart within me is broken. All my bones shake." He then became determined to do something about his hopelessness. It was at this time that he bought land in Judea to show hope in the days, months, and years that were yet to be. Even when his people were in exile and there seemed to be no hope, his faith strengthened him to hear, "Thus saith the Lord. Refrain thy voice from weeping and thine eyes from tears.... There is hope for thy future sayeth the Lord" (Jeremiah 31: 16-17).

taps, pallbearers, and an officer of equal or higher rank than the deceased. Whether the service is held at the grave or a chapel, the U.S. flag is draped over the casket. Sometimes when there are flowers covering the casket, a military representative holds the flag during the ceremony. If there is a memorial service, and the cremains are present, one military representative holds the flag while another holds the urn with the loved one's cremains. The cremains are either sprinkled, buried in the urn, or given to the loved one at this time. At the end of the military portion of the funeral, the flag is given to the primary next of kin.

Normally, the chaplain on the military base where the surviving dependents have lived acts as a support to the grieving family. When asked if there are any support groups for survivors of deaths of military personnel, a military chaplain explained that while military service has a long history and members are dedicated to serving their country and their fellow service members, in actuality they are in the service to do a job and so no support groups are offered. This is their work. Thus, outside support groups, such as those listed within the chapters and the index, are extremely valuable.

Even though it seems unfortunate that the military does not have specific emotional and bereavement support for dependents, it is a reality of our lives. We wouldn't expect IBM or General Motors to offer any type of grief support groups for survivors of their employees. However, the chaplain said that many military base groups do provide short-term support that can be turned into help for dependents, and the CACO or chaplain can provide referrals to grief support groups, too.

SURVIVING THE DISTANCE WHEN A LOVED ONE DIES AWAY FROM HOME

"By itself, the list that follows will not do much for you and is certainly not meant as a checklist for 'ten quick steps to triumphant surviving,'" says psychologist Ann Kaiser

Stearns. "However, the guidelines are an aid to dealing with loss, and can be very helpful."

Dr. Stearns explains that people who do move beyond brokenness, overcoming tragedies and hurts, do some unusual things during the grieving and healing process. She says, "Triumphant survivors think and behave in ways that lead to recovery." This "checklist" is especially pertinent when you cannot be with the family or friends after a loved one has died, if you cannot attend the service, and anytime you're feeling alone, and perhaps forgotten. Remember, you can:

- Establish positive memories, loving memories shared with others.
- Search for answers and find whatever help is needed from friends, family, experts, helping professionals, your church or synagogue, books, healing activities, or support groups.
- Develop survival strategies such as dealing with pain in small segments.
- Make an early decision to go forward and actively reinvest in the future.
- Examine events fully and acknowledge the full range of your human emotions.
- Decide to grow in self-acceptance and take active steps in that direction.
- Experience a crisis of faith and encounter feelings of terror and a continuing struggle, yet become aware that forward movement is taking place.
- Leave encumbrances behind—old resentments, grievances, axes to grind, remembered injustices— the harbored memories that grow increasingly heavy. You can decide not to waste your life by permanently losing yourself in sorrow, defeat, anger, fear, or guilt.
- Work on getting a good mental picture of your loss or crisis event. Gradually, you can form a clear sense

Death used to announce itself in the thick of life but now people drag on so long it sometimes seems that we are reaching the stage when we may have to announce ourselves to death.... It is as though one needs a special strength to die, and not a final weakness.

—Ronald Blythe, from
The View in Winter

Our community of saints, living and dead, is testimony that the gates of hell shall not prevail against us. We can endure. We can survive, and we can take up hope again.

—Jack Silvey Miller,
senior minister, Mount Kisco
Presbyterian Church

of the emotional issues and make concrete plans for your future based on your changed circumstances and the "new person" you have become.

- Plan ahead.
- Look for inspirational role models.
- Associate with and learn from people who have the ability to laugh, enjoy, and see humor.
- Make a firm decision that you *want* things to work out well, *want* to recover, *want* to build a new life for yourself.
- Recall individuals and events in your past that can provide strength, hope, and encouragement in difficult, discouraging times.
- Open yourself to serendipitous events.
- Use rituals and symbolic acts as an aid to healing.
- Find a variety of fitting ways to say good-bye—frequently and fully.
- Accept the best life within reach.
- Go forward, knowing the sorrows and hardships you've had to come through, but looking ahead far more than looking back.

An Emotional Note When Dealing with Death at a Distance

Just because you're unable to attend the funeral service or just because the memorial services is in a city you've only heard of in geography class, doesn't mean that you will not feel the pain of the death. Often when we receive a notice of the death of those we love, even if the relationships had to span half the globe, we cry. Crying and working through the emotions of grief are very real whether we attend the visitation at the funeral home or sit alone at the kitchen table pondering our futures without our loved ones. This often brings up thoughts of the meaning of life and the meaning of death.

THE MEANING OF DEATH

When we are not able to be a with a loved one when he or she dies, when the death occurs out of the city, state, or country, when it happens suddenly and there's no time, we often feel a triple dose of shock, disbelief, and numbness. "He was going on vacation....this couldn't have happened." But it did. "She was just going into the city to see a play....this couldn't have happened." But it did. Rabbi Maurice Lamm, president of the National Institute for Jewish Hospice and professor at Yeshiva University's Rabbinical Seminary in New York, talks about death and the value of life.

"What is death? Is it merely the cessation of the biological function of living?" asks Lamm, the author of *The Jewish Way in Death and Mourning*. "Is it but the tragedy to end all other tragedies? Is it simply the disappearance of the soul, the end of consciousness, the evaporation of personality, the disintegration of the body into its elemental components? Is it an end beyond which there is only black void? Or, is there a significance, some deep and abiding meaning to death—one that transcends our puny ability to understand?

"With all of modern man's sophistication, his brilliant technological achievements, the immense progress of his science, his discovery of new worlds of thought, he has not come one iota closer to grasping the meaning of death than did his ancient ancestors. Philosophers and poets have probed the idea of immortality, but stubbornly it remains, as always, the greatest paradox of life.

"In practice, however, we must realize that what death means to the individual depends very much on what life means to him. If life is a stage, and we the poor players who strut and fret our hour upon the stage and then are heard no more; if life is a tale told by an idiot, full of sound and fury, signifying nothing; if life is an inconsequential drama, a purposeless amusement—then death is only the heavy curtain that falls on the final act. It sounds its hollow thud: *Finita la comedia* and we are no more. Death has no significance, because life itself has no lasting meaning.

YESTERDAY
by Robert Kastenbaum and Ruth Aisenberg, from *The Psychology of Death*

ᔥ

We are told that it is futile to contemplate death. "Ignore death" is the advice, for to dwell upon this subject sickens heart and mind, and to no good purpose. And we are told that the only proper way to conduct one's life is through the daily, if not hourly, contemplation of that inevitable moment toward which all flesh moves.

We are told that death is a biological fact that is no more important than the punctuation at the end of the supreme fact of our existence, a fact that shapes the meaning of everything else in our lives.

We are told that fear of death is instinctive, deeply rooted in human nature. And we are told that in the depths of our psyche none of us can truly accept or even understand the proposition that we are mortal.

Healthy people who contemplate death do so with nervous laughter, or with composure, or with denial, resignation, intensity, indifference, doubt, certainty. Critically ill people and others who face imminent death maintain a silence. Sometimes this is an agitated silence—at other times, it is stoical, tranquil, or enigmatic. Or, they face death with desperate maneuvers, eager anticipation, dread, apathy, or rather mixed sentiments.

THE TIMES AS IT KNOWS US

by Allen Barnett, from *The Body and Its Dangers and Other Stories*

૨**ঔ**

You let go of people, the living and the dead, and return to yourself, to your own resources, like a widower, a tourist alone in a foreign land. Your own sense becomes important, and other people's sensibilities become a kind of Novocain, blocking out your own perceptions, your ability to discriminate, your taste. There is something beyond understanding, and I do not know what it is, but as I carried the phone with me to the couch, a feeling of generosity came over me, of creature comforts having been satisfied well and in abundance, like more than enough to eat and an extra hour of sleep in the morning. Though I hadn't had either, I was in a position to anticipate them both.

The time being seeps in through the senses: the plush of a green sofa; the music we listen to when we attempt to forgive ourselves our excesses; the crazing pattern on the ginger jar that reminds us of why we bought it in the first place, not to mention the shape it holds, the blessings of smells it releases. The stretch of time and the vortex that it spins around, thinning and thickening like taffy, holds these pleasures, these grace notes, these connections to others, to what it is humanly possible to do.

"But if life is the creation of a benevolent God, the infusion of the Divine breath....then death is a return to the Creator at the time of death set by the Creator, and life after death the only way of a just and merciful and ethical God. If life has any significance, if it is not mere happenstance, then man knows that someday his body will be replaced, even as his soul unites with eternal God.

"In immortality man finds fulfillment of all his dreams. In his religious framework, the sages equated this world with an anteroom to a great palace, the glorious realm of the future. For a truly religious personality, death has profound meaning, because for him life is a tale told by a saint. It is, indeed, full of sound and fury which sometimes signifies nothing, but often bears eloquent testimony to the Divine power that created and sustained him.

"The rabbis say *hai alma k'bei hilula damya*; this world can be compared to a wedding. At a wedding two souls are united. In that relationship they bear the seed of the future. Ultimately, the partners to the wedding die—but the seed of life grows on, and death is conquered, for the seed of the future carries the germ of the past. This world is like a wedding."

Whether the death occurred in your arms or far away from the place you call home, Rabbi Lamm speaks clearly and echoes the thoughts of many: Death has meaning if life has meaning. If one is not able to live, will he be able to die?

૨**ঔ**

The pain of your loved one's death may now have reached the point of numbness and you ache with the knowledge that you are grieving deeply. More so, you instinctively know that you will shortly be responsible for the practical matters. This can be a tremendous stress at a time when your emotions are taut. If you have not done so, it is time to clear up financial matters, perhaps settle the estate, and hire a financial consultant. The practical matters of your loved one's death are the topics for the following chapter.

Chapter

8

Practical Matters of the Death

During the time when grief is especially painful and the death of your loved one seems to be the only thing you can think about, just getting through each day is exhausting enough. Practical matters such as settling an estate, changing the title on an automobile, or sorting your loved one's possessions are, for most people, as far from reality as the urge to scramble up the side of Mount Everest.

All too soon, however, you will be asked to make decisions regarding the disposition of your loved one's possessions and property, perhaps finalize his or her taxes, file for veterans and Social Security benefits, apply for continuation of health insurance, arrange for a tax return to be filed. These practical matters can be simple or go on for years. In our mobile society, family members often live in two locations, own property out of the state, and have outstanding debts. All these technical details must be resolved after the death, and often before grieving can be resolved.

The assignment can be formidable. Once more many of the tasks and responsibilities can be shared with other family members, yet sometimes others are unable to cope with the more realistic side of death and the details are left in your

There is a great deal of pain in life and perhaps the only pain that can be avoided is the pain that comes from trying to avoid pain....

—R. D. Laing, psychologist

It's natural to see signs and hear voices. Don't feel crazy, but be a little careful how you interpret them. Some people hang onto these signs as living proof that the one who died is still very near, physically. They want to believe that he or she is communicating with them from the other world and that our two worlds are very close together. A more healthy reading of signs is to see them as reminders that the love which was will always be.

—Rev. Jack Silvey Miller, from *The Healing Power of Grief*

hands. Since this may be the first time you've had to deal with the practical matters of death, the fundamental decisions, and the basic issues of life, it's encouraged that you seek professional legal and financial advice whenever an issue is in question.

Within this chapter, we'll provide an overview of what needs to be done to settle an estate along with how to apply for benefits and select the professionals to aid in the tasks ahead.

WHEN IT'S TIME TO SORT A LOVED ONE'S BELONGINGS

If you haven't done so already, it is now probably time to collect, sort through, and make decisions regarding the disposition of a loved one's belongings. For some, it's so tempting to avoid dealing with this matter; others simply throw out everything that was ever touched or owned by the one who died. The temptation to get rid of everything stems, many believe, from the illusion that if you can deal with and dispose of the possessions, you will make quick business of disposing of the pain and hurt of grief. However, grief can be hidden away for days, months, and years, but it must be processed through our consciousness if we are to move ahead and turn the grief into memories.

When should you begin to organize and decide what to keep and what to give away? The first few weeks after the death of a loved one are probably far too soon for most of us. It is a hard job and when the death is fresh in our minds, it may be too difficult.

Your loved one's personal belongings do not magically disappear with death. Seeing, touching, and smelling your loved one's clothing and other possessions will bring back a flood of feelings. Whether or not you had a positive relationship with your loved one, the feelings may mirror what you are thinking—guilt, loss, anger, reconciliation, or acceptance.

For one woman, helping her mother sort through Dad's things brought tears and smiles. Tucked within pages of his favorite books, included in the paid medical bills, and even stashed in jacket pockets, Katherine's father had left notes for his daughter as they had previously agreed. He knew that she would fly to Ireland to be with her mother after his death. She found messages such as, "Kate, I love you more than a father could ever hope to love a child," and "I'm very proud of you." She also found lovely poems; the scribbled words to the lullaby he had sung to her as a baby. Folded in the envelope with his will was a faded photograph taken during World War II. It was of a smiling, handsome RAF captain in dress uniform balancing a blond toddler on his shoulders—lilliputian Katherine and her beloved parent. The notes from her father were both heartwarming and heart-wrenching, but she cherishes the remembrances and gifts he left for her all the same.

After helping her mother sort through her father's possessions, another woman returned to Chicago and her law practice with her father's stained and work-worn gardening shirt. "I didn't want Mom to wash it. I wanted to keep that smell of Dad and sweat and dirt and sunshine....just like he smelled when he was alive." Even now, once in a while, she'll take the shirt out of the box, squeeze it and rub it. The fragrance of her father, most likely, is gone, but the memories are there.

Unless you absolutely must sort through the possessions by yourself out of desire or necessity, it's very comforting to have a close friend or family member with you. It's often better to have only a few people. Like chefs making soup, too many well-intended recommendations can be exasperating. While you need help, too much can just cause arguments and upset you needlessly. Take breaks often. You may want to stop for lunch or dinner to lessen the intensity of the chore.

THE TASKS OF GRIEF
by Elaine Vail, psychology professor at Western Illinois University, from *A Personal Guide to Living with Loss*

ॐ

Grief has been likened to "cleaning out our closets." We slowly, item by item, go through our memories and emotions. We relive the significance of each bit of the past relationship we have lost and then put it away, retaining only the essence.

As we go through the closets of our minds, we discard the worn-out ideas and commitments to make room for new perceptions and involvements. The effect of this cleaning process is, appropriately, "cleansing." We slowly begin to feel renewed as we assess and appreciate the value of our previous experiences and begin to see the potential for a new and necessarily different future.

We make room in our "closet" for a fresh wardrobe of interests and relationships, to be integrated with the mainstays which have survived the years. We are reborn.

Actually, if you can do any of the organization beforehand, such as putting all important papers in one box, or washing up dishes and taking out the trash, the better you will be able to handle the task. Becoming organized about the job will make you feel more in charge, less overwhelmed as you sort through those things which belonged to your loved one.

Don't be afraid to reminisce about when a piece of clothing was worn, or how hard it was to find a particular color, or how silly some item was to you at the time as you look at your loved one's possessions and clothing. Everyone buys something silly. Maybe she had an obsession for salt and pepper shakers in the shape of cartoon characters. Maybe he loved tools and had a wrench for every possible use under the sun. And who over forty doesn't remember bell-bottoms, miniskirts, and tie-dyed T-shirts?

As you begin the responsibility, allow your emotions to move through the process with you and laugh over the funny memories. Cry, if you need to, because you miss the person. And as you review the entire job ahead, decide which of your favorite mementoes you want to save, and which to give to family members, close friends, charities, churches, or yard sales. After you complete the job, or the first hour of the job, you may want to reward yourself for a responsibility now completed. Do something to reaffirm life—crunch an apple, take a walk, turn up your favorite music and dance.

John W. James and Frank Cherry, authors of *The Grief Recovery Handbook* and cofounders of the Grief Recovery Institute, an internationally recognized authority in the areas of death, education, and grief counseling, recommend a specific plan for disposing of a loved one's clothing and possessions. They suggest that you use the ABC approach for clothing and other items that belonged to your loved one. They lovingly refer to this as the "Pile Plan," and suggest that your objective is to end up with what you really want to keep without having a lot of stuff you think you ought to keep but really do not want. Again, they suggest that you have a helping partner with you during this cleaning out and sorting process, if you want or think you may need assistance.

They tell grievers to take all the clothing out of the closet and put it all in the living room or other large area. You are to go through everything, one item at a time.

"Make three piles of clothes," they write. "If you want to talk about a memory that one of these articles stimulates for you, please do so with your partner." The piles should be grouped as follows:

Pile A: Contains the items and clothing you are sure you want to keep.

Pile B: Contains the things you are certain you want to dispose of. These are the things you will want to sell, give to other family members, or give to charity or the church.

Pile C: Contains all the things that you have yet to make up your mind about. If there's any doubt regarding the item, put it in Pile C.

James and Cherry, consultants and lecturers who have been working with grievers for over ten years, say not to consider this a race. "We are employing a clear plan that works. As you stand in the room looking at all the clothes, it may dawn on you why some people refer to this as the Pile Plan." They suggest that we would dispose of the piles as follows:

Pile A: Goes back into the closet.

Pile B: Is given to individuals and groups.

Pile C: Goes into bags and boxes and to the garage or attic.

They say to congratulate yourself and thank your partner. If your partner is also a survivor, next week go to his or her house and do the same. "One month later bring all the Pile C bags and boxes into the living room and work the plan over again. Once again, never alone!

"Pile A is for the few things you find that you want to keep. Pile B is for those things you are sure you want to discard. Everything else goes back in the bags and boxes and back into the garage or attic. Doing this task one more time will accomplish your goal of keeping what you want to keep and not retaining things that you don't need."

If your loved one prepared a letter of instruction, a list of how, when, and where he or she would like property given or divided, then you should follow this directive when sorting personal things and belongings. The following information on letters of instruction should help you know how to handle property disposal, too.

THE LETTER OF INSTRUCTION

A letter of instruction sometimes is prepared along with a will. The letter of instruction explains how disposition of the body should be performed, the type of funeral service (if any), and other specific wishes not included in the will. A letter of instruction allows family and friends to carry out the immediate wishes of the loved one who died exactly as the loved one wished.

For instance, if Aunt Tilly wants only a simple burial with just the close family attending, she may call this out in the letter of instruction. If she wants Spike, her pet boa constrictor, to be given to a niece, she will advise this. If she wants to be buried in a specific outfit or wants to have the cremains of her cat, Fluffy, buried with her, she will indicate this. The letter of instruction is typically discussed before the death with those who will care for the immediate arrangements after the death so that everything can go smoothly.

Sometimes in a letter of instruction the writer typically calls out specifics on how to dispose of or divide personal property, such as clothing, family photos, plants, and pets. Items and property of value, such as stocks, bonds, artwork, and real estate property, are normally excluded in the letter of instruction because they are a part of the estate and must be probated if not held jointly. Estate attorneys often encourage their clients to set up a living will (a legal documentation that specifies what dramatic life-sustaining measures an individual may or may not want to be taken in case of incapacitation or severe illness), set up a living trust (a legal document that transfers specific assets and property when an individual dies), and list assets and liabilities in the letter of instruction so that the estate can be settled and probate (the action or process of proving that a will is genuine) can be avoided or proceed more smoothly.

The National Funeral Directors Association offers information on specifics it recommends be included in the letter of instruction. Depending on how your loved one's letter of instruction is written, you may want to organize it as follows:

- Full name
- Maiden name
- Date and place of birth
- Names and birthplaces of parents, if living, and address and phone number
- Social Security number
- Date and place of marriage
- Name and address of spouse
- Names and addresses of any previous spouses
- Names, addresses, and phone numbers of brothers, sisters, dependents, or children
- Other relatives to be contacted
- Friends, employers, colleagues to be contacted
- Religious affiliation
- Memberships in professional and fraternal organizations
- High schools/colleges attended, including place and dates

Writing a will is probably one of the nicest things you can do for the people you love. An effective will can insure financial security, name a preferred executor of the estate, minimize costs of settling the estate, minimize estate taxes, and provide peace of mind for the testator during his life and for his heirs upon his demise. But the complexity of modern law places certain restrictions upon preparation of the will and almost eliminates the opportunity for a do-it-yourself last will and testament. Even in small or modest estates, legal counsel can provide helpful perspectives and advice that can result in a far more suitable document for all concerned.

—Elaine Vail
from *A Personal Guide to Living with Loss*

- Which newspapers or publications should run an obituary
- Part of the body to be donated to medical science
- Funeral director/funeral home
- Clergyperson or other to preside over service
- Instructions for visitation
- Type of service
- Special instructions, hymns, and readings for service
- Donations made in his or her honor
- Names, addresses, and phone numbers of casket bearers
- Location of will, along with name, address, and phone number of attorney and/or executor
- Location of the key to the safe-deposit box and name and address of the bank where the box is located
- Location and account numbers of all checking and savings accounts
- Location of checkbooks, passbooks, and other certificates
- Location, name, and number for charge accounts and credit cards
- Location of insurance policies, ownership title to cards and other property.

If your loved one was a veteran, then you may also want to include the following:

- Date and place of enlistment
- Rank and service number
- Organization or outfit
- Commendations received
- Location of discharge papers
- Flag desired to drape casket

HOW TO FIND IMPORTANT PAPERS

If your loved one died having completed a letter of instruction and a will, your work will be much easier. However, if your loved one did not organize his or her estate before the death occurred, you may feel overwhelmed with the funeral details, the thought of settling the estate, and the grief you are experiencing. Additionally, before an estate can be settled or property disposed of according to the law of your state and the wishes of your loved one, you must find documentation.

Before you begin to search out papers you believe are necessary, you may want to talk with your loved one's estate attorney, or the executor. You may be lucky; perhaps he or she has copies of everything that is necessary to settle the estate. If not, typically, a safe-deposit box is the logical place to keep stock certificates, birth certificates, jewelry, and other valuable items. Often you can figure out at what bank the box is located by check stubs or statements from a bank.

You will also need tax returns, records of loans, and titles to cars and property. Experts suggest looking in desk drawers, closets, dressers, the garage, attic, and, yes, even under the mattress. You may have to become Sherlock Holmes if your loved one was like the elderly woman who sewed thousands of dollars worth of savings bonds into the liners of her living room drapes and stored one hundred dollar bills in the books in her den.

Before you dispose of any property which is not to be covered in the estate or which must go through the legal procedure of estate settlement, look at it closely. Sometimes what we consider to be the ugliest knickknack ever created is a valuable piece of Americana. Contact an antique appraiser or other knowledgeable professional on any questionable items. Remember, stranger things have happened than finding a Picasso sketch buried beneath a pile of 1953 *National Geographics*.

YOUR LOVED ONE'S WILL

If your loved one had a will, that is, a legal document written by your loved one or his or her attorney specifying how property or estate should be distributed after death, and you are the spouse or closest next of kin, you should obtain a copy. If you have not told his or her attorney that your loved one has died, do so now. If the attorney prepared the will, he or she will also have a copy on file.

Some people mistakenly place their wills in a safe-deposit box which, in some states, is sealed until after the estate is settled. If the safety deposit box has been rented in your loved one's name alone, a court order will have to be obtained to get into the box, and only papers pertinent to the estate may be removed until the will has been probated. Your attorney can help you get the court order to remove the papers. Your loved one's property will be dispersed according to the will.

If your loved one died without a will, this is called dying "intestate." The property of your loved one will be dispersed according to the laws of the state in which he or she died. If there was property held jointly (such as with a married couple), that property is immediately turned over to the survivor and does not have to go through probate. This includes property held with "right of survivorship," and money from life insurance or other insurance or pension benefits. Also if there are no stocks, bonds, or other property or assets and/or other items have been transferred to a jointly held situation *before death,* then the family can often probate the will themselves, simply by filing a modified probate form. The county court or probate court can provide information as to how to handle the disbursement of the estate.

For example, if Mother was living in a nursing home for the last two years, any property or valuable possessions have been transferred to others. If the family home has long since been sold to support your parent's medical needs, your mother gave you and your sister her antiques, and you both have contributed to her support, the family will probate all that is left. Any outstanding medical bills will have to be absorbed by those who have previously accepted the financial responsibility before the death.

If your loved one died without having filed a will or if there is valuable property which is not held jointly, you will probably have to hire an attorney to help in the probate process. Most states regulate the fees for probate, but this doesn't mean that the fees are low, and they vary from location to location. Sometimes, for considerably less, you can hire a paralegal, sometimes called a legal assistant, who specializes in probate cases. You can also ask your attorney if his or her paralegal can help with the case and perhaps reduce the financial burden. Or you can find out if you can do some of the work yourself, which can also reduce the cost. Your local legal aid office or senior center may have probate help available at a greatly reduced cost, too. You can contact the probate court in your state for details on how to handle this situation. (In some states the probate court is called a surrogate, chancery, or orphan's court.)

Whenever possible, the heirs should be told of any land mines that will detonate when the will is read. "Parents who intend to leave most of the estate to the child who looked after them should explain that up front to take the pressure off that child and let the others understand their reasons," says Peter Brown, senior vice-president at Chase Lincoln First Bank in Rochester, New York. Typically, parents shy away from this situation in hopes that peace will be maintained while they are alive. Actually, conflicts, arguments, and severe breaks in the family structure are often passed down along with the stocks and bonds.

TRUSTS AND WILLS

Sometimes there is confusion between what a will does and what a trust can do. Both wills and trusts are set up prior to the death. Basically, with a trust specific assets and property are transferred to the trust. There are revocable

WILLS AND LIVING WILLS
by Mark A. Edinberg, Ph.D., from *Talking with Your Aging Parents*

ॐ

Will: A will is a legal document that specifies how you wish your assets to be distributed upon your death. It may include provisions for trusts; usually names an executor or individual who will oversee the distribution of assets; and can list contingencies such as who will be executor if the named executor is unable to fulfill that obligation.

Living Will: The living will is recognized by some states as a legal indication of what dramatic life-sustaining measures an individual may or may not want to be taken in case of incapacitation or severe illness. The reason for having such a document is to spare an individual from physical suffering he or she does not want, or secondarily, to preserve assets from being spent fruitlessly to maintain life when there may be little advantage in doing so.

trusts (ones which can be changed) and irrevocable trusts (which cannot be changed). A trust typically must be formatted by an attorney and is a legal document. Both types of trusts avoid probate and, depending on the terms of the irrevocable trust, it may remove assets from taxable income and reduce income tax.

A will is a legal document that distributes property. A will does not give assets to an heir without paying possible taxes, depending on the inheritance.

Various types of trusts, including testamentary trusts (established in your will) or living trusts (established during your lifetime) can be used to protect an estate at death.

Trusts and other estate planning strategies can help you avoid probate. If probate can be avoided with adequate consumer protection, it will help you save the cost of estate administration and the time it takes a court to complete the work.

Trusts are formal, sophisticated planning devices which require guidance of an attorney extremely knowledgeable in the field. Do not let the formality of most trusts cause you to avoid this planning instrument. Trusts can meet certain goals and provide significant benefits which well justify the professional assistance they require.

Where to Get Help

Offices of The Grief Recovery Institute
P.O. Box 6061-382
Sherman Oaks, CA 91413
(818) 907-9600

The Institute creates and establishes grief recovery programs for junior and senior high schools throughout North America. The institute delivers workshops and seminars for the Compassionate Friends, the National SIDS

Foundation, the National AIDS Network, THEOS, and offers seminars each year for the public.

• The following books may be helpful:
• *The Complete Book of Wills & Estates* by Alexander Bove, Jr. (New York: Henry Holt and Co., 2000), provides advice on the management of wills, what to do should a will be contested, how to go about probating an estate if the will is lost, and how to hire a probate or settlement attorney. The helpful book also provides a checklist and timetable of how to disperse an estate if you find yourself in the role of executor, or if you want to make sure your executor is proceeding effectively.
• *The Widow's Handbook: A Guide for Living* by Charolette Foehner and Carol Cozart (Golden, CO: Fulcrum, 1989) is a very practical book, one which takes the reader through real-life situations and provides clear, nonlegalese information on how to cope with the financial and legal aspects of being widowed.
• *Probate: Settling an Estate, a Step-by-Step Guide* by Kay Ostberg (New York: Random House, 1990), gives valuable information on the will and probate process. It also identifies the probate rules for each state.

HALT
An Organization of Americans for Legal Reform
1612 North K St. NW, #510
Washington DC 20006
(888) FOR-HALT
(202) 887-8255
This national public interest group champions simplified low-cost or reduced-cost probates.

While they will not respond to questions and inquiries on probate practices over the telephone, they will do so in writing.

American Association of Retired Persons
AARP
601 E St., NW
Washington, DC 20049
(800) 424-3410

The organization offers many programs and publications for the widowed and retired individual including the informative brochure, *Final Details*. A free publication list is available on request.

Local bar associations, referrals through legal aid, and senior associations in your area can also recommend a probate attorney or advice if you believe that you should change attorneys during probate.

Commission on Legal Problems of the Elderly
740 15th St. NW
Washington, DC 20005
(202) 662-8690

This organization provides information, low-cost, or perhaps free legal services to senior citizens. The association also publishes information on wills and probate practices, and a bibliography is available on request.

DEALING WITH PROBATE
Probate is the legal process authenticating an

individual's will, of paying a deceased's outstanding debts, and distributing his or her estate to the rightful heirs according to the law of the state in which he or she was a resident when the death occurred. Generally, property that is not held in joint tenancy, transferred previously into a trust, or held with a right to survivorship, must go through probate. It is a way to legally settle an estate.

Property, (including automobiles), which is located in another state owned by the loved one who died, must be probated according to the laws of that state. For example, if your father lived in North Dakota but owned an apartment house in Mississippi, the property would become part of the total estate, but it would have to be transferred according to the laws of Mississippi.

All expenses, including those of the attorney and the executor, as well as taxes, filing fees, and other debts, are deducted from the proceeds of the estate. If you require funds to support yourself or dependent children or adults while assets and property in the will are being probated, your attorney and executor can advise you of how to get those funds.

It is up to the family to notify a loved one's attorney that he or she has died and the attorney will file the will with the court, or you may have to hire an attorney to help you through this legal red tape. In your loved one's will, he or she had probably appointed an executor or representative to be in charge of these proceedings. If there's no will, the spouse of the deceased or parent of the deceased (if the deceased was unmarried) usually is appointed. It is up to the executor to inform all who need to know of the death so that they can file claims against the estate. If a claim is not filed (meaning that an outstanding debt is not recorded or asked for) and the will is probated, the debt is cancelled.

When you meet with the attorney, bring along your questions and all unpaid bills and/or outstanding debts. You may want to bring life insurance policies, mortgage insurance policies, pensions, labor union benefits, veterans benefit claims, and other paperwork so your attorney will have all the information readily available—and you won't have to make two trips.

Whenever you have a meeting with an attorney or executor (or another professional regarding the disposition of your loved one's estate such as an accountant or financial planner), it may be beneficial to take someone else along. After a death, friends and family ask how they can help; this is one way. The good friend will not be in the way. On the contrary, he or she can help remember what transpired in the meeting, perhaps ask some of the questions, and be a sounding board when you discuss the best course of action to resolve the facets of the estate.

Before you sign anything involving your loved one's estate, make sure you clearly understand the paperwork. If you don't understand specific terms, ask. The attorney is supposed to be there for you as well as to represent your loved one. If you do not feel your best interests are being served, you will want to talk to the attorney about the problem, then perhaps seek the services of another estate attorney.

Under the guidance of the attorney, the executor or spouse must file a petition with the court after the death, and there is a fee for this filing. If the estate is extensive, an attorney who practices estate law is almost essential. Although there will be a fee involved, probate attorneys are regulated by law. You should ask about the attorney's fee and what the probate will probably cost (and entail) before doing business. It's just wise. The fee can often be paid in installments, deducted from the estate, or paid as a percentage of the estate.

Proceeds from accounts such as Individual Retirement Accounts (IRAs) or life insurance policies are payable directly to the beneficiary and need not go through probate. You must file for these benefits and will need copies of the death certificate to do so.

THE ROLE OF THE EXECUTOR

Disposing of the estate is one of the jobs of the executor whether it is according to the letter of instruction, the will, or the laws of the state. Depending on the state and law of the county, sometimes an executor is the male gender term used, while executrix is the female gender term used; estate administrator or estate administrix are also used.

Typically a surviving spouse is the executor; often an adult child or close family friend is named an executor. A loved one who foresees the rivalries between his or her children after the parent's death often names someone who will not directly benefit from the estate, such as a colleague. A family attorney can be the executor, but one does not have to be an attorney or know the law to take on this job. In a situation where there has been a death of the surviving spouse and the children are under legal age, another individual is appointed as executor.

The executor will not only perform the services required by law, but will follow what he or she believes were the intentions of your loved one. The executor is entitled to be paid a fee for his or her service, although some executors do not accept payment. Again, it's wise to confirm this point.

It is the job of the executor to take an inventory of the estate, to search out property owned or indebted, and to let creditors know of the death. The executor pays off debts, helps to transfer property, and administers the funds according to the wishes of the will and the laws of the state in which the loved one was a resident.

At the end of this process which can take months to years, the length of which depends on the vastness or complications of the estate, a closing statement is filed with the probate court. A copy is sent to those who have an interest in the estate and then the estate is closed. Although it's tempting to throw away all the receipts and bills and tax forms and assorted "important" papers from your loved one estates, most probate lawyers advise against it. Check with the attorney

THE OPENING OF ANOTHER DOOR
by Therese A. Rando,
from *Loss and Anticipatory Grief*

❧

A sage who was about to die saw tears on the faces of his disciples and he asked, "Why do you cry? I'm leaving by one door only to enter by another."

When we begin life it is stretched before us like a corridor with many doors. We open and close the doors of infancy, adolescence, maturity, and old age. As we walk down the corridor, the doors close behind us one by one, year by year. We finally open the door for death and, as we do, we open yet another door for eternal life.

There are so many doors we never touch, and never open. Before it is too late, let us open the doors that lead to truth, comfort in our sorrow, and faith in immortality. More than anything else, let us open the doors to those things in life which abide eternally, those that give life meaning—the doors of tenderness and love.

It is not too late to love and it is not too late to live. It is not too late to thaw ourselves out of our chilling sorrow for the opportunities of living. It is not too late for those who are frozen by the coldness of grief, whose hearts have been made icy and unfeeling, to be warmed by giving life, hope, and love to others.

before disposing of any documents.

The executor is not a custodian of the property, although he or she is in charge of the estate. Likewise, the executor is not a guardian of minor children or dependent adults.

THE ROLE OF THE GUARDIAN

A guardian is often identified in the letter of instruction and must be specifically appointed in the will of the loved one who has died. A guardian is directed to care for minor children and other dependents such as a mentally disabled adult or parent or other dependent relative who has been under the care of the deceased. If a guardian is not named, the court will name someone to care for these dependents.

He or she is sometimes paid by the estate to care for the dependents and typically agrees to the responsibilities before the death of the parent or caretaker.

SOCIAL SECURITY AND YOUR LOVED ONE'S ESTATE

You may be entitled to benefits from Social Security. If you have not done so yet, and your spouse or parent was covered by Social Security, you must apply for these benefits. They are not automatically given to you.

Your loved one was covered by Social Security if he or she paid into the program for at least forty quarters. You can check with the Social Security office at (800) 234-5772 or the local number listed in your telephone book under Department of Health and Human Services, in the government office section.

To make a claim, you will need to know your loved one's Social Security number. If you don't have the actual card, you can often find this information on tax return forms or other tax statements.

If your loved one was covered and you are eligible,

there are two possible benefits:

1. There is a death benefit of about $255 toward burial expenses. You must complete forms available at the Social Security office. Sometimes the funeral director at the mortuary you are using will have the forms. Obviously, this benefit is paid only to an eligible spouse or eligible children.

2. A survivor's benefit for a living spouse or eligible children is available if:

   - The deceased spouse was age sixty or older and eligible for benefits. The amount of benefit received will be less if it is received before age sixty-five than after age sixty-five.
   - A disabled spouse is age fifty or older.
   - The spouse of the deceased is under sixty, but cares for dependent or disabled children under sixteen.
   - The children of the deceased are under age eighteen, or disabled.

When applying for benefits, you will need your loved one's birth certificate, death certificate, and marriage certificate (if you are a spouse), birth certificates of dependent children, the deceased's Social Security number, and copies of the deceased's latest federal income tax return. You will also need your own identification.

When you go to the office of the Social Security Administration, it sometimes helps to:

   - Make a list of questions you want to ask.
   - Ask a friend go with you to the office.
   - Make sure you write down the name and telephone number of the individual assigned to your file. You may have other questions when you return home.

In addition to their many services, the Social Security Administration provides free information on Medicare and Medicaid. The following free pamphlets are also available from the U.S. Government Printing Office or your local Social Security office. The telephone number is in the "government section" or white pages of your telephone book: *Your Medicare Handbook; Your Social Security; Medicaid-Medicare: Which Is Which?*; and *Introducing Supplemental Security.*

INSURANCE POLICIES AND OTHER BENEFITS

Your loved one may have had life insurance, mortgage (or loan) insurance, accident insurance, auto insurance, credit card insurance, and other types of insurance sometimes offered by an employer. In order to obtain benefits from these policies, if applicable, the named beneficiary must apply. You should file a claim as soon as possible as it often takes time to be processed. Sometimes you have options regarding how you will receive the funds, either in a lump sum or in payments. You may want to talk with your financial advisor or attorney with regard to what is best for your situation.

The proceeds of life insurance, if a living person is named as a beneficiary, do not need to be included in the estate which is probated. However, if your loved one named his or her estate as the beneficiary for the life insurance proceeds, it will have to be included as an asset in the estate.

To file a claim, you will need to present a copy of the death certificate to each policy holder and sometimes other requirements must be met. If the text of the policy is too complicated for you to understand, talk with an expert. Sometimes the funeral director you used when your loved one died can help in these matters, too.

If your loved one was employed, he or she may have been covered by other insurance policies or various pension plans at work. Additionally, there may be money due from sick leave pay, vacation pay, or other vested retirement or stock plans. You can talk with a representative at the company's human resources department. Sometimes after a death, the deceased's survivors continue to receive a pension, although it may be reduced. The American Association of Retired Persons suggests that you contact all previous employers regarding any pension or life insurance benefits that may be available.

If you cannot find a policy, but believe there is one, you can contact the insurance carrier, Mutual of Omaha for example, and ask to have their records searched under the name(s) of your loved one. The insurance company will forward a form on which you must verify that you are the beneficiary before the claim can be processed.

If you have hired an estate attorney, how to handle a lost or misplaced insurance policy, along with other assets you believe to have been owned by your loved one, is one of the items you should discuss.

There are times when major insurance companies and their representatives fail to understand the needs of the individual, or times when a claim is being mishandled. Each state has a regulatory commission or insurance board which oversees the ethics of the insurance business. If you believe that your claim has not been handled correctly or you have not received the benefits you believe are due, you can file a protest or claim with your state's insurance board. (Your estate attorney, if you have one, can handle this, too.) You can find information on your state's insurance board by looking in the government section of your local telephone book's white pages. As with other legal actions, often the threat of an action will produce miraculous results in straightening out a tangled claim.

Keep in mind that premiums on any insurance must continue to be paid while the claim is being processed or the policy may become invalid. Record amounts and dates of the money paid after the death of your loved one so that you can ascertain if all money is refunded.

VETERANS' BENEFITS

If your loved one was once in the military and was a veteran who received a discharge (other than dishonorable), you may be entitled to benefits toward burial expenses, currently $300 and $150 toward a plot in a private cemetery. Burial in a national cemetery is free to a veteran, spouse, and dependent children. Keep in mind that not all national cemeteries have grave sites available so if your loved one wanted to be buried in a national cemetery, you may have to keep an alternative cemetery in mind should a grave in the first be unavailable.

Veterans are also eligible for a grave marker at no cost or about $60 toward a marker or headstone. Again, the funeral director or a staff member at the local Veterans Administration office can advise you as to the procedure for this benefit.

Your funeral director should be able to help you apply for these benefits or you can contact the Veterans Administration nearest you. The estate attorney or the estate's executor can also help you. You can locate the Veterans Administration by looking in the government section of your local telephone book's white pages. You may have to ask the funeral director to contact the VA. You must file a claim or no benefits will be paid.

The VA puts out two helpful booklets, *A Summary of Veterans Administration Benefits* and *Federal Benefits for Veterans and Dependents*. You can obtain these by contacting your local Veterans Administration office.

When you apply for benefits you will need a copy of the

death certificate, Social Security number or service number (which can be different depending on the years your loved one served in the military), and your own identification and connection to the veteran who died. As when you apply for Social Security benefits, it's always helpful to write down a list of questions and the names and phone numbers of the people you have talked with at the VA. Make sure you have a pad and pen so you can take notes of what needs to be presented to the VA in order to get the benefits. Additionally, you may find it helpful to have a friend go with you so that you can discuss what happened after the visit.

YOUR LOVED ONE'S TAX OBLIGATION

With recent changes in the federal tax structure, few estate taxes are required to be paid. Your best advice on this topic comes from an attorney, accountant, other financial expert, or an IRS representative. You may be entitled to claim a five-thousand-dollar death benefit exclusion on your income tax return, so it will be worth your while to inquire. A federal estate tax return must be filed and taxes paid within nine months of your loved one's death.

Additionally, a federal tax return of the deceased's income must be filed for the year in which he or she died at normal filing time, unless there has been a request for an extension. A surviving spouse may still file jointly for the year of the death. A spouse with dependent children may file jointly for the next two years. Contact your Internal Revenue Service office (the phone number is in the telephone book under Federal Offices) for booklet #559, *Information for Survivors, Executors, and Administrators*, for more information on filing.

Tax obligation laws vary from state to state. As the AARP points out in their informative brochure *Final*

Details, if you have to file a federal estate tax return, there may also be state inheritance taxes to be paid. Your regional state tax office or your financial expert can help you determine if you must file and/or pay taxes. Other brochures offered free from AARP include: *Will Your Social Security Benefits Be Taxed?, A Woman's Guide to Pension Rights* and *The Social Security Book: What Every Woman Absolutely Needs to Know.*

AARP Tax-Aide

The Tax-Aide program is a free, nationwide service offered by AARP between February and April 15 of each year to low-and moderate-income taxpayers. As part of the program over twenty-five thousand volunteers are trained in cooperation with the IRS to counsel older people about their income taxes. The counselors are specifically trained to deal with tax problems encountered by retirees—Social Security benefits, sale of the family home, and credit for the elderly or disabled.

Tax-Aide counseling is offered in some ten thousand sites around the country, and in twenty different languages. Special arrangements can be made to provide tax counseling to the homebound and the disabled. For the location of the counseling site nearest you, telephone the IRS information number in the government pages of your telephone book, or write to the IRS office nearest you.

CHANGING OWNERSHIP, NAME, OR TITLE

After the death of your loved one, if you are the surviving spouse or the individual who has inherited the property, you will want to inquire about changing ownership or title. The AARP suggests you check or make changes on the following:

- *Insurance policies*: You'll need to change beneficiaries or you may decide to change the amount of the insurance policy. For example, if there would have been a large benefit paid to your spouse after your death, but he or she died before you, you may want to change the amount since the situation has changed. You will want to change auto insurance and the name on your home insurance policy, too. Remember to continue to pay on the policy even when the paperwork is being transferred, otherwise it might become invalid.
- *Health insurance*: Under a federal law known as COBRA, you and your dependent children may continue a spouse's work-related medical insurance policy up to thirty-six months, providing you pay the premiums. Check with your spouse's employer (if applicable) to see if you can continue on the group policy indefinitely, then shop around to see if you can get better coverage, or less expensive coverage other places. You'll probably have to contact the insurance carrier for more information on these changes. You may need to purchase health insurance if you are not now covered.
- *Automobile title*: You may have to change the title on a car owned by the deceased. You will need to contact your state's Department of Motor Vehicles for instructions, and most likely you will need a copy of the death certificate to make the change.
- *Your will*: Now that your loved one has died, if he or she was a beneficiary of your will, you will want to make a change. You may want to talk to your legal expert for assistance.
- *Bank accounts, stocks, bonds, trust funds*: On joint bank accounts, the funds will automatically pass

to the spouse or joint account holder. You will want to fill out a new signature card at the bank and perhaps put another's name on the account with you. If you are the next of kin and have a safe-deposit box, you may want to add another name on the safe-deposit box that you have.

• *Credit cards*: Those held only in the deceased's name should be cancelled. Outstanding debts must be paid by the estate. If you hold joint credit card accounts, you must continue to make payments and you will want to inform the credit card holder about your spouse's death as you have the name changed on the account.

Where to Get Help

Depending on the estate your loved one has bequeathed, you may have to select and work with attorneys, accountants, and experts.

The American Association of Retired Persons has a pamphlet on how to choose an attorney, financial adviser, accountant, and other professional entitled *Money Matters*. You can obtain it by sending a postcard with your request to:

AARP Fulfillment
601 E Street, NW
Washington, DC 20049

You may also want to refer to:
Our Money, Our Selves: Money Management for Each Stage of a Woman's Life by Ginita Wall, C.P.A., C.F.P., and the editors of Consumer Reports Books (Yonkers, NY: Consumer Reports Books, 1992). An excellent all-around financial book, written in plain English, the appendixes at the end

are most valuable for planning for the future. You'll get information on topics such as when to sell assets, how to keep track of financial advisors, planning the funeral, and formatting a financial worksheet.

Personal Finance for Dummies, Eric Tyson, (Hoboken, NJ: John Wiley & Sons, 2000). *Personal Finance for Dummies* offers sound and practical advice for those who want to get control over their personal financial lives. Great section on common mistakes that we all make in our approach to money and prescribes ways to save and invest for a secure future. Using worksheets, the book helps you to measure your own financial health by looking at factors such as how much debt you carry, your savings rate, as well as investment and insurance checkups.

HANDLING THE DEBT YOUR LOVED ONE INCURRED

According to accounting experts, depending on your relation with the deceased you may or may not be obligated by the debts incurred before the loved one's death. For example, if you are a spouse, hold joint property, or are listed as a cosigner on a note with the individual who died, you will be responsible and you will probably be held accountable for the debt. There are "credit counseling" services advertised in the newspaper and telephone book that can help you set up a payment plan. You may want to contact the local senior center. Often through senior citizen organizations there is help available for senior citizens to straighten out unpaid or complicated medical bills left after the death of a spouse. These services also advertise in the Yellow Pages of the telephone book and/or your physician may be able to make a referral.

WORDS OF WISDOM
by Dick Davis, stock market
analyst and author, from
*Tilting the Investment
Odds in Your Favor*

ૐ

*I offer this bit of advice:
Speak softly about your
winnings, always be aware of
your limitations, be flexible,
patient, tolerant, and
maintain your sense of humor.
And most of all, keep things in
perspective. This investment
game is important—but when
you come right down to it, it's
just numbers. We try and
make the numbers as good as
we can.... but some people let
numbers control their lives—
save the twenty-five dollars,
but for a quarter point less,
earn another eighth of a
percent.*

*It may seem vital at the
time—but looking back over
the course of a lifetime, the
pursuit of numbers is likely to
prove less important than the
quest for such values as love,
health, and service.*

*So keep your priorities.
Maybe a lesser return on your
investments makes sense in
exchange for a higher return
on your life.*

As long as your name isn't on the deceased's debts or credit accounts, you will not owe on the accounts after the death. However, if you are entitled to inherit any money or property from the estate, you will have to wait to collect until the will has been probated and creditors are paid.

Your best advice comes from an accountant who is familiar with the laws and procedures in your state. You may want to talk to an attorney or other expert on how best to handle the outstanding debts left when your loved one died and debts that were incurred jointly, such as the mortgage on your home.

Some widowed people prefer not to take their deceased spouse's name off utility bills or telephone bills. It is not necessary to inform companies with whom your loved one has done business that he or she has died, and many people continue to have a spouse's name listed in the telephone book well after the death.

FINDING A FINANCIAL ADVISOR

The estate attorney you have selected to work through the probate for your loved one's estate may be able to advise you on how best to handle the money generated by the estate or bequeathed to you. Often, an attorney will defer to a financial planner or adviser or certified public accountant or tax accountant. Because you may be able to avoid paying sizeable amounts of taxes if the money you inherit is invested, it behooves you to make a financial plan and perhaps find a financial advisor.

However, if you have been advised that you need extra assistance, you may want to seek the advice of an investment manager. People who choose to hire an investment manager, an individual who charges a fee to advise you and to buy stocks, bonds, and mutual funds, often do so because:

- They believe that they can make more money from the money they are investing.

- They believe that someone with more experience can evaluate the potential of various investment opportunities more effectively.
- They want to rely on someone with more education, formal training, and background in the investment field.
- They believe that investment managers do a better job than individuals.

C.P.A. Ginita Wall, author of *Our Money Our Selves: Money Management for Each Stage of a Woman's Life* and a practicing certified financial planner, recommends interviewing financial advisors as you would any other professional with whom you would have financial dealings.

You will do well to ask the following questions, take notes, and compare the answers when you meet with other prospective financial advisors:

- How long has the company been in business?
- How long has the advisor been in business? Will he or she furnish references?
- What services does the company provide?
- How will the services be provided?
- Will the advisor help set up financial goals, decode the investment portfolio you will now manage, or work with you to invest the money you've inherited?
- Who are his or her other clients?
- What are the clients' financial needs and requirements?
- How has the financial planner advised them?
- What amounts and types of investments has he or she suggested?
- What are some of the investments he or she generally recommends to clients? Some financial advisors recommend only mutual funds, bonds,

government tax-free bonds, and others help set up a diverse program for investment.

- How is the advisor compensated for his or her advice?

Wall suggests you ask your advisor, "Do you handle your clients' assets directly?" Be wary of financial advisers who want you to hand over all your investment assets. She also points out, "Some financial advisers have a vested interest in selling you products that will earn them commissions, and that may not be in your best interest. To find a competent and trustworthy financial adviser, ask friends, family members, and colleagues in your general financial situation for their recommendations, then interview those advisers to see how well their style meshes with yours."

Financial planning and consulting is a business, and after an initial consultation you will be expected to pay for advice. According to Michael Stolper, president of the financial firm Stolper & Company, "Depending upon portfolio size and the management in question, annual fees can range from 1/2 percent to 3 percent of the assets under management. However, the question of fees is often subordinate to more pressing considerations such as the search to find the right person to manage your money. One of the few valid clichés in the investment management business is, 'The fee is only significant if the manager is doing a poor job.' "

PRACTICAL MATTERS CONTINUE

Practical matters often continue throughout the grief process. There's not one cutoff date when you can say, "Phew—I've finally finished resolving all the details regarding my loved one's death." As time goes on there will be less and less to do. For many, after the practical matters are completed, they begin to get their own "houses in order." They take time to write their letters of instruction, update their wills, choose a guardian for their minor or handicapped children, and do all the small things they wished their loved ones had done before death.

੨&

In the next chapter, the focus is on death after a terminal illness. We will discuss the effects of long-term illness on the survivors, anticipatory grief, the hospice program, and how to prepare children and others for the death of a loved one. Self-proclaimed "jollytologist" Allen Klein, a nationally known inspirational speaker, offers a loving, sensitive slant on the heartfelt effect of laughter on health, love, and death.

Chapter 9

Death After a Terminal Illness

Dr. Elisabeth Kübler-Ross says, "People die in character." If a loved one has always been warm, loving, and giving, that most likely will not change when death is near. On the flip side, if a loved one has been known for the last five years as the most cantankerous resident in the nursing home, in the final few weeks or days of life, he or she probably won't change. However, these changes do happen; it's simply not typical of the human species.

When facing the death of a loved one, there are often an infinite number of feelings that swirl through our minds, some relieving, some terrifying, knowing our life course has been altered. This chapter concerns itself with preparing for the death of a loved one, focusing on this special person as well as the effect of death on the survivors after a loved one dies of a terminal illness. While we'll talk about Alzheimer's disease, cancer, and other terminal illnesses in a general format, some aspects of AIDS will be addressed separately.

FACING THE PROSPECT OF DEATH

People react similarly when faced with the prospect of a terminal illness. Often, according to experts such as Dr. Kübler-Ross, the terminally ill patient and his or her family, especially the immediate caregiver, go through the five stages of the dying process beforehand. Some authorities believe there is no set order or pattern. One family member may feel the depression, immediately followed by intense anger; another may stay in the denial stage for months, then finally move into acceptance. Other experts believe that the stages can be experienced simultaneously.

Similar to the stages of grief outlined in chapter 3, according to Dr. Kübler-Ross, the five stages of the dying process are:

1. *Denial*: Refusal to accept the evidence that a loved one is dying. "She was fine just last week—we talked on the phone." "You're crazy. I was with him yesterday, and he didn't tell me about the cancer." "You're wrong—the doctor just made a terrible mistake. Those are someone else's test results."

2. *Anger*: The "God, why me!" stage when the intensity of the facts overcomes all other emotions. "It's not fair—she is so young and has so much to live for!"

3. *Bargaining*: "If I live (or if the baby lives), I'll never drink again....go on vacation without her again....go to synagogue every week....attend mass every day." Or "Let me live long enough to see the kids graduate from college." This is an attempt to postpone death or alter the schedule of death. Often unreasonable, family and the one who is terminally ill will pledge, promise, and plead for a reversal of the imminent death.

4. ***Depression***: The hopelessness of denial, anger, and bargaining begins to become a reality and depression overcomes the thoughts of those who are dying and the loved ones who will survive the death. This is the stage when hopelessness sets in, "I can't eat—why bother." "If he is not going to live, why should I?" During this time, the family may constantly want to talk about the disease, the medication, the care the hospice or physicians are giving. The family is caught up in the death, unable to move to the next step.

5. ***Acceptance***: According to Dr. Kübler-Ross, this is often a peaceful, even joyous, stage of the anticipatory process of the death of a loved one. Some people come to the ultimate conclusion that death will bring a release from pain, anguish, and suffering.

There are those who are unable to move through the stages. With some, it seems that they continue to deny the inevitable, yet, when questioned, they have had the other emotions. They hold onto denial for security. It is at this time that many, if they are not currently involved in it, seek outside help with support groups, available through their local hospice. Specific groups for survivors provide expert help and a nonjudgmental place to talk through the events, long after other family and friends may be tired of hearing about the death.

You let go of people, the living and the dead, and return to yourself, to your own resources, like a widower, a tourist alone in a foreign land. Your own sense becomes important, and other people's sensibilities a kind of Novocaine, blocking out your own perceptions, your ability to discriminate, your taste.

—Allen Barnett,
from *The Body and Its Dangers and Other Stories*

Where to Get Help

The following organizations and books may be helpful at this time:

Concern for Dying
200 Varick Street
New York, NY 10014
(212) 366-5540

This organization works to improve the care of the dying and provides referrals and counseling on the right-to-die issue.

The Hemlock Society USA
P.O. Box 101810
Denver, CO 80250-1810
(877) HEMLOCK

The most public of euthanasia groups, the society provides newsletters, a reading list, and information on how to contact local chapters.

Dying with Dignity
55 Eglinton Ave. East, Suite 705
Toronto, Ontario M4P 1G8
CANADA
(416) 486-3998 or (800) 495-6156

Dying with Dignity is an organization that distributes living wills and durable power of attorney forms to Canadians. Makes some referrals and provides counseling.

Notes on Living Until We Say Good-bye: A Personal Guide by Slone G. Nungesser with William D.

Bullock (New York: St. Martin's Press, 1988) is a practical guide when terminal illness is the diagnosis. It addresses the questions of Who should I tell? How should I go about it? and What do I do when...? The tone is warm, friendly, and comforting and can be beneficial at an extremely hard time for patients as well as caregivers and family members.

When Is It Right to Die: Suicide, Euthanasia, Suffering, Mercy by Joni Eareckson Tada (San Francisco: Harper San Francisco/Zondervan Publishing, 1992) offers practical experience and answers on the right to live, the right to die. Tada shares her philosophy and gives comfort from God, as well as her experience, to meet the cold realities of those facing and considering death. Filled with anecdotal stories of life-and-death questions and issues.

Final Gifts: Understanding the Special Awareness, Needs, and Communications of the Dying by Maggie Callanan and Patricia Kelly (New York: Poseidon Press, 1992) gives an insightful overview of the supposed confusion suffered by the terminally ill in their final days and helps readers "uncode" the special messages that the loves ones are offering.

The Rights of Patients: The ACLU Guide to Patients' Rights, second edition, by George J. Annas (Carbondale, IL: Southern University Press, 1989). Valuable information including appendixes on the Patients Bill of Rights Act and the Right to Refuse Treatment Act.

Intensive Care: Facing the Critical Choices by Thomas A. Raffin, M.D., Joel N. Shjurkin, and Wharton Sinkler III, M.D.(New York: W. H. Freeman, 1989). Easy to read, the book talks about the risks, benefits, and responsibilities of intensive care. It discusses when it is appropriate and includes costs.

How each of us experiences grief is a highly individual matter, and we should not feel strange if we react differently than our friends or family members react to their own losses. Each relationship is unique and the death of one individual will be perceived uniquely by a spouse, mother, father, sister, brother, daughter, son, or best friend. While we may share our grief with others who feel the loss, too, no other person can know exactly the impact this loss has on our own life.

—Elaine Vail, from *A Personal Guide to Living with Loss*

❧

For years, before I ever started medical school, I had a very particular picture of how I was going to die. I find that I'm too superstitious to write down all the details, even now, if I write them down, then will the death happen right? Or else I'll die in some completely alien way, and everyone will know that it wasn't my death of choice, because I went and told the world about my death fantasy. So I'll merely say it's a fantasy that's triggered when I see those headlines they run in newspapers: "Bus Plunges off Embankment in Pakistan."

The interesting side to all this is that I suspect that the very old and the very sick often feel the same way I do. They may know many of the rules of the road, they may know how they'll die—but they aren't ready to come to terms with death, any more than I am. The healthy, watching the sick in the hospital, tend to announce that they hope someone will shoot them before they get as sick as so-and-so. But perspective shifts, and you end up with a critically ill patient who isn't interested in any planning for the possibility of death.

KNOWING WHEN DEATH IS NEAR

In the final stages of life, there are no rights and no wrongs. The stages may come suddenly, within hours, or a loved one may move slowly through these facets, or may skip over some. There's no particular order. Like many other hospice programs, the Neighborhood Visiting Nurses Association based in West Chester, Pennsylvania, provides home health care. They share the following information with those families who are involved in the hospice program or with in-home care for the terminally ill. Knowing what to expect during the final stages of life can help families comfort themselves and their loved ones in the same supportive manner as through the terminal illness.

The following are guidelines, offered by the Neighborhood Visiting Nurses Association, to supplement, only, the information you should receive from your doctor or hospice staff. These professionals are your best source for the care of your loved one during the final stage of life.

What to Expect

When a person enters the final stage of the dying process, two different dynamics are at work which are closely interrelated and interdependent. On the *physical* plane, the body begins the final process of shutting down, which will end when all the physical systems cease to function. Usually, this is an orderly and undramatic series of physical changes where there are not medical emergencies requiring invasive intervention. These physical changes are a normal, natural way in which the body prepares itself to stop.

The other dynamic of the dying process is at work on the *emotional-spiritual-mental* plane. The "spirit" of the dying person begins the final process of release from the body, its immediate environment, and all attachments. This release also tends to follow its own priorities, which may include a resolution of whatever is unfinished of a practical nature and permission to "let go" from those gathered. These "events" are the normal, natural ways in which the spirit prepares to move from this existence into the next dimensions of life. The most appropriate kinds of responses to the emotional-spiritual-mental changes are those that support and encourage this release and transition.

When a person's body is ready and wanting to stop, but the person is still unresolved or unreconciled over some important issue or with some significant relationship, he or she may tend to linger, even though uncomfortable or debilitated, in order to finish whatever needs finishing. On the other hand, when a person is emotionally-spiritually-mentally resolved and ready for this process, the person will continue to live until the physical shutdown is complete.

The experience we call death occurs when the body completes its natural process of shutting down, and the "spirit" completes its natural process of reconciling and finishing. These two processes need to happen in a way appropriate and unique to the values, beliefs, and lifestyle of the terminally ill person.

Therefore, as families seek to prepare themselves as this event approaches, the members of the hospice care team let them know what to expect and how to respond in ways that will help the loved one accomplish the transition with support, understanding, and ease. This is the greatest gift of love to be offered a loved one as this moment approaches.

Signs and Symptoms in the Final Stage of Death

The physical and emotional-spiritual-mental signs and symptoms of impending death that follow are offered to help you understand the natural kinds of things which may happen and how to respond appropriately. Not all the signs and symptoms will occur with every person, nor will they occur in this particular order. Each person is unique and

Needless to say, you don't get to choose your death. I think of good deaths and bad deaths in the hospital sense now, and I judge many of my decisions against my what-I-would-want-done-for-me index. There's an unexpected familiarity with death that comes with the job I do, one that still shocks me at times. But you see deaths and you cope with deaths and at times you even orchestrate deaths, and you think a little about how you might face your own. What you might die from. And you know, old age still isn't a bad answer.

HEALING DOESN'T ALWAYS MEAN CURE
by Rabbi Maurice Lamm

ॐ

It would be cruel and misleading to many people with terminal illnesses such as cancer or AIDS to insist that a positive attitude can guarantee them physical cure. In fact, many illnesses cannot and will not be cured, and the longer you live the more likely it is that you will eventually die from a fatal degenerative illness such as cancer.

The fact that some illnesses do reach a terminal stage does not discount the importance of attitude for shaping the quality of the life that remains. Further, it is unfair for cheerleaders on the sidelines to exhort the patient to fight for goals that are no longer appropriate, realistic, or even possible for their loved one, because they cannot bear the thought of his or her death.

needs to do things in his or her own way. This is not the time to try to impose change, but the time to give full acceptance, support, and comfort.

Fluid and food decrease: The person may have a decrease in appetite and thirst, wanting little or no food or fluid. The body will naturally begin to conserve energy which is expended on these tasks. Do not try to force food and drink into the person or try to use guilt to manipulate him or her into eating or drinking something. Since normal hydration is often not feasible, it is more peaceful to decline in a state of dehydration than fluid overload.

Small chips of ice, frozen juices, or Popsicles may be refreshing in the mouth. Be aware of decreases in swallowing ability, and do not force fluids if the person coughs soon after. Reflexes needed to swallow may be sluggish. The person's body lets him or her know when it no longer desires or can no longer tolerate food or liquids. The *loss* of this *desire* is a signal that the person is making him- or herself ready to leave. Dehydration no longer makes the person uncomfortable. Glycerine swabs, used to apply a water soluble lubricant, may keep the mouth and lips moist, comfortable, and hydrated.

Decreased socialization: The person may want to be alone, with just one person, or with very few. It is natural not to feel like socializing when one is weak and fatigued. As well, the path seems a solitary one of progressive detachment. It appears that our words can sometimes arouse a person to be present with us, so be careful to allow as much quality rest time as possible. Reassure your loved one that it's okay to sleep.

Sleeping: Your loved one may spend an increasing amount of time sleeping, and appear to be uncommunicative, unresponsive, and, at times, difficult to arouse. This normal change is due in part to changes in the metabolism of the body.

Sit with your loved one, hold his or her hand, do not shout or speak loudly, but rather speak softly and naturally. Plan to spend time when he or she is most alert. At this point, *being with* is more important than *doing for*. Speak directly and normally, even though there may be no response. Never assume that the person cannot hear you. Hearing is said to be the last of the senses to be lost.

Restlessness: Your loved one may make restless and repetitive motions such as pulling at bed linen or clothing. This often happens and is due in part to the decrease in circulation to the brain and metabolic changes. Do not be alarmed, or try to interfere or restrain such motions. To have a calming effect, speak in a quiet, natural way, lightly massage the hand or forehead, read to the person, or play soothing music.

Disorientation: The person may seem confused about the time, place, and identity of the people surrounding him or her, including close and familiar people and animals. Identify yourself by name before you speak rather than asking the person to guess who you are.

Speak softly, clearly, and truthfully when communicating something important for the loved one's comfort. For example, you might say, "It's time to take your medication." Explain the reason for the communication, such as, "So you won't begin to hurt."

Urine decrease: Your loved one's urine output normally decreases and may become tea-colored, referred to as concentrated urine. This is due to the decreased fluid intake, as well as decreased circulation through the kidneys, and fluid loss in breathing and respiration. Talk with your doctor or hospice nurse to determine if there is a need to insert or irrigate a catheter.

Incontinence: During the final stage of life, your loved one may lose control of urine and/or bowels as the muscles in that area begin to relax. Protective measures should be taken to keep the patient clean and comfortable.

Breathing pattern change: Your loved one's regular breathing patterns may change with the onset of a different breathing pace. A particular pattern consists of breathing irregularly with shallow respirations, or periods of no breath for five to thirty seconds, followed by a deep breath. The terminally ill family member may have periods of rapid, shallow panting-type breathing. Sometimes there is a moan-like sound on exhale. This is not distress, but rather the sound of air passing over relaxed vocal cords.

These patterns are very common. They indicate a decreased circulation in the internal organs. Elevating your loved one's head and/or turning onto the side may bring comfort. Hold his or her hand. Speak gently and reassuringly.

Congestion: In this final stage of life, your loved one may develop gurgling sounds coming from the chest, much like a coffee percolator. Sometimes these sounds become very loud and they can be very distressing to hear until you are prepared and aware of this facet of death.

Watch your loved one closely and note that he or she is usually unaware of his or her bodily processes. It is probably harder for you to watch than it is on the patient. Raise the head of the bed so the secretions pool low and therefore the gag reflex is not stimulated. Elevating the head, and/or turning onto the side may bring comfort. Hold your loved one's hand. Speak gently and reassuringly.

Color changes: Your loved one's arms and legs may become cold, hot, or discolored. The underside of the body may become discolored as circulation decreases. This is a very normal indication that the circulation is conserving core energy to support the most vital organs.

Irregular temperatures can be the result of the brain sending unclear messages. Keep the patient warm if he or she appears cold, but do not use an electric blanket. If your loved one continually removes the covers, then allow him or her just a light sheet.

Permission to go: Families giving permission to a loved one to let go—without making him or her feel guilty for leaving or trying to keep the loved one with the family to meet their own needs—can be extremely difficult. A dying person will commonly try to hold on, even though it brings prolonged discomfort, in order to be assured that those left behind will be all right. A family's ability to reassure and release the dying person from this concern is the greatest gift of love they can give at this time.

Saying good-bye. When a loved one is ready to die, and the family is able to let go, this is the time to say good-bye in personal ways. This closure allows for the final release. It may be helpful to just lie in bed with the person, hold a hand, and/or say everything you need to say.

Tears are a natural part of making peace and saying good-bye. They do not need to be hidden or apologized for. They are expressions of love.

Although the death of a loved one is a stressful event, if you can free yourself from anxiety and fear, then you can help the terminally ill to experience the final stage of life in an atmosphere of calmness and peacefulness.

The following will be evident at the time of death:

- Breathing ceases.
- Heartbeat ceases.
- The person cannot be aroused.
- The eyelids may be partially open with the eyes in a fixed stare.
- The mouth may fall open as the jaw relaxes.
- There is sometimes a release of bowel and bladder contents as the body relaxes.

Where to Get Help

Films for the Humanities and Sciences
P.O. Box 2053
 Princeton, NJ 08543-2053
(800) 257-5126

DYING WITH DIGNITY
by Mark A. Edinberg

One of the great lessons that has been learned from people who work with the dying is that there are specific things that can be done to improve the quality of life for the dying person. These are all subsumed under the idea of "death with dignity." By this, I mean that the dying person has the right to:

• Privacy.

• Control over as much of his or her life as possible (including when to get up, when and what to eat, what clothes to wear, what activities to do, what topic to discuss).

• Make decisions.

• Decide whether or not to discuss his or her death at a given moment with health professionals, clergy, or friends.

• Have any wishes granted by others, within the limitations of resources and the dying person's condition.

This organization provides videos on a wide range of topics for those who have experienced a loved one's death. *Difficult Decisions: When a Loved One Approaches Death* and *Dying Wish* are two of the most timely if your loved one is dying of a terminal illness. Call or write for a free catalog. The videos can be rented as well as purchased. You can also contact your public library, hospice, or hospital to find out if they have these and other videos.

The American Cancer Society
1599 Clifton Road, NE
Atlanta, GA 30329
(800) 227-2345
The ACS headquarters will direct you to the local chapter.

The National Hospice and Palliative Care Organization
1700 Diagonal Rd., #625
Alexandria, VA 22314
(703) 837-1500

This organization serves as a clearinghouse for referrals and information on hospice. The operator at NHO can also direct you to a local hospice for information, support, and referrals for the dying and after death.

PREPARING CHILDREN FOR THE DEATH OF A LOVED ONE

The feelings and emotions when death is eminent can often be more confusing to children than adults. Children, disabled older adults, and those who are mentally handicapped can be prepared for the death of a loved one before the death actually occurs, and doing so will help them weather the storm of grief.

Most young people who are informed about the condition of the loved one who is dying or terminally ill are able to cope more easily if they have some experience with death and know exactly what is happening (to the best of your knowledge) before the event.

The death of a loved one, while extremely hard on you personally, can be an opportunity for instruction on one of life's greatest lessons including how to effectively process grief. When talking about death to children and others who do not have the mental capability of an adult (including the elderly and infirm), you can include examples of plants that are dying and the leaves of fall that change color and die. You can point out dead insects or snails on the sidewalk. You can talk about a pet dying. You can also read some of the children's books about death. Becoming familiar with the concept of dying before children actually experience the death of an important person in their lives may help children better understand death and help them cope with death a little more easily.

When a loved one has been sick, and death becomes a possibility, your children should be told. The sooner they are told, the easier the eventual death may be for them. You, or perhaps another close family member with whom they share a comfortable relationship, should be the one to prepare the children.

Before you begin, it may be helpful to ask what they know about the loved one's illness. "What do you think about Daddy's illness?" "What do you know about the disease that Mommy has?" "What do you think will happen to Grandma now that she is very sick?"

If the reply is "I don't know," you shouldn't be too surprised. This is a way children and others ask for more information or avoid talking about a topic. But you can still help. You may want to say, "Let's see what we can know together...." and begin to discuss the illness that is affecting the loved one.

You can then tell them, in a way that they will understand, to the best of your knowledge what will happen. Children can understand medical terms if you explain them. Be gentle and calm when talking. Let the children (or others) ask questions. Be honest about the loved one and the fact that he or she is not ever going to get well. Be open and share emotions and feelings or concerns that you have, and accept and help children with their feelings.

It is important not to give too much information at one time. It is helpful for children to have time to think about what you have told them, to process the information, to play and act out their feelings, and to be able to return to you for more information. Children need some time to think about the ramifications of what you've told them. After a time they will usually ask more questions. If they don't, you can ask questions to help them verbalize what they know, think, and feel about a loved one's impending death.

Throughout the illness, it is helpful to talk with your children about any changes that occur. While it's tempting to send them out to play, go to their rooms, etc., they will profit by being included in some of the discussions and decisions. If possible, allow them to care for the terminally ill loved one. Children and others can bring blankets, supply a box of tissues, carry a cup of broth or tea, hold a hand, and sit and watch television. Children often talk openly to terminally ill loved ones when left alone, but do not force children to do anything they are not comfortable doing. Assisting with the care of a terminally ill loved one will help children prepare for the eventual death.

Telling Children That a Loved One Has Died

Soon after the death of a loved one, children should be told the death has occurred. Explain the death in terms that they will understand. You may want to say, "Mommy was very sick. She had a very bad disease called cancer. Mommy's disease made her very weak and she couldn't get better. Mommy is unable to feel, move, talk, eat, go to the bathroom, or hurt anymore."

Older children will require concrete explanations and honesty. If you don't know exactly what happened, why, where, or when, tell them the truth. Avoid words such as departed, passed away, and expired, or other sugarcoated terms that only confuse children and disabled adults. Use the correct words such as dying, died, and death.

The American Cancer Society provides some suggestions on how to reassure children at this time. They say:

- Share your feelings and explain that all feelings are okay. "I'm very sad right now. I still love Daddy and always will. Could you hug me and let me hug you?"
- Include the children in what will be happening. "After dinner tonight I'm going to the funeral home to meet some of Uncle Bob's friends. Do you want to come too? Uncle Bob's body will be in a wooden box. It's called a casket. Some people will look at Uncle Bob's body inside the casket. You know he's dead, honey, and his face will look different and peaceful now that he doesn't hurt anymore."
- Explain why you or others in the family may be upset or sad. "At the funeral home and the funeral lots of people will be there. Will you hold my hand? Some of the people will be crying. This is a sad time and it's okay for men and women and kids to cry."

- Explain the reason why you may be away for a short period of time. Tell them what you will be doing when you are gone. (Children often feel abandoned at a time of death and become intensely concerned that you may die, too.) "I have to go to the nursing home where Grandmother used to live and get her Bible. She wanted to be buried with it. I'll show you her handwriting where she added all our names inside the pages when I get home. I'll be gone about an hour."
- Reassure your children that if you cannot be there with them, that someone else will be there for them. Try to have someone familiar stay with the children. "Martha will be here until I get back later tonight. It will be past your bedtime, but I'll wake you up when I come in for a good night kiss." Explain that they will not be left alone.
- Explain that crying and being angry, frightened, or upset are all okay. Tell them how you feel and how a person can talk about emotions and have them, too.
- Explain that they can still laugh and run and play. Just because they do not cry does not mean that they didn't love the person who just died.
- Most importantly, reassure your children that they are not responsible for the death.

Where to Get Help

In addition to talking with your clergyperson or spiritual advisor or other listening friend, the American Cancer Society may be able to help you by providing information on how to tell a child about the forthcoming death of a loved one. You can call the national headquarters and ask for the location of a chapter in your area.

Other groups, such as the American Lung Association, National Hospice Association, the Lesbian/Gay Community Services Center, a local AIDS project, and your local hospital may have information and/or referrals to counselors or therapists to help you during this time.

PREPAYING A FUNERAL

Paying a portion of the funeral costs or the entire funeral in advance of death *can* save money; however, many find that what has been purchased doesn't cover their needs or desires once the loved one has died. These services are sometimes sold door-to-door in senior living complexes and often called "preneed" services.

"While the arrangement of a funeral is clearly an important financial transaction for the consumer," says the Federal Trade Commission, "it is a unique transaction, one whose characteristics reduce the ability of consumers to make careful, informed purchase decisions. Decisions must often be made while under the emotional strain of bereavement."

The American Association of Retired Persons publishes a report called *Product Report: Prepaying Your Funeral?* which may be helpful if you have a loved one who is terminally ill and you want to take care of some of the arrangements before the death. AARP, as with many consumer groups, suggests that you shop around and don't allow anyone to manipulate you into buying anything you don't want and can't afford. Prepaying for a funeral or cremation may save money from your estate, but many people, including seniors, have been cheated of their funds.

Sometimes, the loved one does not discuss or inform those who will be handling the arrangements that prepayment has been made. Thus, while all expenses would be covered, the family is unaware of the purchase and buys the services for the funeral and burial. Before you go ahead and make arrangements for disposition of your loved one, review his or her letter of instruction or personal paperwork to ascertain if a prepaid funeral and burial are included. If you're unaware of the plans your terminally ill loved one has made, try to communicate with him or her (or other caregivers) on this topic. You could save a considerable sum just by asking a few questions. Informative as well as cost-conscious, the pamphlet is available by contacting AARP.

Before prepaying for a funeral for your terminally ill loved one, it's advisable to review this booklet and get as much information as possible. Most experts agree that preplanning, like the letter of instruction a loved one writes to supplement a will, can take some of the pressure off survivors after the death.

LEGAL ISSUES OF DEATH

Whether the terminal illness is a genetic defect or a disease such as Alzheimer's, you will need to tell your family. Don't underestimate them. Yes, your statements may be received with, "No, I don't believe it—I wouldn't have known that he was diabetic!" "How could she have died of AIDS? You're wrong." Anger, denial, and fear are the emotions to expect when the announcement of the death is made. However, if you cover up the cause of death only to be found out later, you will probably generate an even bigger ratio of negative emotion.

This is especially so with AIDS, since the topic even in this "enlightened time" is still taboo and causes fear. The death certificate may identify the cause of death as something other than it actually was. Depending on where you live, the death certificate may or may not identify the exact cause of death. For example, the certificate may state cardiac arrest, when your loved one was slowly dying of complications from diabetes. Or it may indicate a long technical term that means AIDS or the cancer that was destroying her lungs.

If your life partner or other loved one has died of a terminal illness and you want to make sure that the portion or the entire estate clearly goes to whomever your loved one indicated in his or her will, it's wise to talk with an attorney to clarify your rights. You can often get a referral through the local legal aid organization. Most experts caution that you need to make sure the attorney you select is fair and contemporary in his or her thinking about the disease, and is experienced in dealing with these types of cases.

If your partner or longtime companion has included you in his or her will, you may not have trouble inheriting property or assuming it. It depends on the location where you live and those who might protest your relationship.

Since life partnerships, without a marriage ceremony, are not legally valid, some families have been known to contest or challenge the wills of those dying from a terminal illness when a life partner is the sole beneficiary. Your most effective course of action is to have the very best constructed will drawn up by a professional, and definitely have a letter of instruction included.

After the death of a loved one, don't feel victimized and don't give up. Paul Kent Froman, Ph.D., author of *After You Say Good-bye: When Someone You Love Dies of AIDS*, says, "If you and your life partner had a deeply committed relationship, you are morally and ethically every bit as much his spouse as if you were heterosexual and legally married."

Dr. Froman does explain that if you've really exhausted all legal recourse, then possibly you must step back and get on with life. He admonishes to do it with "....as much dignity as you can muster. Starting over again isn't a pleasant thought, especially if you are walking away from a home that you and your partner lovingly put together." But he says, "If you have to start over, don't waste time being bitter and resentful, even though you have a right to feel bitter and resentful."

WHEN A LOVED ONE DIES OF AIDS

Just a decade or so ago, few of us had heard of AIDS. Today it is discussed at almost every kitchen table, as well as on television, in the news, and perhaps even over the back fence. It is an illness that affects every family and every human being to some extent and continues to change the world.

Because AIDS has many losses in addition to the life of the person you loved, you may be experiencing stresses far greater than you ever anticipated. It is important for you to understand what is happening to you and your family in order to better cope with the process.

Guilt and Blame with AIDS

Guilt and blame are a way to deal with anger. They are a means of gaining control when we feel helpless to make changes. By transforming anger into guilt, we tend to find the means of the death within ourselves. There had to be something which we did or should have done to have altered this death. If we blame others it transfers the burden of guilt to someone or something and allows us to focus on what otherwise may be an overwhelming experience. Grief expert Sherry Williams says, "It is healthy for you to be clear that you may be feeling *mad* and that guilt and blame are a way of dealing with mad feelings."

Williams says that most of us are afraid of intense emotions. And something like AIDS robs us of our ability to keep the world and our reaction to it on an even keel. Therefore we do our best to close out, cover up, or deny these emotions. "Find someone who will listen and try to sort out the information you have, someone who will listen to guilt, blame, and questions of 'why?'." Williams encourages people who have a loved one dying of AIDS or who has died of the disease to contact and join the support groups specifically for families.

An Exhausting Disease

Financially and emotionally, AIDS is an expensive disease. Most people who have AIDS have depleted their own resources or that of family and friends long before death. Just as the bank account may have dwindled, so may the emotional bank you feel personally.

Many families and the loved one with AIDS find themselves isolated from others in their community; many do this by choice. "People are afraid of AIDS, they are suspicious of anyone who has been around someone with the disease," remarks Williams. When people are afraid, they tend to run away. When people stay away from us, or don't say much, we tend to think we have done something wrong. Some families even feel ashamed that their loved one had AIDS, and interpret their own sense of shame as a disgrace.

"You are not disgraced," continues Williams. "AIDS has infected all races, all economic levels, males and females, children and adults. Assume that your friends, family, and neighbors are simply uninformed and self-protective." Unfortunately, you may need to educate them because information gives everyone a better sense of control.

Family Conflicts because of AIDS

If your loved one has died of AIDS, you may need each member of your family more than ever. If you were close before, you should find comfort in a network of loved ones to support your emotional grieving process. However, even if you were close before the death, you may find yourself in conflict or even not speaking to each other now. Remember that severe stress can cause communication problems—this has nothing to do with your loved one. And if you were not close or experienced conflicts before your loved one died of AIDS, don't expect a miracle to happen. The dynamics of your family will probably not change.

Says Williams, "Grieve the death of the one you loved, not the method of dying or the reason for death. These you must deal with, and will, but take care not to allow your thoughts to overcome your feelings. Whether son or daughter, husband, wife, lover, or friend has died, you will miss that presence in your life. "Remember your loved one for his or her sorrows, hopes, angry moments, fears, and joys."

Where to Get Help

In addition to Dr. Froman's exceptional book, *After You Say Good-bye: When Someone You Love Dies of AIDS* (San Francisco: Chronicle Books, 1992), another book recommended on the topic of AIDS specifically addressing the legal concerns is *A Legal Guide for Lesbian and Gay Couples* by Hayden Curry and Denis Clifford (Berkeley, CA: Nolo Press, 1990). It is a practical guide to the laws that affect lesbian and gay couples. It comes complete with sample forms and agreements, along with information on estate planning, and relating to previous spouses and the children of former marriages.

For those who would like to read Dr. Kübler-Ross's ideas on and experience with AIDS, the library as well as bookstores should have copies of *AIDS: The Ultimate Challenge* (New York: Macmillan Publishers, 1997).

The Caregivers Journey When You Love Someone with AIDS by Mel Pohl, M.D., Deniston Kay, Ph.D., and Doug Toft (New York: Hazelden/HarperCollins Publishers, 1990) is well recommended. It addresses the special needs of caregivers, providing information on feelings, developing tools for acceptance, and understanding the common stages in caring for those battling AIDS or other chronic diseases.

The Federation of Parents and Friends of
Lesbians and Gays, Inc. (PFLAG)
1726 M St., NW, #400
Washington, DC 20036
(202) 467-8180

They provide information and referrals for local chapters.

The following is a list of AIDS hotlines and information lines for your reference:

National AIDS hotline	(800) 342-AIDS
Spanish AIDS hotline	(800) 344-SIDA
Hearing Impaired AIDS hotline	(800) 243-7889
National AIDS Information Clearinghouse	(800) 458-5231
Project Inform	(800) 822-7422
Women Alive	(323) 965-1564

Every state has an AIDS hotline and AIDS project. By calling, you can get information, referrals, local hospice care information, and the availability of support groups for you and your loved ones. You can often find the number in the telephone book, through telephone information, or by calling the toll-free number at the National AIDS hotline.

EASING TERMINAL ILLNESS

Often we are at wit's end as to how it's possible to ease the pain and discomfort of the terminally ill. Drugs such as morphine are often the prescribed way, yet many family members want to do more or supplement the medication.

This may be the time to suggest that your terminally ill loved one begin writing a journal (perhaps with your help). Other families video or record family memories that would otherwise be lost when a loved one dies. A family in New Mexico helped as the matriarch, Grandma Wills, completed her final landscape paintings.

Bonnie Gray of Hospice of North Coast says, "While the patient may not realize it and think that no one is listening to him or her, the family cherishes the advice and words he or she shares near the end. I tell the dying person, 'What you say now is being turned into lasting memories for the future. This is what everyone will remember.' With that responsibility, many dying people are able to talk vividly about the past, the good times, and those things that they feel are too important to be lost with their death." One excellent resource to help you preserve memories is *Recording Your Family History* by William Fletcher; it's extremely helpful with how-tos on video and audio tape recordings, suggested topics, thousands of questions to help you ask just the right one, plus interview techniques.

If you have yet to become involved in the local hospice program, whether your loved one has chosen to die at home or in a care facility, you may want to contact these professionals for information as well as support.

There are many alternative programs supported by the medical community that others may frown on. As with all alternative methods of self-help, carefully examine the promises and review the results. Talk with your doctor or hospice staff member and make wise consumer decisions even in the face of death.

One program is the domain of four-footed therapists. The volunteers throughout the United States who work through the Delta Society look to animals when helping the terminally ill (along with shut-in residents, the disabled, and children and adults with learning handicaps). It's called animal assisted therapy. Still on the cutting edge of scientific documentation, it has long been known that being with and petting animals can lower human pulse rate, ease the breathing, and relax the terminally ill. Through the Delta Society, (580 Naches Ave. SW, #101, Renton, WA 98055-2297, [425] 226-7357) — a nonprofit organization that promotes research and activities relating to the human-animal bond, and other programs such as Therapy Dogs International—trained service dogs (much like the dogs trained to help the blind and hearing impaired) visit Alzheimer's homes, AIDS hospices, hospitals, and nursing facilities. You can contact Therapy Dogs International at 6 Hilltop Rd., Mendham, NJ 07945.

Marsha's father, a wonderfully vibrant man in his late sixties, died last summer of an inoperable brain tumor. There was no pain, but bit by bit he lost the ability to remember. "His greatest joy during that very long year at the nursing home was having the service dogs visit," Marsha recalls. As a tribute to the memory of Marsha's father, a friend began to go through the time-consuming training so her own Welsh terrier could become a therapy dog. When visiting convalescent homes, the plucky twenty-three-pound ball of energy sits peacefully and lets the patients pet her, hold her paw, and whisper to her. "It's like the dog can connect to the patients' spirits," says Marsha, who is moving through the grieving process and now regularly visits the facilities with the therapy dogs and their owners.

Marsha explains, "Through his love of animals and the difference they made to him in the final days, the tribute continues. This legacy has quietly mushroomed. More people and dogs are volunteering time to spend with people who are dying. It makes happy tears come to my eyes. Dad would be so proud."

RECORDING HISTORY
by William Fletcher, from *Recording Your Family History*

Conducting a life history interview.... gives you a chance to do something about this loss, both by intensifying the communication that does occur, and by preserving personal and family histories for future generations. The problem of intergenerational communication is very great in the modern world; it is difficult enough in stable, conservative societies, so it's no wonder that it's difficult in ours.

Only thirty-five years ago, with the invention of audio- and videotape recorders, it became possible for an ordinary person, just by talking informally with another person, to pass on a unique legacy to enrich future generations. Perhaps one person in ten thousand will ever actually write an autobiography, but virtually everyone can talk one, in his or her own words, to a sympathetic and interested listener. This is a means for you, that interested and sympathetic listener, to help your parents or grandparents tell their life stories.

HOSPICE

"Dying at home, surrounded by family, friends, and comfortable environs and with pain and suffering reduced, is now a viable choice for the terminally ill," says Deborah Chase, author of *Dying at Home with Hospice*. "Hospice is a philosophy that provides an entire framework for caring for both the dying and the family of the dying, returning this natural and deeply personal process back to the realm of privacy and dignity."

Hospice is a comprehensive program of care that provides compassionate support and practical assistance to individuals and families facing life-threatening illnesses. While other programs focus on recovery through medical treatments, hospice aids people as they cope with the physical and emotional pain of dying from a terminal illness. The goal of hospice is not to cure the dying, but to enhance the quality of life remaining by respecting the choices of the patient and family. This is done through humanitarian care and by controlling pain and other symptoms of the disease.

The Services Provided by Hospice

The various services that a hospice provides often include:

- Prevention or control of pain and other symptoms of the disease
- Caregiver education and assistance so the patient can live at home
- Emotional and spiritual counseling for the patient and family
- Practical support such as helping the family locate a service to straighten out medical billing
- Relief time for the caregiver
- Assistance with legal and financial issues
- Coordination with other community services
- Grief counseling for the patient and the surviving family

The services are provided by professionals as well as volunteers who coordinate the efforts with the patient's personal physician.

Those who work with the hospice program often say that hospice affirms life. Hospice exists to provide support and care for persons in the last stages of incurable disease so that they might live as fully and comfortably as possible.

Who Pays for Hospice

The price to participate in a live-in hospice or in an at-home hospice program differs greatly from one part of the country to the other, from being totally covered by Medicare to private programs that are quite costly. Yet, even when there is a charge, it often costs far less than a stay in a hospital. Sometimes the services of a hospice are provided without charge to the patient or family; sometimes all or part is covered under health insurance or Medicare. Before you make a decision to enter the hospice program in your city, talk to the counselor or nurse about the fees. It's just good business.

Hospice and the Medicare Hospice Benefits Program

The Medicare hospice benefits program is designed to expand services covered by Medicare for people with a life expectancy of six months or less who have decided against curative treatments and have a designated primary caregiver.

The goals of the Medicare hospice benefits program are to:

1. Help terminally ill individuals continue life with minimal disruption in normal activities while they remain at their home.
2. Make the individual as physically and emotionally comfortable as possible.

Under the Medicare hospice benefits program and at no charge to the patient, the plan includes:

- Prescription medications related to the terminal illness
- Durable medical equipment
- In-home medical supplies
- Home health aid/certified nurse assistant visits
- Therapy services including physical, occupational, respiratory, speech, ostomy, and dietary
- Short-term inpatient respite care to provide the primary caregiver a break from home care responsibilities
- Short-term hospitalization for pain or other symptom control
- Twenty-four-hour home nursing care if required during a medical crisis

Where to Get Help

For referrals or more information contact your local hospice program, often found in the telephone book or through your local hospital. Their staff takes pride in being happy, nurturing, friendly, and personable while providing straight answers on the health of your loved one.

Your personal physician should be able to make a referral or tell you how to locate the hospice near you as well as indicate whether or not you and your loved one are good candidates for the program. You can also call the National Hospice Association for a referral and more information. You may want to talk with someone at the Social Security Administration to see if you are covered by any programs to offset the cost. Ask your personal insurance carrier about picking up the charges, specifics on coverage, and other benefits for which you've been paying.

SAYING GOOD-BYE AFTER THE DEATH

Dr. Paul Kent Froman says, "Like grieving, saying good-bye is a process rather than a simple act. Just as we all grieve differently, we all need to say good-bye differently." Thus, Dr. Froman comments that for some just saying the word will do, others need to express their good-byes over and over. He believes that the important part of saying good-bye after the death is that you express it, not that your loved one actually hears it.

While you can say good-bye in a letter or through a song or poem, it's perfectly sane to talk with your loved one who has died, just as if you were sitting across a table sharing a cup of afternoon coffee. "It may feel a little strange and you may be self-conscious about it, but it isn't crazy. Say whatever you have to say." You may feel like saying "I love you," or "I hate you," or "I miss you so much," but definitely do not "sit" on any negative feelings simply because people typically don't speak ill of the dead.

"Tell the truth," says Dr. Froman, "even if it's ugly. Once you've expressed it, then you can effectively challenge it, let go of it, and get on with your life." He explains that if you have trouble saying "I love you," then you are probably holding onto anger as if to hold onto a loved one. Releasing the anger will provide an opening in your heart to find the love you had for the person who died and fill it with memories.

"Rejoining life as valiantly as possible is one of the most effective ways for us to honor someone's memory," says Dr. Froman. "Living today well is not a betrayal, it is a gift in honor of the memory of the one who died."

THE TIE AND THE CUT OFF
by R. D. Lang,
from *The Voice of Experience*

ào

Many people say they feel cut off not only from others, but from themselves, from the whole universe, from God. Some have felt cut off for as long as they can remember. Some take it so for granted that they never realize it. Others are tormented by these feelings. Some can remember when, and how, and why it happened. The cut-off feeling can be so awful that some say they would rather be dead than have to live with it.

The cut-off feeling is specific. It is not the same as being turned off. It is not the same as a sense of remoteness, or nostalgia, or pining for lost or absent love.

When someone says he or she has to keep people at a distance, one knows that person is not cut off. The cut-off person need keep no distance. There is no possibility of intimacy, or dread of losing oneself in the other. There are no coils to be caught in. One is never more together than apart. All others are on the other side. No flow, or interchange, nothing, is felt to go on across the irremediable, irrevocable divide.

THE HEALING POWER OF HUMOR

"My wife always had a great sense of humor. Seventeen years ago, Ellen became ill with a terminal liver disease, but she never lost her joy in laughing. She continued to use it throughout those very difficult years before her death, to make herself feel better and me and everyone else around her feel better," says Allen Klein, the author of *Quotations to Cheer You Up When the World Is Getting You Down* and *The Healing Power of Humor.*

That humor never changed, even when she was hospitalized. "She wanted the nude centerfold of a male model from *Playgirl* put on the wall across from the bed. I knew the staff would have a problem with it, so she suggested I go get a leaf to stick it to *the* appropriate spot. All was fine the first day and the second day, but then the dry heat of the hospital began to shrivel the leaf....even that made everyone chuckle." He recalls that even a few seconds of laughter over that slowly shriveling leaf helped with the pain and brought the couple closer.

Not that there weren't lots of tears, recalls Allen. "But looking back there was also lots of laughter. I realized after she was gone that it was the laughter that helped both she and I and our friends get through a most difficult period."

After his wife died, Klein set out to share her laughter. From the experience of laughing with his wife, he realized that even a few moments of humor can make troubles easier to bear. It gives a breather and a chance to regain strength and pull fragile physical and mental resources together again.

A former hospice volunteer and home health care aid, Klein now puts all his energy (and he has a lot) into writing about the power of humor. A much-sought-after speaker on humor, Klein travels extensively sharing the power of humor and helping the terminally ill, those with major life challenges, and the people who help them understand the strength of a giggle or three.

Through his work, Klein submersed himself in death and dying. Finding there was little material to draw from, he decided to research and write how people use humor in difficult situations. He says, "I sometimes saw laughter squelched, however, because people thought that anything connected to death and dying had to be 'serious.'" He contradicts that statement vehemently. "In fact, any nurse or undertaker will tell you that humorous incidents frequently occur around intense death-related situations. What is important for all of us to remember is not to close ourselves off and exclude laughter because we think death *must be solemn.* So many funny things can happen during a funeral but often we feel guilty for laughing."

Klein quickly points out that he's not the first to suggest the use of laughter during the dying process and the stages of grief. He explains that in several tribes in West Africa it is the tradition to assign someone to restrain, entertain, and distract the bereaved. In the three days before the burial, this "joking partner" helps shifts the emphasis from stopping the grief of the survivors to promoting the exact opposite emotion....laughter.

When lecturing, Klein does his laugh speech. "I go through the word and we do exercises for every letter. For example, L is for 'let go' and the participants learn to let go with laughter. A is for 'attitude' and I show how to take the troubles life has tumbled on them to change their attitude. U is for 'you'—only you can do the work, no one else can do it for you. G is 'go do it' and I provide ways to begin. H, of course, is for 'open your humor eyes and ears' and look for ways to brighten your day with laughter. It is indeed all around us, but we get so stressed out that we forget to hear and see it."

"Put on a happy face," is a lyrical line from a song written in the Depression, and Klein says that putting on a happy face is one part of feeling the power of laughter. "There has been some smiling research done at Clark

University and it has been shown that when you're smiling—even faking it—your body doesn't know the difference! So it's generally good to even put on a phony grin."

Life isn't all smiles and laughter, and Klein says, "Go with the grief. It's an important, healthy process." But when it gets in the way of your life or your work, Klein cautions that professional help may be warranted.

ཨ

Because death and grief come in many wrappings, not only do we suffer when a loved one dies, but often the death of pets has a profound effect on our lives. Family pets often become a major focus in our hectic lives; they bring us joy and make us laugh, and eventually we feel great sadness when they die.

The next chapter will be devoted to the topic of pet death. It will focus on the grief process, making arrangements for a caring disposal, talking to children about the death of a pet, and what to do when death occurs to the ones who give us their unconditional love.

Chapter 10

When Pets Die

Anytime we walk through that front door, down to the stable, out in the yard, our pets are delighted to be with us. While our human companions sometimes make subjective judgements or offer gratuitous advice, our pets offer love, pure and simple, with no strings attached. And when their death occurs, it can be as profound or even more profound than when a human loved ones dies. Psychologists and those involved in the study of the human-animal bond can guess the scientific reasons. For animal lovers, it's clear. Our pets give us unconditional love. They are confidants, companions, therapists, playmates, challenges, and a warm, snugly addition to the family.

They love us when our teeth aren't brushed, when our hair is a disaster, when the biggest deal of the century falls in the Dumpster, when we have had one of the worst days on record, and even when we succeed. They expect so little in return.

This chapter focuses on the effects of the death of our animal loved ones. When we talk about our pets, it should be understood that we are not exclusively referring to dogs and cats, but to all those in the animal kingdom from goldfish to boa constrictors. If you love or have feelings for an animal, the grief you experience at its death needs to be acknowledged whether it has scales or Persian fur, a long, skinny rat tail or the plume of a peacock.

We will also keep a warm place in our hearts for the amazing Irish setter who licked away the tears of our first ill-fated romantic episode, or the hamster who squeaked to wake us up each morning. We accept our pets for what they are with a far shorter life span than human loved ones, and their death can often teach us about the grieving process.

The death of pets is included in this book for a very special reason. When we adopt a pet into our family, we become closely involved in the full cycle of life—the terrible babyhood time, the awful adolescence, the adults years, and then the time Cookie's muzzle begins to gray or when arthritis is evident. These are the precious years in which we can begin to give back some of the constant care and joy that our pets have given to us.

Loving a pet and facing its death can be compared to a dress rehearsal for the death of a human loved one. The death of our wonderful pets doesn't make the death of a family member easier—that's like comparing two shades of black for the deepest color. But it allows us to know that we can get through the experience of a human death, survive the mourning, and find a new normal in life.

Why does the death of a pet hit so many people so hard? For adults as well as children, this is their first experience with the final transition, the experience of death. All death hurts. Knowing that you will hurt, that it's okay to feel what you're feeling, and with the information on how to cope, you can move to the resolution stage. And it is this reality that makes you realize that you can go on and love again.

Where to Get Help

If you are contemplating the eminent death of a loved pet and need help *now,* the Pet Loss hotline, (800) 565-1526, is staffed by counselors and veterinary students at the University of California-Davis. The hotline is available Monday through Friday from 6:30 P.M. to 9:30 P.M. Pacific Time. No question is too trivial. All conversations are confidential. Referrals to counseling and grief support groups are available. The Delta Society, at (425) 226-7357, also maintains a listing of pet loss support groups.

Bonnie Mader, M.S., associate director of the Human-Animal Program at the School of Veterinary Medicine on the University of California-Davis campus, says the following are some of the issues you may want to explore with the staff member who answers your hotline call:

- The right time to say good-bye
- The feeling that losing a pet is like losing a member of the family
- Extended grieving for an animal you lost some time ago but have still not resolved
- Why you often feel guilty at the death of your pet
- What specific arrangements can be made for euthanasia
- How to care for the animal's remains
- How you might memorialize your pet
- How to know when it's the right time to get another pet

Says Mader, "The hotline serves two purposes—the need to offer emotional support to those experiencing grief and the need to better prepare future veterinarians to respond to the human side of veterinary medicine. For the cost of a phone call, individuals facing the loss of an animal can contact the hotline and discuss their particular situation with a veterinary student volunteer who has been specially trained in supportive listening skills."

IT STARTED LONG AGO

Often it seems that our love for pets started with the last two generations when it suddenly became okay to think of your animal as a best friend, but that's not true. The Greeks had pets as early as 400 B.C. The ancient Hebrews had small house dogs. The ancient Egyptians used domesticated cats to safeguard supplies of grain from marauding rats and mice. Because of this great value, cats became sacred as well as a routine part of any Egyptian household.

In ancient Egypt, the cat goddess Bastet was worshiped and every year there was a holiday in her honor. Domesticated cats were revered as personifications of Bastet, dressed in jewels and allowed to eat from the same dishes as their owners. Thus, anyone who killed a cat or caused its death was put to death.

When the death of a pet cat occurred, members of a household shaved their eyebrows and went into deep morning. The master of the household put the body on a linen sheet, and took it to a sacred house for embalming and anointing. Then the funeral was held and all those in the household, friends, and neighbors joined in the grief ritual. Cats were buried. Some were wrapped as mummies and placed in special vaults in cat cemeteries outside each city. The bereaved family, it is documented, would bury food with the dead cat that it would not go hungry, and often continued to bring fish and milk offerings to the grave site or entombment for many years.

Companion dogs of the ancient Egyptians were also revered, many authorities say often more than cats. Dogs were so much a part of the family that when they died, they were buried at sacred dog cemeteries. When a dog died, household members shaved their entire bodies, including their heads.

FACING THE DEATH OF YOUR PET

Do you consider your pet to be part of your family? Do you talk to your pet? Do you celebrate its birthday? If you've answered yes, join the club.

Surveys show that 84 percent of all pet owners consider their animals part of the family. Almost 99 percent of those queried disclose that they talk to their pets. And more than half celebrate their pet's birthdays, with gifts at the holidays, too. A companion animal is a member of the family, a part of your life.

In addition to the obvious rituals of talking to and walking your pet, animals have been scientifically shown to lower blood pressure, help heart attack patients regain their health, break through mental handicaps of children and adults, and bring comfort and aid to the terminally ill. They alleviate feelings of intense loneliness, help promote responsibility, and connect us with the world. Just try walking a dog in any suburban area or on a city sidewalk without having at least one neighbor stop to talk. It is impossible.

According to author and educator Dr. Alan Wolfelt, "With your capacity to love your pet comes the necessity to grieve when that 'best friend' dies. The death of a pet is, without a doubt, a traumatic experience." As any household member it's not just a dog, or just a cat, or another horse or canary, but a part of our lives.

"With the death of that pet, the family experiences a significant loss. A difficult problem, however, is that society often denies you the need to grieve for your pet. You may even be chastised for openly and honestly expressing your feelings. As a result, your grief may be hidden, buried, or ignored."

Dr. Wolfelt points out that although denied understanding and support, your family needs to grieve the death of your pet. Grieving means expressing feelings, regardless of the pain and anguish which accompany them, and doing so without being criticized. Unlike the ancient Egyptians who shaved body hair when grieving the death of a pet, we do not visibly show that we are grieving. We often hide it from the world and grieve silently, so much more alone than necessary. This, too, can be counterproductive to our health and can often make the grieving process of human death more difficult.

Dr. Wolfelt warns that when a beloved family pet dies, you and your family will probably be greeted with many trite phrases. Although these comments are intended to somehow soothe the bereaved, often they only insure a response of anger. "Get another cat." "But I heard you complain that she always tore up the rose garden—and you're crying because that old mutt died?" "Hey, now you

Don't berate yourself for recovering too quickly or too slowly. Each individual needs a certain amount of time to handle this challenging mix of emotions, and you'll only feel worse if you think your progress doesn't match some improbable norm. Your relationship with your animal, built over years of living together, was distinct and personal—too special to be locked into a category now....

—Jamie Quackenbush, M.S.W., from *When Your Pet Dies*

don't have to care for him anymore—no more vet bills or lugging those bags of pet food home." These are not constructive comments—they hurt and make the grieving process often more difficult because we feel chastised for having loved a being with such intensity.

Grief and the Death of Your Pet

As with human death, our memories eventually fill the void left by the death of a pet. Experts on the human-animal bond explain that we should look toward these memories as we move through the grieving process. Often the memories will make us laugh. "Remember how Quaker got his name that first morning we had him? Remember how he put his front paws up on the counter to lick out my oatmeal while I was getting the milk?" Dr. Wolfelt likes to say, "Memories made in love can never be taken away."

When a pet dies, we experience the emotions of grief.... anger, confusion, denial, sadness, guilt, disorientation, depression, and eventually resolution and acceptance. Repressing these feelings can make the process more intense. You may blow up at coworkers or your kids weeks later for no apparent reason. You may be too distracted to work, go to school, or sleep. The death of a pet brings a significant change in your life and the dynamics of the family, too. You are grieving a loss and that meaningful change, too.

Don't repress your feelings. Don't try to ignore anyone, even well-meaning family members and friends, who tell you what to do. "Don't overanalyze your response," says Dr. Wolfelt. "Just allow your feelings to find expression. As strange as some of these feelings may seem they are normal and healthy." As each family member probably had a specific relationship with the pet, each one will experience grief in a unique way. Mary may cry for days. Bill might become sulky and nonverbal. After crying for hours, Joe may act as if nothing is wrong, and question his parents as to when the family can get another dog. Counselors recommend that we should be careful to honor each person's need to grieve in his or her own way.

When older adults adopt a pet, the animal often becomes the source of sole companionship. When death occurs, the owner may take the death extremely hard. As with other age groups, when a pet death happens it can trigger memories of unresolved grief for loved ones and feel doubly painful. Sometimes joining a bereavement group or talking with a therapist can help focus the unresolved grief where it needs to be worked out so that a resolution can be found.

The Death of a Pet for Children

For children, as well as adults, the death of a pet may be the first experience encountered with the end of a life. As difficult as it is, the death of a pet is a real opportunity to talk about life and death with children. It's also a time to talk about grief and explain that whether we grieve for an animal or a person whom we loved we feel many of the same emotions.

Depending on how the death of a pet is handled, it can be a positive experience or one filled with dissolution. Give your children the time and space to grieve for their pet. (You may want to talk with their teacher since he or she will probably see a difference in your child.) Many children love the family pet with their full, tiny hearts and look to you for information and as an example. You need not hide your tears; simply explain why you are crying. You can share the depression and the glimmer of hopefulness when it arrives.

Some Dos and Don'ts on Coping with Pet Death

Like the keepsake book project discussed in chapter 4 which can help survivors work through grief, family members may want to make up a scrapbook or design a photo collage in memory of their pet. Here are some other ways to cope with the death of a beloved family animal:

- Do be honest with all involved. This is especially true with children and handicapped adults who may misunderstand or be unable to acknowledge the finality of death.
- Do explain why the pet died and try to use the correct terms.
- Do show your own emotions. Death makes us sad.
- Do refer to other chapters on grieving and ways to

ৰ্জ

When he came to live with us, he was a timid mixed breed— an All-American in need of love. An abused dog, he had been turned into the Animal Rescue League; he lay there, head between his paws, solemnly surveying the world. Maybe it was because he had been placed in a large cat cage that he had been overlooked. Whatever the reason, I'm glad I took time to peek at the cats and found him.

Stooping to peer into his cage, I softly asked, "Want to go home, boy?" A sudden twinkle came into his big brown eyes, a timed wag to his tail. It was love.

We named him Cardozo after the New York Supreme Court Justice, Benjamin Cardozo. Dad was in law school and it seemed appropriate, but as with most appropriate names, we shortened it to Dozo.

Dozo became my first baby. We went everywhere together. He was my protector and playmate as we romped the beaches and he was a fellow adventurer as Dad and I canoed down the White Mountain's Saco.

When the cherubs came along, Dozo was almost four and I assumed the role of nursemaid. He would patiently sit while his ears were pulled or lie still as an

cope as the examples will help you during this difficult time, too.

- Don't hide from grief. Find an animal-loving friend or a staff member at the Pet Loss hotline to help you discuss the issue of death.
- Don't tell children that the pet got sick and died, unless this is true. It's often helpful to explain the bad disease that caused the pet's death.
- Don't say that the pet ran away and won't be coming back—unless that's true.
- Don't try to rush through grief. Give it time, cherish your memories, and concentrate on all the years you spent together, not just the last few months or days when your pet was close to death.

THE CHOICE OF EUTHANASIA

Loving a pet is a responsibility. When the pet is in pain, after an accident or at another time when the quality of life is questionable, our thoughts often consider a humane death. It is a topic and decision that is more difficult than most to be faced. There are hardly any right answers, and some people continue to emotionally flagellate themselves years after they've chosen to help end their pet's life.

Those who love animals and adopt a pet in their lives also take on the responsibility for this decision. Sometimes euthanasia is the right choice when there's no hope for recovery, the cost of the surgery or medical attention is tremendous, or a disease is terminal.

According to Bruce Fogle, D.V.M, author of *Pets and Their People*, the following are among the valid reasons for ending a pet's life:

1. Overwhelming physical injury
2. Irreversible disease that has progressed to a point where distress or discomfort cannot be controlled
3. Old age wear and tear that permanently affect the "quality of life"
4. Physical injury, disease, or wear and tear resulting in permanent loss of control of body functions

5. Aggressiveness with risk to children, owners, or others
6. The carrying of untreatable disease dangerous to humans

Your best advice comes from a caring veterinarian. If your vet seems cold and uncaring when you bring up the topic, it is time to consider getting a second opinion. There are a few veterinarians whose bedside manner leaves lots to be desired, but these are few and far between.

Euthanasia is humane and painless for the pet and can curtail needless suffering for you both. A drug, given in a shot, is used. The drug is an overdose of a medication to ease pain and the animal relaxes from the drug and dies. The animal quietly and peacefully is finally released from distress. If you have loved your animal and provided care, warmth, and friendship throughout the years, the decision, while difficult, will not be impossible.

But before making that decision, talk with your vet, review the alternatives, and discuss the procedure. This can be done over the telephone or personally. Often your vet will not charge you for the consultation. Before you begin the conversation, you may want to ask if there will be a fee. While there will be tears, you and your family can make a decision that is right for your pet as well as yourselves.

Saying good-bye. These may be the toughest words you've ever had to speak, but doing so helps you move through the grieving process. Some people say good-bye once the decision has been made. This can be as simple as spending quiet time together or talking with your pet out loud about the decision. As you recount memories, you'll laugh and perhaps even cry. Tell your pet why you've made the decision, tell your pet how deeply you feel for it and express your love. Explain to children what will be happening and give them the opportunity to say good-bye, too.

Should you be there? This is an individual decision, but most pet owners prefer to continue their lifelong commitment to their pet. They accept the responsibility to be with their pet when the injection is given. Talk to your vet about exactly what will go on and what you should expect and do. You may

exhausted toddler napped on his back. By the time cherub number four arrived, he was ten and gray around the muzzle. As he watched the baby being placed in the cradle, he slowly lowered his head and sighed as if to say, "Oh, no, not another one!"

In the last few years, Dozo's age caught up with him. His eyes lost the sharpness of his youth, his hearing was less than perfect (although I believe it was more selective), and arthritis had invaded his joints. This, however, didn't stop his wag each time we called him to us.

Dozo had become the oldest member of our family. At age sixteen his dog years numbered more than one hundred.

As I rubbed his ears for the last time, I looked into his now-cloudy brown eyes. "Want to go home, boy?" I whispered. His tail gave the slightest tremor of a wag as I kissed him good-bye.

want to hold your pet, or stroke it, or speak to it softly as the injection slowly works. Do not feel guilty if you choose not to be with your pet. There is no right decision, but do give yourself some time to say good-bye.

PET DISPOSITION

If your pet is a goldfish rather than a quarter horse, you will have a different view of the proper way to dispose of the body. One woman, who has four cats in her home, decided to place the body in the care of the Humane Society (which in her area cremates dead animals). Another man elected to bury his box turtle in the garden where it loved to be and where it spent most of its life.

Depending on where you live, it may be impossible to bury the body or the cremated remains of your pet in your garden. Your vet, health department, or the local Humane Society can answer questions about regulations for burying animals.

You can talk to your vet before your pet dies or when the end is near. Consider the alternatives. There are over five hundred pet cemeteries in the United States and they do serve a purpose for many. And pets are either buried with an earth burial or placed in an entombment, or their remains are sprinkled or placed in an urn and buried in an urn garden. Some pet lovers prefer taking the cremated remains back home with them after the cremation to be sprinkled somewhere personal or at a later date. One elderly woman requested (in a letter of instruction) to have the remains of her dear cat Libby buried with her so that they'd be together forever.

Costs to bury or cremate pets vary depending on the size of the animal and the location in this country. The cost to bury a pet at a cemetery can range from fifty dollars to well over one thousand dollars, depending on the extras you wish to include. On the West Coast, to cremate a medium-sized dog is about one hundred dollars; it is usually calculated per pound. "A very general rule of thumb," says Wendell Morese, a veterinarian and executive director of the International Association of Pet Cemeteries, "is that pet burial costs 10 percent of what it may cost to bury a human." The association has voluntary standards which include that a good pet cemetery should consist of at least five acres, possess an endowed care fund, be well maintained, and be restricted by a deed of trust.

Keep in mind that you do not have to incur any expense when your pet dies. The Humane Society often does not charge to dispose of the body of an animal; be sure to ask if there is a cost or if a donation is expected. Do not feel guilty if this is the right choice for you—it is for many people. Also do not feel guilty if you choose to buy a casket lined with pink satin and purchase a marker for the grave. If this is the direction your grief takes and you are moving through the stages well, then continue. If, however, you're stuck in any of the stages, seek professional advice.

Your local Yellow Pages, your vet, or the county Humane Society can make referrals to pet cemeteries and/or crematoriums. If you plan to sprinkle the ashes of Rover in the rose garden, it's senseless to buy a pricey urn.

You may also want to compare prices and services. Keep in mind that pet cemeteries and cremation services are in business and, at the time a beloved pet dies, you may be at an all-time low when it comes to making rational decisions. These services make money when you spend money. If you are not presented with a price list, ask for one and match what one business offers to another.

PET FUNERALS

Rituals after a loved one has died help make the natural occurrence of death a reality. As we often see our pets more than, and love as much as, family members, it seems fair that we take time to say good-bye. A funeral or other memorial service can serve this purpose. Whether you do or do not believe in holding pet funerals, don't allow well-meaning friends to alter your decision. Pet funerals are not for everyone.

For a family pet who has been loved by all, this can be a family affair. The decision of where and when to hold the service, perhaps even what to say, can be mutually considered. You may want to say a prayer, read a poem, recall fond memories, especially those that include laughter, and say, "I love you."

BEREAVEMENT
by Bruce Fogle, D.M.V.,
from *Pets and Their People*

২৯

In compassionate surroundings, human death brings to those who are grieving an open and genuine support from others. It is a time of maximum communication. It is a busier time than normal. Friends and relatives are more open and less inhibited than they otherwise are. And, of course, there are ritual and ceremony. All of these things help those who are grieving. They give both physical and mental support.

But such is not the case when a pet dies. In fact, it is sometimes the reverse. People are embarrassed to commiserate with someone whose pet has died. If anything, there is probably less communication than normal. The routine of the rest of the family is expected to continue, with simply a void where the pet used to be. The barriers that come down when a human dies, if anything, go up when a pet dies. Instead of visitors, telegrams, phone calls, letters, and flowers, there is loneliness.

OTHER WAYS TO COMMEMORATE YOUR PET'S DEATH

Herbert A. Neiburg, a psychotherapist specializing in grief therapy and coauthor of *Pet Loss*, explains that there are many ways to pay tribute to the special place in your life that your pet shared.

Dr. Neiburg says, "More and more people are memorializing their pets, recognizing that this satisfies a need to keep good memories alive." Some of the suggestions he offers are:

- Plant a small tree or shrub in your yard or local countryside. You might even affix a plaque with the pet's name, dates of birth and death, and a simple message.
- Donate funds for equipment to an animal hospital, shelter, or other pet-related facility.
- Donate funds for medical research in the disease that claimed your pet's life.
- Make a donation or set up a scholarship to a veterinary school.
- Donate cash to a breed rescue fund.
- Provide a trophy for a breed or obedience competition in your pet's memory.
- Arrange to have a painting or sketch of your pet copied from a photograph. Or you can arrange for handiwork such as needlepoint to be designed in your pet's likeness.
- Commemorate the anniversary of your pet's death according to your religious traditions or in other less formal ways such as visit to a burial site.

THE QUESTION OF REPLACEMENT

For many pet lovers, replacing a loved animal before the grieving process is completed is wrong. As you know, grieving is work and takes time. There are no quick fixes whether you are five or fifty-five. If a replacement animal is adopted too soon, before grief is resolved, the new pet is often unjustly compared to the old one, and pushed aside because it's nothing like Sparky. Sometimes our unresolved anger at the death of the previous pet is inadvertently displayed to the new pet, which is unfair.

However, if you've known for a long time that your pet was dying, you may want to consider when you'll be ready to adopt a new animal. There is no right time; we are all special in our grief. Whether you want to adopt a pet before your old pet dies or wait until the death occurs is a decision you, your family, and your vet can discuss together.

Dr. Wolfelt says, "Be especially careful about premature replacement of pets with children. It sends a message to a child that says when something is lost all that you have to do is buy another one. In reality, that is often not the case. It also devalues the significance of the pet that just died."

Most grief therapists who deal with the death of family pets recommend strongly that individuals and families wait just slightly longer than necessary or they think possible to adopt a new pet. During this time, you and your family can:

- Talk about the pet who died without any comparison.
- Research the type of pet you may want next.
- Go to dog, cat, or bird shows to talk with breeders.
- Consider changing breed or variety.
- Decide on a new name.

The pet who died will never be usurped. The new pet will take time to adjust to the family and bond as closely as the previous one. Remember your old pet didn't become your best friend overnight, and the new one won't either.

Where to Get Help

Dogwise has a free catalog of dog and cat books and includes many of the titles on pet bereavement listed here.

Dogwise
701 B Poplar
P.O. Box 2778
Wenatchee, WA 98807-2778

Orders: (800) 776-2665, Direct: (509) 663-9115

The following books should be available at bookstores or by ordering directly from the publisher:

Saying Good-bye to the Pet You Love: A Complete Resource to Help You Heal by Lorria A. Greene, Ph.D. and Jacquelyn Landis (Oakland, CA: New Harbinger Publications, 2002). Written by a psychologist who is a leader in the field of pet bereavement, this practical but sympathetic guide validates the survivor's often misunderstood feelings.

The Loss of a Pet, Wallace Sife (Hoboken, NJ: John Wiley & Sons, 1998). Author and professional bereavement counselor Dr. Wallace Sife updates and expands the widely successful 1993 version for readers who need help coping with and understanding this particular kind of grief.

The following books are recommended by those who staff the Pet Loss hotline:

Pet Loss: A Thoughtful Guide for Adults and Children by Herbert A. Neiburg and Arlene Fisher (New York: Harper & Row, 1996). A gentle book that deals openly with the feelings that the death of a pet can have on a life. An excellent section on pet loss and children and older adults with whom pets often bond closely.

When Your Pet Dies: How to Cope with Your Feelings by Jamie Quackenbush, M.S.W., and D. Graveline (New York: Simon and Schuster, 1985). Suggestions and strategies for moving through the grief process from one of the country's leading vets.

The following are recommended for children:

The Tenth Good Thing about Barney by Judith Viorst (New York: Antheneum, 1975). Simply written, a classic for children of all ages. In an attempt to overcome grief, a boy tries to think of the ten best things about his dead cat.

A Snowflake in My Hand by Samantha Mooney (New York: Delta/Dell, 1997). For teenagers and older children, this is a gently touching story of young veterinarians in the life-and-death struggles of their education and love of animals.

Although there are no right or wrong decisions when it comes to euthanasia, disposition, or replacement, you do need to take the time to grieve the loss of this important family member. Address your needs now—talk about the pain, recall the fond memories, smile at the joy your pet brought you. Like we've said so many times before, although it may not feel like it now, eventually you *will* heal. In time the grief will turn into a soft spot in your heart.

❧

Chapter 11 addresses the kinds of healing that take place after the death of a loved one, and how you can move toward acceptance, resolution, and finally peace. Eventually life does get back to normal, but often the hurdles are painful and frightening. We'll talk about adjustment, making it through all the "firsts," and new beginnings. We'll talk about how to get on with the rest of your life, and the beauty and happiness that tomorrow brings. No matter where you are in the grief recovery process, take a moment to acknowledge your growth and know that you will do more than survive—you will live.

That wasn't the last time I cried, but it was the most healing, because I was with friends who understood and cared.

Watachie still has a special place in my heart and always will, but his loss doesn't hurt anymore—unless I poke too hard. (Some tears went into this essay.) Talking with family and friends along with good memories plus a new puppy and time have helped heal the heartache.

Moving On

Hopefulness.
Resolution.
Acceptance.
Acknowledgment.

It may be impossible to believe that you will experience these feelings with regard to the death of your loved one. They are tough concepts and ideas and you may or may not be ready to accept them. However, when you can accept that you will at some time be ready for a transition to a new normal life, then you have made the first step toward resolution.

There will still be many unanswered questions and you may feel like you're floundering without a direction. This is normal; this is expected. The information in this chapter may help guide you through some of the events that will happen as you move to the final stages of grief and eventually see that flicker of hopefulness become a flame in your life. We'll focus on the personal adjustment death demands, suggestions on coming to know the you of today, getting through the holidays and other anniversaries, and how to make and keep emotional promises for a healthier you.

PERSONAL ADJUSTMENT

Learning to live alone or feeling alone after the death of a loved one is part of the process of death. You are stronger from the experience of death. You now know how crazy, angry, and horrible you can feel and you know that you can live through it. Even with the intense sadness can come a unique feeling and knowledge of personal independence.

Grief expert Dr. Paul Froman says that we need to accept the memories we have of our loved ones, and yet be ready to move on "without castigating ourselves for being weak or unstable. Too many people I talk with tell me that such sadness over memories makes them feel inadequate, as if they're not handling it.

"They are handling it. 'Handling it' doesn't mean never feeling sad again. Let the memories come up. Just don't get lost in the pain. Memories can be sweet as well, as you remember the wonderful times you had together."

Although you may still feel like it at times, most likely you know that you're not really alone. Yes, some of the friends who were close to you before the death have faded away, but they would probably have done so in the natural progression of time anyhow. Now there are new people in your life who accept you as you are, even with that slightly mended place that binds together the permanent perforation in your heart. When that realization comes— and it comes in its own time—it's a gratifying and satisfying feeling to know acceptance of self.

Becoming Your Own Friend

It may sound too sugarcoated, too "quick fix," to consider that after a loved one who meant so very much has died you could ever live without that person. But you are living proof that it's possible. No, you may not be happy, go a day without crying, ever think you could entertain a happy thought again. However, resolution does come about. For some, depending on the circumstances of the death, it can happen within days or weeks. For example, after a lengthy, painful terminal illness when the death of a loved one is expected, often the grief has begun months or years before, and plans have been formalized for the future. This doesn't make it pleasant, yet it makes the future a possibility.

Resolution sometimes takes years. A successful realtor recalls that she still gets a twinge of anger when she sees women and their daughters shopping and lunching together or women playing with their children at the park near her condo. Her only child, a daughter, died at sixteen of leukemia. She says, "I'm 99 percent resolved—I'll probably always feel that stab of envy. But it's okay now, because the stab makes me think of Tiffany." And she adds with a knowing chuckle, "What a dry wit that child had!"

Resolution of grief can often consume us, and emotional support groups and counseling may provide a means to work through the feelings. Therapists and survivors recommend the following do-it-yourself techniques and tools:

Talk it out. For those things that are left unsaid, whether it's "I love you" or "How could you leave me with this mortgage and three kids in college!" get the words out. Set up two chairs facing each other. Talk to your loved one; it can help. This is a time to say all the things you meant to say, wanted to say, were unable to say, and now know you should have said.

Write your feelings out in a journal. This is another tool to help you work through the resolution of any loss, including death. Keep a record of where you went, who you saw, what you ate, as well as what's happening inside. One survivor always began her entries with what birds she saw in her garden. While consciously knowing that she was resolving the grief of the homicide death of her father, and in order to identify each bird correctly, instead of writing down "a pretty red crested something-or-other," she began to study ornithology. She bought a bird book, joined a bird-watchers organization, and recently made a career move to accept a position with the National Audubon Society.

Another woman, a fashion coordinator for a magazine, chronicled what she wore to work among other things in her journal. After a month she reread the entries and realized it was time to move from a stretched-out sweatshirt and jeans back to the more avant-garde combinations she wore before her miscarriage.

In both cases, the grief had not disappeared, but progress toward acceptance of the loved one's death was being made, and each woman in her own way was making headway.

Even though I may have regrets, I can remember the ways I did show my love and appreciation. I can trust that they knew my feelings. I can also tell them how much I love them by sharing thoughts even now, through writing, prayer, or letting my soul speak to them....

—Elizabeth Levang, Ph.D., et al., from *Remembering with Love*

Complete a project your loved one started. Did he have half of the photos placed in the album? Did she have the garage "almost" organized? Did she finish copying all the poems she loved into a special book? Did he want to build a shed for the gardening tools? At this time you may be able to take steps to accomplish your loved one's projects or dreams. Even though you may physically be able to complete some projects your loved one started, others like the gardening shed may not be possible. However, with a little ingenuity perhaps you can barter to have the work completed or find a friend who has genuinely wanted to help do the job with you.

Start a new hobby or learn a new skill. Don't worry if this new adventure isn't like the old you—you are a different person now. Those "friends" and family members who may raise an eyebrow only deserve your smile and perhaps a shrug. If your new hobby or skill doesn't hurt you, jeopardize your life or others' lives, then it's acceptable.

Bert recalls that after Millie died and he believed that most of his grief was resolved, he took up skydiving. "It was plucky. It was terrifying. It helped me to recapture my own inner strength. You don't have anyone to depend on when you're freefalling through nothing but air," Bert assures.

"Our adult kids were horrified. After telling them it really wasn't their business, I countered with, 'How do you think I felt right after getting a driver's license, I saw one of you pull the family car out of the driveway and burn rubber down the street?' End of discussion. However, after the fifth jump, I decided I'd rather fly the plane than jump out, so I'm taking lessons to do that now."

Set realistic goals as you resolve grief. Make tiny goals to support the heftier ones. For example, if during this resolution period you look in the mirror and see a reflection that's twenty pounds overweight, don't crash diet to loose it all by next week at four o'clock. Instead, talk to your doctor (one goal), modify your food intake slowly and cut out sweets (one goal), and walk for twenty minutes every day (one goal). Within a month, using these small goals will begin producing results to achieve the big goal.

Take a personal dare. Have you always been scared silly to ride a horse? Take riding lessons. Have you always been frightened to talk in front of a group? Join Toastmasters International. Have you always (secretly perhaps) wanted to be a blond? Wear black underwear? Eat snails? Visit New York City? Write down your dare, your personal challenge, and take small steps in that direction. You could, for example, look in the phone book for riding lessons, visit a ranch to touch the horses, talk with a riding instructor, and take a short ride to see if you even like it.

You may find that something you thought was so impossible to accomplish by your old self—the person you were before your loved one died—is not really so difficult now. Surviving the death of a loved one may be the most difficult thing you ever have to do—making all the other scary stuff pale in comparison.

Be kind to yourself. Treat yourself to the most pampering experience you can seriously afford—a week at a health spa, a cruise, a manicure, a haircut, a triple scoop of double Dutch chocolate ice cream. One survivor treats herself to something special every day—nothing too fattening or expensive—a pack of her favorite sugarless gum, a bouquet of carnations, five minutes on the drive home from to work to watch the sun set in the Pacific. In the beginning, she had to push herself to do these things and become creative about them. "But now they are part of me—my treats—my life as it is now that Jake is dead."

Make yourself feel special, wear "up" colors, force your face into a smile, watch only funny movies, bake cookies (take them to the local elementary school if you're on a diet), or start the day reading the comics instead of the front page.

Locate your spiritual self. Begin reading about various religions or beliefs, meditate, and become attuned to the world within.

If you've always attended one church, try another or try a different one every third Sunday. If you've never been to church and feel awkward, visit those in your area as if you're a visitor from another planet. You may find serenity in the peace and fellowship that religion holds.

Another possibility as you locate your spiritual self is that a whole new world of meaningful work is out there to

There is a major difference between denying real problems and the avoidance of agonizing over those things we cannot change. Denial is dangerous, for it results from failure to acknowledge facts. Avoidance is healthy, because avoidance is the dismissal from our living of those implications and speculations about which we can do nothing.

—Paul Pearsall, Ph.D.,
from *Super Joy*

ACCEPTANCE
by Mel Pohl, M.D., et al.,
from *The Caregiver's Journey*

❧

Reaching our goals will take time, patience, trials, and errors. We may often fail. We may still experience emotional or physical pain. At times we may forget what we've learned, sink into despair or depression, or forget to act on what we know.

Even so, we can forgive ourselves, just as we would forgive the people for whom we care. We can seek help from others. We can return to the sources of hope and strength in our lives, and we can keep in contact with them. What's more, we can be grateful. We can treasure moments of joy, laughter, ease, and contentment with people we love, knowing that these are ours forever.

be done. Of course, there's "church" work, like caring for the altar or running the Saturday night bingo games, but look further. Many spiritual and religious organizations have a desperate need for people like you.

There are thrift stores to be staffed, soup kitchens to be run, disabled to be assisted in everyday tasks, and thousands of other possibilities for those involved with helping others, all organized through religious organizations. Not only will you be helping the organization and those whom it serves, but you'll discover a sphere of comradeship with others as you serve your spiritual self.

Adopt a pet into your life. Having a pet there at home when you return may help alleviate that shock of loneliness when you walk through the door. A pet makes you responsible to another being and (depending on the creature) will provide unconditional love—obviously, you'll get more response from a cat or dog than a newt or a guppy.

When thinking about adopting a pet, consider the ways the pet can help you to regain confidence or make new connections with this new world you now inhabit without your loved one. If you've ever walked a dog down a suburban sidewalk, you already know it's impossible to make it for more than twenty minutes without someone talking to you or your dog. Others respond to people with animals, regardless of the type or the breed. Pets are always a topic for any conversation.

Additionally, when adopting a pet, you can join a club or organization specifically for the species, such as a cat club, or bird fanciers association. After training, you can show a dog in conformation or obedience trials, herding competitions, and agility meets. You can work with organizations such as the Delta Society and take your pet to nursing homes and work with the handicapped.

Depending on your circumstances, you may even want to consider being a foster parent to a dog who will eventually be training for the blind, hearing impaired, or disabled. It's very hard work, but the love and caring you provide to start this training is priceless.

Recognize yourself. You are an individual with style and talents that are unique. Often during this time people realize they don't fit the traditional roles any longer, and you may not fit the mold of wife, mother, daughter, husband, father, or son as you did before the death. This can be intimidating since you no longer have an exact role. Am I still a mother after my child dies? Am I a brother without a sister, an aunt without a niece, or a wife without a husband? Yes, you will always hold this position as you hold the memory of your loved one in your heart, but you will also grow into other roles. Just like at one time you were a high school senior, then a college freshman, then a thirty-year-old office worker, you can be lots of things in your lifetime. A survivor of a loved one's death is one of those roles.

Accept compliments about your "new" self with grace. The new self isn't necessarily better, prettier, more confident, simply new after the death of a loved one.

"After the baby's death, people kept remarking at how beautiful and blue my eyes were. I thought they were inferring that there was a contrast between my eyes and the black rings underneath caused by sleeplessness. One day I caught my reflection in a department store mirror and there was a difference in my eyes. It was as if my eyes mirrored my soul—and the empathy for others who have lost children and the deepened love I have for my husband and surviving children."

Getting Active Again

If you have yet to do so, you're past due to become involved *outside* of yourself. Refer to the sections on self-help support groups, volunteer, and become a joiner if you enjoy being with people. Remember as you become more active, the new people in your life will accept you as you, sometimes sad, sometimes happy. Additionally, as you begin living more in the outside world, your social opportunities will be extended.

Getting active can mean putting more energy back into surviving relationships—making plans with family and friends who have been waiting for you. As often happens, relationships with surviving loved ones falter after a death.

CREATIVE WORK
by Ed Bordeaux Szekley, philosopher and philologist, from *Creative Work–Karma Yoga, A Western Interpretation*

In the highest sense, work is meant to be the servant of man, not the master. It is not so important what shape or form our work may take, what is vitally important is our attitude toward that work. With love and enthusiasm directed toward our work, what was once a chore and hardship now becomes a magical tool to develop, enrich, and nourish our lives.

"Work makes the man" is an old proverb with much more truth in it than appears on the surface. Work can indeed make the man, if the man will use his God-given powers of reason to transform work into the sacred partnership with the Creator it was originally meant to be.

SIX PROMISES FOR EMOTIONAL WELL-BEING
by Susan Forward, Ph.D.

❧

1. I promise myself to begin to recognize those beliefs about myself and other people that make me feel sad, guilty, anxious, or inadequate.

2. I promise myself to remember that I am an adult. I am not helpless and I have options and choices. I have the ability to change.

3. I promise myself to remember that nothing is more important than my self-esteem and that I will have people in my life who are loving and will nourish good feelings about myself.

4. I promise to take responsibility for my own cruel, critical, hurtful, or victimizing behavior and to stop trying to manipulate others with it.

5. I promise myself to confront those people in my life who have injured me and if they are not willing to work with me toward healthier relationships, I have the right to decrease my contact with them or get them out of my life altogether, whomever they may be.

6. I promise myself to recognize that there will be times when I feel depressed or overwhelmed and if these feelings continue for long I will get professional help. To do so is an act of courage and honesty.

As the old adage goes: You can pick your friends, but you can't pick your relatives. And although Aunt Mildred, Mom, or big brother Jim may be thorns in your side, it may be time to become reacquainted. Could that anger and contrariness also stem from grief? Have others close to this person died? Did this recent death have a more profound effect? Why?

Sometimes talking with a therapist about difficult or confusing family members may make the situation clearer in your heart and mind. Self-help books on resolving relationships and healing the inner child often make the journey more sensible.

Getting active can also mean dating again, going to parties, singing in the church choir, traveling, and joining the local theater group. You may discover a whole range of new talent, but unless you take the first steps, your gifts may go undiscovered.

A good place to start gathering ideas for activities is the listing of community groups often found in the Sunday paper. You can also call your local chamber of commerce for groups and ongoing volunteer needs. You may want to approach a self-help group specific to the illness or event that caused your loved one's death. Everybody welcomes volunteers.

If you're unsure of what you want to do or know definitely what you don't want to do—make a list. For every entry that's an activity you want to try, write one down that you absolutely do not want to participate in—golf versus bungee jumping. The "don'ts" will at least make you smile as you come up with some wild alternatives. You may also want to go back and revise the goals you made months ago, or format a new set.

Be sure to include participation in a regular exercise program as one of the pleasurable goals on your list. Exercise is a proven method to help lift a mood. Just how, even the scientists are unsure. However, from a biochemical viewpoint, exercise increases the brain's level of beta-endorphins, the body's natural painkillers. It also makes us feel more powerful. Often in a state of depression, we feel helpless; exercise challenges that belief. Check with your doctor first. Then start slowly, join a gym, get instruction, or simply walk off your mood. Keep in mind that losing unwanted body fat (not necessarily going on a diet) will help you feel more in control and thus improve your self-confidence. There is nothing quite so wonderful as fitting comfortably into clothing that was previously snug.

Where to Get Help

Bookstores are now carrying daily meditation books and calendars for those who are survivors. Some of the meditations are for those involved in a Twelve-Step chemical recovery program, others are for harried mothers or high-stress career people, and some have religious connotations. All are pleasant and positive to read and contemplate. They're worth looking at during this time of resolution.

Your bookstore or public library will also have a section of self-help books. Here are but a few survivors often recommend.

Remembering with Love: Message of Hope for the First Year of Grieving and Beyond by Elizabeth Levang, Ph.D., and Sherokee Ilse (Minneapolis: Deaconess Press, 1995). The collection of essays provides thoughts and inspiration as the reader moves through the very first days of grief toward the final acceptance.

Chop Wood Carry Water: A Guide to Finding Spiritual Fulfillment in Everyday Life by Rick Fields, et al. (Los Angeles: Jeremy P. Tarcher Publishers, 1984). Providing ancient wisdom with contemporary thought, this book talks about work, play, love, and learning as we proceed through our own inner journey living each day at a time.

Life Skills 101: A Practical Guide to Leaving Home and Living on Your Own, by Tina Pestalozzi (Cortland, OH: Stonewood Publishing, 2001). *Life Skills 101* is an indispensable guide to the complete spectrum of skills .

The punctuation of anniversaries is terrible, like the closing of doors, one after another between you and what you want to hold onto....

—Anne Morrow Lindberg, from *Locked Rooms and Open Windows*

DECISIONS

This may also be the time when you're thinking of moving, changing jobs, going back to school, or completing a major project. Do some research before you jump into this change. Perhaps the university will give you "life credit" because of career experience and you'll be two-thirds of the way to achieving that degree. Or by talking with your boss, you'll find that the company is considering opening an office in another part of the country—a place where you always thought you'd like to live. Make your needs known and investigate all the options, including seeking out professional advice from attorneys, accountants, and career advisors before you make any drastic decisions.

More personally, this may be the time when you're considering marrying again, having another child, or accepting a new partner. Before this decision is made, you may find that you want to talk with a counselor, clergyperson, or listening friend. It's scary to make another commitment, but often it's far worse to go through life without having made a choice.

When Denise died of breast cancer, Barry never thought he could fall in love with anyone again. Denise was capable, a real spitfire with a ready laugh, and she had a pithy comment for just about everything. Then a year after her death he met Jan. And although initially she seemed to resemble his wife, Jan's sensitive side was the characteristic that won his love.

"Asking Jan to marry me was the most difficult thing I've done—at times it seemed harder than the initial days of grief when I mourned Denise. I wanted to share my life with Jan, but I had a life full of memories with my first wife." Prior to agreeing, Jan and Barry spent six months in counseling. "I'm blessed to have Jan and have her accept that Denise will always be part of our lives."

MAKING IT THROUGH THE HOLIDAYS AND ALL THE FIRSTS

We all have favorite memories like that really hot Fourth of July when the family had a watermelon eating contest. Or you may remember the time you and your loved one spent a quiet Thanksgiving evening pushing cloves into pomander balls, and how that simple time turned into a tradition as the kids grew up. Or the joy that comes with celebrating Christmas and Hanukkah and other religious holidays. These are the times to be with family and those with whom we love to celebrate.

Now that a loved one has died, these times, and especially the holidays, may seem hollow. Your feelings about celebrating any occasion may have vanished. This is normal and you're not alone. As therapists tell us, the depression stage of grief can often remain for years and even after we believe we've moved on, flashes of what life once held do return. Often the tears return, too.

Holidays make us face a crisis in our loss. Who wants to do something when the event seems meaningless without our special loved one to share the time, the chatter, the food, the meaning of the day?

Sherry Williams and Dr. Sandra Graves, founders of ACCORD, explain that holiday grief is very real. They say, "We grieve not only the person we loved who has died, but also the life we lived with that person, our roles and responsibilities, our companionship, the physical space we occupied together.

"We also grieve the time we spend living the important moments and those important events took on a life and identity of their own. Christmas, Rosh Hashanah, Easter, all had a flavor, color, and sound of their own, that we created with our loved ones." Since the death, that identity is gone and with it we grieve not only for the person who died, but for the event that will always now be different. Holiday grief isn't limited to those holidays marked on the calendar, but includes birthdays and anniversaries, or the first day you planted spring flowers, or raked the fall leaves.

Knowing this, it makes sense that we face the holidays, with the stages of denial, anger, despair, and resolution. "I don't want to be a part of any of that fuss." "I'm not going to put up a tree.... why bother? It's a waste of time. Phooey!"

Williams and Graves point out, "We may feel mad, sad, and scared at the same time, resulting in being just plain overwhelmed. Our anger may be toward others who do care

ﾗ▰

When I was very young and confused, I thought that when I reached my thirties I would finally be all wise and knowing, my values would be intact, and my life would be complete. Instead, my marriage ended, I began to question my values, and Cari died. So then I looked forward to my forties. Yet by the time I was forty, I was no longer selling real estate, I was no longer with MADD, my children had left home, and I did not know what I was going to do when I grew up. The future was a blank to me, but before I could move ahead, I had to look back. I had to grieve.

If there is one thing I have learned.... it's that we all grieve in our own ways and on our own schedule. When I interviewed psychologist Dr. Jerri Smock.... she told me that you know you've made significant progress when you can go to the cemetery, you can look at the pictures, you can talk about that person without feeling overwhelmed by pain or sadness or tears. I've finally reached that place with Cari.

Today I don't dwell on how my daughter died. I don't seek out opportunities to say, 'My daughter was killed by a drunk driver.' And I don't

that the seasons exist and seem to enjoy them! These are normal feelings. Our anger is trying to serve its healthy function of making change in our lives, yet we are out of control of those changes."

Alone at the Holidays

Holidays are typically a time for food, fun, excitement, celebrating, and faith....they are not a time to be alone. Often it's very frightening to be alone when "everybody else has somebody." We are alone, frightened, with no power to remedy the situation because our loved one is dead and will not be coming back.

Fear is one of our most basic instincts and when fear is aroused, it produces hormones that trigger our nerves to be on edge, as we become alerted to danger. Fear may also hide our worry about being abandoned, and while intellectually we know that our loved one has died because of an accident or disease, we often feel like we've been rejected and deserted. This is very natural. Children also experience these feelings of being forsaken during the holidays. They may even have trouble expressing why they are mad or fearful, especially when they see others celebrating the days and know that theirs will not be anything like what they see on television or in commercials.

"I know it's stupid, but I'm angry that there are so many shoppers. Sure it's Christmas, but everybody's in my way." "I'm not coming to your house for Thanksgiving dinner—turkey always makes me sick." These are not silly excuses, but real feelings used when the fear and grief become more intense with upcoming holidays.

Williams and Graves say that there are four ways that we make ourselves miserable at the holidays. If we feel

- Anticipation of the pain on the holiday
- Fear of preparation for the holidays
- The wish to avoid the whole season
- Pressure regarding expectations

then the holidays will be hard on us. "These fears may increase or decrease in intensity depending on the significance the holiday has." We may also feel some portion of each of the four and/or feel different about the holidays from one day to the next. Additionally, other family members may have a difficult time coping with other survivor's reactions to the holidays because they are fearing them, too.

Anticipation of pain on the holiday: After the death of a loved one the approach of the holidays can be depressing and often we use up vast quantities of energy worrying how we'll cope. We live in fear and anticipate that bad things will surely happen. We are not living for the moment, but worrying over what *might* be in the future. Through this method of anticipation of pain, we distort reality; however this is all quite human as we attempt to gain some control over our lives that may seem totally out of control. Say Williams and Graves, "The problem is, we miss living while we are doing it.

"It is probably true that the actual holiday itself, or some part of it, will be painful. You may feel sad, or mad, or scared. Your emotions may be more intense, because you are grieving the loss of your loved one and the loss of the holiday you loved at the same time. It is also true that if you think about an event you may sensitize yourself to that event. You cannot, however, plan your pain. Your body doesn't work that way. You can only experience pain right now. If you are anything, like other grievers, you are very good at making yourself feel very bad."

They explain that right now, as you are reading this section, you can make yourself very uncomfortable, perhaps nauseous or sweaty by concentrating on the worst possible things that will happen to you during the holidays. You can conjure up thoughts of the worst holiday, in minute detail, and since that's what you are expecting to happen, nine times out of ten, you'll get your "wish." Live for *this* moment, not next week or December or Super Bowl Sunday, but now.

Fear of preparation for the holidays: It's quite normal to fear getting ready for the holidays. Even though the actual day of the holiday is important, the preparations are part of the tradition.... buying just the perfect size turkey, making

avoid them. My focus is no longer on the past, no longer on drunk driving. I'm relieved to be able to say that.

Yes, there is life after MADD. It's in Southern California by the sea. It's taking time to know my children better and developing relationships based on who I am and not what I do. Ten years ago I could barely make it through the day. Now I look forward to the future.

special cakes, and wondering if the store will finally stock the right brand of poppy seeds. In addition to thinking about the plans, there's shopping, decorating, sending cards, listening to music, and exchanging gifts.

Within the preparation, we anticipate how our loved ones who died played an integral role in our lives. "Even after I left for college, Mother and I always made butter cookies. We called them 'dunking cookies' because they were so hard."

"Mark and I always bought each other a special tree ornament. Sometimes we'd shop all day and have lunch. In the evening, we made a tradition of sipping hot chocolate and exchanging the decoration which we'd immediately put on the tree." But Mark and Mother are no longer alive and the intimate tradition that was shared died, too.

We grieve for the people who helped fill our holidays with pleasure. The pain arrives when we anticipate doing the preparations. Sometimes we feel trapped, and being trapped makes us angry and ready to escape or lash out at others.

The wish to avoid the whole season: With the emotion of fear, we attempt to survive by turning our backs on the holiday, ignoring it, skipping it. Williams and Graves explain, "Sometimes avoiding takes the form of forgetting or procrastinating, putting off making painful decisions." In addition to the urge to get angry at people who seem to be enjoying themselves, we sometimes want to simply hide, isolating ourselves so that there's no holiday interaction at all.

Pressure regarding expectations: "We don't know what to say if we can't say 'happy' birthday, Easter, Hanukkah, anniversary, etc.," say Williams and Graves. But people, family, friends, colleagues, expect us to do certain things at the holidays. If we are parents with young children, we still expect ourselves to make the season bright-eyed and wondrous. "We want to make things better. We put tremendous pressure on ourselves because of our expectations. Expectation is much like anticipation. We can be very judgmental about our expectations—the best Christmas, the loveliest Thanksgiving, with the perfectly cooked turkey. We tend to think in absolutes and create fantasies about events. We embrace the 'shoulds' and the 'ought ofs' of life and try to do what is right. If we don't, we are wrong. That's bad. Pressure builds and stress increases. Dread may be the natural result."

What Can You Do?

Understand the stages of grief and review other coping mechanisms mentioned in previous chapters. Eating sensibly, getting sufficient exercise, avoiding drugs, alcohol, and caffeine, talking with sensitive friends, and being good to yourself are essential at any time of stress, particularly at the holidays.

Williams and Graves provide some handles to help survivors cope during the holidays.

Stop yourself from anticipating pain. They say, "Become aware that when you think about a certain holiday you are experiencing an emotion. Ask yourself, What am I feeling—mad, sad, glad, scared? After you have identified the emotion, it's helpful to express the emotion out loud. If you are comfortable screaming or crying, do so. You can also say, "I am feeling…." Ask yourself, What do I need right now? You may need a hug, a friend, or to tell yourself that you're okay." Inventory your needs and act on your needs.

Fear of preparation for the holiday can be realistic "if you look at the possibility of activities you can generate." They suggest making a list of activities you've always wanted to do. Start new traditions, and make significant changes in the traditions you always did "before."

The wish to avoid the season is natural. "Be aware that you are experiencing a normal process. If you feel like you want to run away from it all, this could be a signal that you are not taking care of yourself and need some more nurturing and compassion." They suggest that if you're feeling this way, you may want return to the support circle that embraced you after the death. "Emotions can trick you to think you are scared when you are mad and mad when you are really sad." And they recommend that you use your emotions effectively and efficiently. "Use anger to make

ONE TULIP
by Joan Jacobsen

๕๏

It was Mother's Day. All week I dreaded this day. My sons had sent cards and gifts and telephoned, but Don, my husband, wasn't here. He died in April, a year ago, of cancer. That first Mother's Day went well, so much to do, but this Mother's Day was lonely and sad. My youngest son was coming home from college, but not until late afternoon.

I decided to mow the yard. When I was done, I looked out the back window and saw a flash of bright orange and red peeking out from behind a tree in the yard by the fence. I thought, That's strange. I just mowed and didn't notice anything.

I never had any flowers in the backyard and neither did any of my neighbors. I walked out to the tree and there was one large red-orange fluted tulip with yellow accents, with the sweetest fragrance. I was so thrilled and immediately thought of Don. He didn't forget Mother's Day, and every Mother's Day he bought for me the flowers we transplanted around the house.

I plucked that beautiful tulip and brought it in the house and put it in a vase by the sink. It lasted four days. Beautiful and fragrant, and each of those days I smiled and thanked Don for a wonderful Mother's Day.

HELPING OTHERS MOVE BEYOND LOSS

by John W. James and
Frank Cherry, from
The Grief Recovery Handbook

❧

In helping others, you must go first. Don't ask others if they are ready to recover. It won't make any sense to them. They don't know if they'll even survive. You didn't think you'd survive the pain, but with the right information you did. Do what you know you need to do. Ask them to lunch. Call once a day and ask how they're doing. Don't judge, preach, or give advice. Just tell the truth about your own experience. Start putting their significant anniversary dates in your calendar. Call on those days. Share your feelings with them. Remember to share your feelings first, then ask how they're feeling. Don't ask them to go first; they've been evaluated and judged a lot. Tell the truth about your feelings and volunteer some of the small recovery actions you've taken.

changes. Use fear to gain knowledge. Use sadness for finding meaning in the past and to develop new values. Joy and laughter will be your rewards."

Just because a loved one has died, it does not mean that his or her name should be taboo. Grief therapists always suggest that we use the names of our loved ones. Don't pretend your loved one never existed; he or she was a wonderful part of your life. "Concentrate some moments into creating memorials to your loved one as part of the holiday celebrations." You may want to donate toys to disabled children in his name, take flowers to the cemetery after midnight mass on Christmas Eve, or take peanuts to the wild birds at the park on New Year's morning....just like your loved one always did.

Pressure regarding expectation comes from within us. Williams and Graves explain, "We have somehow decided that there are things we *should* be doing or *should* be feeling." Thus we judge ourselves and probably come up short; we are often our own worst critics.

"We add details to our lives which we could probably live very well without. As human beings, we take a hallway that is straight and simple and build complex mazes. Are you doing that for the holiday? Are you building your fantasy memory of the perfect Christmas or Hanukkah that sparkles and tingles and brings nothing but childlike joy?" We often forget the gravy stains on the antique white linen table cloth. That expensive toy or piece of electronic equipment that was neglected before the first day of January. That tinsel, ribbon, or pine cone that broke the vacuum cleaner. And the turkey that was tough and stringy.

"Are you forgetting to laugh at yourself and your memories? Learn from what you are telling yourself you should do, then gently tell yourself no. Give yourself permission to keep your life more simple while enriching it with thoughts and things that are beautiful to you."

THE END AS YOUR BEGINNING

Take time to recall and rejoice in the progress you've made since that moment when someone you loved died.

Call back the memories of the good times and the great times. And if there were trying, soul-wrenching and horrifying times, perhaps as you witnessed your loved one slowly, even painfully move to the final transition to death, put these experiences in among the many displayed in your own kaleidoscope of life.

You have something no one can take away. You've had the privilege and the pleasure of knowing and loving that special person. There still may be times—for years in the future—when you will miss the one who died. Anyone who believes there's a quick fix to grief has never experienced death or never really experienced life.

Throughout your continuing journey to resolutions, there may be times when you'll want to seek out more information. Nineteenth century American writer Henry David Thoreau said, "If you have built castles in the air, your work need not be lost; that is where they should be. Now put the foundations under them." You now have the tools to build that foundation. Some jobs and tasks can be shared, another such as bereavement is work each individual must do alone. But the hammer is in your hands, the blueprints and directions are in this book and other self-help books on grief and recovery.

It is said that there is a time for every purpose. Don't push too hard to find it. Instead, be gentle with yourself and the purpose will come to you.

Move on at your own pace, to your own rhythm, with the words of your own song. And continue to listen to the music that plays in your heart.

Appendix

Condolence Letters

While our hearts often break when trying to write condolence letters, the actual process may become part of our therapy as we move through the stages of grief. The following samples are available to give you help when words fail. Use just part of the letters or the entire message.

DEATH OF A CHILD

Dear (first name):

    It truly was sad news to learn of the loss of your (deceased's first name). May I express my condolences?

    As touching as your moments are, (deceased's first name) brought joy into the world and affected many lives. People truly cared for him/her, as was evidenced by those who penetrated your desire for privacy during this time to express their feelings to you and your family.

    I believe it is the Almighty who conceives our spirits. (Deceased's name) death is a test to all of us to strengthen our faith and accept, without fully understanding, the reasons why. This is the true meaning of faith above all others, and without it we have nothing.

    My thoughts and prayers are with you (and spouse's name) and I will remember (deceased's first name), who is now at peace, through a contribution to (charity name).

Sincerely,

Dear (first name):

Please accept my heartfelt and most sincere condolence on the loss of your daughter/son (deceased's first name).

You have truly been faced with a most difficult experience to accept and I hope you will be given the faith and strength to accept God's will.

We will someday know the reasons why, but for the present our faith is the only thing that can sustain us. Our mortal life, as ordained by our Maker, is not for us to fully appreciate unless we accept the crosses each of us are given. One day we will all know the reasons why, but in the meantime, must rely solely on our faith, strength, and personal convictions that life does continue in a much more beautiful and meaningful way.

Although we all experience the loss of our family members and loved ones sometime during life, it is tragic to go through the sudden loss of a younger soul in the physical departure from this earth. You may be sure that life continues on and that just as matter can never be destroyed, neither can the soul and spirit of one who has been created.

(Spouse's name) and I wanted to express our feelings and have done so through a donation to (charity) in your son/daughter's memory. We are truly saddened and you may be sure our prayers and thoughts are with you both.

With our love,

DEATH OF A PARENT

Dear (first name):

I was so sorry to hear that your mother/father/grandparent has passed away.

No words can really convey what is in our hearts at a time like this, but please know that I am just one of many who are grieving with you.

With love,

Dear (first name):

    Even though I/we expressed my/our sympathy to you at the funeral home, please accept these condolences on the loss of your father/mother.

    Death is difficult to understand and often more trying to accept, even when one has the benefit of a full life.

    Please know that our hearts and thoughts are with you and your family at this most complicated time. I'll call you soon just to talk.

    Please express my sympathies to your family, too.

Sincerely,

Dear (first name):

    Even though I/we expressed my/our sympathy to you at the funeral home, please accept these condolences on the loss of your father/mother.

    Death is difficult to understand, even when one has the benefit of a full life. Although there is little I can say or do to lessen your grief, I wanted to let you know of my concern. I hope you are given the strength and grace to accept and understand our Maker's privilege to call each of our spirits back to Himself in eternal happiness.

    Time will heal, and we know life really does not end in our spiritual existence, but continues on in a more perfect form. I'm confident she now knows better than we the true meaning of life well lived.

    Again, (first name), my/our sincere sympathy to you and your family.

Very sincerely,

Dear (first name):

Even though I expressed my feelings to you after the service, I wanted to again let you know of my sincere condolences on the loss of your mother.

I know that her life in the last few years has not been of a quality nature and so her departure to eternal happiness is probably a blessing at this time. As we are privileged to know in our faith, it is not the end, but the beginning. I will remember her at Mass this week and I hope you will accept my prayers for understanding and acceptance.

She was truly a wonderful lady and obviously she fulfilled her purpose in life and now goes on to her reward, which I'm sure will be great. I know she had great pride in you and your accomplishments. Be assured her spirit will live on, and even though the temple of her spirit was buried with great dignity, her soul is with us all.

Again, I am very sorry.

Dear (first name):

Even though we shared a few minutes after the service, I wanted to again let you know of my sincere condolences on the loss of (deceased name).

I know that his/her life in the last few years has been complicated and his/her departure to eternal happiness is probably a blessing. Yet his/her passing leaves a gaping hole in so many lives. What a privilege it is to know that this is not the end, but the beginning. I will remember him/her and you in my prayers (at Mass this week). I hope you will accept my prayers for understanding and acceptance.

He/She was a wonderful gentleman/lady. I know he/she had great pride in you and your accomplishments. Be assured his/her spirit will live on. While the temple of the spirit was buried with great dignity, his/her soul is with us all.

Again, I am very sorry.

DEATH OF A SPOUSE

Dear (first name):

(Spouse's name) and I were shocked to learn of (spouse name's) death on (date of death if known).

You have our deepest sympathy on the loss of your wonderful wife/husband. We regret we did not have the opportunity to personally express our sympathy to you as we/I have just heard the news. Be assured we share in your grief.

(Add personal note about community involvement such as: Our community was privileged to have had (spouse name's) strong influence on our way of life. We have lost an outstanding citizen and the dedication to his/her many civic involvements will be missed.)

Your sorrow must be overwhelming, and I/we hope you can take comfort in knowing this is only a temporary separation. One day we will all be together again.

Please know our thoughts are with you.

(First name), if there is anything I/we can do for you during this difficult time, please don't hesitate to let me know. I/we will call in a few days.

Sincerely,

Dear (first name):

It is my/our deepest regret that we will be unable to attend the service for your wonderful wife/husband (spouse name). Please accept our love and sympathy to you at this heartbreaking time. We know it's been a long, hard battle for you with his/her illness. There are no words that can heal the physical loss of one you love so dearly and has been your mate for so many years.

(First name), I/we cannot forget the occasions we enjoyed together. I/we pray you will have the strength and courage to accept and understand God's master plan.

(Deceased's first name) fulfilled his/her purpose very well, and I/we am/are confident his/her spirit lives on in ways we haven't begun to appreciate.

A donation to the (charity's name) has been made in (spouse's name's) memory. I/we share your great sadness. If there is anything we can do for you during this difficult time, please don't hesitate to let us know.

Sincerely,

Dear (first name):

(Wife's or husband's name) and I are so sad that we will be unable to attend the service for your wonderful husband/wife (spouse name). We have a commitment to be out of town.

Please allow me/us to express my/our love and sympathy to you at this challenging time.

There are no words that can heal the physical loss of one you love so dearly and had been your mate for so many years, but I/we pray you will have the strength and courage to accept and understand God's master plan.

Again I/we am/are so very sorry

DEATH OF A BUSINESS
ASSOCIATE/COLLEAGUE

Dear (first name):

I was so sorry to hear (deceased's name) has passed away.

His/her life touched so many in our business and he/she will be truly missed.

No words can really convey what is in our hearts at a time like this, but please know that I am just one of many who are grieving with you. A charitable donation has been made to (charity name) in (deceased's name).

Sincerely,

Dear (first name):

It truly was sad to hear (deceased's name) has passed away.

Please accept my/our condolences. His/her life touched so many in our business and he/she will be truly missed.

At this difficult time, words seem shallow, but is it my/our hope that you know many are grieving with you.

A charitable donation has been made to (charity name) in (deceased's name).

Sincerely,

UNABLE TO ATTEND SERVICES

Dear (first name):

(Wife's or husband's name) and I extend to you our deepest sympathy and condolence in the loss of your remarkable and great man/woman (deceased's first name). She/he was truly an inspiration in our lives as a (include civic or business accomplishment such as executive, leader, and citizen).

He/she was a wonderful life partner, mother/father, and sister/brother. (Deceased's name) will be greatly missed.

It is my/our belief that his/her spirit lives on and it is only through faith that we who are left behind can realize that life does not end. Regardless of one's convictions, I/we feel blessed and privileged to have had the time in years gone by with (deceased's first name). What an incredible individual (lady/gentleman)!

We only wish we could be with you at the service on (date) to recognize his/her contributions to all of our lives. Unfortunately, I/we am/are not able to change my/our plans.

Be assured I/we will remember him/her in prayer and with a contribution to (charity's name). I/we hope and pray that time will allow you to accept and understand this sadness of temporary separation.

Again, I/we am/are so very sorry.

Sincerely,

DEATH OF A PET

Dear (first name):

    (Animal companion's name) brought so much happiness to life, he/she will be greatly missed.

    With their gift of loving us unconditionally, our pets share our joys and our sorrows. Whatever would we do without them?

    Please accept my/our condolences at this time and know that my/our prayers are with you (and your family).

With love,

Dear (first name):

    I/we was/were so sorry to hear that (animal companion's name or type of animal, such as cat or dog) had passed on.

    Our animal friends bring joy, laughter and comfort to our lives and their death is often a time of great sorrow. Please know, (first name), that as pet lovers I/we have felt something similar to what you are going through right now.

    I/we have made a charitable contribution in (animal's or person's name) to (charity) in loving memory of this wonderful animal companion.

Notes

The numbers preceding notes refer to the pages on which the references appear.

૨▲

Chapter 1

3: within the first . . . "Was It Death by Trauma?" ACCORD, Inc., Louisville, KY, 1986.

4: Sandra L. Graves, Ph.D., A.T.R., "I Didn't Schedule Death for Today," ACCORD, Inc. newsletter (1991, Vol. 7, No. 3.).

6: Elaine Vail, *A Personal Guide to Living with Loss* (Toronto: John Wiley and Sons, Inc., 1982).

7: Most people are . . . Fred Jordan, Chief Medical Examiner, State of Oklahoma, "Unshrouding Death's Mystery," *USA Today* (February 1990, Vol. 118, 2357), 10.

7: a checklist of . . . "Signs of Forthcoming Death," Hospice of North Coast, Carlsbad, CA.

8: when the death is expected . . . Ernest Morgan, *Dealing Creatively with Death* (Bayside, NY: Barclay House Books, 12th edition, 1990).

9: Nancy Zeidman, "When You Lose Someone You Love," *Health Scene* (Fall 1987), 7.

9: David A. Crenshaw, *Bereavement: Counseling the Grieving throughout the Life Cycle* (New York: The Continuum Publishing Company, 1990).

12: Ernest Morgan, *Dealing Creatively with Death.*

13: consider this procedure . . . *Autopsy Manual* (New

York: New York Academy of Medicine, Office of Public Health, 5th ed., 1988).

❧

Chapter 2

16: Michael A. Simpson, *The Facts of Death* (Englewood Cliffs, NJ: Prentice-Hall, Inc. 1979).

19: When a loved . . . "The Traditional Funeral," National Funeral Directors Association, Inc., Milwaukee, WI.

20: Theodore E. Hughes and David Klein, "On an Open Casket," *A Family Guide to Wills, Funerals, and Probate* (New York: Charles Scribner's Sons, 1983).

21: A buyer should . . . Consumers Union, *Funerals: Consumers' Last Rights* (New York: Consumers Union of United States, W. W. Norton & Co., 1977).

23: The CCSC is . . . "Having a Problem with a Cemetery?" Cemetery Consumer Service Council, Washington, DC.

25: cremation is the . . . *Cremationist* (November 3, 1991, Vol. 12, No. 11), 16.

25: some people choose . . . "What You Should Know about Cremation," National Funeral Directors Association, Inc., Milwaukee, WI.

26: Michael A. Simpson, *The Facts of Death.*

31: Donation of organs . . . "Anatomical Gifts," National Funeral Directors Association, Inc., Milwaukee, WI.

31: Federal Trade Commission, Embalming Information, FTC Rule, approved 1984.

33: The purpose of . . . "Embalming," National Funeral Directors Association, Inc., Milwaukee, WI.

36: The funeral is . . . "Yes, Funerals Are for the Living," National Funeral Directors Association, Inc., Milwaukee, WI.

38: from the hour . . . Ibid.

41: The schedule of ten standard items . . . Funeral Price Information, NFDA 1991 Survey of Funeral Home Operations.

46: The majority of . . . "A Way to Remember: Choosing a Funeral Ceremony," National Funeral Directors Association, Inc., Milwaukee, WI.

47: The Jewish ceremony . . . "For Families of the Jewish Terminally Ill," National Institute for Jewish Hospice, Palm Springs, CA, 1989.

50: Every day, trained . . . Funeral Service Consumer Assistance Program, "A Consumer's Guide," National Research and Information Center, Evanston, IL.

54: Rasa Gustaitas, "Honoring Lives That Ended on a City Street," Pacific News Service, October 1, 1990.

56: Susan McClelland and Susan McClelland Prescott, *If There's Anything I Can Do: An Easy Guide to Showing You Care* (Gainesville, FL: Triad Publishing Company, 1990).

58: Etiquette experts have . . . "Funeral Etiquette," National Funeral Directors Association, Inc., Milwaukee, WI.

61: You could certainly . . . Susan McClelland and Susan McClelland Prescott, *If There's Anything I Can Do: An Easy Guide to Showing You Care.*

༄

Chapter 3

66: Alan D. Wolfelt, Ph.D., "Tears Are a Sign of Healing," *Thanatos*, (Fall 1989), 28.

66: The following is... "After Death.... The Urgent Details," American Association of Retired Persons, Washington, DC.

68: anyone who has . . . "On Being Alone: Guide for Widowed Persons," American Association of Retired Persons, Washington, DC.

68: Michael Tynan MacCarthy, *San Diego Writer's Monthly* (September, 1992), 3.

69: after a death . . . "Physical Grief," ACCORD, Inc., Louisville, KY, 1986.

72: Alan D. Wolfelt, Ph.D., "Embrace Your Spirituality," *Thanatos*, (Spring 1991), 11.

73: Alan D. Wolfelt, Ph.D., "Helping a Friend in Grief," *Thanatos* (Winter 1990), 28.

78: Dying usually lasts . . . Robert E. Enck, M.D., *American Journal of Hospice & Palliative Care* (July/August 1992), 11–13.

79: Sudden death is . . . David Carroll, *Living with Dying* (New York: Paragon House, 1992).

79: I didn't pass . . . Candy Lightner with Nancy Hathaway, *Giving Sorrow Words* (New York: Warner Books, 1990).

80: A trauma is . . . "Was It Death by Trauma?," ACCORD, Inc., Louisville, KY, 1986.

83: For too long . . . "A Homicide Survivor Speaks Out," The Judicial Reform Foundation, Monterey, CA.

84: The office for . . . "Your Primary Source for Information about Victims of Crime," National Victims Resource Center, Rockville, MD.

86: Sometimes death is . . . Sandra L. Graves, Ph.D., A.T.R., "When Death Seems Like Malpractice," ACCORD, Inc. newsletter, (1991, Vol. 6, No. 3).

88: bad parenting doesn't . . . Andina Wrobleski, *Suicide Survivors: A Guide for Those Left Behind* (Minneapolis: Afterwords Publishing, 1991).

88: Diane Watson, "Tap-Tap-Tap," *Caring Concepts*, The Centering Corporation, Omaha, NE, 1991.

89: There are as . . . Charlotte Foehner and Charolette Cozart, *The Widow's Handbook* (Golden, CO: Fulcrum Publishers, 1988).

89: The guilt of . . . "Are You a Survivor of Suicide?" ACCORD, Inc., Louisville, KY, 1986.

92: You need to . . . John Hewett, *After Suicide* (Louisville: Westminster Press, 1980).

94: is based on . . . Ernest Morgan, *Dealing Creatively with Death* (Bayside, NY: Barclay House Books, 12th edition, 1990).

97: This baby has . . . "Ectopic Pregnancy," La Crosse Lutheran Hospital, La Crosse, WI, 1984.

99: SHARE reaches out . . . "SHARE," Pregnancy and Infant Loss Support, Inc., St. Joseph, MO, 1989.

99: Babies are not . . . Sherokee Ilse, *Empty Arms: Coping with Miscarriage, Stillbirth, and Infant Death* (Maple Plain, MN: Wintergreen Press, 1990).

100: Shaun Lammert, "A Brother's Memories," SHARE, St. Joseph, MO.

102: there are four . . . "Has Your Baby Died?" ACCORD, Inc., Louisville, KY, 1986.

104: Your baby deserves . . . Alan D. Wolfelt, Ph.D., "Helping Yourself Heal When a Baby Dies," Center for Loss and Life Transitions, Fort Collins, CO.

105: Facts about SIDS . . . "Fact Sheet: What Is SIDS?" Federal SIDS Program, National SIDS Clearinghouse, Washington, DC.

107: When a baby . . . "Information Exchange," newsletter of the National Sudden Infant Death Syndrome Clearinghouse, U.S. Department of Health and Human Services, Washington, DC, July 1991.

৯৯

Chapter 4

114: "45 Suggestions to Help Conquer Depression," Teen Age Grief, Inc., Panorama City, CA.

115: After the death . . . "The Stages of Grief," ACCORD, Inc., Louisville, KY, 1986.

118: Elisabeth Kübler-Ross, Ph.D., *On Death and Dying* (New York: Macmillian, Collier Books, 1982); *Questions and Answers on Death* (New York: Macmillian, Collier Books, 1974); *Death: The Final Stage of Growth* (Englewood Cliffs, NJ: Prentice-Hall, Spectrum Books, 1975).

123: All children are . . . Fact Sheet: The Grief of Children, U.S. Department of Health and Human Services, Washington, DC.

126: Here are a . . . "Children and Death," National Funeral Directors Association, Milwaukee, WI.

127: Marcia G. Scherago, M.S.W., L.C.S.W., *Sibling Grief* (Redmond, WA: Medic Publishing, 1987).

128: There was a . . . The Dougy Center, information newsletter, Portland, OR.

129: Joan Borysenko, Ph.D., "Respectful Listening," *Guilt Is the Teacher, Love Is the Lesson* (New York: Viking Press, 1974).

133: Absence of grief . . . Patricia L. Papenbrock, R.N., and Robert F. Voss, M.A., Q.M.R.P., *Loss: How Children and Teenagers Can Cope with Death and Other Kinds of Loss* (Redmond, WA: Medic Publishing Co., 1990).

134: has a more . . . Carol Staudacher, *Beyond Grief: A Guide for Recovering from the Death of a Loved One* and *Men and Grief* (Oakland: New Harbinger Publications, Inc., 1991).

136: Keep on courting . . . Rev. Terry Morgan, Chaplain James Cunningham, Dr. Ray Goldstein and Earl Katz, *Fathers Grieve, Too* (Omaha: The Centering Corporation, 1991).

140: Adults take on . . . Sandra L. Graves, Ph.D., A.T.R., "When a Sibling Dies," ACCORD, Inc., Louisville, KY.

142: Margaret S. Miles, author of *The Grief of Parents When a Child Dies* (Oakbrook, IL: Compassionate Friends, 1978).

146: When a parent . . . Rabbi Marc D. Angel, *The Jewish Orphaned Adult* (Palm Springs, CA: National Institute for Jewish Hospice, 1991).

148: Sheila Cluff, "50-Plus and Feeling Fine," for syndicated column "Fit for Life," 1991.

154: If you can . . . Sandra L. Graves, Ph.D., A.T.R., "Has Your Grandparent Died?" ACCORD, Inc., 1986.

154: Suzanne Howell, M.A.,"Saying the Name, Sharing the Memories," ACCORD, Inc. newsletter (1991, Vol. 7, No. 3).

155: There is no . . . Enid Samuel Traisman, *I Remember.... I Remember* (Omaha: The Centering Corporation, 1991).

ঽ᳜

Chapter 5

160: I have noticed . . . Sandra L. Graves, Ph.D., A.T.R., "Borrowed Recovery," ACCORD, Inc. newsletter (1991, Vol. 7, No. 2).

163: Here's an overview . . . "What Will I Be Feeling," ACCORD, Inc., Louisville, KY, 1986.

172: During this time . . . Sandra L. Graves, Ph.D., A.T.R., "How Can I Cope?" ACCORD, Inc., Louisville, KY, 1991.

180: The following guidelines . . . Dr. Ann Kaiser Stearns, *Coming Back: Rebuilding Lives After Crisis and Loss* (New York: Random House, 1989).

181: Sherry Williams, "When We Dream about the One We Love," ACCORD, Inc., 1990.

182: Alan D. Wolfelt, Ph.D., "Dispelling Five Common Myths about Grief," *Thanatos* (Fall 1989), 25–27.

183: many of us . . . Greg Risberg, M.S.W., and Virginia E. McCullough, *Touch: A Personal Workbook* (Oak Park, IL: Open Arms Press, 1989).

ॐ

Chapter 6

188: We have found . . . Parents of Murdered Children, *Survivors* newsletter, Cincinnati, OH, June 1992.

190: "Traveling Memorial Wall," Parents of Murdered Children pamphlet, Cincinnati, OH.

193: Simply treat the . . . Melba Beals, *Expose Yourself* (San Francisco: Chronicle Books, 1990).

194: Don't use the . . . Diane Gage and Henry DeVries, *Self-Marketing Secrets: Winning by Making Your Name Known* (San Marcos, CA: Slawson Communications, 1992).

194: the press wants . . . Herbert Schmertz, with William Novak, *Good-bye to the Low Profile* (New York: Little, Brown & Company, 1986).

195: If the reporter's . . . Stan Sauerhaft and Chris Atkins, *Image Wars* (New York: John Wiley Books, 1989).

195: Richard and Deanne Mincer, "Ideas for Producing Your Issue," *The Talk Show Book* (New York: Facts on File, Inc., 1982).

200: Ed Wohlmuth, "10 Sure-Fire Ways to Give a Lousy Speech," *The Overnight Guide to Public Speaking* (Philadelphia: Running Press, 1983).

205: Ernest Morgan, "Bereavement and Catastrophic Loss," *Dealing Creatively with Death.*

206: The commuter plane . . . Linda Probus, M.A., A.T.R., "We Are Together in Pain and Hope," ACCORD,

Inc., Louisville, KY.

210: we need heroes . . . Sandra Graves, Ph.D., A.T.R., "We Need Heroes!" ACCORD, Inc. newsletter (Vol. 6, No. 2, 1991).

212: Marly Hayer, "Light in the Darkness," *Caring Concepts*, The Centering Corporation, Omaha, NE, 1991.

ֶ♠

Chapter 7

218: If you are . . . "Death Away from Home," National Funeral Directors Association, Milwaukee, WI.

226: Americans traveling abroad . . . "Your Trip Abroad," U.S. Department of State, Bureau of Consular Affairs, Washington, DC.

231: For all who . . . Sandra L. Graves, Ph.D., A.T.R., "Circles of Grief," ACCORD, Inc., Louisville, KY, 1990.

234: When a member . . . Marine Corps Casualty Procedures Manual MCO P3040.4, May 11, 1990.

238: By itself, the . . . Ann Kaiser Stearns, *Coming Back: Rebuilding Lives After Crisis and Loss* (New York: Random House, 1989).

238: Therese A. Rando, M.D., "What You Think—You Are!" *Loss and Anticipatory Grief* (Lexington, MA: Lexington Books, 1986).

241: Robert Kastenbaum and Ruth Aisenberg, "Yesterday," *The Psychology of Death* (New York: Springer Publishing Company, Inc., 1972).

241: What is death . . . Rabbi Maurice Lamm, "The Meaning of Death," *The Jewish Way in Death and Mourning* (New York: Jonathan David Publishers, 1969).

242: Allen Barnett, "The Times As It Knows Us," *The Body and Its Dangers and Other Stories* (New York: St. Martin's Press, 1991).

ֶ♠

Chapter 8

245: Elaine Vail, *A Personal Guide to Living with Loss* (Toronto: John Wiley and Sons, Inc., 1982).

246: Make three piles . . . John W. James and Frank Cherry, *The Grief Recovery Handbook: A Step-by-Step Program for Moving Beyond Loss* (New York: Harper & Row Publishers, 1988).

249: Depending on how . . . "Easing the Burden, Prearranging Your Funeral," National Funeral Directors Association, Inc., Milwaukee, WI.

253: Mark A. Edinberg, Ph.D., "Wills and Living Wills," *Talking with Your Aging Parents* (Boston: Shambhala, 1987).

259: Therese A. Rando, M.D., "The Opening of Another Door," *Loss and Anticipatory Grief* (Lexington, MA: Lexington Books, 1986).

268: recommends interviewing financial . . . Ginita Wall, C.P.A., *Our Money, Our Selves: Money Management for Each Stage of a Woman's Life* (Yonkers, New York: Consumer Reports Books, a division of Consumers Union, 1992).

270: Dick Davis, *Tilting the Investment Odds in Your Favor* (Miami: Dick Davis Digest, 1992).

272: Depending on portfolio . . . Michael Stolper, *How to Select an Investment Manager* (Chicago: Stolper & Company, Inc., 1990).

੨ৡ

Chapter 9

280: Knowing what to . . . The Neighborhood Visiting Nurses Association, West Chester, PA, "Preparing for the Death of a Loved One," *The American Journal of Hospice and Palliative Care* (July/August 1992), 14–16.

280: Perri Klass, M.D., "Dying in Character: The Myth of the Impish Chuckle," *Discover* (February 1987, Vol. 8, 2), 20.

282: Rabbi Maurice Lamm, "Healing Doesn't Mean Cure," The National Institute for Jewish Hospice, Palm Springs, CA.

285: Edinberg, Mark A., *Talking with Your Aging Parents* (Boston: Shambhala, 1987).

287: When a loved . . . San Diego Children's Project,

"Preparing Your Children for the Death of a Loved One," *A Family Guide to Helping Children Cope* (San Diego, CA: San Diego Children's Project, a division of American Cancer Society of California, 1993).

293: If you and . . . Paul Kent Froman, Ph.D., *After You Say Good-bye: When Someone You Love Dies of AIDS* (San Francisco: Chronicle Books, 1992).

294: you may be . . . "Has Your Loved One Died of AIDS?" ACCORD, Inc., Louisville, KY, 1989.

299: William Fletcher, *Recording Your Family History* (New York: Dodd, Mead & Company, 1986).

300: Dying at home . . . Deborah Chase, *Dying at Home with Hospice* (St. Louis: C. V. Mosby Company, 1986).

302: Under the Medicare . . . "Explanation of Medicare Hospice Benefits," Medicare brochure, distributed by the Hospice of North Coast, Carlsbad, CA.

303: Like grieving, saying . . . Paul Kent Froman, Ph.D., *After You Say Good-bye: When Someone You Love Dies of AIDS.*

303: R. D. Laing, "The Tie and the Cut Off," *The Voice of Experience* (New York: Pantheon Books, 1982).

304: My wife always . . . Allen Klein, *The Healing Power of Humor* (Los Angeles: Jeremy Tarcher Publishers, 1989).

306: Compassionate Friends, "Please See through My Tears," 1990.

ॐ

Chapter 10

308: The hotline serves . . . "Emotions When You Lose Your Pet," Pet Loss Support Hotline, University of California-Davis, Davis, CA.

311: With your capacity . . . Alan D. Wolfelt, Ph.D., "Helping Your Family Cope When a Pet Dies," 1992.

314: valid reasons for . . . Bruce Fogle, D.V.M., *Pets and Their People* (New York: Viking Publishers, 1989).

314: Linda Lascelles, "Going Home," *Caring Concepts*, The Centering Corporation, Omaha, NE, Summer 1992.

318: More and more . . . Herbert A. Neiburg and Arlene Fisher, *Pet Loss: A Thoughtful Guide for Adults and Children* (New York: Harper & Row, 1982).

320: Liz Palika, "Fond Memories," *Dog Fancy*, "Living

with Dogs" column, September 1991.

ॐ

Chapter 11

324: we need to . . . Paul Kent Froman, Ph.D., *After You Say Good-bye: When Someone You Love Dies of AIDS*.

328: Mel Pohl, M.D., et al. *The Caregiver's Journey: When You Love Someone with AIDS* (New York: Hazelden/HarperCollins Publishers, 1990).

333: Holidays make us . . . Sandra L. Graves, Ph.D., A.T.R., Sherry Williams, B.A., R.N., "Holiday Helps: Hope & Healing for Those Who Grieve," ACCORD, Inc., Louisville, KY, 1992.

334: Candy Lightner with Nancy Hathaway, *Giving Sorrow Words* (New York: Warner Books, 1990).

337: Joan Jacobsen, "One Tulip," *Caring Concepts*, The Centering Corporation, Omaha, NE, Summer 1992.

Index

ॐ

ॐ

ॐ

ॐ

ॐ

107–109
Suicide, 88–93
 blame, 88–90
 guilt, only for some, 89–90
 religious reflection, 91–92
 telling others, 90–91
 where to get help, 92–93
Support groups, 160–170
 what to expect at a meeting,
  163–164
Szekley, Ed B., 329

❧

Taxes, 265–266
Teen Age Grief, Inc. (TAG), 114–115,
 169–170
Teenage support groups, 169–170
Terminal illness, 275–306
Therapy Dogs International, 299
Tischler, Janet, 98
Traisman, Enid Samuel, 155
Trauma Intervention Program, 6
Trusts and wills, 253–256

❧

U.S. Department of State, deaths
  overseas, 226–230
Ushers, 62

❧

Vail, Elaine, 6, 245
Veazey, Rev. Diana Cole, 212–215
Veterens' benefits, 264–265
Victims Assistance Program, 85
Voss, Robert F., 133–134

❧

Wall, Ginita, 271
Watson, Diane, 88–89
Weston, Rev. Robert Terry, 45
What to say, 154–155
Widowhood, 147–150
Wills, 252–256
Williams, Sherry L., 17–18, 115–118,
 181, 294, 333

Wohlmuth, Ed, 200–201
Wolfelt, Alan D., 66–67, 72–73, 103,
 122, 182–183, 311–312
Worbleski, Adina, 88

❧

Zeidman, Nancy, 8
Zenker, Arnold, 198–199

ABOUT THE AUTHOR

æ

Eva Shaw, Ph.D. is the author of more than seventy books and scores of magazine articles, including *Shovel It: Nature's Health Plan*, a self-help book using gardening for therapy recovery. She specializes in how-to and self-help genres and is a nationally recognized expert, lecturing nationally on garden therapy, recovery, grief management, and wellness topics. She teaches online through Education To Go and at traditional colleges. Dr. Shaw lives in Carlsbad, California, with her husband Joseph, and their sweetly exuberant Welsh terrier, Buttons. Contact Dr. Shaw at www.evashaw.com

Write your thoughts...

Write your thoughts...

Write your thoughts...